NEW OXFORD HISTORY OF MUSIC

VOLUME II

THE VOLUMES OF THE
NEW OXFORD HISTORY OF MUSIC

SACRED AND PROFANE MUSIC
(St. John's College, Cambridge, MS. B. 18.) Twelfth century

EARLY MEDIEVAL
MUSIC
UP TO 1300

EDITED BY

DOM ANSELM HUGHES

LONDON
OXFORD UNIVERSITY PRESS
NEW YORK   TORONTO

Oxford University Press, Walton Street, Oxford OX2 6DP

OXFORD LONDON GLASGOW
NEW YORK TORONTO MELBOURNE WELLINGTON
IBADAN NAIROBI DAR ES SALAAM CAPE TOWN
KUALA LUMPUR SINGAPORE JAKARTA HONG KONG TOKYO
DELHI BOMBAY CALCUTTA MADRAS KARACHI

ISBN 0 19 316302 0

First edition 1954
Revised in 1955 and reprinted in 1961, 1967, 1969, 1976
and 1978

Reproduced and printed by photolithography and bound in
Great Britain at The Pitman Press, Bath

GENERAL INTRODUCTION

THE present work is designed to replace the *Oxford History of Music*, first published in six volumes under the general editorship of Sir Henry Hadow between 1901 and 1905. Five authors contributed to that ambitious publication—the first of its kind to appear in English. The first two volumes, dealing with the Middle Ages and the sixteenth century, were the work of H. E. Wooldridge. In the third Sir Hubert Parry examined the music of the seventeenth century. The fourth, by J. A. Fuller Maitland, was devoted to the age of Bach and Handel; the fifth, by Hadow himself, to the period bounded by C. P. E. Bach and Schubert. In the final volume Edward Dannreuther discussed the Romantic period, with which, in the editor's words, it was 'thought advisable to stop'. The importance of the work—particularly of the first two volumes—was widely recognized, and it became an indispensable part of a musician's library. The scheme was further extended in the new edition issued under the editorship of Sir Percy Buck between 1929 and 1938. An introductory volume, the work of several hands, was designed to supplement the story of music in the ancient world and the Middle Ages. New material, including two complete chapters, was added to volumes i and ii, while the third volume was reissued with minor corrections and a number of supplementary notes by Edward J. Dent. The history was also brought nearer to the twentieth century by the addition of a seventh volume, by H. C. Colles, entitled *Symphony and Drama, 1850–1900*.

Revision of an historical work is always difficult. If it is to be fully effective, it may well involve changes so comprehensive that very little of the original remains. Such radical revision was not the purpose of the second edition of the *Oxford History of Music*. To have attempted it in a third edition would have been impossible. During the first half of the present century an enormous amount of detailed work has been done on every period covered by the original volumes. New materials have been discovered, new relationships revealed, new interpretations made possible. Perhaps the most valuable achievement has been the publication in reliable modern editions of a mass of music which was previously available only in manuscript or in rare printed copies. These developments have immeasurably increased the historian's opportunities, but they have also added heavily to his responsibilities. To attempt a detailed survey of the whole history of music is no longer within the power of a single writer. It may even be doubted whether the burden can be adequately shouldered by a team of five.

The *New Oxford History of Music* is therefore not a revision of the older work, nor is it the product of a small group of writers. It has been planned as an entirely new survey of music from the earliest times down to comparatively recent years, including not only the achievements of the Western world but also the contributions made by eastern civilizations and primitive societies. The examination of this immense field is the work of a large number of contributors, English and foreign. The attempt has been made to achieve uniformity without any loss of individuality. If this attempt has been successful, the result is due largely to the patience and co-operation shown by the contributors themselves. Overlapping has to some extent been avoided by the use of frequent cross-references; but we have not thought it proper to prevent different authors from expressing different views about the same subject, where it could legitimately be regarded as falling into more than one category.

The scope of the work is sufficiently indicated by the titles of the several volumes. Our object throughout has been to present music not as an isolated phenomenon or the work of a few outstanding composers but as an art developing in constant association with every form of human culture and activity. The biographies of individuals are therefore merely incidental to the main plan of the history, and those who want detailed information of this kind must seek it elsewhere. No hard and fast system of division into chapters has been attempted. The treatment is sometimes by forms, sometimes by periods, sometimes also by countries, according to the importance which one element or another may assume. The division into volumes has to some extent been determined by practical considerations; but pains have been taken to ensure that the breaks occur at points which are logically and historically justifiable. The result may be that the work of a single composer who lived to a ripe age is divided between two volumes. The later operas of Monteverdi, for example, belong to the history of Venetian opera and hence find their natural place in volume v, not with the discussion of his earlier operas to be found in volume iv. On the other hand, we have not insisted on a rigid chronological division where the result would be illogical or confusing. If a subject finds its natural conclusion some ten years after the date assigned for the end of a period, it is obviously preferable to complete it within the limits of one volume rather than to allow it to overflow into a second. An exception to the general scheme of continuous chronology is to be found in volumes v and vi, which deal with different aspects of the same period and so are complementary to each other.

The history as a whole is intended to be useful to the professed student of music, for whom the documentation of sources and the bibliographies are particularly designed. But the growing interest in the music of all periods shown by music-lovers in general has encouraged us to bear their interests also in mind. It is inevitable that a work of this kind should employ a large number of technical terms and deal with highly specialized matters. We have, however, tried to ensure that the technical terms are intelligible to the ordinary reader and that what is specialized is not necessarily wrapped in obscurity. Finally, since music must be heard to be fully appreciated, we have given references throughout to the records issued by His Master's Voice (R. C. A. Victor) under the general title *The History of Music in Sound*. These records are collected in a series of albums which correspond to the volumes of the present work, and have been designed to be used with it.

J. A. WESTRUP
GERALD ABRAHAM
EDWARD J. DENT
ANSELM HUGHES
EGON WELLESZ

CONTENTS

ILLUSTRATIONS

INTRODUCTION TO VOLUME II

THE second volume of the *New Oxford History of Music* covers thirteen centuries of European music. For the earlier of those centuries contemporary information is almost non-existent; conclusions have to be drawn from the few authoritative sources of the Dark Ages or disinterred from the writings of early medieval times, writings which are usually verbose and not always free from confusion, inconsistency, and misunderstanding. With the ninth century the contemporary musical documents and theoretical writings begin to multiply; we can trace the beginnings of the polyphony which, in its wonderful development, differentiates European music of the last thousand years from that of all other ages and of the rest of the world. Notation becomes more and more precise, capable of indicating accurately pitch and, later, note values. By the beginning of the fourteenth century, where the volume closes just before the advent of the *ars nova* of Philippe de Vitry and the *Roman de Fauvel*, European music was set firmly on the path that was to lead to Dufay, Josquin, Palestrina, and beyond.

Until comparatively recent times the music of this period was regarded as merely embryonic, interesting only because it contains the seed of later developments. Increasing knowledge has given us a clearer view and deeper understanding. Directly we see music more clearly as it emerges from the Dark Ages, we see it as a living art shaped by contemporary conditions, answering to contemporary needs, and reflecting contemporary ways of thought. It is hardly necessary to labour this point so far as ecclesiastical chant is concerned: in its Gregorian forms, long surrounded by the nimbus of its supposedly divine inspiration, it has answered to the spiritual needs not only of the centuries of its origin and of those that immediately followed, but also—rhythmically interpreted and contrapuntally adorned according to many changing fashions—of every period of the history of the Catholic Church down to the present day. The accretions to this central body of Christian chant—trope and sequence and liturgical drama—have proved more time-bound; yet, characteristically medieval as they are, they still have the power to touch and impress us. So is it also with the high and subtle art of the troubadours and trouvères of the twelfth and thirteenth centuries, which we perceive imperfectly through a notation the interpretation of which is still not beyond dispute. This was one of the finest flowers of a culture remote indeed from those with which we are familiar, the wonderful Provençal culture destroyed by the Albigensian Crusade of 1208; foreign and often artificial in spirit and uncertainly transmitted though they may be, the songs of the troubadours can still strike us by their lyrical freshness. The most primitive beginnings of polyphony may say less to us, but by the end of the twelfth century France, at least, possessed in the work of the Notre-Dame school a polyphonic music admirably suited to the spaces of the great new Gothic cathedrals for which it was composed; and the thirteenth-century motets that have come down to us include a large number whose beauty or humour is quite undimmed and in which the combination of different texts is no more incongruous than the gargoyles or grotesque misericords of medieval churches.

This practice of combining different texts (and even different languages) is typical of that medieval Christendom which, with all its shades and distinctions, was an undivided, all-embracing whole, ordered and (at least in theory) systematic. There was no emphatic distinction between sacred and secular, or between nations. In so far as regional characteristics are noticeable in medieval art, they are due as much to the spread of monastic communities or to pilgrimage routes as to racial boundaries. Irish monks carried their script to Lindisfarne and St. Gall and Bobbio; the great pilgrim road through Conques and Limoges to Compostella is marked not only by similarities of architecture but by similarities of musical notation.

Christian medieval thought and art were theocentric; God stood at the head of the system to which everything was referable. The chief intellectual discomforts of the Middle Ages were occasioned by the need to reconcile the Emperor or some other sovereign with the Pope, and Christian dogma with Aristotelian philosophy. Such conflicts hardly existed in art. The design and imagery of the cathedrals symbolize the all-inclusive oneness, and music was the more easily incorporated in the system of Christian aesthetics since it possessed its own tradition of mystical theory stretching back through the Gnostics and Neoplatonists to the Pythagoreans. We may dismiss the fantastic symbolism and allegorical interpretations of Aribo Scholasticus, Johannes de Muris, and the rest, the parallels between the three kinds of instruments—*vasalia, foraminalia*, and *chordalia*—and faith, hope, and love, between the eight modes and the eight parts of speech or the eight beatitudes, and so on, as completely divorced from the reality of music. But when Marchettus of Padua in his *Lucidarium* likens music to a tree 'whose branches are beautifully proportioned by numbers, whose flowers are kinds of consonances, and whose fruits are the sweet harmonies produced by these same consonances',[1] we recognize a musician thinking about his art in a typically medieval way—for the tree-image was equally popular in philosophy, theology, and the plastic arts—and we apprehend that such thoughts were probably the common furniture of the minds of most intellectual musicians of the time. It may be difficult, perhaps impossible, in the twentieth century to relate the metaphysics of medieval music to the actual sound-material, but the effort is at least worth while. The great bulk of the early medieval music that has come down to us, the music of the Church, was not directed towards an audience or congregation apart from the performers themselves; it mattered only to those who were making it in the spirit of their own devotion, delighting in the reproduction or contrapuntal adornment of the traditional God-given chant, and in a system of sound that seemed to spring from and parallel the divine order of things, much as the carvings on the west front or round the portals of church or monastery often depicted the sacred hierarchy.

ACKNOWLEDGEMENTS

So wide is the range of interests covered by this volume that it is impossible to include thanks to more than a representative selection of those who have helped the editor in his work. Mention must be made first of the staff of the Bodleian Library and particularly the Keeper of Western Manuscripts, Dr. R. W. Hunt. Beyond Oxford Mr. Neil Ker, Reader in Palaeography, has made many journeys in his own line of research and has most kindly notified the editor of hitherto unknown fly-leaf music in early bindings. Mention must also be made of help given at the British Museum by Dr. Bertram Schofield and his assistants, and of the librarians of many other institutions who have supplied photographs or answered questions or given permission for their materials to be quoted. In particular, acknowledgement is due to the Abbey of Montserrat for permission to reproduce the map showing the distribution of neumatic notations from the *Introducció a la Paleografià Musical Gregoriana* by Dom Gregory Suñol; and to the Éditions de l'Oiseau-Lyre for permission to quote from a setting of 'O Maria, virgo Davidica' reprinted in their *Polyphonies du XIIIe siècle*. Thanks are also due to the British Broadcasting

---

[1] Gerbert, *Scriptores*, iii. p. 66b.

Corporation and the Gramophone Company, who have given so much practical encouragement to the live production of early music; and finally to those scholars who have contributed chapters to the present volume.

ANSELM HUGHES, O.S.B.

NASHDOM ABBEY
   April 1954

I

EARLY CHRISTIAN MUSIC

By Egon Wellesz

EARLY CHRISTIAN CHANT

By early Christian music we mean the chant of the Christian Churches up to the end of the fifth century A.D. This chant had its roots in the Jewish Synagogue. It was from the Synagogue that the early Christians took over the cantillation of lessons, the chanting of psalms, and the singing of hymns. We are coming more and more to understand how conservative was the attitude of the early Christian Church, an attitude which led to the preservation of as much as possible of the Jewish service. The first generations of Christians still regarded themselves as members of the Jewish religious community and took part in the services of the Temple in Jerusalem and of the Synagogues, joining in the singing with the Jews. At the *agapae*, the 'love-feasts' instituted in commemoration of the Last Supper, the singing of psalms and hymns heightened the solemnity of the ceremony. In the Acts of the Apostles (ii. 46–47) we are told that the newly baptized continued 'daily with one accord in the Temple, and breaking bread from house to house did eat their meat with gladness and singleness of heart, praising God, and having favour with all the people', and in the next chapter (Acts iii. 1) that the Apostles Peter and John 'went up together into the Temple at the hour of prayer, being the ninth hour'. Converted readers and precentors from the Synagogue instructed the Christian congregation in chanting and singing. In the early days of Christianity the readers may have preserved the rules of Jewish cantillation, which permitted a certain amount of improvisation as long as the traditional formulas and cadences were kept.[1] In the course of liturgical development, however, both the Eastern and Western Church took steps to render any sort of improvisation impossible. By a system of punctuation the Church gave the reader strict indications as to which words and phrases were to be chanted on a high, which on a low, pitch; exactly where a transition from high to low pitch or vice versa should be made; and on which formula the close of a lesson should be sung,

[1] Cf. E. Werner, 'Preliminary Notes for a Comparative Study of Catholic and Jewish Musical Punctuation', *Hebrew Union College Annual*, xv (Cincinnati, 1940), p. 351.

so that the congregation would be aware that it was ending. We shall have to deal more fully with the problem of musical punctuation when we come to discuss Syrian and Byzantine ecphonetic notation.[1]

No document from the Apostolic Age has come down to us from which we can learn the exact nature of the music which was sung at the first gatherings of the followers of Christ. But we learn something from a passage in the Epistle to the Colossians (iii. 16) in which St. Paul tells them to teach and admonish one another 'in psalms and hymns and spiritual songs'. Similar advice is given in the Epistle to the Ephesians (v. 19). These passages have given rise to discussion ever since the days of Origen in the third century, but their meaning could not be established with any certainty until we knew more about the music of the Jewish Synagogue on the one hand, and of the Byzantine Church on the other. St. Paul must certainly have been referring to a practice well known to the people to whom he wrote.[2] We may therefore assume that three different types of chant were, in fact, in use among them, and we can form an idea of their characteristics from the evidence of Jewish music and later recorded Christian chant:

1. Psalmody: the cantillation of the Jewish psalms and of the canticles and doxologies modelled on them.
2. Hymns: songs of praise of a syllabic type, i.e. each syllable is sung to one or two notes of the melody.
3. Spiritual Songs: Alleluias and other chants of a jubilant or ecstatic character, richly ornamented.[3]

1. In these early days of the Church chanting must have kept to simple melodic types.[4] There are no indications of a development peculiar to the new creed, either in words or in music. It was only gradually that a new element was introduced. Words like 'Amen' and short versicles were added to the chants sung by a soloist. These responses were sung by the congregation. This practice was taken over at an early date, as we can see from the version of the *Pater noster* preserved in the Mozarabic chant (see Ex. 30, p. 82). This is cited by Peter Wagner as probably the oldest specimen of ecclesiastical chant which has come down to us in the West.[5] The insertion of whole versicles can

---

[1] See pp. 10–13 and 35–37.
[2] Cf. F. Leitner, *Der gottesdienstliche Volksgesang im jüdischen und christlichen Altertum* (Freiburg, 1906), p. 77.
[3] I have dealt with the problem more fully in *A History of Byzantine Music and Hymnography* (Oxford, 1949), pp. 24–34.
[4] Cf. E. Werner, 'Notes on the Attitude of the Early Church Fathers towards Hebrew Psalmody', *The Review of Religion* (1943), p. 346.
[5] *Gregorianische Formenlehre* (Leipzig, 1921), pp. 58–59.

be studied in its earliest form in the Byzantine *Lectionaria*, books containing the lessons for the day from the Prophets, Epistles, and Gospels. From the rubrics in the *Prophetologium*[1] we can see how the 'Song of Moses', from Exodus xv. 1–19, was sung on Good Friday. One of the chanters goes up to the pulpit and announces 'The Song from Exodus'. Then the deacon says 'Attention!' and the precentor immediately begins:

I will sing unto the Lord, for he hath triumphed gloriously.
People: I will sing unto the Lord, for he hath triumphed gloriously.
Precentor: The horse and his rider hath he thrown into the sea.
People: For he hath triumphed gloriously.
Precentor: The Lord is my strength and song, and he is become my salvation.
          For he hath triumphed gloriously.
People: I will sing unto the Lord, for he hath triumphed gloriously.

All eighteen verses of the canticle are sung in this way. To the last verse is appended the Little Doxology, followed by the refrain, sung by the chanter, and the response, sung by the congregation. Thus, even in the early days of Christian chant we can see a tendency to place more emphasis on the music than on the words, by causing the choir to repeat the musical phrases first sung by the precentor. This tendency develops more and more in Eastern chant and gives it its peculiar character.

2. The singing of hymns, like the chanting of psalms and canticles, was a usage deeply rooted in Jewish liturgy, and consequently familiar to the first generations of Christians. Because these hymns were free paraphrases of the biblical text, and not exclusively based on the words of the Scriptures, there was an orthodox reaction against them in the third century. All new hymns were condemned, and only those to be found in the Scriptures were tolerated. This feeling accounts for the fact that so few hymns survive from the beginnings of Christianity. But they had played too large and important a part in religious life to be completely suppressed. They had embellished the liturgy: their loss was felt to decrease its splendour, and the Church was forced to change its attitude. By altering passages to which orthodoxy could take exception the old practice was restored and hymnography developed even more richly than before. Besides these hymns there were also a few Christian poets influenced by the classical tradition, who wrote in an archaic style, for example, Synesius of Cyrene (*c.* 375–

---

[1] *Monumenta Musicae Byzantinae*, Series *Lectionaria*; *Prophetologium*, fasc. 3, ed. C. Høeg & G. Zuntz (Copenhagen, 1949).

c. 430); but these hymns were not introduced into the liturgy, and had no influence on later hymnology.

The earliest example of a Christian hymn which has come down to us with music is a fragment of a song in praise of the Holy Trinity dating from the late third century and written by a Greek-speaking Christian in Egypt.[1] The strip of papyrus, which contains the close of the hymn, is very much mutilated, but three of the five lines are easily legible, and they enable us to draw some conclusions as to the structure of the music. We give lines 3–5 in modern staff notation:

Ex.1

(*After the first three words in the Greek*: 'While we hymn Father and Son and Holy Spirit let all creation sing amen, amen, Praise, Power . . . to the one Giver of all good things, amen, amen.)

The music of the hymn is written down in letters which form the following series of notes:

R	φ	σ	o	ξ	ι	ζ	ε
f	g	a	b	c′	d′	e′	f′

According to the *Isagoge* of Alypius, a musical theorist of the fourth century, these letters are used for the diatonic Hypolydian scale. Set above the letters are a number of dynamic signs, strokes, dots, hyphens, *leimmata* (pauses), and colons. The Greek notation of the hymn and the anapaestic metre of the text led some scholars to see in it the last example of classical Greek music: they took it as a proof that Greek pagan influence can be traced in early Christian music.[2] Analysis of the structure of the music, however, shows that the melody

¹ *Oxyrhynchus Papyri*, ed. A. S. Hunt, Part xv, No. 1786, pp. 21–25.
² Cf. H. Abert, 'Ein neuentdeckter frühchristlicher Hymnus mit antiken Musik-noten', *Zeitschrift für Musikwissenschaft*, iv (1921–2), pp. 528–9.

is built up of a group of formulas.[1] This principle is characteristic of Semitic melody construction, and is not to be found in ancient Greek music. As Christianity spread to the countries of the Mediterranean basin it carried with it this principle of composition, which is therefore to be found in both Eastern and Western chant, and which constitutes a proof of their ultimate Semitic origin.[2] The fragment of a 'Hymn to the Holy Trinity', therefore, is not only a unique and valuable document of the music sung by Greek-speaking Christians in Egypt: it also proves that a principle of composition which we find to be characteristic of Christian chant was securely established as early as the third century outside the immediate sphere of Palestine.

3. The third group consists of chants of the melismatic type, the most important of which are the Alleluias. In his *Exposition of the Ninety-ninth Psalm* St. Augustine describes the character of the songs of exultation: 'He who jubilates speaks no words: it is a song of joy without words.'[3] The spiritual songs of which St. Paul speaks were obviously the melismatic melodies of the Alleluias and other exultant songs of praise, which, again, the Jewish Christians brought with them into the Christian Church from the Temple and Synagogue. The Hebrew word itself has never been translated by either the Greek or the Latin Church, and it has always been accepted that the chants derived from the Jewish liturgy. As early as 636 Isidore of Seville suggested a Hebrew origin for the *alleluia-jubili*: 'Laudes, hoc est alleluia canere, canticum est Hebraeorum'[4] (the praises, that is to say, the singing of Alleluia, is a song of the Hebrews). This view is supported by the musical structure of the Alleluias of the Ambrosian rite, the oldest specimens of the type which survive in manuscript.

When we consider these three main forms of ecclesiastical music it becomes obvious that from the very beginnings of Christian worship

---

[1] Cf. E. Wellesz, 'The Earliest Example of Christian Hymnography', *The Classical Quarterly*, xxxix (1945), pp. 43–45. Transcriptions of the hymn, but without taking into account the dynamic signs, are given by H. Stuart Jones, *Oxyrhynchus Papyri*, Part xv; T. Reinach, 'Un Ancêtre de la musique d'église', *Revue Musicale*, July 1922, p. 24; R. Wagner, 'Der Oxyrhynchos-Notenpapyrus', *Philologus*, lxxix (N.F. xxxiii), 1923, pp. 201–21; H. Abert, loc. cit., p. 527. A full transcription, showing all the lacunae, is given on pp. 42–43 of my article.

[2] It was at first assumed that the principle of formulas was confined to Arabic music, cf. A. Z. Idelsohn, 'Die Maqamen der arabischen Musik', *Sammelbände der internationalen Musikgesellschaft*, xv (1913–14), pp. 1 ff., but, as I showed in an article, 'Die Struktur des serbischen Oktoechos', *Zeitschrift für Musikwissenschaft*, ii (1919–20), pp. 140–8, it is in fact characteristic of Semitic music all over the Middle East. This problem is also discussed in my *Eastern Elements in Western Chant, Monumenta Musicae Byzantinae, Subsidia*, ii, American Series I, 1947, p. 89.

[3] 'Qui jubilat, non verba dicit, sed sonus quidem est laetitiae sine verbis' (J. P. Migne, *Patrologia Latina*, xxxvii. 1272).

[4] *De ecclesiasticis officiis*, i. 13; *Patrologia Latina*, lxxxiii. 750.

liturgical chant was an integral part of the service. Its development is inseparably bound up with that of the liturgy. Further, though only a few fragments of music are preserved in documents dating from early Christian times, we may assume that there was a substantial body of chant in existence in this period, and that both Byzantine chant and Western plainchant have a traceable connexion with it.

ANTIPHONAL SINGING

It was only later that another element of the Jewish liturgy was introduced. This was antiphonal singing, i.e. chanting in alternate choirs. This practice, however, requiring as it did large numbers of singers, did not derive from the simple service of the Synagogue but from the more solemn worship of the Temple. It seems to have been taken over into the rite of the Synagogue only after the Temple was destroyed, and the first mention of its use by Christians occurs in the *Ecclesiastical History* (vi. 8) of Socrates (b. about 380). It is now generally agreed that it was first introduced into the monasteries of Syria and Palestine at the beginning of the fourth century, and that the monks took over the practice from the Jewish communities which had flourished in these countries, particularly in Antioch, since the reign of Seleucus Nicator, who founded the city in 301 B.C.

In a letter to his clergy written in 375 St. Basil, the founder of the monastic rule of Orthodox Christianity, speaks of the rapid spread of the antiphonal singing of the psalms, and defends the new genre against its critics by pointing out that it was not, as they claimed, an innovation restricted to the Church of Caesarea, but was in general use in Egypt, Libya, the Thebaid, Palestine, Arabia, Phoenicia, Syria, and Mesopotamia.[1] We have, however, no clear reference to the manner in which the alternating singing of the psalms was actually performed. We must distinguish between the antiphon itself, a verse of praise, not necessarily taken from the psalm, and the actual performance of the psalms by two alternating choirs. The problem of the execution remains unsolved: neither the view of L. Petit[2] nor that of J.-B. Thibaut[3] is completely convincing. We shall do best, however, to agree with Thibaut that the antiphonal singing of the psalms was executed in the following way: the first choir intoned the verse of

[1] St. Basil, *Epistolae*, 207, 3–4; *Patrologia Graeca*, xxxii. 763.

[2] In his article 'Antiphone' in *Dictionnaire d'archéologie chrétienne et de liturgie*, fasc. viii (Paris, 1905), c. 2461.

[3] In his study of the Holy Week in Jerusalem from the fourth to the tenth century, *Ordre des offices de la semaine sainte à Jérusalem du IVᵉ au Xᵉ siècle* (Paris, 1926), pp. 57–63.

praise, the antiphon, which was repeated by the second choir. The first choir then repeated it a third time, followed by the first verse of the psalm; the second choir repeated the antiphon once again and sang the second verse of the psalm, and so on. After the last verse the antiphon was sung three times by the two choirs as at the beginning. Thibaut suggests that in this antiphonal performance the psalms were really sung, and not merely cantillated, and that the antiphons were composed in an ornamented style. He supports this view by a quotation from Cassian (c. 360–435), *De institutis coenobiorum*, in which the extension of the psalms by the melodies of the antiphons is mentioned.[1]

The most important document for our knowledge of the liturgy at the end of the fourth century is the *Peregrinatio ad loca sancta* of the nun Etheria, in which a description of the liturgical ceremonies at Easter in Jerusalem is given.[2] The pilgrim mentions the regular singing of hymns, psalms, and antiphons at Matins, of psalms and hymns at the sixth and ninth hours, and of psalms, hymns, and antiphons at Vespers. She also says that it was customary to translate the lessons, which were read in Greek, into Syriac and Latin for the benefit of those who did not understand that language.[3] In the greater part of Palestine and Syria the Syriac language was to become the language of the Church, and through it vernacular melodies influenced the development of ecclesiastical chant. The Syrian monks of the fourth and fifth centuries were the first to develop and extend poetical forms as well as melodies. The importance of Syria as a centre from which Christian chant spread in all directions is becoming more and more evident; indeed, we shall see that the origins of Byzantine hymnography can be understood only when their Syrian antecedents are taken into account. We must therefore give a short survey of Syrian hymnography before we can deal with Byzantine ecclesiastical music and that of other Eastern countries.

THE SYRIAN CHURCH

In Palestine the vernacular was the West Aramaic dialect, in Syria the East Aramaic. The Christians in this country called themselves *Surjâjê*, from the Greek Σύροι (Syrians), an abbreviation of Ἀσσύριοι

---

[1] *Patrologia Latina*, xlii. 78.

[2] *Itinera Hierosolymitana saeculi iv–viii*, ed. P. Geyer in *Corpus scriptorum eccles. lat.*, xxxix (Vienna, 1898). The *Peregrinatio* was attributed by J. F. Gammurini and P. Geyer to St. Silvia of Aquitaine, by Dom M. Férotin to the Spanish nun Etheria, by E. Bouvy to Eucheria, daughter of the consul Eucherinus. At present most scholars connect the *Peregrinatio* with the name of Etheria and fix the date of the pilgrimage between 385 and 388.   [3] Ibid., p. 99.

(Assyrians). The original Semitic name of the people, *Arâmâjê*, was used by the Christian population as synonymous with 'pagans'.

When the Christian faith was introduced Syria already had a rich pagan literature in the vernacular, particularly in Northern Mesopotamia. The nationalistic trend in Syrian civilization favoured the growth of Christian literature in the vernacular. This tendency also affected ecclesiastical poetry, which from earliest times not only assimilated hymns of Gnostic and other sects, but also developed a creative activity of its own. The most important centre of this movement was Edessa, where Ephraem (306–73), the son of a pagan priest and a Christian mother, became the leader of a literary movement in Syriac. Syriac poetry flourished in other parts of Syria also, as well as in the Syrian colonies which had repudiated the authority of the Orthodox Church from the middle of the fifth century and had accepted the doctrines of Nestorius on the two persons in Christ, condemned as heretical by the Council of Ephesus (431). The impassioned dogmatic controversies which followed in the East between the Nestorians and Monophysites, who though opposed to the teachings of Nestorius were also condemned as heretics by Byzantine Orthodoxy, led to the foundation of the Nestorian Church and, in the middle of the sixth century, of the Jacobite, each with its own liturgy. The separation from the Orthodox Church and the development of the two new rites resulted in great activity on the part of the hymnographers to adorn the feasts of the ecclesiastical year with hymns in the vernacular.

THE FORMS OF SYRIAC POETRY

The three main forms of Syriac poetry are (1) the *memrâ*, (2) the *madrâshâ*, and (3) the *sogîthâ*.

The *memrâ* is a poetical homily in lines of five, seven, or twelve syllables. Ephraem wrote most of his homilies in a metre of five syllables, Jacob of Serûgh (451–521) used one of twelve syllables. Baumstark calls the *memrâ* a spoken 'metrical sermon',[1] in contrast to the two other poetical forms, *madrâshâ* and *sogîthâ*, which were sung. It would be more correct to distinguish between the cantillation of the *memrâ* and the singing of the *madrâshâ* and *sogîthâ*, the hymn forms of Syriac religious poetry. We shall see later that Syrian lectionaries show a system of punctuation by which the cantillation of the phrases of the *memrâ* is clearly indicated (see p. 10).

The *madrâshâ* is a strophic poem sung by a soloist; at the end of each stanza the choir responded with the same phrase. Ephraem was

[1] A. Baumstark, *Geschichte der syrischen Literatur* (Bonn, 1922), p. 40.

the master of this style. He used it in theological controversy to refute the arguments of his opponents and to inspire his followers; at a later stage he turned it into a lyrical form and gave it the character of a hymn.[1] The *madrâshâ* became, as far as form is concerned, the forerunner of the Byzantine *kontakion*.

The *sogîthâ* is a poem of dramatic character; it seems to have been sung by two soloists and two choirs. It appears to have developed from songs in which a biblical character was introduced as the speaker. Passages in nativity hymns, in which the Blessed Virgin is introduced, make it clear that these songs must have been composed before the beginning of the Christological dispute.[2] When two persons were introduced it became possible to replace the earlier form of monologue by dialogue. Sophronius of Jerusalem took over the dramatic element of the *sogîthâ* in his Nativity hymns (see p. 20). We cannot now know whether he translated Syriac poems into Greek or based his hymns on older Greek models. It is certain, however, that his work is closely connected with Syriac literature, and therefore, if his models were Greek we must assume that they were also used by Syrian poets.

Besides these major forms of Syrian hymnography a number of smaller forms existed, poems which were inserted between the verses of psalms or sung between and after the reading of the Lessons. These are comparable to the Byzantine *troparia* and *stichera* of which we shall have to speak in the next chapter. The *qâlâ* ('tune') is a poem consisting of several stanzas which have no refrain. Some of the *qâlê*, particularly those sung at funerals, are ascribed to Ephraem.[3] Another group was written by the monophysite poet Jacob of Sĕrûgh, but most of them are anonymous. Another group of poems, of a later date, are the *'enjânê* (*responsoria*) which were inserted between the verses of certain psalms.[4] They are the Syriac equivalents of the Byzantine *kanon*, the main form of Byzantine hymnography.[5]

The Arab conquest of Syria (635–7) and the subsequent Arab domination of Persia had no immediate effect on Syrian Christianity. The attitude of the Caliphs was one of tolerance. The introduction of the Arabic language, however, led to a gradual reduction in the use of Syriac and finally put an end to the once flourishing Syriac poetry.

[1] Ibid., pp. 40–41.
[2] A. Baumstark, *Die christlichen Literaturen des Orients*, i, Sammlung Göschen (Leipzig, 1911), pp. 99–100.
[3] Baumstark, *Geschichte der syrischen Literatur*, p. 47.
[4] Ibid., pp. 244–5.
[5] Cf. O. Heiming, 'Syrische 'Enjânê und griechische Kanones', *Liturgiegeschichtliche Quellen und Forschungen*, Heft 26 (Münster i. W., 1932), pp. 47–52.

The Syriac literary renaissance of the twelfth century produced a belated flowering of Syriac hymnography, particularly among the Nestorians, but in the long run only the Syrian Churches were able to preserve their inheritance. The music of the hymns, too, seems to have kept its original melodic structure up to the present day, although it could not remain unaffected by the Arabic way of singing. From its present state it can clearly be seen that it must have undergone alteration, both melodically and rhythmically; but since it was transmitted orally, we are unable to reconstruct its state in the great period of Syriac hymnography. The only musical signs which are known to us are those which regulate the cantillation of the lessons.

SYRIAN ECPHONETIC NOTATION

The term 'ecphonetic chant' was coined by J. Tzetzes in his study of the cantillation of the lessons in Byzantine liturgy[1] and was extended to Byzantine musical palaeography by J.-B. Thibaut.[2] Today when we use the terms 'ecphonetic chant' and 'ecphonetic notation' we understand by them the solemn reading of the lessons and the signs used to regulate its performance in all the Eastern Churches.[3] The introduction of a system of dots into the Syrian *Lectionaria* is attributed to Joseph Hûzâjâ, a pupil of Narsai, 'the Harp of the Holy Spirit', as he was called by his co-sectarians.[4] One of the greatest of Nestorian hymnographers, he died at Nisibis in 503. The ecphonetic signs of Joseph Hûzâjâ must therefore have been introduced about the year 500.[5] This system, consisting of nine signs, was later enlarged, as we know from a table in a manuscript dated 899.[6] A further development was made by Elijâ ben Sînajâ (975–1049). The main signs are:

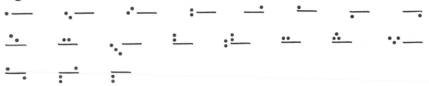

---

[1] 'Η ἐπινόησις τῆς παρασημαντικῆς τῶν κατὰ τὸν μεσαιῶνα λειτουργικῶν καὶ ὑμνολογικῶν χειρογράφων τῶν ἀνατολικῶν ἐκκλησιῶν (The meaning of the musical signs in the medieval liturgical and hymnological manuscripts of the Eastern Churches), Παρνασσός (Athens, 1885), pp. 413–93.

[2] 'Étude de musique byzantine: Le chant ekphonétique.' *Byzantinische Zeitschrift* (Leipzig, 1899), pp. 122–47.

[3] Cf. C. Høeg, *La Notation ekphonétique. Monumenta Musicae Byzantinae, Subsidia*, i. 2 (Copenhagen, 1935), pp. 137–53.

[4] Cf. W. Wright, *A Short History of Syriac Literature* (London, 1894), p. 58.

[5] T. Weiss, *Zur ostsyrischen Laut- und Akzentlehre. Bonner orientalische Studien*, v (Stuttgart, 1933), p. 30.   [6] London, Brit. Mus. Add. 12138.

Barhebraeus,[1] a grammarian of the thirteenth century gives an involved explanation of the signs, but the easiest way to understand their significance is to see how the Syrian scribes placed them in the texts,[2] e.g.:

(1 Kings, xix. 9) What doest thou here, Elijah?.

(1 Samuel, iii. 10) Samuel, Samuel.

(Psalm 51. 1) Have mercy upon me, O God, according to thy loving kindness.

(Psalm 6. 2) Have mercy upon me, O Lord, for I am weak

(2 Samuel, xviii. 33) My son,: my son Absalom.

(Isaiah xxi. 2) Go up, O Elam, besiege, O Media.:

(Matthew vii. 5) Thou hypocrite,:

The Syrian ecphonetic notation was not confined to texts in Syriac, but was also used for texts written in Soghdic, a middle-Persian dialect. This was proved by the discovery of fragments of texts with ecphonetic signs in Central Asia, particularly in Chinese Turkestan. These showed a system of punctuation closely related to the Syrian one attributed to Joseph Hûzâjâ. The ecphonetic notation of the Soghdic texts seems to represent the earliest stage of the signs.[3] It was brought to Central Asia when Nestorianism was accepted as the official Christian Church in Persia and the countries under Persian domination. In contrast to the tolerance which the Persian Kings showed towards the Nestorians, their attitude towards other Christian sects, especially the Manichees, was hostile. Members of these sects were exiled from the Persian kingdom, although the countries dominated by Persia were open to them. This explains the fact that Manichean hymns in praise of Manî[4] were found at the beginning of the present century in Chinese Turkestan as well as Nestorian texts.

The system of punctuation in Manichean hymns is of an even simpler type than the Syrian one. It seems, however, that Manichean

---

[1] Barhebraeus, *Buch der Strahlen*, ed. A. Moberg (Lund, 1907), ch. 6, 'Über die grossen Punkte'.

[2] For the compilation of a list of Syrian ecphonetic signs, from which these examples are taken, I am indebted to Professor P. Kahle, with whom I discussed the question of cantillation in Oxford in 1942–3. Cf. also P. Kahle, *Die Masoreten des Ostens* (Leipzig, 1913) and *Die Masoreten des Westens* (Stuttgart, 1927).

[3] Cf. E. Wellesz, 'Probleme der musikalischen Orientforschung', *Jahrbuch der Musikbibliothek Peters* (Leipzig, 1917), pp. 12–18, and 'Miscellanea zur orientalischen Musikgeschichte. Die Lektionszeichen in den soghdischen Texten', *Zeitschrift für Musikwissenschaft*, i (1918–19), pp. 505–15.

[4] Cf. my 'Probleme der musikalischen Orientforschung', pp. 15–17.

hymns were sung, not cantillated, as we can see from the repetition of vowels and the frequent insertion of the syllables *ygâ*. This group of letters has no meaning, but is used to expand certain words of the text so that they can be sung to a melisma—a proceeding also to be found in African and Asiatic folk-songs, as well as in the *teretismata* of the highly elaborate chants of the late Byzantine period. We give first the facsimile of a Manichean hymn,[1] then the transcription of the text with the inserted vowels and syllables (left), and the reconstructed original text (right):

Ex. 2

[1] The text of the hymn is published in F. W. K. Müller's 'Handschriftenreste in Estrangelo-Schrift aus Turfan II', *Abhandlungen der Kg. preuss. Akademie der Wissenschaft* (Berlin, 1914), p. 29. The transcription and reconstruction of the hymn were given me by H. Jansen of Berlin in 1916, and first published in my article, already quoted, 'Probleme der musikalischen Orientforschung', p. 17, where an additional example of a Manichean hymn is given on p. 16.

Transcribed text	*Reconstructed text*
'a—ygâ	'An ḥêm
na—°—ḥê—ê—mâ°'u	'ûzdêh 'î nakhûstîn
—û—zâ—dê—ê—° 'i-nâ-	frazênd 'î bay Zarvân puš
khû-û-û-stî-î-fâ-	'î šaḥreyârân°°
ygâ—râ° zê-ê-ndî—°	
bâ-yâ-zâ-râ-va—	
ygan° pû-sî—° šaḥrê—	
yâ-ygâ—râ—ygân°°	

(I am the first stranger, the Son of the eternal God, the sovereign child.)

In his *Neumen-Studien*, I (1895) Oskar Fleischer had already stated that musical punctuation had its origin in the East and that it was used in early Christian times. Today, more than fifty years after the publication of his work, our knowledge about the origin of the ecphonetic and neumatic notations of the Eastern and Western Churches has not greatly progressed. The discovery of the Syrian system of ecphonetic signs has definitely destroyed the legends of the origin of neumatic notation in Rome or Constantinople. Much work, however, remains to be done in order to discover the precise relationship of the Syrian and Jewish systems of punctuation, and, once this point has been cleared up, to decide whether both are not derived from an earlier source, which may be found in Babylonian texts.

II

(a) MUSIC OF THE EASTERN CHURCHES
By EGON WELLESZ

THE DEVELOPMENT OF THE ORTHODOX CHURCH

IT must be emphasized that Christian music in the Eastern Empire, though sung in Greek, was a foreign element in a state whose administration was modelled on that of the Western Empire, and whose civilization was Hellenistic. We know that music played an important part in theatrical performances and in the circus. There must also have been a great deal of other secular music of various kinds, particularly folk-songs, which may have left their traces on popular music of the present day. But this kind of music, of which nothing has come down to us in writing,[1] must have belonged to the Hellenistic civilization of the Eastern Empire, whereas Christian chant was a legacy from the early Christian Churches of Palestine and Syria—that is to say, it was Semitic music, originally sung to either Syriac or Greek words.

The history of Byzantine liturgy begins in A.D. 527 with the coronation of Justinian I as Emperor of the Eastern Roman Empire. Constantine the Great, who in 324 transformed the small town of Byzantium into the capital of the Eastern Empire, had made it a Christian city. But the Bishop of Constantinople was under the ecclesiastical jurisdiction of the Metropolitan of Heraclea, and had to struggle for his independence. For political reasons he had also to gain supremacy over the Bishop of Alexandria. On the other hand, the Empire was still to a large extent a pagan one, and heresies threatened to undermine the position of the Orthodox Church. It was not until two hundred years later that Justinian could venture to take the decisive step of suppressing every tendency opposed to his position as priest-king. By his edict of 529 the famous Academy at Athens, which had flourished since the days of Plato, was closed, with other Neoplatonic schools. Books, temples, and statues of the gods were destroyed and the study of philosophy forbidden.

---

[1] A group of thirteen folk-songs in Koukouzelean notation, recently discovered in a Mount Athos manuscript, dates from the fifteenth or sixteenth century.

From the beginning of his reign Justinian made every possible effort to strengthen religious life throughout the Empire. A powerful ecclesiastical administration was set up, churches and monasteries were built and richly endowed. As head of the Church Justinian demanded from the monks strict submission to their rule. By a decree of 528 the daily singing of the three main offices, i.e. Matins (*mesonyktikon*), Lauds (*orthros*), and Vespers (*hesperinos*) was made compulsory. But Justinian was far from attempting to introduce asceticism into religious life. He desired the victory of Orthodoxy to be celebrated by an increased splendour of the service; and as a visible sign of the supremacy of Constantinople as ecclesiastical centre of the Empire he ordered a church to be built which was to surpass all others. On 27 December 537 St. Sophia was solemnly inaugurated. We can get some idea of the splendour of the ritual from a decree of the Emperor Heraclius, of 1 May 612, which ordered the reduction of the number of *Hagiosophitae* to 80 priests, 150 deacons, 40 deaconesses, 70 sub-deacons, 160 lectors, and 25 singers.[1] The splendour of St. Sophia was imitated by all the principal churches throughout the Empire. Churches were built of the most costly materials and decorated with mosaics. Icons of the Saints were painted by the most prominent artists; the books from which the readers chanted were bound in heavy leather and adorned with precious stones mounted in gold and silver. The Morning and Evening Services were enriched with hymns, which were introduced in steadily increasing number, and gradually the music assumed a dominating role in the liturgy. Mass was celebrated frequently but not daily. On the other hand, it became customary to celebrate the Morning and Evening Services with greater solemnity, and the Lesser Hours also, particularly during the fasts which precede Christmas and Easter. During these periods the monks spent most of their time in the choir, and the burden was so heavy that in the laxer monasteries it became usual for the singing to be performed by relays.

The development of monasticism, furthered by Justinian I and his wife the Empress Theodora, suffered a severe setback when the Iconoclastic controversy broke out in the time of Leo III (717–40), the first Emperor of the Isaurian dynasty. It was partly an oriental reaction from the worship of icons, but it soon turned into a violent persecution of the monks, who defended image-worship; and it led to the destruction of icons and statues of saints, and the burning of all liturgical books containing miniatures illustrating the life of Christ,

[1] J. Pargoire, *L'Église byzantine de 527–847* (Paris, 1905), p. 61.

the Blessed Virgin, the Apostles, and the Saints. The fight between the Image-breakers and the Image-worshippers lasted for more than a hundred years, until the death of the Emperor Theophilus in 842 and the reign of his widow Theodora, who acted as regent for his young son Michael III. During the struggle the monks endured persecution, torture, and death. But instead of breaking resistance, persecution only heightened their courage, and the Iconoclastic Age was a period of great activity in hymnography. After the quarrel had come to an end a period of renewed artistic activity set in, in which the damage was repaired, and the *scriptoria* of the monasteries were busy copying those manuscripts which had escaped destruction. From the point of view of our studies we must regret that no musical manuscript of the important period of hymnography from the sixth to the ninth century has come down to us. To this period belong, as we shall see, the growth of the *kontakion* and the beginning of the *kanon*, the two great forms of Byzantine hymnography.

Up to the seventh century the hymnographer was a poet-musician who composed words as well as music, or at any rate adapted the music of an older hymn to fit his new words, which in their turn were always modelled on an earlier hymn which they paraphrased and extended. Attention has been drawn elsewhere to the similarity of the method of the Byzantine hymnographer to that of the painter of icons.[1] According to the teaching of the Christian author who wrote under the pseudonym of Dionysius the Areopagite, the hymnographer transmits to us the echo of the divine hymns which are sung in heaven[2] and can only be passed on through divinely inspired men. The hymnographer, therefore, is bound to follow the pattern of an already existing hymn which is to him the echo of the songs inaudible to uninspired ears. The creative inspiration of the hymn-writer is thus conditioned by this theological conception.

From the seventh century to the eleventh the introduction of new feasts of the Saints, and the extension of already existing ones, brought about an increased production of new poems, which either had their own melodies or were modelled metrically on older hymns and adapted to already existing melodies. With the end of the liturgical development in the course of the eleventh century, at which time the introduction of new hymns was forbidden, this activity came to an

---

[1] Cf. Wellesz, *Trésor de musique byzantine*, i (Paris, 1934), p. 13, and *A History of Byzantine Music and Hymnography* (Oxford, 1949), pp. 47–51. An exposition of the 'Theory of the Icon' is given in O. Demus, *Byzantine Mosaic Decoration* (London, 1948), pp. 5–7.

[2] Pseudo-Dionysius, *Ecclesiastical Hierarchy*, ch. 7.4, in Migne, *Patrologia Graeca*, iii.

end, and it seems that for two centuries the monks restricted themselves to slight and hardly perceptible embellishments of the melodies.
It is true that new hymns were being written up to the twelfth century
in the Greek monasteries in Southern Italy and at Grottaferrata, the
Basilian monastery near Rome, but these hymns had only a local
importance and were not introduced into the Byzantine liturgy. The
last period of Byzantine hymnography coincided with the artistic
renaissance which took place during the reign of the Palaeologan
dynasty (1261–1453). The power of the Byzantine Empire had been
broken by the conquest of Constantinople on 13 April 1204 by the
Crusaders and the establishment of the Latin Empire (1204–61).
During this period the spirit of Byzantium found refuge at the court
of Nicaea, where Byzantine civilization flourished untouched by the
influence of the Western overlords. The situation of the Eastern
Empire seemed hopeless. Parts of Constantinople were in ruins, all
the wealthy quarters were in the hands of the Venetians and Genoese;
the size of the Empire had been considerably reduced, and its financial
state was precarious.

But the situation suddenly changed when, on 25 July 1261, Michael
Palaeologus took Constantinople by a surprise attack. On 15 August
he was crowned in St. Sophia. A spiritual revival began; churches
were built and monasteries were founded; historians wrote annals to
bring back the glory of the past to the memory of their contemporaries. The writings of the theologians covered every field from
mysticism to polemics. Philosophy, rhetoric, and philology flourished
again. The monks began to embellish the music of the hymns with
fioriture. The balance of words and music, so characteristic of the
great period of Byzantine hymnography, was destroyed in favour of
the music, which began to abound in lavish ornamentation. But there
is a certain mannerism to be observed in this new development; for
the music became overloaded with a superficial figuration which
completely obscured the original melodic structure.

From the middle of the fourteenth century onwards the political
situation deteriorated rapidly, until finally the Byzantine Empire
was reduced to Constantinople and its immediate surroundings, with
Morea and a few islands in the Aegean. The end of the Empire became
inevitable. Up to the last, however, the Court maintained its solemn
ceremonial, and cultural life went on as in the days of the Empire's
grandeur. Nevertheless, there was something artificial about it, just
as there was in the coloratura of the music of the *maïstores* (see p. 30,
n. 2). French, Italian, Slav, and Turkish influences had become so

strong in the Eastern Mediterranean, now almost entirely under the domination of foreign conquerors, that even Byzantine ecclesiastical chant took in foreign elements. The monks began to copy foreign melodies and to compose in the Bulgarian, Persian, and Frankish styles. This last development survived the fall of Constantinople in 1453 and the end of the Eastern Empire. In order to earn a living the Byzantine clergy were forced to teach music to the children of their Turkish overlords. Thus it happened that they began to sing in the Turkish manner. As they became accustomed to Turkish music they also began to compose in this style. In musical manuscripts of this period the oriental *ductus* of the Greek letters and of the musical notation is striking. Byzantine musical notation became overloaded with auxiliary signs which eventually ceased to be comprehensible to anybody, so that a simplification of the notation was needed. This reform was undertaken by Chrysanthus of Madytus in 1821.

Unfortunately the liberation of Greece from the Turkish domination had no bearing on the reform of its ecclesiastical music. There was no movement comparable to that which restored the Gregorian melodies at the beginning of the twentieth century. The reason for this is obvious: Gregorian chant had been kept unchanged by the Western Church, and the great majority of the hymns, tropes, and sequences which had flourished for a time in the Middle Ages were eliminated by Pope Pius V in 1568. The tendency therefore in the West, strictly maintained by the Church, was always to preserve Gregorian chant unaltered. The Byzantine Church, on the contrary, from its earliest days encouraged the composition of hymns and did not object either to the introduction of new hymns, or, from the thirteenth century onwards, to changes in the music by the introduction of ever-increasing embellishment. The present state of Neo-Greek ecclesiastical music is, therefore, a legitimate and genuine historical development, whether we approve of it on aesthetic grounds or not, and a reform comparable to that of Gregorian chant is out of the question, since there is no period in its development which can be regarded as representing its purest state. Any date, therefore, which we may suggest to mark the end of Byzantine music proper and the beginning of the music from which Neo-Greek music finally developed must be an arbitrary one and open to criticism. We venture, however, to bring forward the end of the fourteenth century as such a date: that is, the moment when the Byzantine Empire disintegrated and was reduced to the status of an insignificant power. At that moment it had virtually ceased to exist, even before its actual end came with the fall of Constantinople and the conversion of St. Sophia into a Turkish mosque.

THE POETICAL FORMS OF BYZANTINE HYMNOGRAPHY

(i) *Troparion*. The first poetical form which we meet with in Byzantine hymnography is the *troparion*, originally a monostrophic prayer. The *troparia* replaced the versicles which in the early days of the Church had been inserted after each verse of a psalm. Since the singing of whole stanzas after every psalm-verse would have meant an undue lengthening of the service, the *troparia* were inserted only after the last three or the last six verses. From the fifth century onwards special *troparia* were also written for the feast of the day. Soon the form was enlarged and *troparia* of two or more stanzas composed, all the stanzas following the same metrical scheme as the first. Anthimus and Timocles are the first hymn-writers of whom we hear. Both lived in the days of Emperor Leo I (457–74); in neither case have any of their hymns been preserved The only *troparia* of the fifth century which have come down to us are a group of stanzas by Auxentius, beginning:

$$\Pi\tau\omega\chi\grave{o}s \;\kappa\alpha\grave{\iota}\; \pi\acute{\epsilon}\nu\eta s$$
$$\acute{\upsilon}\mu\nuο\hat{\upsilon}\mu\acute{\epsilon}\nu\; \sigma\epsilon,\; K\acute{\upsilon}\rho\iota\epsilon.$$

(We, poor and needy, praise Thee, O Lord.)[1]

A famous *troparion* of the sixth century is the hymn, 'Ο μονογενὴς υἱός (The only-begotten Son)[2] attributed to the Emperor Justinian I. It is a poetical paraphrase of the Constantinople Creed.

Of the innumerable *troparia* of the centuries that follow, a great number have come down to us in the printed liturgical books, especially in the *Menaia*, which contain the Offices for the fixed feasts of the year, in the *Triodion*, which contains those for Lent and Easter, and in the *Pentekostarion*, which contains those for the period from Easter Day to Whitsun.[3] On the great feasts a number of *troparia* on the same theme were linked together to form a unit. Such a group are the twelve *troparia* sung during the Adoration of the Cross on Good Friday. These are attributed to Sophronius, Patriarch of Jerusalem (634–8), but they seem to have their roots in an even older layer of Christian hymnography. Three of them, which treat of the reproach of

---

[1] Cf. J.-B. Pitra, *Analecta Sacra*, i (Paris, 1876), and Wellesz, *A History of Byzantine Music and Hymnography*, pp. 147–51.

[2] The text is taken from W. Christ and M. Paranikas, *Anthologia graeca carminum christianorum* (Leipzig, 1871), p. 52.

[3] The Greek texts of a number of *troparia* can be found in Christ and Paranikas, op. cit.

Christ to his people, are so similar as to suggest that they are in-dependent paraphrases of a common original. One of these *troparia*, Ὅτε τῷ σταυρῷ (When on the Cross), has been preserved in a bilingual version, with the Latin text 'O quando in cruce', in Beneventan manuscripts of the eleventh century. In the Roman liturgy these *troparia* were replaced by the *Improperia*.[1]

Another group of *troparia* is the cycle of the Nativity hymns which are also attributed to Sophronius.[2] The dramatic element in these hymns is so strong that they can be regarded as a kind of Nativity play. The cycle opens with the appeal of the Narrator to Bethlehem, to prepare the manger for God Incarnate. In the third *troparion* Joseph addresses the Virgin, and asks her to explain the strange event which is taking place. In the fourth and fifth *troparia* the chorus pays homage to God, and reflects on the contrast between the Child in the manger and the Lord who holds in his hands the boundaries of the world. In the *troparia* which follow, the miracle which took place at Bethlehem is further expounded until, in the eleventh, the climax of the cycle is reached with the Virgin's answer to Joseph's complaint. The last *troparion*, the epilogue of the Narrator, sums up the miracle of the birth of our Lord and the adoration of the Magi, and ends with an appeal to the congregation to worship Christ's Nativity. A com-parison with Syriac hymnody in the fourth and fifth centuries shows that the Byzantine Nativity cycle derives from an older source. It shows, in fact, that a semi-dramatic form can be traced back to the early days of the Church.

(ii) *Kontakion*. It was the development of the Byzantine liturgy at the end of the fifth and the beginning of the sixth century that gave rise to the *kontakion*,[3] the first great form of Byzantine hymnography. The term *kontakion* (κοντάκιον or κονδάκιον), meaning 'a roll', was applied to the new genre at a later date. St. Romanus, the first hymnographer whom we know to have used the form, called his poems hymns (ὕμνοι), songs (ᾄσματα), songs of praise (αἶνοι), and psalms (ψαλμοί). The *kontakion* consists of from eighteen to twenty-four stanzas all of them modelled on a leading stanza called the *heirmos* (εἱρμός). The *heirmos* either has its own melody or uses an already existing one. In the first place it is called an *automelon* (αὐτόμελον) or an *idiomelon* (ἰδιόμελον), in the second a *prosomoion*

[1] Cf. the chapter 'Greek hymns in the *Adoratio Crucis*' in Wellesz, *Eastern Elements in Western Chant*, where references are given to other studies on this subject.

[2] Cf. Wellesz, 'The Nativity Drama of the Byzantine Church', *Journal of Roman Studies*, xxxvii (1947), pp. 145–51.

[3] Cf. P. Maas, 'Das Kontakion', *Byzantinische Zeitschrift*, xix (1910), pp. 285 ff.

(προσόμοιον). All the stanzas of a *kontakion* have the same number of syllables and the same metre. Acrostic and refrain are obligatory.

The *kontakion* is a poetical homily. Its content was taken from the same sources as the early Byzantine sermons. Most of the early *kontakia* are based on the lessons which were read during the Nativity, Easter, and Pentecost cycles. At a later date *kontakia* for the feasts of the Blessed Virgin, the Apostles, Saints, and Martyrs and the Fathers of the Church were added. Research into the origin of the *kontakion* have shown that it derived from the three main forms of Syriac poetry (see pp. 8–9). From the *mêmrâ*, the festival homily, it took its contents, from the *madrâshâ* and *sogîthâ* its poetical form and its dramatic character. St. Romanus, the greatest of all Byzantine hymnographers, is also the first Byzantine writer of *kontakia*.[1] He grew up at Berytus (Beyrout) in Northern Phoenicia, where he took deacon's orders, and came to Constantinople during the reign of the Emperor Anastasius I (491–518).[2] The decisive impressions of his youth must have come from the poems of St. Ephraem and his pupil, Basil of Seleucia. Many of Romanus's *kontakia* are translations from Ephraem, or are composed under his influence.[3] It has been said that his stanzas are fragments of Ephraem's *mêmrê* put into metre, and that 'he thought in Syriac and sang in Greek'.[4]

Such a statement, however, only explains the origins of Romanus's poetry; it does not help us to understand his genius. If we compare, for example, his *kontakion* on the Second Coming of Christ with that of Ephraem on the same subject[5] we shall find that Romanus uses half as many words to describe the same situation as Ephraem had done, and by his conciseness achieves a greater poetic effect. We know that Byzantine ecclesiastical poetry was closely linked with the demands of the liturgy and that the hymnographer had to express himself within a given framework. If we take these restrictions into account we shall come more and more to admire the achievement of Romanus, whom Tillyard rightly compares with Pindar.[6] His most famous poem is the Nativity *kontakion*, which begins:

[1] Cf. the hymn in honour of the saint by Germanus in the *Menaia*, i (Rome, 1888), p. 305.

[2] The controversy as to whether Romanus lived during the reign of Anastasius I or Anastasius II has now been conclusively settled in favour of the earlier date. Cf. G. Camelli, *Romano il Melode* (Florence, 1930), pp. 11–22.

[3] Cf. C. Emereau, *St. Éphrem le Syrien* (Paris, 1918).

[4] Ibid., p. 104.

[5] Cf. T. Wehofer, 'Untersuchungen zum Lied des Romanus auf die Wiederkunft des Herrn', *Sitzungsberichte d. k. Akademie d. Wissenschaften, phil. hist. Kl.*, 154, 5 (Vienna, 1907), pp. 28–107.

[6] H. J. W. Tillyard, *Byzantine Music and Hymnography* (London, 1923), p. 12.

'Η παρθένος σήμερον
τὸν ὑπερούσιον τίκτει
καὶ ἡ γῆ τὸ σπήλαιον
τῷ ἀπροσίτῳ προσάγει.

(The Virgin today bears the Superessential, and the earth brings the cave to the Unapproachable.)

Up to the twelfth century this hymn was sung every year at Christmas, during dinner at the imperial palace, by a double choir of St. Sophia and the Church of the Apostles. In this poem Romanus introduces the Blessed Virgin, the Magi, and our Lord in direct speech and develops a dialogue between the Blessed Virgin and the Magi which, like the twelve Christmas *troparia* of Sophronius which we have already examined,[1] reminds us of the fully dramatic Western medieval Nativity plays.

Romanus overshadowed all the other hymn-writers of his age— Georgius, Dometius, Kyriakos, Elias, Koukoulos, and Kyprianos— some of whom are known to us only by name. Only the *Acathistus* hymn attributed to the Monophysite Patriarch Sergius, composed probably in 626 when Constantinople was threatened by the Avars, surpassed in fame the Nativity hymn of Romanus. It has survived uncurtailed in the service of the Orthodox Church up to the present day.

The *Acathistus* (Ἀκάθιστος) is a hymn of praise in honour of the Blessed Virgin, who saved Constantinople by a miracle. Until lately the hymn was unhesitatingly ascribed to the Patriarch Sergius, and it was assumed that the hymn was written as a kind of thanksgiving to the Virgin. P. Maas, however, pointed out that the hymn itself shows the style of an earlier period and that only the prooemium may have been composed on the day of the raising of the siege by the enemy.[2] It is sung during the night before Passion Sunday. No manuscript containing music has come down to us from this early period of Byzantine hymnography, probably because such manuscripts were illuminated, and were therefore destroyed by the Iconoclasts. Consequently we do not know anything definite about the music of the *kontakia*. Judging from the present state of Greek music, however, we are led to assume that it was of the same simple syllabic type to which the few stanzas of *kontakia* still in use in the Office of the Greek Orthodox Church are now sung.

(iii) *Kanon*. At the end of the seventh century the *kontakion* sud-

[1] See p. 20.
[2] Cf. P. Maas's review of Dom Placide de Meester's *L'inno acatisto* in *Byzantinische Zeitschrift*, xiv (1905), p. 646.

denly disappeared from the service and was replaced by a new poetical genre, the *kanon*, which has remained in use until the present day. The *kanon* (κάνων) consists of nine odes, each composed in a different metre and sung to a different melody. Each ode (ᾠδή) has from six to nine, or even more, stanzas all modelled on the first, the *heirmos*. The term *kanon* was originally applied to the collection of the nine canticles or odes chanted in the Morning Office. Each of the new poems had to have some connexion with one of the nine canticles.

All writers on Byzantine hymnography consider the period of the *kontakion* to be the highest achievement of Greek ecclesiastical poetry and regard the introduction of the *kanon* as a decline. The reason for this view is that they consider the poetic diction of the *kanons* as aesthetically inferior to the concise diction of the *kontakia*. But this view is only justified if both *kontakion* and *kanon* are regarded as purely literary forms, without taking into account their liturgical function or their music. It is evident that they cannot be so regarded; we must consider both genres as intrinsic parts of the Office, and this leads us to ask why the *kontakion* suddenly disappeared and why the new genre, the *kanon*, was introduced. The reason for the change is to be found in the nineteenth Canon of the Council *in Trullo* (692), in which daily preaching, especially on Sundays, was made obligatory for the higher clergy. But, like the sermon, the *kontakion* had its place in the Morning Office after the reading of the Gospel, of which it was an explanation. Preaching, before or after it, would therefore have meant a duplication of part of the liturgy: so the *kontakion* had to be dropped to make way for the sermon. But it was still felt necessary to embellish the liturgy with hymns, and the daily singing of the *kanons* was therefore introduced. Hitherto it had been customary only during Lent and between Easter and Pentecost.

From the musical point of view the *kanon*, compared with the *kontakion*, was certainly an enrichment of the service. Instead of one melody, as in the *kontakion*, repeated through from twenty-four to thirty stanzas, the *kanon* consisted of nine melodies, each of which ran through nine stanzas. At an early date the second ode, based on the Song of Moses, 'Attendite coeli', was omitted, except in Lent, because of its sombre character. In order to give added variety several monostrophic hymns were added at the beginning and the end of the *kanon*, and others were inserted between the odes. In the first few centuries of *kanon* singing the melodies of the *heirmoi* were of the simple syllabic type, as we know from the manuscripts. When more hymns were introduced into the service, and the melodies became more embellished and therefore sung in a slower tempo, the *kanons* were felt to be too long, especially during Lent and Holy Week. It became necessary to shorten them by reducing the number of the stanzas to three.

We must now return to the question of whether the *kanon* is inferior to the *kontakion* as a work of art. The answer is that the two genres cannot properly be compared, for they have a different purpose. The *kontakion* is dynamic, the *kanon* static. In the former the poem is more important than the music; in the latter the music is more important than the poetry. It is for this reason that writers of *kanons* make extensive use of two principles peculiar to Eastern art: reiteration and variation. By the use of these two principles the content of the stanza— and the whole content must be taken as a unit—acts on the mind of the congregation like a meditation; though a word here and there may be missed, the idea of the stanza, contained in words and music, will still impress itself on the faithful. We must therefore take the words and music of the hymns together as a single entity and consider their liturgical function. This is the only way in which we can come to understand the beauty and richness of this art, so strange to the Western mind if approached from the literary side alone.

We must not, however, blame the first generation of Byzantine scholars for failing to find the right approach. When investigations into Byzantine hymnography began in the middle of the nineteenth century nothing was known about the melodies of the hymns, which had been transmitted in a type of neumatic notation which it seemed impossible to decipher. The metrical structure of Byzantine hymns had only just been rediscovered; the knowledge that they were written in accordance with a metrical scheme had been completely lost during the dark age of Greek history which followed the conquest of Constantinople in 1453. In the liturgical books, both in the manuscripts and in the editions printed at Venice from 1500 onwards, hymns, of whatever form, are given in a running text, divided up by dots or asterisks. These marks, it was assumed, were intended to facilitate reading and singing. The discovery that the dots were always placed after the same number of syllables in all the paragraphs of a hymn was made by Cardinal Pitra during his stay in St. Petersburg in 1859. 'Le pèlerin', as he describes himself, 'était en possession du système syllabique des hymnographes.'[1] The importance of the discovery

---

[1] Cf. J.-B. Pitra, *L'Hymnographie de l'Église grecque* (Rome, 1867), p. 11. In fact, the discovery was first made by F. J. Mone in his *Lateinische Hymnen des Mittelalters*, 3 vols. (1853–5), but this collection was not used by Pitra or other scholars who worked on Byzantine hymnography.

was immediately evident. Pitra found that the hymns were composed in a metre no longer based on quantity, as had been the case in classical poetry, but on the principle that the accents of the lines must coincide with the accents of the words. His work was taken up and developed further by W. Christ, K. Krumbacher, P. Maas, and G. Camelli. We are now able to examine in detail the structure of Byzantine hymns and to compare the metre of the stanzas with that of the melodies of the *heirmoi*. It is obvious that as the same melody is used for all the stanzas the accents must be on the same syllable in the line in each. The present writer's investigations into the metre of the poetry and the music have clearly shown that the tonic accents of the lines coincide with the accented notes of the melody. These notes are marked either by a large melodic interval or by a dynamic sign which demands accentuated singing of the note on which it is set. This principle is strictly observed in the *idiomela*, or odes which have their own melody. Slight deviations from it can be found in some of the *prosomoia*, or odes written to an already existing melody. Indeed it is possible to tell at once from the way in which words and melody fit together whether both were written by the same hymnographer.

Andrew of Crete was the first writer of *kanons*. He was born at Damascus *c*. 660. In his youth he lived as a monk in Jerusalem, and later became a deacon of the Great Church in Constantinople. During the short anarchic reign of Philippicus Bardanes (711–13) he obtained the archbishopric of Crete and attended the Pseudo-Synod of Constantinople, at which the Monothelite heresy won a short-lived victory. Later he repudiated his heretical errors and returned to orthodoxy. He died *c*. 740. The Orthodox Church forgave him, admitted his *kanons* to the liturgy and made him a saint. His most famous work is the 'Great Kanon' of Mid-Lent Week, consisting of 250 *troparia* divided into four sections. There can be no doubt that Andrew of Crete owed much to Romanus, and it will be seen from a comparison of the *proemium* Ψυχή μου of Romanus with its paraphrase in the fourth ode of the 'Great Kanon' how he worked on a given pattern:

Ψυχή μου, ψυχή μου,
ἀνάστα, τί καθεύδεις;
τὸ τέλος ἐγγίζει
καὶ μέλλεις θορυβεῖσθαι·
ἀνάνηψον οὖν,
ἵνα φείσηταί σου Χριστὸς ὁ θεός.
ὁ πανταχοῦ παρὼν
καὶ τὰ πάντα πληρῶν.

ROMANUS.

(My soul, my soul arise; why sleepest thou? The end is coming, and thou wilt be confounded. Be sober, that Christ the Lord may spare thee; for he is everywhere and filleth all things.)

Ἐγγίζει, ψυχή, τὸ τέλος,
ἐγγίζει καὶ οὐ φροντίζεις,
οὐχ ἑτοιμάζῃ·
ὁ καιρὸς συντέμνει, διανάστηθι·
ἐγγὺς ἐπὶ θύραις ὁ κριτής ἐστιν·
ὡς ὄναρ, ὡς ἄνθος ὁ χρόνος
τοῦ βίου τρέχει·
τί μάτην ταραττόμεθα;

Ἀνάνηψον, ὦ ψυχή μου,
τὰς πράξεις σου, ἃς εἰργάσω,
ἀναλογίζου,
καὶ ταύτας ἐπ᾽ ὄψεσι προσάγαγε
καὶ σταγόνας στάλαξον δακρύων σου·
εἰπὲ παρρησίᾳ τὰς πράξεις,
τὰς ἐνθυμήσεις
Χριστῷ καὶ δικαιώθητι.

ANDREW OF CRETE.

(The end is near, O soul, it is near, and you take no heed. You make no preparation. The time is growing short; arise. Near, at the door, stands the Judge. Like a dream, like a flower, the time of life is running out. Why are we confused by vain thoughts?

Be sober, my soul, consider the works which thou hast done, and bring them before thine eyes, and let thy tears run down. Confess thy works and desires freely to Christ and be justified.)[1]

Damascus was also the birthplace of the two other great hymnwriters of this period, St. John Damascene (c. 700–60) and his foster-brother, St. Kosmas of Jerusalem (also called Kosmas of Crete) (d. c. 760). They grew up together and having completed their studies at Jerusalem both became monks in the monastery of St. Sabas near the Dead Sea. Here flourished the first school of *kanon* writers, a group of eighth-century Greek, Syrian, Armenian, and Coptic monks, among whom John Damascene and Kosmas were the most outstanding. The hymns of John Damascene and Kosmas of Jerusalem show a marked difference from those of the first period, and also from those of Andrew of Crete. The classical education which both had received in the house of John's wealthy father influenced the thought and style of their poems, and we may take it as significant that John is the only one of all the *kanon* writers to reintroduce classical iambic trimeters in his three *kanons* for the Nativity, Epiphany, and Pentecost. They are, however, constructed in such a way that the Byzantine principle

[1] Cf. Wellesz, *A History of Byzantine Music and Hymnography*, p. 175.

of tonic accentuation can also be regarded as the basis of the metrical scheme.[1]

Unlike Andrew of Crete, both John Damascene and Kosmas of Jerusalem were strong supporters of Orthodoxy. In his writings *Against Heresies*, in his *Precise Exposition of the Orthodox Faith*, and in his other treatises John Damascene laid a firm basis for Eastern theology, summarizing the doctrines of the Eastern Fathers of the Church, and putting them into a form which from his time onwards was considered authoritative. But he played an even more important part in his defence of Image-worship in the first phase of the Orthodox Church's fight against the Iconoclast Emperors. His three *Apologetic Discourses against those who reject the Holy Images* (726–30) had a great influence on the Eastern clergy and rallied them to resistance against the Emperor, whom they anathematized in 730. John Damascene's attitude in the iconoclastic controversy had far-reaching consequences. Owing to his authoritative position in the Eastern Church, both as theologian and as hymn-writer, it came about that Byzantine hymnographers were the strongest supporters of the Orthodox creed, and professed it in the face of defamation, torture, and death throughout the long period of the conflict until the final victory of the Image-worshippers in 843.

Tradition attributes to John Damascene the introduction of the *Oktoechos* or eight-week cycles of hymns composed in one of the eight modes. In the Byzantine Church the music of the hymns was collected in eight groups according to the mode in which it was composed. Each group, beginning at Easter with the hymns of the First Mode, was sung for a week, so that after a period of eight weeks the modal cycle was repeated with a fresh set of hymns. We now know that these cycles go back to Jewish tradition,[2] but John Damascene must have played an important part in building up the repertory, as in the manuscripts which contain the model stanzas, the *heirmologia*, the first of the melodies in each group of *heirmoi* is attributed to him, usually under the name 'John the Monk' (Ἰωάννης μοναχός). Among his numerous *kanons* the Orthodox Church gives the highest praise to his Easter *kanon*, called the 'Golden Kanon' or 'Queen of Kanons'. This hymn is familiar to the English-speaking world in J. M. Neale's verse translation,[3] which begins:

[1] Cf. Christ, *Anthologia graeca carminum christianorum*, p. xlvi.

[2] Cf. E. Werner, 'The Doxology in Synagogue and Church', *The Hebrew Union College Annual*, xix (1946), p. 332.

[3] The Greek text of the Easter *kanon* is given in full in Christ's *Anthologia Graeca*, pp. 218–21. Neale gives a prose translation in his *A History of the Holy Eastern Church*,

The day of Resurrection:
Earth, tell it out abroad!
The Passover of Gladness!
The Passover of God!

We give here the *heirmos* of the first ode:

Ex. 3

Cod. Iviron

As often happens, a number of *kanons* by unknown writers of a later
date have been ascribed to John Damascene, and the same is true of
a number of *heirmoi*, ascribed in the manuscripts to 'John the Monk',
some of which are the work of John Mauropus (d. 1060) and not of
John Damascene.[2]

Kosmas of Jerusalem is the author of nineteen *kanons* for the great
feasts of the year, among them the 'Great Kanon' sung on the Thurs-
day of Passion Week at Lauds after the fifty-first psalm, 'Have mercy
upon me, O God'. The penitential mood of the psalm is kept throughout the *kanon*, as can be seen from the first two stanzas of the eighth
ode:[3]

Ὅν στρατιαὶ οὐρανῶν δοξάζουσι καὶ φρίττει τὰ Χερουβὶμ

καὶ τὰ Σεραφίμ, πᾶσα πνοὴ καὶ κτίσις

ὑμνεῖτε, εὐλογεῖτε, καὶ ὑπερυψοῦτε

εἰς πάντας τοὺς αἰῶνας.

i, pp. 880–5. The music of the hymn has been studied by Dom H. Gaisser in his article
'Les Heirmoi des Pâques', first published in *Oriens Christianus*, iii (1903), pp. 416–510,
by Tillyard and by the present writer. Cf. Wellesz, *A History of Byzantine Music and
Hymnography*, pp. 177–92, where the music of all the odes is given.

[1] A later, slightly more ornamental version is recorded in *The History of Music in
Sound* (H.M.V.), ii, side 1.

[2] Cf. Tillyard, *Byzantine Music and Hymnography*, pp. 35–36.

[3] Ibid., p. 22.

'Ημαρτηκότα, σωτήρ, ἐλέησον διέγειρόν μου τὸν νοῦν
πρὸς ἐπιστροφήν, δέξαι μετανοοῦντα,
οἰκτείρησον βοῶντα· ἥμαρτόν σοι, σῶσον·
ἠνόμησα, ἐλέησόν με.

(Him whom the hosts of heaven glorify, and of whom the Cherubim and Seraphim stand in awe, let all life and creation praise, bless, and exalt throughout all ages.

I have sinned, Saviour; have mercy upon me, raise my mind to conversion, receive me penitent, have pity upon me when I cry: I have sinned against Thee, save me: I have transgressed, have mercy upon me.)

Towards the end of the eighth century the centre of hymnography shifted from St. Sabas to the Studium monastery in Constantinople. Here the monks were in the thick of the battle against the Iconoclasts. St. Theophanes (759–c. 842), the first of this group, seems to have come from Jerusalem. He and his brother Theodorus were branded on the forehead by order of the Emperor Theophilus (829–42), the last of the Iconoclasts, and they were therefore given the name of οἱ γραπτοί, the branded ones, by the Orthodox Church. The fate of their contemporary, St. Theodore of the Studium (759–826), was not as cruel as theirs, but he, too, was persecuted by the Emperor Leo V, 'the Armenian' (813–20), and imprisoned and exiled. St. Theodore was the greatest of the hymnographers of the Studium school; a number of his hymns have found their way into the service-books of the Orthodox Church, and are sung at the present day. He was most successful as a writer of *kanons*, among which that for Sexagesima Sunday on the Last Judgement has won the highest praise.[1] Another member of this first generation of hymn-writers in the Studium was St. Methodius I (d. 846), who was born at Syracuse. He was sent as legate by Pope Paschal to Constantinople and was kept in close confinement by the Emperor Michael III (820–9) for his defence of the Icons.[2] After the end of the Iconoclast movement and the restoration of Orthodoxy Methodius became Patriarch of Constantinople and convoked the Synod which is celebrated on Orthodoxy Sunday.

The last of the great hymnographers of the Studium was St. Joseph (d. 883), a Sicilian by birth. In an attempt to reach Rome in order to escape the persecutions of the Image-breakers he was captured by pirates who held him prisoner for a long time. He was finally released and subsequently lived in Constantinople as a writer of hymns. Though he was not as original as his forerunners his style must have appealed greatly to the taste of his contemporaries, since more than

[1] J. M. Neale gave a verse translation of the *kanon* in *Hymns of the Eastern Church* (London, 1863), pp. 104–12.
[2] Ibid., p. 119.

D

two hundred of his *kanons* are retained in the printed *Menaia* besides those to be found in the *Triodion* and in the *Oktoechos*. One of the last of the famous hymn-writers was John Mauropus (d. *c.* 1080), Metropolitan of Euchaïta,[1] who composed 151 *kanons* of which all but three have acrostics ending with 'John' and often with 'John the Monk'. Only a small number of these, however, have been included in the printed liturgical books. By the eleventh century Byzantine service-books were so crowded with hymns for every feast of the ecclesiastical year that the Church forbade the introduction of new ones. In the thirteenth and fourteenth centuries the monks concentrated on the embellishment of the existing melodies by *fioriture*, and on the composition of new ones in an ornamented style. Among the *maïstores*[2] of this period John Glykys, Manuel Chrysaphes, John Lampadarios, and John Cucuzeles were the outstanding figures. The only places where new *kanons* and *troparia* were still written in the twelfth century were the Basilian monasteries in Southern Italy, particularly the Badia of Grottaferrata, founded in 1004 by St. Nilus the Younger. This local school, however, represented by Bartholomew, Arsenios, Germanus, and other minor hymnographers, had no influence upon Byzantine hymnography.

MINOR HYMNOGRAPHY

The writing of *troparia* went on during the whole period of Byzantine hymnography. The *kontakia* and *kanons* are preceded, interspersed, and followed by monostrophic poems, which are often more beautiful than the more important poetic forms. To this group belong, for example, the *theotokia* (Θεοτόκια or, more frequently, Θεοτοκία), monostrophic hymns in praise of the Blessed Virgin. The following is an example from the *Oktoechos*.[3] The music, composed in the fourth plagal mode, is of the slightly ornamented syllabic type. Where two or three notes are set to a syllable older manuscripts often have only one note:

Ex. 4

Mode Pl. IV

Ἀ - νύμ - φευ-τε Παρ - θέ - νε   ἡ   τὸν θε - ὸν   ἀ - φρά-στως συλ - λα - βοῦ - σα

---

[1] Cf. J. Hussey, 'The Canons of John Mauropus', *The Journal of Roman Studies*, xxxvii (1947), p. 71.

[2] This name was given in the late period of hymnography to the composers who embellished the earlier simple melodies.

[3] Cf. H. J. W. Tillyard, *The Hymns of the Octoechus*, Part I, *Monumenta Musicae Byzantinae* (Copenhagen, 1940), pp. 143–4.

σαρ-κί, Μή-τηρ. θε-οῦ ... τοῦ ὑ-ψί - στου, σῶν ἱ-κε-τῶν
πα-ρα-κλή-σεις δέ-χου, παν-ά - μω-με ἡ πᾶ-σι χο-ρη-γοῦ - -
σα κα-θα-ρι-σμὸν τῶν πται-σμά - των .. νῦν τὰς ἡ-μῶν ἱ-κε -
σί-ας προσ-δε-χο - μέ - νη δυσ - ώ-πει σω-θῆ-ναι πάν - τας ἡ-μῶν.

(O Virgin, unwedded, who didst ineffably conceive God in the flesh, Mother of God most high, receive the entreaties of thy servants. Blameless one who dost minister to the cleansing of sins unto all, accept our supplications and plead for the salvation of us all.)[1]

There are, however, other hymns in the Office which are more interesting from the musical point of view because they show a more developed structure. These are the *stichera*. A *sticheron* (στιχερόν) is a monostrophic hymn which follows the verse (στίχος) of a psalm. The *stichera* were collected in a bulky service-book called the *Sticherarion* of which only a few copies have come down to us: these date from the tenth to the thirteenth centuries; and the Codex Dalassinos of the Vienna National Library has been reproduced in facsimile in the *Monumenta Musicae Byzantinae* (1935). The melodic structure of the *stichera* shows great variety. A large number are of the syllabic type, particularly those for the minor feasts. Others show some ornaments, mostly on the last syllable of a word before a caesura. The most elaborate *stichera* are those for Holy Week and the Nativity, as can be seen from the opening of the *stichera* sung during Vespers on Good Friday:

Mode II Plagal   Ex.5 [2]

"Ω .... πῶς .... ἡ πα-ρά -
νο - - μος συν-α-γω-γὴ τὸν βα-σι-λέ - α τῆς κτί-σε -

[1] Ibid., p. xv.
[2] Codex Dalassinos, fo. 293. Cf. Wellesz, *A History of Byzantine Music and Hymnography*, pp. 284–5 and p. 314.

ως . . κατ - ε - δί - κα - σεν θα - νά - τῳ,

(How could the lawless council condemn to death the King of Creation?)

The richly developed melodic form of these melodies in the twelfth-
and thirteenth-century manuscripts is the achievement of several
generations of musicians who gradually embellished the originally
simpler structure.[1] From comparative study of the different states of
the notation, however, it can be shown that the earlier versions in the
tenth-century manuscripts also made use of ornaments which can be
traced back to the sixth century, as, for example, in the case of the
bilingual hymn, *Ὅτε τῷ σταυρῷ—O quando in cruce*.[2]

In the final period of the Byzantine Empire and under the Turkish
domination the technique of embellishing the melodies, and of introducing a rhythm originally alien to them, became more and more
obvious. This late development of Byzantine hymnography, however,
has not yet been made the subject of musicological research and it
does not belong to the sphere of Byzantine music proper. At present
it is necessary to concentrate our efforts on the transcription of music
from the manuscripts of the twelfth, thirteenth, and fourteenth centuries. These manuscripts contain the stage of Byzantine notation
which can be deciphered without difficulty. When this task has been
achieved we shall have proved that the music of the Byzantine Church
was in no way inferior to that of the Church in the West.

THE ACCLAMATIONS

The Emperor was the head of the Church. His daily life and that
of the imperial family was therefore regulated by innumerable ceremonies of a semi-religious or even religious character: they are described in the *De Caeremoniis* of Constantine VII Porphyrogennetos
(912–59).[3] This cycle of ceremonies formed a counterpart to the cycle
of the feasts of the ecclesiastical year. Music, both vocal and instrumental, played an important part in heightening the solemnity of the
ceremonies. It consisted of acclamations, processional songs, hymns,
and dances, of music played on the organ either to accompany the
chants or to fill in the intervals between the stanzas of the songs, and

[1] Cf. Wellesz, *Eastern Elements in Western Chant*.

[2] Ibid., pp. 68–110. Recorded in *The History of Music in Sound*, ii, sides 1 and 2.

[3] *De Caeremoniis aulae byzantinae*, ed. J. J. Reiske, *Corpus scriptorum historiae
byzantinae* (Bonn, 1829–30). Two volumes only have been published of the new edition
by A. Vogt, *Constantin VII Porphyrogénète, Le Livre des Cérémonies, Collection byzantine* (Paris, 1935, 1939).

of music played by the imperial band. The processional songs, which had the form of the *troparion*, were given different names when they were sung on the way from the palace to the church, and when they were sung on the way back. The same chant is called *phone* on the way to the church, and *apelatikos* on the way back.[1] Chants which accompanied the Emperor and his suite as they rode back to the Palace at a quicker pace than that of the outward journey are called *dromika*. On the evening of 11 May, the birthday of Constantinople, hymns were sung to the dance of the torch-bearers. During the *Gothikon*, the play performed on the ninth day of the Christmas celebrations, dance tunes accompanied on lutes were sung to the war-dances of the players, who were disguised as Goths.[2]

Among these groups of ceremonial chant the acclamations seem to have occupied the most prominent place. We are, at any rate, most fully informed by the *De Caeremoniis* about the part they played in Byzantine life, and about their texts. Unfortunately only a few pieces of ceremonial music dating from the fifteenth century have come down to us. As these were composed for the reception of an Emperor, Empress, and the Patriarch at a monastery they are modelled on liturgical music and cannot be regarded as typical specimens of the music of the ceremonies. We may, however, assume that the acclamations, which were sung on religious or semi-religious occasions by clerics called *psaltae* (ψάλται), were similar to these surviving specimens. The acclamations sung by the *kractae* (κράκται), who were court officials and laymen, may have been of the same type, but were probably less elaborate.

The *kractae* belonged to the retinue of the Emperor. When the Emperor took part in a procession[3] or went to church the *kractae* and *psaltae* sang the acclamations together and the responses were sung by the crowd. On Christmas Eve[4] the singing of the two groups in church was accompanied by instruments, one of the rare occasions when instrumental music was admitted to the church. The imperial band consisted of trumpeters (σαλπιγκταί), horn-players (βουκκινάτορες), cymbal players (ἀνακαρισταί), and pipers (σουρουλισταί). None of the 'weak-sounding' instruments (τῶν λεπτῶν ὀργάνων) were used.[5] To the

---

[1] Cf. J. Handschin, *Das Zeremonienwerk Kaiser Konstantins und die sangbare Dichtung* (Basle, 1942), pp. 8–17.

[2] *De Caeremoniis*, ed. Vogt, ii, pp. 182–5.

[3] Cf. the list of processional hymns in Handschin, op. cit., pp. 11–14, 68.

[4] Codinus Curopalata, *De officiis*, in *Corpus scriptorum historiae byzantinae*, pp. 33–55.

[5] Cf. Wellesz, *A History of Byzantine Music and Hymnography*, p. 93.

Western mind it seems strange that the organ was forbidden in the church.[1] The Byzantines had a portable pneumatic organ which was played in processions but had to be left in the porch when the procession entered the church. It was also played in the Hippodrome and during banquets at the Imperial Palace.[2] Organs were used in pairs, one accompanying the choir of the Greens (*Prasini*, πράσινοι), another that of the Blues (*Veneti*, βένετοι), the two leading factions. The Emperor had his own organs which were covered with gold. Those of the Greens and Blues were covered with silver.[3] The institution of the circus with its chariot races, games, and fights, and of the factions[4] who cheered the Emperor when he appeared in public in the circus, goes back to the Roman Caesars, some of whom took a passionate interest in the races. We find also that *laudes* in praise of Caligula, Nero, Domitian, and Trajan were shouted by the senators. The elaborate form of salutations organized by Nero was introduced by him after his return from the Greek East, where he had been acclaimed in this way.[5] When the whole system of Roman administration was transferred by Constantine the Great to his metropolis, the 'New Rome' of the Eastern Empire, he also transferred the system of the factions or *demes* among which the Blues and the Greens were the most powerful.

From the time of Heraclius I onwards, as a consequence of the victory over Persia, Byzantine court ceremonial became more and more orientalized, and the acclamations developed into panegyric formulae. An acclamation with which the crowd wished long life to the Emperor, the Empress, and the Princes was called *polychronion*, that with which they were greeted by the clergy *euphemia* or *euphemesis*.[6] We give an example of the music of an *euphemesis* from the last years of the Byzantine Empire, from a manuscript in the library of the Pantocrator monastery on Mount Athos. It is in honour of John VIII Palaeologus (1425–48), of his third wife Maria Comnena of Trebizond, and of the Patriarch Joseph II.[7] According to the rubrics the first phrase sung during the ceremony of the blessing is

---

[1] Cf. Wellesz, *A History of Byzantine Music and Hymnography*, pp. 94–98.

[2] Cf. J. Marquart, *Osteuropäische und ostasiatische Streifzüge* (Leipzig, 1903), pp. 217 sqq.

[3] *De Caeremoniis*, i, ed. Reiske, p. 571.

[4] Cf. S. Runciman, *Byzantine Civilisation*, 2nd ed. (London, 1936), p. 71.

[5] Cf. M. P. Charlesworth, '*Pietas* and *Victoria*', *Journal of Roman Studies*, xxxiii (1943), p. 5.

[6] Cf. H. J. W. Tillyard, 'The Acclamations of Emperors in Byzantine Ritual', *Annual of the British School at Athens*, xxiii (1911–12).

[7] Cf. Tillyard, *Byzantine Music and Hymnography*, p. 59, and Wellesz, *A History of Byzantine Music and Hymnography*, pp. 104–5.

repeated three times, first by those inside the church, then by the crowd outside, then again by those inside the church. The acclamations, both to the Emperor and Empress and to the Patriarch are first sung by those in the church and then repeated by the crowd outside:

Ex.6

(Many be the years of the Sovereigns [*three times*]. Many be the years of John, the most religious King and Emperor of the Romans, the Palaeologus, and of Mary, the most religious Empress [*twice*]. Many be the years of Joseph, the most holy Oecumenical Patriarch [*twice*].)

From the text of this acclamation we learn that this panegyric style was used to greet a high dignitary of the Church as well as the Emperor and Empress. After the fall of Constantinople acclamations were only used to greet bishops when they visited a monastery. At present they are only sung in honour of an archbishop.

BYZANTINE MUSICAL NOTATION

We have to distinguish between two systems of Byzantine musical notation—one for the formal reading of the lessons, and the other for the singing of the hymns. The first, the so-called ecphonetic notation, seems to have been introduced towards the end of the fourth century.[2]

[1] Translation by H. J. W. Tillyard.
[2] Cf. C. Høeg, *La Notation ekphonétique* (Copenhagen, 1935), pp. 38–39.

Owing to the lack of manuscripts we know nothing about its develop-ment. It appears fully developed in manuscripts of the eighth century and is maintained practically unchanged until the end of the thir-teenth. From the beginning of the fourteenth century it begins slowly to disintegrate, and by the beginning of the fifteenth the meaning of the signs has become obscure. As in the Syrian ecphonetic system (see p. 10) the signs are set at the beginning and at the end of a phrase in order to regulate the cantillation. This, it is clear, became real singing on the more solemn feasts, as can be seen from a table in Codex Sinaiticus 8, fo. 303, where the neumatic signs are superimposed on the ecphonetic.[1] A complete list of the ecphonetic signs and their names has come down to us in a table in Codex Leimon. fo. 318. Unfortunately its discoverer, Papadopoulos-Kerameus,[2] gave only part of it in facsimile, and misplaced some of the signs in his tran-scription so that the list made no sense. His erroneous interpretation was accepted by J.-B. Thibaut in his *Origine byzantine de la notation neumatique*, p. 20, and in P. Wagner's *Neumenkunde*, pp. 24–26, and in J. Wolf's *Handbuch der Notationskunde*, i, p. 63. From these books it found its way into many other books. From the investigation of manuscripts containing ecphonetic signs the present writer realized that some of the signs listed by Thibaut did not actually occur any-where in the manuscripts. This conclusion led him to examine the reproduction of the table in Papadopoulos-Kerameus's essay and he found it necessary to assume that the original table must contain a different placing of the signs. He also realized that the original table was a kind of 'primer' giving the signs arranged as they might occur in a lesson.[3] The photographs of the manuscript which Høeg made some years later and reproduced as table I of his *La Notation ekphonétique* showed the correctness of this view. The correct list of the ecphonetic signs is as follows:[4]

Simple Signs		Compound Signs	
⌒	Oxeia	⫽	Oxeiai
∿	Syrmatikē	⟍	Bareiai
⟍	Bareia		
⌣	Kathistē	⋯	Kentemata

[1] Cf. C. Høeg, *La Notation ekphonétique* (Copenhagen, 1935), table III and pp. 26–35.
[2] Μαυροκορδάτειος Βιβλιοθήκη (Athens, 1884), p. 50.
[3] E. Wellesz, 'Die byzantinischen Lektionszeichen', *Zeitschrift für Musikwissenschaf.*, xi (1929), pp. 513–34.
[4] Ibid., p. 521 and *A History of Byzantine Music and Hymnography*, p. 221.

✓	Kremastē	⌐····· ⌃	apeso exo
⌐	Apostrophos	⌐⌐	Apostrophoi
‿	Synemba	ᐳ ᐳ	
⋎	Paraklitikē		Hypokrisis
✛	Teleia	ᐳ ᐳ	

The simple signs are used in the first part of the lesson. But towards the end the compound signs are used. These are emphatic[1] and are probably sung in order to prepare the congregation to respond with the doxological formula.

The *Lectionaria*, which contain the lessons for the ecclesiastical year with ecphonetic signs, form two groups of codices, the *Prophetologia* and the *Evangeliaria*. The *Prophetologium* contains the lessons from the Old Testament, mainly from the Prophets, among whom Isaiah is prominent, but also from the Octateuch and Proverbs. The *Evangeliarium*, the *Epistolarium*, and the *Praxapostolus*, contain the lessons from the New Testament. These books are written for the most part in a calligraphic hand, but the ecphonetic signs are inserted by another hand in a reddish ink which has usually turned brown. The signs are always less carefully written than the text, which suggests that they were inserted by a skilled precentor.

The Byzantine musical notation of the hymn-books shows three phases: (1) an early one represented in manuscripts of the tenth to twelfth centuries, in which the signs have no interval value; (2) a later one extending from the eleventh to the fifteenth century in which the signs give clear indication of the size of the intervals and their dynamic and rhythmical significance, and (3) a final phase, beginning in the fifteenth century, in which an increasing number of additional signs in red ink are added to the interval notation. A certain development can be observed within these three phases, and they are linked together by manuscripts in which the transition from the first phase to the second and from the second to the third can be observed. It can be clearly seen from the earliest manuscripts that many of the signs of Byzantine musical notation originated in the Greek accents. This theory was put forward by O. Fleischer in his *Neumen-Studien*, I (Berlin, 1895) and by J.-B. Thibaut in his *Origine byzantine de la notation de l'église latine* (Paris, 1907), and has been generally accepted.

[1] E. Wellesz, *A History of Byzantine Music and Hymnography*, pp. 222–6.

There are, however, some signs to be found in this early phase of notation which make it difficult to accept fully the accent hypothesis.

We do not think that the Byzantine neums were originally intended to indicate the flow of music, for we know from the earliest manuscripts that these signs were not set for every note but only for the formulas typical of the mode. As these were known to every singer we may assume that the signs, or at any rate some of them, had the function of regulating the dynamic and rhythmical interpretation of the formulas, which were sung to many different texts and therefore needed indications as to how the melody was to be fitted to the words. It will be sufficient to give here a short introduction to the Middle-Byzantine system of musical notation, since we can read music only when it is written down in an interval notation. This middle phase has been deciphered independently by H. J. W. Tillyard and the present writer. Riemann's transcriptions of early Byzantine neums in his book, *Die byzantinische Notenschrift im 10. bis 15. Jahrhundert* (Leipzig, 1909), and those of Gastoué in his *Catalogue des manuscrits de Musique byzantine* (Paris, 1907) are purely hypothetical and misleading.

The Byzantine hymnographers of the eleventh century developed a clever and economical system of indicating the interval which was to be sung, together with its dynamic and rhythmical interpretation. They distinguished between the most frequently recurring intervals, the ascending and descending seconds which they called *somata* (bodies) and the intervals of the third and fifth which they called *pneumata* (spirits). For all the other intervals combinations of these two were used. The sign for the repeated tone was called *ison* (equal). To these, two other signs were added which were neither *soma* nor *pneuma*: the *aporrhoë*, a descending third performed in a *glissando*, and the *kratemo-hyporrhoon*, a sign indicating the same movement executed more vigorously, with the first note lengthened and accentuated. Thus we get the following table of neums for the intervals for which a single neumatic sign existed:

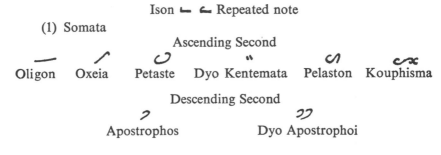

Ison ⌐ ⌐ Repeated note

(1) Somata

Ascending Second

Oligon   Oxeia   Petaste   Dyo Kentemata   Pelaston   Kouphisma

Descending Second

Apostrophos   Dyo Apostrophoi

(2) Pneumata

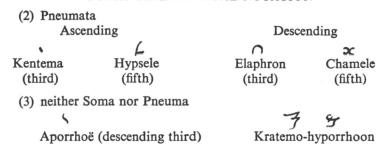

Ascending   Descending

Kentema   Hypsele   Elaphron   Chamele
(third)   (fifth)   (third)   (fifth)

(3) neither Soma nor Pneuma

Aporrhoë (descending third)   Kratemo-hyporrhoon

It will be seen from the table that six different signs were used for the ascending second, while for the ascending and descending thirds and fifths only one sign existed. For the descending second also, in fact, only one interval sign was used; the *dyo apostrophoi* meant nothing else but the doubling of the time of the *apostrophos*, i.e. an unaccentuated quaver becomes a crotchet. From the study of the theorists[1] we learn that each of the six signs for the ascending second had a different meaning and demanded in each case a different execution from the singer. If we take the quaver as the basis we can see how the neums can best be transcribed into modern staff notation:

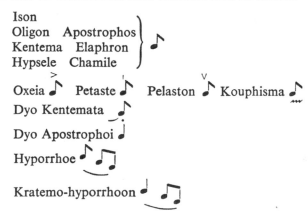

Ison
Oligon   Apostrophos
Kentema   Elaphron
Hypsele   Chamile

Oxeia   Petaste   Pelaston   Kouphisma

Dyo Kentemata

Dyo Apostrophoi

Hyporrhoe

Kratemo-hyporrhoon

In addition to the interval signs, an ever-increasing number of dynamic and rhythmical signs were used. The most common of these are:

Bareia ＼ Diple ∥ Parakletike ≏ Kratema ⁄ℓ Kylisma ˙⌣⌣
Gorgon ⌐ Argon ⌐ Antikenoma ⇁ Tzakisma ⌣
Xeron Klasma ⌒⌐ Piasma ⑊ Apoderma ⌒ (⌣⌣)
Thematismos eso ⊕ Thematismos exo ⊕ Thema haploun ⊕

---

[1] Cf. E. Wellesz, *A History of Byzantine Music and Hymnography*, pp. 237–43. A collection of the theoretical treatises is published in L. Tardo, *L'Antica melurgia bizantina* (Grottaferrata, 1938), pp. 151–247. A critical edition of the treatises is still badly needed.

The Byzantine theorists give indications of the meaning of these additional signs, but fully satisfactory explanations are given only for those occurring in manuscripts from the twelfth to the fourteenth centuries. They are rendered in our transcriptions as follows:

Bareia ♪

Diple ♩　Kratema ♩

Tzakisma ♪　Parakletike ♪　Seisma ♪

Gorgon = *accel.*　Argon = *rit.*　Apoderma ⌢

Xeron Klasma = *mezzo stacc.*　Kylisma ♩♩♩♩

In order to mark the interval of the ascending fourth, sixth, seventh, and the octave, two or three signs were combined and written one above the other, and a similar method was used to indicate the descending fourth. In some combinations, however, the signs are set one after the other. This happens when a *pneuma* (an ascending third or fifth) is combined with a *soma*. In this setting, i.e. *soma* followed by *pneuma*, the *soma* becomes 'soundless' (ἄφωνον). It loses its interval value but gives its dynamic nuance to the *pneuma*. This is the reason why in Byzantine notation relatively few signs are needed to give a great variety to the intervals.

The first musicologists who tried to decipher Byzantine musical notation were not aware of the meaning of ἄφωνον. Some of them, for example Riemann, treated the 'soundless' *soma* as a grace-note. Others ignored it and therefore failed to decipher the notation properly. Fleischer came nearest to the solution of the problem when he published and commented on the most important theoretical treatise on Byzantine musical notation, the *Papadike*, in his *Neumen-Studien*, III (Berlin, 1904), but he failed to draw the right conclusions from his discovery and gave only skeletons of the melodies in his transcriptions, completely neglecting their rhythmical shape. It was the discovery that the Byzantine *melodoi* used the signs for the most frequently occurring interval, the ascending second, also as rhythmical signs in combination with other intervals, which made a satisfactory transcription of Byzantine neums possible.[1] The following table shows the way in which those intervals are built up which are to be transcribed by a quaver without an expression mark. If the note needed to be

[1] Cf. E. Wellesz, 'Zur Entzifferung der byzantinischen Notenschrift', *Oriens Christianus*, N.S. vii (1918), pp. 97–118, and *A History of Byzantine Music and Hymnography*, pp. 226–68. The best practical introduction to Byzantine musical palaeography is Tillyard's *Handbook of the Middle Byzantine Musical Notation* (Copenhagen, 1935).

emphasized, shortened, or lengthened the *oligon* had to be replaced
by the *oxeia, petaste, pelaston,* or *kouphisma*:

Interval	ascending	descending
Repetition ⌣		
Second	—	ɔ
Third	—＼	ɔ∩
Fourth	↲	⑤
Fifth	_L	ɔ x
Sixth	L̲	...
Seventh	L̲＼	...
Octave	L̲̣	...＼

The *dyo kentemata* is the only sign for an ascending second which was
never used in these combinations but was attached to the preceding
note by a slur.

THE STRUCTURE OF BYZANTINE MELODIES

In front of the first line of the musical notation and often in the
middle of the hymn we find one of the first four letters of the Greek
alphabet, α, β, γ, δ, followed by a stroke which indicates that they
are to be regarded as ciphers. In some hymns these ciphers are preceded by the letters πλ. These combinations of letters and neums are
called in Greek *martyriai* (μαρτυρίαι). The ciphers α', β', γ', δ', indicate that the melody belongs to the first, second, third, or fourth
authentic mode. The letters πλ are an abbreviation of πλάγιος
(*plagios*), and indicate that the melody belongs to one of the four
plagal modes. Neums added to the letter indicate the note of the
mode on which the melody is to begin. In many cases, however, these
groups of neums were abbreviated or replaced by signs whose meaning was for a long time obscure. It was the great achievement of
Tillyard that he succeeded in solving the riddle of the *martyriai* and
made possible the correct transcription of a melody headed by one
of the more complicated *martyriai*.[1] Further progress towards solving
the problem of the Byzantine intonation formulas was made by O.
Strunk.[2] These intonation formulas are:

[1] Cf. Tillyard, 'Signatures and Cadences of the Byzantine Modes', *Annual of the
British School at Athens,* xxvi (1923–5), pp. 78–87, and *Handbook of the Middle Byzantine
Notation,* pp. 30–36.

[2] O. Strunk, 'The Tonal System of Byzantine Music', *The Musical Quarterly,* xxviii

Mode I	Ananeanes	Mode I Plagal	Aneanes
Mode II	Neanes	Mode II Plagal	Neanes
Mode III	Aneanes	Mode III Plagal	Anes
Mode IV	Hagia	Mode IV Plagal	Neagie

These formulas stand for fixed intonation melismata which begin on the 'starting note' of the mode and lead to the initial note on which the hymn begins either (a) directly or (b) by leaps, as is indicated by a neum.[1] This can be seen from two beginnings of hymns in the fourth plagal mode:

In the intonation formulas the singers had a guide to help them over the beginning of a new hymn. This was particularly necessary when the hymn began with a note which did not belong to the initial formula of the mode.

The question of the origin of the Byzantine modes and their significance still needs further investigation. This, however, cannot be undertaken until the corpus of the Byzantine treatises on musical theory has been made available in critical editions.[2] We can, however, say definitely that the old theory of the survival of classical Greek music in Byzantine music, based on the fact that the latter was composed on a modal system, can no longer be regarded as valid. The essential feature of Byzantine music is that melody construction is based on the linking up of certain melodic formulae characteristic of a mode, not on the principle of the *ethos* which, according to Greek philosophy, exists in every mode and reacts upon the listener.[3] The speculations of Byzantine theorists on the modes have nothing to do with Byzantine musical practice. The theorists merely repeated and

(1942), pp. 190–204, and 'Intonations and Signatures of the Byzantine Modes', ibid. (1945), pp. 339–55.

[1] Ibid. (1945), p. 346.

[2] This part of the editorial programme of the *Monumenta Musicae Byzantinae* had to be postponed. The best survey of the subject is O. Gombosi's 'Studien zur Tonartenlehre des frühen Mittelalters', *Acta Musicologica*, x (1938), pp. 149–74; xi (1939), pp. 28–39, 128–37; xii (1940), pp. 21–52.

[3] Cf. H. Abert, *Die Lehre vom Ethos in der griechischen Musik* (Leipzig, 1899), pp. 3–5.

expanded their predecessors, who had assimilated the essentials of Neoplatonic philosophy to the doctrine of Pseudo-Dionysius, who wrote at the end of the fifth or the beginning of the sixth century.[1] This fact becomes evident from a treatise of Nicolas Mesarites on the Church of the Apostles in Constantinople, from which we learn that in the precincts of the Church musical theory was taught in the philosophy classes, whereas in the elementary classes children were instructed in grammar, dialectic, and music. From this and other evidence we conclude that the music of the Byzantine Church which, in the main, was a legacy from the music of the Synagogue, was treated by Hellenistic and Byzantine philosophers only in the course of their metaphysical speculations on numbers.

The question which arises from these facts is: are the modes the ruling principle of Byzantine melody construction, or was it the formulas which gave the specific character to each of the eight groups into which the Byzantine melodies were classified in accordance with the views of Neoplatonic writers on Greek musical theory?[2] The modal hypothesis was the only one accepted by scholars before transcription had been carried out on a large scale. Once this had been done it became evident that the principle of composition lay in adapting a group of formulas for use in a *heirmos*, a *troparion*, or a *sticheron*, and in connecting them by simple passages. On the other hand it is becoming more and more apparent that the system of modes was not a feature peculiar to ancient Greek music, but was also typical of the Orient. In Byzantine music it was made the basis for collecting the melodies into eight major groups with many subdivisions, all the melodies in each group belonging to the same type. The similarity, indeed, is so strong that the hymnographers are by some scholars accused of lacking creative power. This view is wrong. The Byzantine composer had to work within the framework of Orthodox theology, which taught that the prototypes of the melodies were the songs of praise of the angels, inaudible to human ears, but transmitted and made audible by the inspired hymnographers. Like the prototypes of the icons, the prototypes of the melodies are pre-existent in God.[3]

An analysis of the melodic structure of the melodies from the *Heirmologion* and from the *Sticherarion* shows that all the melodies in one of the eight modes contain a number of formulas characteristic

---

[1] Cf. the chapter on the survival of Greek musical theory in Wellesz, *A History of Byzantine Music and Hymnography*, pp. 38–66.

[2] Cf. A. Heisenberg, *Grabeskirche und Apostelkirche* (Leipzig, 1908), pp. 20–21.

[3] Cf. John Damascene, *De imaginibus oratio*, i. 10–11; Migne, *Patrologia Graeca*, xciv. 1241.

of that mode.[1] The same formulas can be used at the beginning, in the middle, and at the end of a melody. The accented notes coincide with the main accents of the line of the stanza. If one or more unaccented syllables precede the accented one, one or more unaccented notes will precede the accented note of the formula:[2]

Ex.8

The hymn-writers developed great skill in adapting words to music. Ornaments, as in plainchant, were mostly set to words which could be emphasized but which were not of primary importance for the understanding of the phrase. Thus the ornament had the function of preparing a tension by means of which the listener's attention was directed to the words which were important for the understanding of the text. In some instances, however, the coincidence of ornament and important word was essential both for musical and poetical reasons, as can be seen from the beginning of the Christmas *sticheron* 'Come, Christ-bearing people, let us look upon the marvel which confounds thought and holds it bound':[3]

Ex.9

Now that a steadily increasing number of hymns from the *Heirmologion* and *Sticherarion* is being made accessible in modern staff notation we can study Byzantine chant more closely than has hitherto been possible, and compare the achievement of Byzantine hymnographers with that of the anonymous monks who gave Western chant

[1] Cf. the list of the formulas of the first mode in Wellesz, *A History of Byzantine Music and Hymnography*, pp. 272–3.

[2] Ibid., pp. 274–7.

[3] Codex Dalassinos, fo. 91[v]. For the full text cf. *A History of Byzantine Music and Hymnography*, pp. 309–10.

its form. Such a study will show how profoundly the Byzantine melodies reflect the spirit of Eastern piety, just as plainchant does that of the West. It will also destroy the legend of the sterility of Byzantine music, in the same way as modern investigation put an end to the legend of the sterility of Byzantine art. The music of the Byzantine Church, indeed, is no less great than that of the Western Church: it may even be said to surpass it in its power of passionate expression and its dramatic force.

COPTIC MUSIC

As far as we can see from the present state of their music, three among the Eastern Churches had an independent and highly developed chant. These Churches were (1) the Coptic, (2) the Abyssinian, and (3) the Armenian. Up to the present all attempts to reconstruct the early state of the music of these three Churches have failed, and there is no prospect that we shall ever succeed in discovering anything definite about the music of the first two: Coptic music was handed down orally from one generation to the next, Abyssinian music was written down at a relatively late date. Only the Armenian Church possessed, in the twelfth century, an elaborate system of neums, similar to the Byzantine one, and one day the clue to its interpretation may be found. As we cannot give any examples of the music of the Eastern Churches in the Middle Ages we must restrict our survey to some general remarks about its development.

The term Copt is used for the Christian Egyptian. It is an Arabic mutilation of the Greek name [Αἴ]γυπτος (Aigyptos) to Qibṭ. The home of Egyptian Christianity was in Upper Egypt, in the Thebaïd, as it was called by the Greeks, or Saïd as it was called by the Arabs. Here a literature flourished in the Egyptian language, written down in Greek letters with some additional signs, and a Christian literature developed in the Saïdic dialect which became the liturgical language of the whole of Upper Egypt. This part of the country was not affected by the Hellenization which had made the Delta of the Nile a Greek-speaking country; its conversion to Christianity was easier than that of Hellenized Lower Egypt. The Christianization of Upper Egypt began about A.D. 200 and was complete in both Upper and Lower Egypt towards the middle of the fourth century.[1] The hostile attitude of the Egyptians towards the Greeks was inherited by the Coptic Church, which, in the middle of the fifth century turned

---

[1] Cf. A. Baumstark, *Die christlichen Literaturen des Orients*, i, Sammlung Göschen (Leipzig, 1909), p. 137.

Monophysite in opposition to Greek Orthodoxy. In their opposition to Constantinople and the imperial court, the Copts went so far as to encourage the invasion of the Arabs in 641, a step which proved fatal for them.

The Coptic Church in Lower Egypt took over its rite from the Church of Jerusalem. In its later development it was influenced by the Byzantine Church. In Upper Egypt, where in A.D. 320 Pachomius had instituted the coenobitic life and had given it a rule, the rite, taken over from Syriac, developed in the Coptic language. Here the opposition to the Hellenized Delta of the Nile was strong, and constant contact with Syria opened the way for the introduction of the Mono-physite heresy which had developed in Syria.[1] Among the numerous forms of the Mass three liturgies stood out, and survived. These were the liturgy of St. Gregory the Theologian, the liturgy of St. Basil, and the liturgy ascribed to St. Mark and known as the liturgy of St. Cyril.[2] Fragments of old Egyptian liturgies have come down to us on strips of papyrus, showing the great variety of the rite in the early days of Christianity. Today the main form of the Mass is the liturgy of St. Basil: on festival days that of St. Gregory is used, on solemn feasts that of St. Cyril.

As far as can be seen from the remnants of Coptic poetry which have escaped destruction, three genres were developed: (1) liturgical chants, (2) hymns, and (3) religious folk-songs. The last group comprises poems probably sung at feasts or public gatherings. A large number of these popular songs have come down to us in manuscript collections. They are written in stanzas and in the titles of most of them reference is made to the melody to which they are to be sung and to the mode.[3] From a few lines of Coptic hymns with musical signs which survive and are reproduced by W. E. Crum in the *Catalogue of the Coptic Manuscripts in the Collection of the John Rylands Library* (Manchester, 1909), p. 10, we know that the Copts possessed a primitive system of musical notation in the tenth and eleventh centuries. From four to six *oxeiai* (acutes) were set to the syllable which had the tonic accent:

ΛΕΓΟΝΤΕΣ ΠΡΟΣΚΥΝΗΣΟΜΕΝ

They also had signs like the Byzantine *apostrophos*, the circumflex,

---

[1] Cf. Dom B. C. Mercier, *La Liturgie de Saint Jacques. Patrologia Orientalis*, xxvi. 2 (Paris, 1946), p. 128.

[2] Cf. F. E. Brightman, *Liturgies Eastern and Western*, i (Oxford, 1896), pp. 111–88.

[3] H. Junker, 'Koptische Poesie des 10. Jahrhunderts', *Oriens Christianus*, vi, pp. 339 sqq.

and a sign which cannot be identified.[1] This notation is similar to Byzantine ecphonetic notation, and both may have derived from the same source, i.e. the Greek *scriptoria* in Alexandria, but we can speculate no farther about the origin and nature of Coptic neums, because there is too little palaeographical evidence available to support any more definite hypothesis. We know nothing about the character of Coptic music in the days when Egypt was a flourishing country. The present state of Coptic liturgical music is remarkable for its beauty and for the richness of its melodies: and we may assume from this that it must have once attained a high level, especially when we consider that in spite of the persecution which the Copts suffered for more than a thousand years their music was so little contaminated by that of the Arabs. We may therefore conclude that it still retains features of a great past civilization.

ETHIOPIAN MUSIC

Ethiopian is the name given to the Christian literature of Abyssinia. Its language is a South Arabian dialect called *Ge'ez*, which remained the language of the liturgy after it had ceased to be spoken by the Abyssinians. From Greek sources we learn of the existence of a Semitic kingdom in northern Abyssinia in the first century A.D. It seems to have been founded some centuries earlier, as epigraphical documents discovered in Aksum, its capital, go back to pre-Christian times.[2] The conversion of the country to the Christian faith seems to have started from Alexandria soon after 328, when St. Frumentius was ordained bishop of this centre of African Hellenism.[3] About A.D. 500 another mission was undertaken by Syrian monks, but finally it was the Hellenic influence, or rather the Coptic, which was important in shaping the liturgy, and up to the present day the Church of Abyssinia is under the sovereignty of the Coptic Church. Athanasius Kircher was the first scholar to mention Abyssinian Church music in his *Musurgia universalis* (1650). He gave an example of a hymn, but distorted it by harmonizing it and adapting it to fit the Anacreontic metre ('ad formam Anacreontici accommodatum').[4] Kircher gives no indication as to where he got the melody, but we may assume that it was sung to him by one of the Portuguese Jesuits who

---

[1] Cf. Høeg, *La Notation ekphonétique*, p. 146.
[2] E. Littmann, 'Geschichte der äthiopischen Litteratur', *Die Litteraturen des Ostens*, vii. 2 (Leipzig, 1909), p. 191.
[3] A. Baumstark, *Die Messe im Morgenland* (Nijmegen, 1906), p. 74.
[4] A. Kircher, *Musurgia universalis*, ii, pp. 134–5.

were exiled by King Fasiladaz (1632–67), when, after a short interruption, Monophysitism again became the official creed.

More than a hundred years later some further information about Ethiopian music was given by M. Villoteau in his *Description de l'Égypte* (Paris, 1808).[1] But this survey cannot be regarded as a reliable source, since Villoteau had no knowledge of the liturgy and music of the country, and the priests whom he consulted did not have the necessary training in musical theory to answer his questions. The most important part of his treatise is a table of musical signs which he compiled after having heard the chants and compared the manuscripts. Here, too, he admits the possibility of error, and indeed it is clear that he made mistakes. It is therefore unfortunate that the sections on Ethiopian music in the fourth volume of Fétis's *Histoire générale de la musique* and in the first volume of Ambros's *Musikgeschichte* are based on Villoteau's study, summarizing his statements and repeating his mistakes. The first attempt to complete the list of musical signs was made in H. Zotenberg's *Catalogue des MSS. éthiopiens de la Bibliothèque Nationale*. He gives a list of all the musical signs and their combinations in the course of his description of the Ethiopian Codex Paris 67. Another attempt was made by A. Dillmann, who gives a sample from a Berlin codex in his *Verzeichnis der abessinischen Handschriften*.[2] A corrected list of the Ethiopian musical signs, taken from Codex Aethiop. 24, Vindobonensis, is given in the present writer's study of Ethiopian Church music.[3]

According to an Ethiopian chronicle musical notation was introduced in the middle of the sixteenth century. Up to that date the chant was obviously transmitted orally, as is still the case in the Coptic Church. In the musical manuscripts sufficient space is left by the scribes between the lines of the poetry for the insertion of the musical notation, which is written as carefully as the text of the hymns. The notation consists of letters and accents which are set sparingly, i.e. rarely more than one sign to a word, as can be seen from the example opposite, taken from the hymnal Codex Aethiop. 24, Vindobonensis. If Villoteau's explanation is right in principle this would mean that the signs are set for a group of notes in the same way as signs for the cantillation are set in Hebrew texts. The accents are written in black ink like the text, the letters in red ink. We may assume that the red signs have the same significance as those of the late Byzantine nota-

---

[1] Cf. E. Wellesz, 'Studien zur äthiopischen Kirchenmusik', *Oriens Christianus*, N.S. ix (1918–20 p. 80.),

[2] *Die Handschriftenverzeichnisse der Kgl. Bibliothek zu Berlin* (Berlin, 1878), table iii.

[3] Wellesz, 'Studien zur äthiopischen Kirchenmusik', pp. 97–100.

AN ABYSSINIAN HYMN BOOK

The notation consists of neums and letters in brown ink with superimposed letters in red ink. (Cod. Vindob. Aethiop. 24, fo. 80.) Sixteenth century

tion where they indicate the manner of execution, whereas the black signs are the musical signs proper.

According to Villoteau the basis of Ethiopian music is the three modes, 'ezel, arāraj, ge'ez. The meaning of these names is obscure. Villoteau mentions that the mode ge'ez was used on weekdays, arārāj on the great feasts, 'ezel on days of fasting and mourning. The Church ascribes the invention of these three modes to St. Jārēd. Thus we read in the Homily for the Saint that 'nobody can invent a new mode which could be added to the three modes of the priest Jārēd'.[1] The voice of Jārēd, it is added, could not be compared with that of a man cantillating the Bible or other prayers but was 'like a strong noise, very beautiful when singing the hymns. When the priests and deacons sing as they have learnt from Jārēd, they do it up to the point of complete exhaustion, until sweat bursts from their pores, until their limbs are out of their control, their muscles are relaxed, their throats are hoarse, their knees tremble and their hands, with which they clap while they sing, are raw.'[2] This kind of singing is still usual in Abyssinia during the service, which consists of chanting the liturgical songs for hours at full strength. Priests and deacons form a circle. In the middle are two or three priests who execute a kind of dance to the rhythm of drummers who stand behind them. The rhythm of the chants and the movements of the priests in the centre are followed by all the priests in the circle with a rhythmical movement of their staffs and rattles. This liturgical dance obviously comes from Egypt,[3] and was taken up by the Coptic Church, whose rite, as we have said, was closely connected with that of the Ethiopia Church. We may assume that this kind of dancing to the rhythm of rattles and drums goes back to the early days of the Church in Abyssinia, for the rattle is derived from the saïschschit of the Egyptians, which the Greeks took over and called σεῖστρον (seistron). The drum has the same egg-shaped form as the Egyptian drum and, like it, was beaten with the ball of the thumb.[4]

The Abyssinian rite certainly kept more closely than any other to the earlier pre-Christian ritual of the country. The ecstatic style of dancing is only one of many signs of this. This style of dancing, and the ecstatic singing which the Ethiopians took over from the Copts

[1] Corpus scriptorum christianorum orientalium. Scriptores Aethiopici, series II, xvii, Vitae sanctorum antiquiorum, ed. C. Conti Rossini (1904), p. 4.
[2] Ibid., p. 6.
[3] Cf. F.-J. Fétis, Histoire de la musique, i, p. 210.
[4] Cf. V. Loret, 'Note sur les instruments de musique de l'Égypte ancienne', Encyclopédie de la musique, i, p. 12.

throws light on the attitude of some of the early Fathers of the Church who were strongly opposed to singing in church. We can understand, for example, the attitude of Clement of Alexandria who, during his stay in Egypt (180–203), witnessed the melomaniac frenzy of the Alexandrians,[1] and condemned it in many passages of his *Paedogogus* and *Stromata*. These, and other passages in the writings of the Fathers refer to the frenzy for music which they had witnessed in the East, not only in the great Hellenistic centres of Africa, but also in the interior where Christianity was only a thin covering for the old pagan rite. Later writers followed the Fathers in this attitude, understandable only so long as it referred to the East, and applied it to music in the West, where conditions were entirely different.

ARMENIAN MUSIC

The conversion of Armenia to the Christian faith began in the Apostolic age. It was carried out by Syrians from Edessa and Nisibis and by Greeks from Caesarea in Cappadocia. The final victory of the Christian mission was due to Gregory the Illuminator (*c.* 257–*c.* 337) who, according to Armenian hagiography suffered thirteen years' imprisonment for teaching the new creed but was released when King Trdat was converted by a miracle. Gregory and Trdat converted the whole country in a short time; the nobility followed the lead of the King and the people gradually conformed. The office of *Katholikos*, the head of the Armenian Church, became hereditary among certain families. Thus Armenia was the first country to accept Christianity as the official religion of the state. Hellenism became the leading spiritual influence, but in the sphere of politics the influence of Syria was most important. But Gregory had already given the Armenian Church its national character. Its opposition to that of the Eastern Empire was increased by the close relationship with the Georgian Church which came about under Gregory's grandson. Under Sahak the Great, who was made *Katholikos* in 390, Armenia severed its links with Syria. Supported by King Vramšapuh (395–416), Mesrob, the greatest Armenian scholar of his age, introduced an Armenian alphabet, and both he and Sahak inaugurated a literary activity in the vernacular. Before their day books were written in Greek, Syriac, or Persian. No translation of the Bible into Armenian had been made. Now, however, it was possible to create a literature in the vernacular which mainly consisted of translations from the Bible, the liturgical books, the lives of the Saints and of the Martyrs, and chronicles. The

[1] T. Gérold, *Les Pères de l'Église et la musique* (Paris, 1931), pp. 89–90.

Armenian liturgy is based on the text which was used in Caesarea and Cappadocia, the early form of the Byzantine liturgy of St. Basil. The liturgy of St. Chrysostom and the liturgy of the Presanctified were also translated from the Greek, both being introduced from Constantinople. From this early period also dates the main part of the Hours.

The fifth century is called by the Armenians the Golden Age. The following centuries, up to the eleventh, lived on its achievements. In the sixth century literary activity came practically to a standstill, and only began to move forward again in the seventh. The political quarrels of the eighth century left no time for literary activities. A new period, however, began in the ninth century, and led to a second flourishing period of translations from Greek into Armenian, which led gradually to a climax of activity in the twelfth century. The final redaction of the so-called Maštotz Ritual was undertaken in the second half of the ninth century by the *Katholikos* Maštotz (d. 897). The renaissance of the twelfth century was caused by the foundation of a new Armenian kingdom in Cilicia under the Rubenid dynasty. A new literary life began, though it was dependent for appreciation on the highly educated upper class. Its protagonist was Nerses Šnorhali (1102–73) the last important contributor to the Armenian *Šarakan* (hymn-book), which contains more than a thousand hymns, arranged in three groups: (1) *kanons*, (2) hymns consisting of a group of stanzas, and (3) monostrophic hymns. Nerses Šnorhali, who enlarged the *Šarakan* by a fifth of its former content, composed *kanons* for Good Friday, St. John Baptist, Whitsun, the Ascension, and other feasts for which *kanons* had not previously been written. He seems, however, to have been unable to complete his task, as the final shape was given to the *Šarakan* by Arakel, Bishop of Siuni, about 1300, a hundred years after his death.

From Lazarus of Parb, an author of the fifth century, we learn that the Armenians used letters to fix the music of their chants.[1] According to a later source, however, the music was transmitted orally up to the twelfth century. The introduction of neumatic notation is ascribed to Katšatour, a priest from Taron who lived in the twelfth century.[2] We do not know whether these musical signs stood for a group of notes or whether they indicated the approximate course of the melody. From Kirakos, an author of the thirteenth century, we gather merely that the signs did not have a fixed interval value, and that they were

[1] Cf. P. Wagner, *Neumenkunde*, 2nd ed. (Leipzig, 1912), pp. 70–71.
[2] Cf. P. Aubry, 'Le Système musicale de l'Église arménienne', *La Tribune de St. Gervais*, viii (1902), p. 327.

a guide to those who knew the music, but that they were of no use if one wanted to sing a new melody.[1] This applies not only to signs which are set for a group of notes but also to the early stage of the neumatic notation, which seems to have been derived from the Byzantine system and to have been developed independently into a system of fifty-four signs.[2] This stage of notation can be seen from the example opposite, taken from an Armenian hymn-book of A.D. 1377.[3] Unfortunately, even the fully developed system known to us from manuscripts of the fourteenth and fifteenth centuries cannot be read, because there are no theoretical treatises available which, like the Byzantine *Papadike*, would help us to understand the significance of the neums and to decipher them. In this instance our ignorance is particularly regrettable because the highly developed state of Armenian ecclesiastical music as we know it from present-day practice[4] suggests that the music of the Armenian Church in the Middle Ages must have been of outstanding beauty, comparable in quality only to that of the Byzantine Church, if not superior.[5] Indeed we might go farther and say that we shall never be able to understand fully the development of Eastern church music until we know more about Armenian music and its role in the development of Eastern chant.

(b) RUSSIAN CHANT

By ALFRED J. SWAN

Ex. 10

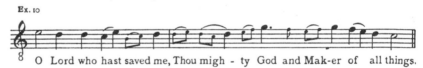

O Lord who hast saved me, Thou migh - ty God and Mak-er of   all things.

This short quotation contains most of the characteristics of the old Russian *znamenny* chant (so called from *znamya*, a sign): (1) It is

[1] Cf. P. Wagner, *Neumenkunde*, p. 71.

[2] A list of the main signs is given in Aubry's article, quoted above, opposite p. 324. P. Wagner, *Neumenkunde*, pp. 72–75, also gives a list and attempts to explain the signs.

[3] Preuss. Staatsbibl., Berlin, Codex orient. oct. 279, fo. 3ᵛ.

[4] The best collection is that made by M. Ekmalian, *Les Chants de la sainte liturgie* (Leipzig, 1896). The versions of the chants from the monastery of San Lazzaro, edited by P. Bianchini, *Les Chants liturgiques de l'Église arménienne* (Venice, 1877) and by Amy Abcar, *Melodies of the Holy Apostolic Church of Armenia* (Calcutta, 1897), are much inferior to those in use in Edchmiadzin, which are published by Ekmalion. A new edition of the Armenian chants, edited by P. Leonzis Dayan of San Lazzaro, is in progress.

[5] Cf. E. Wellesz, 'Die armenische Messe und ihre Musik', *Jahrbuch der Musikbibliothek Peters* (Leipzig, 1921), pp. 10–16, and *Aufgaben und Probleme auf dem Gebiete der byzantinischen und orientalischen Kirchenmusik* (Münster, 1923), pp. 84–90.

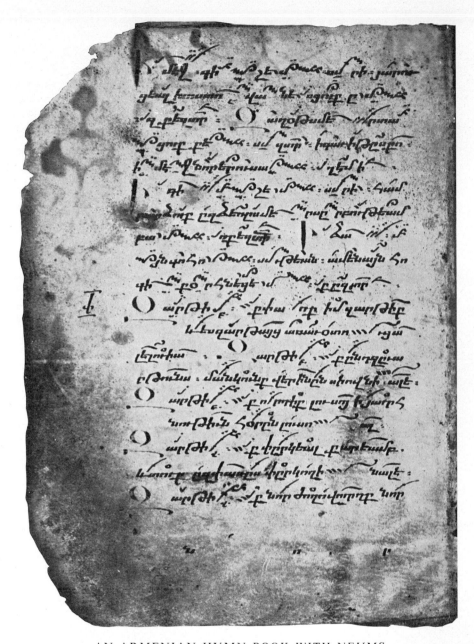

AN ARMENIAN HYMN BOOK WITH NEUMS

Written by the scribe Ter Nerses in A.D. 1337; ordered by the Metropolitan Sargis in the
days of Leo IV of Cilicia. (Cod. Berlin. Orient. 279, fo. 3ᵛ.)

strictly diatonic, having no chromatic intervals. (2) It is broad and noble in feeling: the note values are long, and there is no undue vocalization. (3) It has a free prose rhythm: the length of the bar is determined by the text lines, which are prose lines of uneven length. (4) It is highly dignified: there is no repetition here of words or syllables, as we often find in folk-song. (5) Its flow is smooth and legato (in contrast with some of the accented, staccato passages found in recent transcriptions of the Byzantine chant). (6) In range, it can go down to G below the middle C and up to B♭ above it (rarely C or D): twelve notes lying roughly in the tenor register, although the pitch of the chants was relative and not strictly determined in the old notation. (7) In character it is very distinct from the Byzantine or Gregorian chants, and its intervals are similar to those of Russian folk-song, except for an avoidance of wide leaps.

EARLY HISTORY

The conversion of Russia to Christianity began in 988 or 989, when Vladimir of Kiev and his army were baptized at Kherson by Greek priests. The Byzantine chant was naturally imported into Russia with the Christian ritual. There were, however, not enough Russian priests, while the Greek missionaries did not understand the vernacular; monks had therefore to be brought from Bulgaria— where the Christian faith had been introduced in 864—to instruct the Russians in liturgy and chant. Hence the melodies taken over from the Byzantine chant-books were sung in Old Slavonic as in Bulgaria.[1] According to the *Nikonov Chronicle* (under the year 993) 'the Metropolitan Michael [a Bulgarian by birth] went from Kiev into the Rostov country, baptized great multitudes of people, erected many churches and installed presbyters and deacons, founded a choir, and laid down regulations'.

The earliest Old Slavonic hymn-books with musical notation date from the eleventh century. Their notation is identical with that of the earliest phase of Byzantine neumatic notation, dating from the ninth century (see table on pp. 38–9 and chart facing p. 54)[2], so we may assume that from the earliest days of Christianity in Russia liturgical chant was sung from song-books with musical notation. Step by step, however, an indigenous notation was evolved. As the

[1] R. Palikarova-Verdeil, 'La Musique Byzantine chez les Bulgares et les Russes', *Monumenta Musicae Byzantinae*, Subsidia, iii (Copenhagen, 1953), pp. 64–70.

[2] See O. von Riesemann, *Die Notationen des altrussischen Kirchengesanges* (Leipzig, 1909); Palikarova-Verdeil, op. cit.; and E. Koschmieder, *Die ältesten Norgovoder*

fully legible chant of the fifteenth century sounds entirely different from the Byzantine,[1] and as the outline of that legible chant can be faintly recognized in the manuscripts of the twelfth and thirteenth centuries, the process of moving towards a national type of liturgical song (the *znamenny* chant) must have continued from the formation of the Kiev choir mentioned above. In 1072 the first Russian saints—the Princes Boris and Gleb—were canonized, and new canticles in their honour were composed on Russian soil. This is where the beginnings of Russian music lie, and not seven and a half centuries later, in the operas of Glinka. The new canticles—called *stichera* (see p. 31) in Byzantine and Russian terminology—were soon followed by others, in honour of St. Theodosius and the transfer of the remains of St. Nicholas to Bari. They are all to be found in the oldest Russian manuscripts.

From 1237 to 1480 Russia was under the Mongol yoke. The number of extant manuscripts is no more than five for the whole of the fourteenth century—the time of the most disastrous fires and destructions; then it increases again. A theory has been advanced[2] that it was precisely that peculiar period in Russian history, one of enforced isolation from the rest of the world, that is responsible for the great difference between the *znamenny* chant and its predecessor. Towards the end of this period the Russian chant becomes fully readable (see the table opposite).

DEVELOPMENT AND DECLINE

The period of the highest development and decline is from 1480 to 1652. With the transition to the sixteenth century the number of manuscripts of Russian chant increases to hundreds, if not thousands. Many of them have theoretical manuals of the period (so-called 'informations' or 'interpretations') attached, which give somewhat crude indications about the performance of the musical signs above the text. Ivan IV was keenly interested in music; to him we owe the foundation of schools, which in a remarkably short time began to produce famous singers. The copyist of a *sticherarium* (collection of *stichera*) of the seventeenth century which was formerly in the library of Prince Obolensky, has preserved some of their names, ascribing to

Hirmologien-Fragmente (Munich, 1952), where parallel tables of a twelfth-century Old Slavonic Hirmologion (Cod. Paris, Coislin 220), the Hirmologium Athoum (*Monumenta Musicae Byzantinae*, ii), and a late sixteenth-century manuscript are given.

[1] *Monumenta Musicae Byzantinae. Transcripta*, i–vi.
[2] D. Allemanov, *A Manual of the History of Russian Church Singing* (Moscow, 1914).

CHART OF RUSSIAN NOTATIONS AND THEIR SOURCES

NAME	Palaeobyzantine notation of 11th century from Cod. Graec.136 of Vienna National Library	Early 'znamenny' notation from the Statutes of the 11th or 12th centuries of the Library of the Moscow Synodal Printing Press	'Kondakarian'	Later 'znamenny' post-Mongolian	Latest 'znamenny' with Shaidurov's red cinnabar marks	'Demestvenny'
TIME AND PLACE OF ORIGIN		This codex (126 pages) comes either from Kiev (Metallov) or Novgorod (Volkova, Lissitzyn), and belongs either to the end of the 11th or the beginning of the 12th century.	Appears in five of the pre-Mongol Russian codices in Kiev, Suzdal, and Vladimir (possibly also Novgorod).	Northern Russian, 15th century: readable (according to Smolensky), but never explained or transcribed.	16th and 17th centuries. It is from these codices (of which there are many hundreds) that Tihon Makarievsky transcribed about 1690.	Akin to 'znamenny': was noted down at a very late stage (17th century). Hence it also has the cinnabar marks of Shaidurov.
NOTATION						
COMMENTS	Preobrazhensky in 1909 compared the Palaeobyzantine and the early znamenny notations and showed their great similarity. He compared the Vienna codex above with those of the Synodal Library (589) and the Uspensky Cathedral in Moscow. Both notations are as yet unreadable.		Completely unreadable and soon abandoned. It is possibly the highly mannered Byzantine chant referred to by Zonaras and perhaps imported into Russia by the 'three Greek singers' under Yaroslav the Wise (1051) (see *The Musical Quarterly*, xxvi (1940), pp.532–3).	The Heirmoi, which are model stanzas for the Odes of the *Kanon*, are the oldest fully readable bits of the chant. They have been least subjected to later ornamentation - and are probably contained in this 15th-century notation.	Created by Novgorod masters, the Rogovs, Ivan Noss, Stephen the Pauper, &c., under Ivan IV, and brought to Moscow by them or their immediate pupils. It is essentially an elaboration of the preceding stages of the znamenny chant.	*Either* non-liturgical chant used in private houses for religious gatherings (see Chronicle for 1442 and description of the death of Prince Dmitry Krasnoy) *or* semi-liturgical chant used on most solemn occasions in cathedrals. May be *both*.

them the setting of the various parts of the services. He says in his
preface:

I have heard ... about the old masters ... Feodor the pope named
Christian, who was famous here in the town of Moscow ... and greatly
skilled in the chanting of the *znamenny* chant ... and he, Christian, was
wont to tell them (his pupils) that in Novgorod the old masters were
Savva Rogov and his brother Vassili, Karelians by descent ... and Savva
had for his pupil the above-named pope Christian, and Ivan Noss, and
Stephen called the Pauper. And Ivan Noss and Christian lived in the reign
of the righteous Tsar Ivan Vassilievich (the Fourth) ...

These were the 'classic' masters who inserted their *fioriture* into a
given fixed pattern with measure and wisdom, never allowing the
balance and proportions of the canticle to be disturbed by excess of
virtuosity. But by the beginning of the seventeenth century a period
of decline had set in, and the contours of the chant were marrred by
the insertion of long *vocalises* (*thetai*).[1] What form did their compositions take?

Outwardly the Russian canticles are identical with the Byzantine.
There is the traditional system of eight modes—the *Oktoechos* (Russian *Osmoglassiye*), based in this case entirely on the oriental *maqam*
(pattern) principle.[2] Russian scholars have for long been on the wrong
track in trying to derive the Russian modes from the medieval scales
or even from the ancient Greek modes. They were unaware of the
oriental pattern-principle which St. John Damascene—the Eastern
St. Gregory—obviously followed when he systematized Eastern
church singing in the eighth century. It was only about 1900 that the
pattern-principle was pointed out by Metallov. Medieval Russian
singers were, of course, quite ignorant of any such concepts as Dorian
or Mixolydian, and moulded the chant entirely in conformity with
their popular practices. They knew every one of the patterns (*popevki*)
and gave them picturesque names, such as 'little valley', 'rocking',
'break' (*dolinka, kachka, lomka*) and so on. Each of the eight modes
of the *znamenny* chant, as it sounds to us from the early transcriptions
on to the staff, possesses a very definite musical physiognomy,
derived from the sum-total of the patterns constituting each mode.
Some modes are richer in such patterns (the first mode has as many
as ninety-three), some are poorer (the seventh has only thirty-seven),
but in nearly every case the mode can be detected from the actual

[1] Melodies that departed too much from the original were designated as 'wanton'.
One such 'wanton' singer was the precentor of the Troitsk-Sergievsky monastery,
Loggin, nicknamed 'the Cow' (d. 1635), about whom the Archimandrite Dionysos once
said: 'Is there any good in Loggin's singing? He treats the melody as he pleases.'
[2] Cf. H. Besseler, *Die Musik des Mittelalters und der Renaissance* (Potsdam, 1931), p. 53.

sound of the canticle, as most of the patterns are characterized by great beauty and expressiveness. They vary in length:

Ex. II

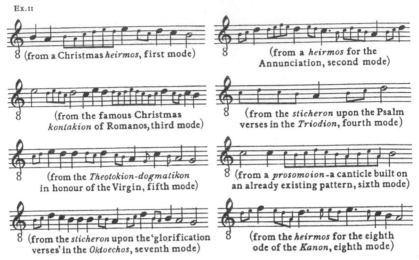

(from a Christmas *heirmos*, first mode)

(from a *heirmos* for the Annunciation, second mode)

(from the famous Christmas *kontakion* of Romanos, third mode)

(from the *sticheron* upon the Psalm verses in the *Triodion*, fourth mode)

(from the *Theotokion-dogmatikon* in honour of the Virgin, fifth mode)

(from a *prosomoion*-a canticle built on an already existing pattern, sixth mode)

(from the *sticheron* upon the 'glorification verses' in the *Oktoechos*, seventh mode)

(from the *heirmos* for the eighth ode of the *Kanon*, eighth mode)

The transcriptions on the staff were made from the last stage of the neum notation, late in the seventeenth century, the time of the introduction of the staff into Russia. Our authority is one Tikhon Makarievsky, bursar to the Patriarch Adrian. Tikhon was still alive in 1705, and he explained his method in his *Klyuch* (key). In 1772 these transcriptions were printed in four separate books (the *Obikhod*, the *Oktoechos*, the *Heirmologion*, and the holy-day *Menaia*), but Smolensky in 1888 challenged the accuracy of Tikhon's transcriptions.

It is premature, as yet, to speak of the structure of the canticles as a whole. Up to now the bulk of the Russian chant is untranscribed and the source material has not yet been examined. Not enough attention has been given to the North Russian style in architecture. A Pskov or Novgorod church or chapel is a seeming paradox: the architect's method is clearly an improvisation. He seems to have proceeded on his task as the spirit moved him, and suddenly to have pasted on an extra arch or belfry; here a vault that appears like an afterthought, there a stairway out of nothing. But the effect is one of rare beauty and harmony, and any correction by technical standards would mean the ruination of the structure. The same might be said of the architects of the northern chant. There may be forms of an enviable clarity and symmetry,[1] but any general deductions about the structural intentions of the Russian masters would be dangerous.

---

[1] See some of the analyses in A. J. Swan, 'The *znamenny* chant of the Russian Church', *Musical Quarterly* xxvi (1940).

MANNER OF PERFORMANCE

The bulk of the *znamenny* chant is contained in manuscripts with only one line of neums above the text. Only among the manuscripts of the latest period—the seventeenth century—do we find some that reveal three and even four lines of neums, one above the other. Russian palaeographers have not succeeded in deriving from them a system of Russian harmony or polyphony.[1] Must we conclude from this that the *znamenny* chant, in its century-long expanse, was performed in unison, as one line of melody?

It is hard to believe that the Russian singers ever clung to unison singing. The practice of the singers up to the present day is so firmly rooted in 'harmonizing' the principal melody, that it would be unnatural to assume that this practice never found its way into church singing. Here again we have the everlasting clash between theory and practice. The manuscripts are the work of copyists and theorists bent on preserving tradition and conforming strictly to the canons of church observance. At no time has the Russian Church formally admitted part-singing into its services. Nevertheless, as in the Western Church, part-singing triumphed over monody. The Russian singers even had their own names for 'singing in lines' (*strochnoye peniye*) and for the various separate lines—the 'way', the 'catch', the 'grasp'. Thus the seventeenth-century manuscripts with several lines of neums are a belated attempt on the part of the theorists to recognize reality. But the attempt remained misshapen because of the absence of any method of writing polyphonically in neums. Modern authorities on the *znamenny* chant, realizing that it could not have existed in practice as monody for six and seven centuries, have been anxious to derive the laws of its harmonization from methods of performing folk-songs which have not yet died out. Others, however, are advocates of an uncompromising unison performance.[2]

---

[1] See a transcription in D. Razumovsky, *Church Singing in Russia* (Moscow, 1868), part ii, pp. 215–16. The lowest voice can be established as a melody of the second *echos*, but the upper voices form with it passages of consecutive seconds, along with the usual consonances. The solution is not obvious. It may be that the fault lies in the absence of any adequate way of expressing polyphony in the Russian neums.

[2] A. D. Kastalsky (1856–1926) has here opened up a new path, and the present writer has followed it farther, relying also on his observations of the practices of folk-singers.

III

LATIN CHANT BEFORE ST. GREGORY

By HIGINI ANGLÈS

EARLIEST TRACES

IT was not until about the end of the third century that the Greek
language was replaced in the Roman liturgy by Latin. By this time the
Vetus Latina or *Itala* translation of the Scriptures—so-called to distinguish it from the Vulgate of St. Jerome—had been finished, and
up to the time of St. Gregory this text was always used for the singing
of the Psalter. Evidence for the use of the dialogue introducing the
great Eucharistic Prayer or Canon, known today as the Preface, is
found in Hippolytus (235) for Rome, and in Cyprian (258) for North
Africa. Sacred song was also used in the celebration of the Vigils in
the second and third centuries, and some chants have actually been
preserved from the *agape*, such as 'Ubi caritas et amor',[1] which
might be taken as the beginning of Latin hymnody in Christian worship: but these compositions are sporadic, and nothing is known as
to the antiquity of their melodies. The hymn has been from early
times a 'confessional' chant, used to state and affirm the belief of the
worshippers: and because of its popularity it was much employed by
heretics as a most effective means of proselytism.

The alternation of reading and singing presupposes two officials,
a lector and a cantor (*psalmista*), and the number of ministers increases as time goes on. Cantors are mentioned by the Council of
Laodicea (*c.* 350) and Carthage (390). We read in the *Liber Pontificalis* that Pope Stephen I (254–7)—a tenacious defender of the Roman
tradition who declared: 'Nihil innovetur nisi quod traditum est'—
laid down that only priests and clerics might wear sacred vestments
in church, thus implying that other persons were active in the performance of divine worship. The Roman Marcellinus (296–304), who
used to gather up the bodies of the martyrs at night-time with his
priests and deacons, buried them 'cum hymnis' (with hymns): and
Pope Marcellus (307–8), after being miraculously loosed from prison,
converted the house of his patroness Lucina into a church, where they

---

[1] *Graduale Vaticanum*, p. 175.

used to pray and sing hymns night and day ('die noctuque hymnis et orationibus').

AMBROSIAN CHANT

(i) *Origins*. The fourth century, as we shall see in the next chapter, was the epoch of the great liturgical and musical reforms in Italy, starting on the one hand from Rome and on the other from Milan. The chant of Milan is called 'Ambrosian' after its bishop, St. Ambrose (374–97) in spite of the fact that this chant and its corresponding liturgy were fixed in times later than those of the great bishop. The Ambrosian chant is one of the four classes of liturgical chant in the Latin Church—the other three being the Roman, the Gallican, and the Mozarabic—and like these it has no little dependence upon the Eastern Church. The city of Milan was the residence of the Emperors and had several Greek bishops. It fell into bad repute during its occupation by Auxentius (355–74), an Arian bishop and the immediate predecessor of St. Ambrose, but regained its position as a metropolitan city during the fourth and fifth centuries. Bishops from southern Italy, Gaul, and Spain turned to it for instruction. This almost patriarchal influence was due to the activities of St. Ambrose, who was the counsellor of the Emperors and one of the most eminent personages of his time. Trained in the theology of the Greek Fathers and a stubborn champion of orthodoxy, he placed himself at the head of the faithful against the Arians; and at the same time he came to the front as a reformer of the Milanese liturgy and chant, by which his name has come down to us as the originator of several musical forms.

In the first place we know that during the days of religious struggle St. Ambrose introduced more elaboration and perhaps a new arrangement in the celebration of the Vigils, so as to encourage popular interest; and that he established the singing of hymns and antiphonal psalmody. According to his biographer Paulinus, the Saint,[1] because of the persecution of the Empress Justina, locked himself up with the faithful in the Basilica Portiana, and 'hoc in tempore primum antiphonae, hymni ac vigiliae in ecclesia Mediolanensi celebrari coeperunt' (at this time antiphons, hymns, and vigils first began to be used in the Church of Milan); and according to St. Augustine[2] 'excubabat pia plebs in ecclesia . . . Tunc hymni et psalmi ut canerentur secundum morem orientalium partium ne populus moeroris taedio contabesceret, institutum est' (the faithful kept guard in the church . . .

---

[1] *Patrologia Latina*, xiv. 31.   [2] *Confessions*, ix. 7.

It was then ordained that hymns and psalms should be sung after the manner of Eastern parts [i.e. the Syrian Church], so that the people should not faint away through the weariness of their grief). St. Ambrose also began to write Latin hymns in order to popularize the orthodox doctrine of the Holy Trinity. Hymns of this kind were sung for the first time at the nocturnal Vigils celebrated on the occasion of the siege of the Basilica. By their words and their melody these chants produced a magical effect upon the minds of the multitude.

Much discussion has taken place upon the origins of the chant and liturgy of Milan. There have been two principal tendencies, one looking in a purely Oriental direction (Duchesne) and the other in a purely Latin and classical (Cagin). Modern historians hold that the years of the Lombard invasions of the sixth and seventh centuries were—after the Ambrosian period—those of greatest importance for the development of the Milanese rite and chant: but it is in the eleventh and twelfth centuries that we find them finally systematized. Extant documents show that northern Italy depended upon the Syrian Church. According to Duchesne, the Gallican rites, among which he classes the Ambrosian, have many points of contact with the Eastern rites, both Syrian and Greek: they are the same ancient Christian rites, with modifications brought about by the passage of time and the variation of place.

This theory of the great liturgiologist Duchesne is in full accord with the conclusions reached by Gregorian and musical scholars at the present day. Suñol, after studying Wellesz's *Die Hymnen der Sticherarium für September* (Copenhagen, 1936), declared that he had found among the hundred melodies there given a clear confirmation of the thesis which holds the origin of a large number of the Latin melodies to be Eastern; and especially so in the case of the Ambrosian.[1] Dom Gajard, finding many pieces with the same melody in both Ambrosian and Gregorian (the Introits 'Puer natus est', 'Lux fulgebit', and 'Misericordia Domini', the Graduals 'Tecum principium', 'Universi', and 'Benedictus Dominus', the Offertory 'Precatus est', the *Communio* 'Ecce Virgo' and others), cannot deny that there is a relationship in origin for both sources, 'without being able to state precisely and scientifically which of the two is the original, the problem being very difficult'. Dom Gajard (without alluding to the common Eastern origin) adds: 'The Roman chant is made of measure, equilibrium, order . . . more beautiful than the Ambrosian.'[2] On the

[1] *Ambrosius*, xiii (1937), p. 169.
[2] *Revue grégorienne*, May–June, 1937.

other hand, Peter Wagner, comparing the Gregorian chant with the Ambrosian in passages where the same melody is used, affirms that the Ambrosian melodies display a more ancient character, 'in which case the Ambrosian chant is probably closer to the Latin pre-Gregorian chant of the oldest period'.[1]

The oriental character of the Ambrosian chant has been underlined by Wellesz, who says, after examining the relation of Byzantine and Ambrosian melodies:

This seems to be a new and valuable verification of the thesis, formulated by P. Wagner, J. Thibaut, and the editors of the *Paléographie musicale*,[2] that the Ambrosian melodies represent the oldest form of Plainchant, as they have not undergone the process of artistic transformation made or ordered by Pope Gregory the Great and his successors ... We learn from the comparison of Byzantine melodies on one side, and Ambrosian and Gregorian on the other, that a great number of the formulae and cadences of which both are built up are identical, or, if identity cannot be proved, through lack of manuscripts of an earlier date than the end of the ninth century or from the fact that Byzantine notation of an earlier date than the twelfth century cannot be deciphered, the analysis of these formulae and cadences still makes it evident that they are closely related and that they must derive from a common source. The results of comparative liturgiology show this to have been the Church of Jerusalem.[3]

This specimen is typical:

Ex. 12 (b)

[1] *Lexikon für Theologie und Kirche* (1930), i, p. 346.
[2] P. Wagner, *Einführung in die gregorianischen Melodien*, i (3rd ed. Leipzig, 1911) and iii (1921); J.-B. Thibaut, *Origine byzantine de la notation neumatique de l'Église latine* (Paris, 1907); *Paléographie musicale*, v and vi.
[3] *Eastern Elements in Western Chant* (Oxford, 1947), p. 126.
[4] *Antiphonale Missarum*, p. 38.

(Alleluia. Unto us a Son is born, unto us a Child is given.)

In the time of Charlemagne and Pope Hadrian an effort was made to unify the European liturgies and chants with those of Rome. The Emperor presented himself personally at Milan with the avowed object of doing away with any music or rite not in conformity with Rome, and of destroying or removing its books, and it was only the zeal and energy of the bishop Eugenius that saved the ancient heritage of Milan. Other attempts at unification were made in the eleventh century under Nicholas II, St. Peter Damian, and Gregory VII. After the liturgical reform of Pius V the Ambrosian rite and music were protected by St. Charles Borromeo and by his nephew Cardinal Frederick Borromeo. Since that time the Ambrosian rite has been followed in Milan and in some churches of the Swiss Cantons of Ticino, as well as in the three Italian valleys of Blenio, Leventino, and Riviera, all in the diocese of Lugano.

(ii) *Sources.* Although Ambrosian chant, as it has come down to us, may be regarded as a fair representative of what it was at the turn of the fifth century, the earliest manuscripts known to exist are much later. The chief documents are the Codex Sacramentorum Bergo-mensis of the tenth or eleventh century, edited by Dom Cagin (Solesmes, 1900), the *Antiphonarium Ambrosianum* of the twelfth century now in the British Museum[1] (published as vols. v and vi of *Paléographie musicale*), which contains the *pars hiemalis*, and another antiphoner discovered subsequent to the publication of *Paléographie musicale*, vols. v and vi, now at Bedero Valtravaglia (Lake Maggiore, near Luino). The last of these also dates from the twelfth century; it is written in a slightly cursive neumatic notation, and fortunately

[1] Add. 34209.

contains the *pars aestiva*, so that it is the complement of the British Museum manuscript. Cardinal Schuster found another manuscript of the Mass and the Office, also copied in the twelfth century, at Porlezza.

In addition to these principal sources fragments from the tenth century have been found, and other fragments of a seventh-century palimpsest, now indecipherable. By comparing the known manuscripts Suñol was able to see clearly that the twelfth-century version was melodically identical with that of the tenth century, an interesting light on the reliability of the Ambrosian tradition. There are other manuscripts preserved which date from the twelfth to the fourteenth century, and many more from the fifteenth century and later.

(iii) *Modern Restoration.* Though the Ambrosian rite resisted suppression in the days of Charlemagne, the reforms then in the air were not without influence. The feasts and texts that the Ambrosian Sacramentaries of the ninth and tenth centuries have borrowed from the Gelasian Sacramentary of the eighth century prove this. The *Missale Ambrosianum* was printed in 1475: a new edition was published in 1902, followed by a critical edition by Achille Ratti (later Pope Pius XI) and M. Magistretti. The liturgical reforms initiated by St. Charles Borromeo were of high importance, as his object was to restore the Breviary (1582 and 1588) and the other books of the Ambrosian rite in conformity with the primitive tradition. But from the musical point of view the efforts of Borromeo and his nephew were not a reform: nor can we expect much from the theoretical writers of the seventeenth century. It was Dom Guerrino Amelli (1848–1933) who first began the real work of reform in 1881, publishing in 1883 the *Directorium Chori* and a collection of Masses with text and music. He had but few sources from which to work, the oldest being of the fourteenth century, and he himself lacked a thorough knowledge of musical palaeography. The publication in 1896 of the Ambrosian antiphoner in facsimile with a study by Dom Cagin as vol. v of the *Paléographie musicale*, followed by a transcription in vol. vi, marked a definite step towards a modern restoration.

Some years ago Cardinal Schuster, Archbishop of Milan, entrusted this work of reform and restoration to Dom Gregory Suñol, who devoted himself to the laborious study of about forty existing Ambrosian manuscripts for the purpose of preparing new editions. Speaking of them himself, he says:

The codices that proclaim the antiquity of the Ambrosian chant are not the Gothic manuscripts of the fourteenth century, nor the semi-Carolingian manuscripts of the twelfth century in Guidonian script, nor even the few known fragments of the tenth century with cheironomic and rhythmic neums, though these are all precious witnesses to the Ambrosian melodic tradition; they are rather the palimpsest fragments of the seventh century, which testify to the existence in those early days of Ambrosian neums and melodies, even if it has been impossible so far to decipher a single phrase.[1]

The editions published by Suñol are the *Praeconium Paschale* (Milan, 1934); the *Antiphonale Missarum* (Rome, 1935); *Canti Ambrosiani per il popolo* (Milan, 1936); *Liber Vesperalis* (Rome, 1939); *Officium et Missa pro Defunctis cum exsequiarum ordine* (Rome, 1939). Suñol was preparing the *Directorium Chori* and the *Processionale* when death overtook him, and he left almost finished a monograph on the editorial method and research lying behind his editions. In both the *Antiphonarium Missarum* and the *Liber Vesperalis* a certain amount of patchwork was necessary in order to complete the volumes. The hymns number 65, but there are only 23 melodies used for them. In Suñol's editions the Ambrosian music has made a great contribution to the treasures of the Latin Church, preserving for us precious jewels of this most ancient popular chant, hitherto unknown. Surviving the persecutions and crises of many centuries, the only source outside Rome to be saved from the wreck, this Ambrosian chant has, in our own day, found a glorious resurrection, thus:

Ex. 13 (a)[2]

Psalmellus

Hæc di-   es*quam fe- cit Do- mi- nus: ex- sul-te-   mus   et læ-

te-   mur   in e- a.   ℣. Confite-   mi-ni Domi-   no

Ex. 13 (b)

Hæc di- - - - es * quam fe- - - cit Do -

- mi - nus: ex - sul- te- - -mus

---

[1] *Ambrosius*, xii (1936), p. 68. The present whereabouts of these palimpsests seems to be unknown.   [2] *Antiphonale Missarum*, p. 208.

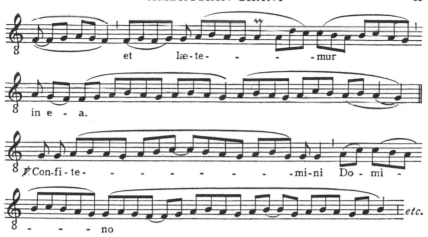

et læ-te- - - -mur

in e - a.

℣. Con-fi - te - - - - - - - -mi-ni Do - mi -

- - - no

etc.

(This is the day which the Lord hath made: let us rejoice and be glad in it.
O give thanks unto the Lord.)

(iv) *Musical Forms.* Most of the Ambrosian melodies have texts
from the Bible, especially from the Psalter: like the Old Roman chant
of which we have spoken, the Old Latin version was used. It was
replaced by the Vulgate at Milan in the seventh century, but the
liturgical books retain many reminders of the older translation. The
Ambrosian recitatives are distinguished from the Roman by ending
on the fourth instead of the fifth below:

Ex. 14 (a) [1]

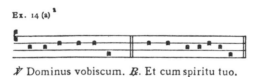

℣ Dominus vobiscum. ℟. Et cum spiritu tuo.

Ex. 14 (b)

℣. Do-mi-nus vo-bis - cum ℟. Et cum spi-ri-tu tu - o.

(The Lord be with you. And with thy spirit.)

Ex. 15 (a) [2]

Ju-be, dom-ne, be-ne-di-ce-re. A-men.
De-o gra-ti-as.

[1] *Liber Vesperalis,* p. 1.
[2] Ibid., p. 851.

Ex. 15 (b)

Ju - be, dom - ne, be - ne - di - ce - re.　　A - men.
De - o　gra - ti - as.

(Bid, sir, a blessing. Thanks be to God. Amen.)

The psalmody consists of *incipit*, reciting note, and final cadence, without any intermediate cadence; and it has a numerous variety of cadential endings for the purpose of linking up with the antiphon which follows:

Ex. 16 (a) [1]

Quam ad-mi-ra-bi-le * est no-men tu-um, Do-mi-ne.　Do-mi-ne, Do-mi-nus

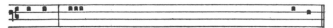

nos-ter,* quam admirabile est nomen tuum in universa ter-ra!

Ex. 16 (b)
(Transposed)

Quam ad - mi - ra - bi - le　est　no - men tu - um, Do - mi - ne.

Do - mi - ne,　Do - mi - nus　nos - ter,　quam admirabile

est nomen tuum in universa ter - ra!

(How admirable is thy name, O Lord. O Lord, our Lord, how admirable is thy name in all the world.)

Ex. 17 (a) [2]

Psal-li-te　De-o no-stro, psal-li-te: psal-li-te Re-gi no-stro, psal-li-te.

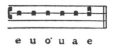

e　u　o̓　u　a　e

---

[1] *Liber Vesperalis*, p. 17.
[2] Ibid., p. 250.

Ex. 17 (b)

(Sing ye unto our God, sing ye: sing ye unto our King, sing ye.)

These six vowels are those of 'saeculorum. Amen', the second half of the last verse of *Gloria Patri*, forming the almost invariable termination of a psalm or canticle in all forms of the Latin rite. As such, they provide a handy formula on which to quote the variant endings of psalm-tones. In medieval and some later writers the formula is called the *evovae*.

The principal chants of the Mass are the *Ingressa* (the Roman Introit, but without any psalm-verse); the *Psalmellus* (Gradual), *Alleluia*, during Lent the *Cantus* (Tract); *Antiphona post Evangelium*, which does not occur in the Roman liturgy; *Offertorium*; *Confractorium*; and *Transitorium*, the latter equivalent to the Roman *Communio*. As in the Roman liturgy, these chants can be divided into three classes: antiphons, responds, and tracts. There are four antiphons: *Ingressa, Antiphona post Evangelium, Confractorium*, and *Transitorium*; on some feasts a fifth antiphon is added *ante Evangelium*. The responds are the *Psalmellus* and the *Offertorium*, some of them keeping one or more verses, with the repetition of a portion of the first part. The *canti* or tracts are from the same melodic source as those in the Gregorian corpus.

Ex. 18 (a)[1]

Fa-ctus est *re-pen-te de cœ-lo so - nus ad-ve-ni-en-tis spi-ri-tus ve-he-men-tis,

u-bi e - ,rant se-den-tes, hal-le-lu-jah.

Ex. 18 (b)

Fac - tus est re - pen-te de cœ - lo so - nus

¹ *Antiphonale Missarum*, p. 253.

ad - ve - ni - en - tis · spi — ri - tus ve - he — men — tis,

u - bi e — rant se — den - tes, hal - le — lu - jah.

(Suddenly there came from heaven the sound of a mighty wind coming upon where they were sitting, alleluia.)

The Office links antiphons with psalms, responds with hymns. Confining our remarks to the hymns, we can say that it is generally agreed, following the studies of Biraghi, Dreves, Steiner, and Blume, that the hymns known without any question to have been composed by St. Ambrose are fourteen in number, three of which have also found a place in the Roman rite—'Aeterne rerum conditor', 'Splendor paternae gloriae', and 'Aeterna Christi munera'. They are written in eight stanzas of four lines in iambic octosyllabics (the English 'Long Metre') and they were received with such acclaim that later on the name of Ambrosian was applied to them: for centuries afterwards they were regarded as models. St. Benedict uses 'Ambrosianum' as a synonym for a hymn. It is impossible to say at the moment whether the extant melodies of the hymns which are genuine productions of St. Ambrose are the same as those actually sung at Milan in the fourth century. The chant of the hymns has no more importance in the Ambrosian liturgy than in the Roman. E. Jammers, basing his opinion on the internal characteristics of the melodies, thinks the hymn-like melodies sung to the Ambrosian texts of the Milanese liturgy are perhaps the oldest of this epoch.[1]

Ex. 19 (a)[2]

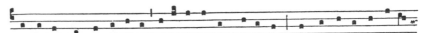

Ae-ter-na Chri-sti mu-ne-ra, A-po-sto-lo-rum glo-ri-am, Lau-des fe-ren-tes de-bi-

-tas, Læ-tis ca-na-mus men-ti-bus.   A-men.

Ex. 19 (b)

Ae-ter-na Christi mu-ne-ra,   A - po - sto-lo-rumglo-ri-am,   Lau-des fe-ren-tes

[1] *Archiv für Musikforschung*, viii (1943), pp. 32 ff.
[2] *Liber Vesperalis*, p. 444. Another Ambrosian hymn—'Veni Redemptor gentium'—is recorded in *The History of Music in Sound* (H.M.V.), ii, side 2.

de - bi - tas,   Læ - tis   ca - na-mus men-ti-bus.   A - men.

(The eternal gifts of Christ the King,
The Apostles' glorious deeds we sing:
And while due hymns of praise we pay,
Our thankful hearts cast grief away.)[1]

(v) *Characteristics.* No methodical and scientific study of the Ambrosian melodies has yet been made, nor any comparative study of this chant in relation to other types from East or West. As we have suggested, Ambrosian chant may possibly represent a melodic source common to the whole Latin Church prior to the reforms of St. Gregory. The antiphon 'Sitientes', which has been preserved in Ambrosian, Mozarabic, Gregorian, and pre-Gregorian neums (the last named preserved in Vatican manuscripts), provides the best evidence for this theory. According to Suñol, whose knowledge of the Ambrosian chant was unrivalled, it is not (as used often to be said) an absolutely primitive and archaic form of art without any elaboration, style, or refinement. It has its own style, in fact, homogeneous, and with melodic and rhythmic formulas. At the same time it must be said that Ambrosian chant contains many melodic and rhythmic formulas that reveal a most archaic style and may be substantially earlier than the time of St. Gregory. Compared with Gregorian chant, Ambrosian has a flavour of originality and of profound simplicity. The text is often treated with more freedom, and there is more elasticity in the use of intervals and in modality. The manuscripts never indicate the mode of the pieces.

Ex. 20 (a)[2]

Do-mi-nus*di-xit ad me: Fi-li-us me-us es tu, e-go ho-di-e genu-i te.

Ex. 20 (b)
(Transposed)

Do - mi - nus   *di - xit ad me: Fi - li - us me - us   es   tu,

e - go   ho - di - e   ge - nu - i   te.

(The Lord hath said unto me: Thou art my Son, this day have I begotten thee.)

[1] Translation by J. M. Neale.   [2] *Antiphonale Missarum*, p. 39.

Ex. 21 (a)[1]

Can-te-mus Do-mi-no, hal-le-lu-jah, hal-le-lu-jah, hal-le-lu-jah. ℟ Can-te-mus.

℣. Can-te-mus Do-mi-no glo-ri-o-se, qui-a fa-ctus est no-bis in sa-lu-tem. ℟. *as before*

Ex. 21 (b)

Can - te - mus Do - mi - no, hal - le - lu - jah, hal - le - lu - jah,

hal - le - lu - jah. ℟ Can - te - mus *etc.*

1.Can - te - mus Do - mi - no glo - ri - o - se,

qui - a fac - tus est no - bis in sa - lu - tem. ℟ *as before*

(Sing we to the Lord, alleluia. Sing we gloriously to the Lord, for he is become our saving health.)

Formulas are found in Ambrosian chant both syllabic and neumatic in type: also initial and final formulas, and short bridge-phrases between groups, found in the same form in various tonal and modal contexts. Again, it is most interesting to notice the frequent occurrence of the 'word melody', that is to say, one and the same melodic phrase used to clothe one particular word, stereotyped in all the modes. Extended formulas, or types, are found in the *Ingressa*, *Psalmellus, Alleluia, Cantus*, and so on of the Mass, and in many of the Office chants. Another aspect worth notice is that the Ambrosian manuscripts contain many examples of mosaic or patchwork composition (known in French as *centonisation*) following more or less the same rules as are observed in Gregorian chant (see p. 110). Furthermore, many Ambrosian responds are based on the Latin *cursus*, as in Gregorian chant.

Seeing that the eight-mode classification is certainly later than the time in which these melodies were written, and that the chief object of this classification was to settle the psalm-chant which follows the

---

[1] *Liber Vesperalis*, p. 877.

antiphon, Suñol wisely followed the manuscript practice of not indicating the modality of individual items. The chants of the *Liber Vesperalis* seem more popular and less sophisticated than those of the *Antiphonale Missarum*. As in the other families of Latin chant, Ambrosian chant has the threefold range of syllabic,[1] semi-syllabic, and melismatic chants, the last being neither so elaborate nor so finished as the Roman, and often showing close affinity with Eastern melodies; for example, in the frequent use of the interval of the fourth, both ascending and descending. Sometimes the ascending fourth is followed by an ascending third.

Ex. 22 (a)[2]

Confractorium

Da-ta est mi-hi *om-nis po-te-stas in cœ-lo, et in ter-ra. Halle- lu-jah. E-un- tes

etc.

do-ce-te o-mnes gen-tes

Ex. 22 (b)

Da - ta est mi - hi *o-mnis po - te - stas in cœ -

-lo et in ter - ra. Hal - le - -

-lu - jah. E - un - te; do-ce-te om-nes gen-tes, *etc.*

(There is given unto me all power in heaven and in earth, alleluia. Go ye and teach all nations.)

Ex. 23 (a)[3]

Transitorium

Ma-ria et Martha *dum ve-ni-rent ad mo-nu-men-tum, An-ge-li splenden-tes pa-

etc.

-ru-e-runt, di-cen-tes: Quem quæ-ri-tis? vi-ven-tem in-ter mor-tu-os?

---

[1] An example of syllabic chant—'Pater noster'—is recorded in *The History of Music in Sound*, ii, side 3. [2] *Antiphonale Missarum*, p. 215.
[3] Ibid., p. 226.

Ex. 23(b)

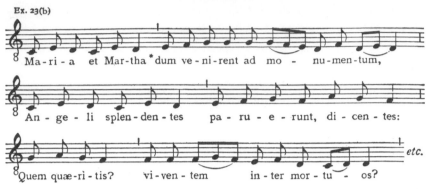

Ma - ri - a   et Mar-tha *dum ve - ni - rent ad mo - nu -men-tum,

An - ge - li splen-den - tes   pa - ru - e - runt, di - cen - tes:

Quem quæ - ri - tis?   vi - ven - tem   in - ter mor - tu - os? *etc.*

(To Mary and Martha, as they came to the sepulchre there appeared bright angels, saying: 'Whom seek ye? the living among the dead?')

GALLICAN CHANT

(i) *Historical Importance.* The music of the ancient liturgies used in France for about 400 years from the beginning of the fifth century is called Gallican. In spite of the fact that authentic examples are so few in number, study of the Gallican chant throws much light on the musical and literary aspects of civilization in Aquitaine, Provence, and southern France in general; and this over a period when we know that culture was fertile in those regions—a culture which has not yet been fully investigated from the musical point of view. Three important points stand out in this respect. First, there is the Aquitanian notation, a type of neumatic writing known as far back as the ninth century and spreading over the south of France, found in Catalonia at least as early as the tenth century, and in Castile and the rest of Spain after the abolition of the Mozarabic chant in the middle of the eleventh century. Secondly, there is the literary and musical school of St. Martial of Limoges, investigated by Hans Spanke and others. Thirdly, and allied to the last, there are the sequences associated with the centre of St. Peter of Moissac, into which inquiry has been made by Clemens Blume, H. M. Bannister, and other scholars. These facts (not to mention here a fourth, trouvère and troubadour music, discussed in Chapter VII) are very significant in themselves, and suggest the extent of the unexplored territory.

Just as the worship, liturgy, and music of the African Church in the time of St. Augustine lay hidden under the incursion of the Vandals, so did that of Southern France from the middle of the fifth to the middle of the sixth century, when the Visigothic culture of the Spanish Church began to develop. Before the Carolingian era France was divided, liturgically speaking, into four regions, among which those of Narbonne and Aquitaine were specially important. In the first case the metropolitan churches of Narbonne and Toulouse were in close contact with Visigothic liturgy and chant in the sixth and seventh centuries: in the second, the region included the Lyonnais and Provence, thus taking in the famous churches of Lyons, Autun, Vienne, and Arles.

Aquitanian notation was known and used here from early times. Gennadius,[1] speaking of the work of the priest Musaeus of Marseilles, who died after 450, says: 'Hortatu sancti Venerii episcopi excerpsit ex sanctis scripturis lectiones totius anni festivis aptas diebus: responsoria etiam psalmorum capitula tempori et lectionibus congruentia' (by order of the saintly bishop Venerius he selected lessons from Holy Scripture meet for the feastdays throughout the year; also responsorial verses of the psalms suitable to the day and the reading); and he adds that for the use of Eustasius, the successor of Venerius, 'composuit sacramentorum egregium et non parvum volumen per membra quidem pro opportunitate officiorum et temporum, pro lectionum textu psalmorumque serie et cantatione discretum' (he compiled a fine, large sacramentary in several sections corresponding with the offices and seasons, arranged for the text of the readings and for the order and singing of the psalms). The two last words indicate that if the sacramentary did not have a definite notation it had at least some signs intended to facilitate the singing of the chant. In 1936 Dom Alban Dold of Beuron published a Gallican *Lectionarium*, transcribed from a palimpsest of the fifth or sixth century, indicating the chants to be sung: and in the respond 'Cantemus Domino' for Easter Eve can be seen the spaces left blank in order to be filled in. The importance of this discovery for the story of musical notation is sufficiently obvious.

A significant figure of this time is the great St. Caesarius of Arles, born in 470 or 471, bishop of Arles from 502 or 503 until his death in 542, and in 514 appointed vicar apostolic 'per Gallias Hispaniasque' by Pope Symmachus. He was outstanding in his efforts to encourage the people to take their part in the chant, as is shown by many of his sermons and told in the life written between 542 and 549 by Cyprian, bishop of Toulon, and four other priests who had been intimate with Caesarius. A typical and pertinent passage is this: 'Adjecit etiam atque compulit, ut laicorum popularitas psalmos et hymnos pararet'

[1] *De viris illustribus*, lxxx; ed. E. C. Richardson in *Texte und Untersuchungen zur Geschichte der altchristlichen Literatur*, xiv (Leipzig, 1896), p. 88.

[i.e. disceret] 'altaque et modulata voce instar clericorum, alii Graece, alii Latine prosas antiphonasque cantarent, ut non haberent spatium in ecclesia fabulis occupari' (furthermore, he ordained and constituted that the congregation of lay people should learn hymns and psalms, and should sing with clear and tuneful voice (like the clergy) both proses and antiphons, some in Greek and some in Latin, so that there be no occasion given in the church for idle talk).[1] As may be inferred from this quotation, Caesarius arranged that chants should be set in Latin words for the Gallo-Roman population, and in Greek for the Greek-speaking people who came perhaps from the Greek colony of Marseilles.

The meaning of *prosa* in this passage is obscure; it can hardly mean a text written in prose, as this is also true of psalms and antiphons; nor can it very well be taken to refer to the *prosa* which was an alternative title for the sequence of the ninth century, as Dom Leclercq seems to suggest.[2] At least the passage shows that in the early sixth century psalmody in two choirs with antiphons was sung in the church of Arles, as well as in the monastery of Lerins, with which Caesarius was connected. The long retention of solo psalmody in French churches is noteworthy. Arles, as we have seen, used antiphony at an early date: in Avignon it was not until 700 that the Bishop Agricus introduced the antiphonal form with two choirs, in imitation of Lerins; and that in spite of the fact that the metropolitan church of Arles, not so very far off, had been using that form for nearly two centuries.

(ii). *Sources*. The Gallican rite was the most short-lived of those used in the west, and relatively few documents have been preserved; the reason being that after the introduction of the Roman rite neither cantors nor liturgists had any reason for wanting to keep the old manuscripts any longer, still less for having them copied. No single musical manuscript of the Gallican liturgy has been preserved, so that to get any idea of the importance which music had in the Frankish liturgy we can only have recourse to non-musical writings. The chief sources of our knowledge are the *Sermones de Symbolo* of St. Caesarius and his *Regula ad Monachos*, the *De cursibus ecclesiasticis* of St. Gregory of Tours (d. 594) and the works of Venantius Fortunatus (d. before 610). The *Expositio brevis antiquae liturgiae gallicanae*, attributed until recently to St. Germanus of Paris and

---

[1] Cf. the edition of B. Krusch, in *Monumenta Germaniae Historica, Script. rer. Merov.* (1896), iii, pp. 33 seq.; Migne, *Patrologia Latina*, lxvii. 1001–42.
[2] *Dictionnaire d'archéologie chrétienne et de liturgie*, vi, p. 534.

serving as a starting-point for the study of the Gallican liturgy, is the work of an anonymous writer of the middle of the seventh century and has only minor value.

The few actual specimens of Gallican music known are mostly pieces from the Mass. They are detected by a process of elimination in later French manuscripts, where the Gregorian chant enshrines, or is replaced by, certain items of Gallican and Visigothic (Mozarabic) origin. These come from Toulouse, Albi, Narbonne, Carcassonne, Saint-Yrieix, Conques, Limoges, and Aurillac. The most important of these are the early eleventh-century Gradual of Albi Cathedral,[1] the St. Yrieix Missal,[2] and some of the manuscripts from St. Martial at Limoges, most of which are now in the Bibliothèque Nationale at Paris. These manuscripts show that in spite of the efforts made by Charlemagne and his successors to abolish the Gallican rite there were chants so loved by the people that when the Roman rite was imposed some of them were retained in the Gregorian books. Some of them even outlived the passage of time and the processes of suppression, as can be seen in traces which have survived until quite recent times in some French dioceses. The same thing happened in Spain with the Mozarabic rite.

There was a close connexion between the Gallican and Mozarabic rites, so that if it ever became possible to transcribe the early Spanish notation we should be able to learn a good deal about Gallican chant. Such Gallican melodies as have been preserved are quite different from their Roman counterparts. Some of them display close analogy with Ambrosian chant, others with Mozarabic, while others again seem specifically Gallican. Sometimes the text is identical in the various Latin liturgies, but the music varies. In character it is like that of all the other Western liturgies—based on prose and on poetical texts, monodic, and written in free rhythm.

(iii) *Chants of the Mass.* Up to the present it has been impossible to discover very much about the music of the Gallican Office; but there is some information available about the chants of the Mass, derived from liturgical texts which have been preserved. These were:

1. The *Antiphona de praelegendo* (Roman Introit, Ambrosian *Ingressa*, Mozarabic *Officium*—a title also used in some medieval English books) which was a psalmodic antiphon followed by *Gloria Patri*: in the sixth century one verse only followed the antiphon.

---

[1] Paris, Bibl. Nat. lat. 776.
[2] Paris, Bibl. Nat. lat. 903: facsimile edition in *Paléographie musicale*, xiii.

2. The *Aius* or *Agios*: after the bishop's salutation 'Dominus sit semper vobiscum' (exactly as in the Mozarabic rite) he intoned the *Trisagion*, 'Agios o Theos', in Greek and Latin; in 529 the council of Vaison recommended that it be sung at every Mass, and in Spain it was also sung before the lessons on solemn feasts.[1]

3. *Kyrie eleison*, sung by three boys and repeated by the choir. Similar chants were those of the *preces* and litanies so widespread in Gallican and Spanish uses, and the fact that so many examples were preserved until much later times is a witness to their popularity:

Ex. 24 (a)

Ky-ri-e e-le-i-son.*ij.* Chri-ste e-le-i-son.*ij.* Ky-ri-e e-le-i-son.*ij.* Chri-ste au-di nos.*ij.*

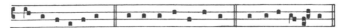

Chri-ste ex-au-di nos.*ij.* Pa-ter de cœ-lis De-us. ℟ Mi-se-re-re no-bis.

Ex. 24 (b)

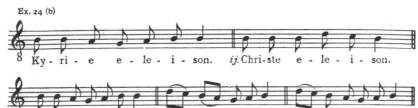

Ky - ri - e e - le - i - son. *ij.* Chri-ste e - le - i - son.

ij. Ky-ri - e e - le - i-son. *ij.* Chri - ste au-di nos. *ij.* Chri-ste ex-au-di nos.

ij. Pa-ter de cœ-lis De-us. ℟. Mi - se - re - re no - - -bis.

(Lord, have mercy, Christ, have mercy, Lord, have mercy. O Christ, hear us. O Christ, do thou hear us. O God the Father of Heaven, have mercy upon us.)

4. *Benedictus*, sung before the lections, by alternate choirs.

5. After the first two lessons, from the Old Testament and the Epistles (or Lives of the Saints on their feasts), came the *Benedicite opera omnia*, or Song of the Three Children, followed by the Responsory Gradual. This was a very ornate chant, sung by choirboys (*parvuli*) according to pseudo-Germanus, though Gregory of Tours implies that it was sung at Orleans by the deacon. The Alleluia was sung after, not before, the Gospel, which followed with full ceremonies, accompanied by the *Trisagion* or on feast-days by an *antiphona ante evangelium*, as at Milan. Musical examples of these anti-

---

[1] Cf. Wellesz, op. cit., pp. 11–18.

phons, which were also sung at Magnificat on the preceding evening,
are preserved in French manuscripts, thus attesting their popularity;
and their typical phrases—such as 'Hodie illuxit nobis' or 'Dicamus
omnes', are even found in twelfth-century tropers at Madrid. One of
the most interesting of these is the 'Insignis praeconiis' of the
martyrs St. Denys and his companions; the abbey of this dedication
dates back to the seventh century:

Ex. 25 (a)

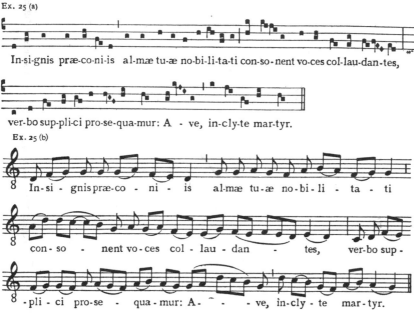

In-si-gnis præ-co-ni-is al-mæ tu-æ no-bi-li-ta-ti con-so-nent vo-ces col-lau-dan-tes,

ver-bo sup-pli-ci pro-se-qua-mur: A - ve, in-cly-te mar-tyr.

Ex. 25 (b)

In-si - gnis præ-co - ni - is al-mæ tu-æ no-bi-li - ta - ti

con - so - nent vo-ces col - lau - dan - tes, ver-bo sup -

-pli - ci pro-se - qua-mur: A - - ve, in-cly - te mar-tyr.

(Let the voices of them that praise thee ring out with noble proclamation in
honour of thy bountiful dignity: let us follow on with the voice of prayer: Hail,
illustrious martyr.)

6. **Chants after the Gospel.** On the way back to the altar the
Trisagion was repeated: then followed the sermon, after which a
Litany to which the people responded 'Precamur te, Domine,
miserere'. This ended the first part of the service, the *Missa catechu-
menorum.*

Ex. 26 (a)

Di-ca- mus o-mnes, ℟¹ Do- mi-ne, mi-se- re-re. ℟² Do-

-mi- ne, mi-se-re-re.

Ex. 26 (b)

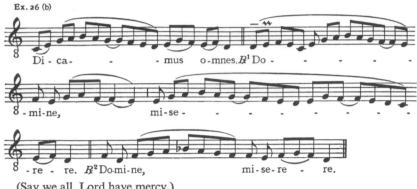

(Say we all, Lord have mercy.)

7. The second part of the service opens with the *Sonus*, sung while the deacon brings the offerings to the altar. The *Sonus* ends with Alleluia, and is thus parallel to the *Laudes* in the Mozarabic and the Song of the Cherubim in the Byzantine rite. This Alleluia (also called *Laudes*) is threefold. No examples have been preserved, but indications from Spain point to it having been like the Roman Alleluia but much more florid.

8. After the Offertory (as in the Mozarabic rite) was sung the Creed, in the Nicene form but in the plural, opening 'Credimus', in conformity with the Council of Toulouse in 589. A fragment of this can be given here:[1]

Ex. 27 (a)

Cre-di-mus in u-num De-um, Pa-trem o - mni-po-ten-tem, Fa-cto-rem cœ-li et ter-ræ

Ex. 27 (b)

Cre-di-mus in   u-num De _ um, Pa-trem o   -   mni-po - ten-tem,

Fa - cto - rem cœ-li et ter - ræ,   *etc.*

(We believe in one God, the Father Almighty, Maker of heaven and earth.)

9. *Immolatio* (Roman Preface, Mozarabic *Illatio*), followed as in all liturgies by the *Sanctus*: no specifically Gallican music for this is known.

¹ Paris, Bibl. Nat. lat. 776, fo. 92: printed by A. Gastoué, *Revue du Chant grégorien* (1938), p. 61.

10. Antiphon of the *Fractio panis* (Ambrosian *Confractorium*). The people recited the *Pater noster* with the celebrant, after the Greek fashion. Just before the Communion came a blessing from the bishop, preceded by 'Humiliate vos benedictioni', sung by the deacon; this blessing was rather long and was divided into short phrases, to each of which the people replied 'Amen', as in the Mozarabic *Pater noster*.

11. Three verses of a psalm were sung antiphonally during the Communion of the people, called *Trecanon* or *Tricanon* by pseudo-Germanus; this was followed by the 'Te laudamus':[1]

Ex. 28 (a)

1. Te lau-da-mus, Do-mi-ne o-mni-po-tens: qui se-des su-per Che-ru-bim et Se-ra-phim,

ex-au-di nos. Te be-ne-di-cunt An-ge-li et Arch-an-ge-li, et ve-ne-ran-tur Pro-phe-

-tæ et A-po-sto-li. 2. Te ad-o-ra-mus, te de-pre-ca-mur ma-gnum Red-em-pto-rem,

quem Pa-ter mi-sit o-vi-bus pa-sto-rem. Al-le-lu-ia, al-le-lu-ia.

Ex. 28 (b)

1. Te laudamus, Domine o - mni-po - tens: qui sedes super Cheru -

-bim et Ser-a-phim, ex-au - di nos. Te be - ne-di -cunt An-ge -

-li et Arch-an - ge - li, et venerantur Prophetæ et A - po-sto - li.

2. Te ad-o - ra - mus, te de-pre-ca-mur ma - gnum Red - em-pto-rem,

---

[1] Gastoué, op. cit., p. 79.

quem Pater misit   ovibus pa-sto-rem. Al - le-lu - ia,   al - le - lu-ia,

(We praise thee, almighty Lord; thou that sittest above the Cherubim and Seraphim, hear us. The angels and archangels bless thee, and the prophets and apostles worship thee. We adore thee, we pray to thee our great Redeemer, whom the Father has sent as shepherd to the sheep. Alleluia, alleluia.)

We reproduce also the well-known 'Venite populi', an Easter hymn also given in the manuscripts as a Communion chant:[1]

Ex: 29 (a)

Ve - - - ni-te,   po-pu-li, ad sa-crum et im-mor-ta-le... Al- - -

- - - - le -   - lu - ia

Ex. 29 (b)

Ve- - - - - - -ni - te,   po-pu - li,

ad sacrum et immor - ta - le.... Al - - - - - -

- - - - le - - - - - - - - lu - ia.

(Come, ye people, to the holy and everlasting [banquet], Alleluia.)

(iv) *Chants of the Office.* Very few specimens of the psalmodic and antiphonal melodies of the Gallican Office have come down to us. *Gloria in excelsis* was sung at the end of Lauds on Sundays and festivals before it was transferred to its present place after the *Kyrie* of the Mass. Hymns, of the Ambrosian type, were sung in some churches, forbidden in others. The hymns for the feasts of the Holy Cross, *Vexilla regis prodeunt* and *Pange lingua gloriosi praelium certaminis*, composed by Venantius Fortunatus (d. before 610), were certainly written for the Gallican liturgy. The dramatic *Popule meus*

---

[1] Printed by Dom P. Ferretti in the *Proper of the Papal Masses* (Rome, 1922) as 'ex antiqua liturgia gallicana'.

with the oriental *Agios o Theos* is another example of a Gallican-Mozarabic chant which has passed over into the Roman liturgy.

(v) *Suppression of the Liturgy.* The suppression of Gallican chant meant a very real loss to the history of music in France. Its abolition was due to different causes, of which the principal one was undoubtedly the Roman attempt at unifying the various liturgics of the West. The immediate motive and the definite cause must be looked for in the intimate relations which existed between the France of Pepin and the Rome of Stephen II. Pressed by the attacks of Astolph, king of the Lombards, the Pope was obliged to call for the help of Pepin, king of the Franks. Chrodegang, bishop of Metz and uncle of Pepin, was charged with the negotiations in Rome, and on his return he introduced the Roman liturgy and chant in his cathedral. In 754 Stephen II went to Paris to crown Pepin, and on that occasion the superior attractions of the Roman liturgy and chant induced the King—instigated also perhaps by his uncle—to request that the Pope would order the Frankish liturgy to be laid aside in favour of the Roman. Under Charlemagne the unification was completed. The Roman Pontiffs sent into Gaul books of their rite and singers from their *schola*: and very soon the Gallican books were forgotten.

MOZARABIC CHANT

(i) *The Visigothic Period.* The music of Roman Spain and its Church was influenced by the civilization of pagan Rome between the first and fifth centuries of the Christian era. There are a few historical records bearing witness to the existence of pre-Christian music, but no examples of its chant or of secular music have been found. Paulus Orosius, a native of Lusitania, had worked with St. Augustine in Africa and with St. Jerome in Palestine. His presence in Spain may well have served as a link between the liturgical and musical practice of the Iberian peninsula and that of the Churches of Africa, Antioch, and Jerusalem. It is worth noticing that St. Damasus, whom we shall meet in connexion with Gregorian chant reforms in the next chapter, was of Spanish origin. Aurelius Prudentius (d. about 405), one of the earliest Christian poets, was writing in Spain at about the same time: he was followed by Caelius Sedulius (d. about 450), who is most famous for his 'Salve, sancta parens, enixa puerpera'. The Spanish pilgrim Etheria visited Jerusalem at the end of the fourth century and has left us an account of her impressions of some of the ceremonies she saw there (see p. 7), from which it is evident that others of them were known in her native land, seeing that she thought it unnecessary to describe them. According to Cabrol traces of the Mozarabic *Illationes* can be seen in some of the treatises attributed to the heretic Priscillian, a native of Galicia and bishop of Avila, who died in 385.

Recent investigations have shown that, as we might expect, the Spanish liturgy of the sixth and seventh centuries enshrines elements of the highest antiquity: and that the oldest Latin version of the Scriptures preserved comes from Spain, to which it had passed in the time of St. Cyprian (third century) or even of Tertullian (second century). Furthermore, the oldest Latin secular songs with music that have been preserved come from seventh-century Spain, as does the oldest liturgical Latin hymn with a refrain (given with its music in the Visigothic hymnal of the ninth or tenth century); and Peter Wagner thought that the Mozarabic *Pater noster* might very well date from the fourth century:

Ex. 30 (a)[1]

1   Pater noster,   qui es in cœ - lis,   A - men.
2   Sancti-fi - ce-tur no-men tu - um.   A - men.
3   Ad-ve- ni - at   regnum tu - um.   A - men.
4   Fi - at vo-lun-tas tu-a,   sic-ut in cœ-lo et in ter - ra.   A - men.
5 Panem nostrum   quo-ti-di - a-num   da no-bis ho-di - e.   A - men.
6 Et dimitte   no-bis de-bi-ta nostra, sic-ut et nos
                                        dimittimus debitoribus no - stris. A - men.
7   Et ne nos in-du-cas   in ten-ta-ti - o - nem:

℞. sed li - be - ra nos a ma - lo.

Ex. 30 (b)

1   Pater noster,   qui es in cœ - lis,   A - men.
2   Sanctificetur nomen tu - um.   A - men.
3   Adveniat regnum tu - um.   A - men.
4   Fi - at voluntas tua,   sicut in cœlo et in ter - ra.   A - men.
5   Panem nostrum quotidianum   da nobis   ho-di - e.   A - men.
6 Et dimitte   nobis   debita nostra,   sicut et nos
                                        dimittimus debitoribus no - stris.   A - men.
7   Et ne nos inducas   in tentati - o - nem:

℞. sed li - be - ra nos a ma - lo.

[1] Recorded in *The History of Music in Sound*, ii, side 3.

(Our Father, who art in heaven, Amen. Hallowed be thy name, Amen. Thy
Kingdom come, Amen. Thy will be done, as in heaven, so on earth, Amen. Give
us this day our daily bread, Amen. And forgive us our debts, as we forgive our
debtors, Amen. And lead us not into temptation: but deliver us from evil.)

The music of the Visigothic Church was fixed and in order by
the time of the Arab invasion of 711. In spite of this fact it is more
usually known by the name of 'Mozarabic' (from *musta'rib*, meaning a
Christian living under the Moorish yoke) because the Christians went
on using it during the time when the Arabs ruled, and because its manuscripts date back to the time of Islamic domination. The music of the
Spanish liturgy was worked out from the fifth to the seventh centuries,
and the process of its elaboration may be dated between 550 and 660.
Famous names in this connexion are those of the bishops of Seville
(Leander, d. 599, and Isidore, d. 636), Toledo (Eugenius II, d. 657,
Ildefonsus, d. 677, and Julian, d. 690), and Saragossa (John, d. 631,
and Braulius, d. 651), all accomplished musicians and liturgists,
according to the contemporary records.

(ii) *Sources*. Almost the entire cycle of the music used by the Visigothic or Mozarabic Church has been preserved, mostly in manuscripts copied from the eighth to the eleventh century, which contain
the chant of the sixth and seventh centuries together with certain
elements even pre-Visigothic: and these give us the full product of
the scriptoria of Toledo, San Millan de la Cogolla, Santo Domingo de
Silos, &c. About twenty of these manuscripts have been preserved,
of which seven come from Toledo. Of the others the most important
by far is the Antiphoner of Leon Cathedral, copied in the early tenth
century from a seventh-century exemplar written for the Toledo
parish of St. Leocadia. All the others come directly or indirectly from
the same church of Toledo, except for some fragments elsewhere.

In addition to these main sources there are others from the south
of France which should be mentioned: notably the eleventh-century
Gradual of Albi Cathedral[1] and the Gradual of St. Yrieix.[2] These
contain a substratum of Visigothic chant as well as of Gallican. There
are similar manuscripts from Toulouse and Narbonne, and perhaps
some traces can be seen in those from St. Martial at Limoges.
Gastoué noticed in a tenth-century manuscript at Paris[3] the hymn
'Inventor rutili' of Prudentius, with Spanish neums. Again, Paris,
Bibl. Nat. lat. 8670 contains the distich 'Scande coeli templa' with

[1] Paris, Bibl. Nat. lat. 776.
[2] Ibid., lat. 903; facsimile edition in *Paléographie musicale,* xiii.
[3] Ibid., lat. 8307, fo. 6–7.

Visigothic neums, one of the earliest instances of the kind: it is a ninth-century manuscript of the works of Martianus Capella, an African writer of the end of the fourth century. Paris, Bibl. Nat. lat. 8093 (eighth century) contains several distichs in Mozarabic neums— among them 'O mortalis homo', by Eugenius of Toledo, and 'Sum et miser' (written in the same metre as the 'Salve festa dies' of Venantius Fortunatus) by Isidore of Seville.

(iii) *Notation.* The notation of Mozarabic plainsong in the early manuscripts is neumatic, with Eastern and Byzantine elements. There are two schools of notation, one writing horizontally, the other vertically. The horizontal manuscripts belong to the Toledo school: there are fewer types of neums, their form is more primitive and there is no trace of 'careful height': the simple neum has not more than one or two forms, and compound neums are found but rarely. The second school, the vertical, presents its neums much more clearly and in a form easier to read: its manuscripts come from Silos, from San Millan de la Cogolla (in which traces of 'carefully heighted' or diastematic neums may be seen) and include the important Antiphoner of Leon; and with them must be mentioned the two manuscripts in the British Museum[1] which come from the monastery of San Domingo de Silos and give Roman texts and melodies in Visigothic script. Though the Toledo style of writing seems the older, it does not follow that the vertical type did not originate in Toledo as well, judging from the Antiphoner of Leon. One thing must be noticed, namely, that after the Arab invasion of 711 until the introduction of the Roman chant in the second half of the eleventh century there was little or no development either in the music or in its notation. The scribes contented themselves with copying the existing manuscripts.

(iv) *Musical Forms of the Liturgy.* (*a*) The Mass. There are four choral chants, together with *Gloria, Credo, Agios,* and *Sanctus,* antiphons of the *Pax* and the Communion, salutations by the celebrant and biddings by the deacon, the Diptychs, and the Consecration. In all, the Mozarabic sacramentary includes 240 formularies for Mass. This Offertory salutation occurs before (12) on p. 87:

Ex. 31 (a)[2]

Adjuvate me, fratres, in o-rati-onibus vestris, et orate pro me ad Deum. ℟. Adjuvet

[1] Add. 30848 and 30850.
[2] *Missale Mixtum* (1500).

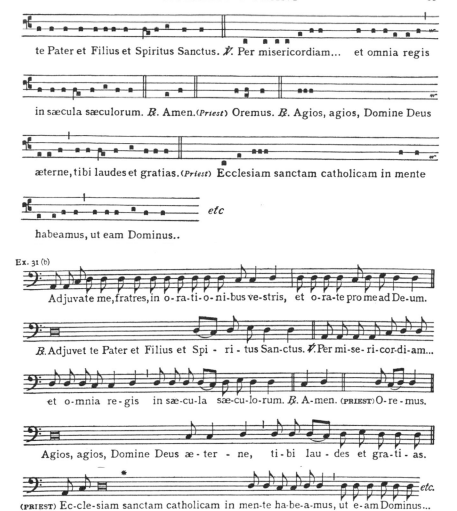

te Pater et Filius et Spiritus Sanctus. ℣. Per misericordiam... et omnia regis

in sæcula sæculorum. ℟. Amen.*(Priest)* Oremus. ℟. Agios, agios, Domine Deus

æterne, tibi laudes et gratias. *(Priest)* Ecclesiam sanctam catholicam in mente

etc

habeamus, ut eam Dominus..

Ex. 31 (b)

Adjuvate me, fratres, in o-ra-ti-o-ni-bus ve-stris, et o-ra-te pro me ad De-um.

℟. Adjuvet te Pater et Filius et Spi - ri - tus San-ctus. ℣. Per mi-se-ri-cor-di-am...

et o-mnia re-gis in sæ-cu-la sæ-cu-lo-rum. ℟. A-men. (PRIEST)O-re-mus.

Agios, agios, Domine Deus æ-ter - ne, ti-bi lau-des et gra-ti-as.

(PRIEST) Ec-cle-siam sanctam catholicam in men-te ha-be-a-mus, ut e-am Dominus...

(Assist me, brethren, in your prayers and pray for me to God.
May the Father and the Son and the Holy Spirit assist thee,
Through the mercy . . . and rulest all things for ever and ever, Amen.
Let us pray, Holy, holy, Lord God eternal, to thee be praises and thanks.
Let us bear in mind the Holy Catholic Church, that the Lord may . . .)

The choral chants are as follows:

1. The *Praelegendum* (or *Prolegendum*), corresponding to the Roman Introit, and having like it a verse and *Gloria*. It is written in simple style and was sung before the first lesson. The name now given to it, *Officium*, is not found in the earliest manuscripts.

2. *Gloria in excelsis.* When used, this hymn follows the *Praelegendum*.

In early days it was rarely used, and there are only three or four melodies for it in the books.

3. *Trisagion* ('Agios o theos'). A distinctive mark of the Spanish liturgy was the insertion of the *Trisagion* after the *Gloria*, and the *Benedictiones* before the *Psallendum* with the *Clamor* after it. There are several ornate chants for the *Gloria*, which was sung in Greek and in Latin.

4. The *Benedictiones*, sometimes consisting of certain verses of the canticle 'Benedictus es, Domine Deus'.

5. The *Psallendum*: sung after the *Benedictiones* if they were used, but on lesser days coming after the first lesson. It was a solo chant, sung in the 'pulpit', with passages for full chorus. In its psalmodic form and melismatic style it is very similar to the Gregorian Gradual.

6. The *Clamor* occurs in no other rite and is peculiar to the Spanish liturgy. Sometimes it extends the text of the *Psallendum*, differing from it by an acclamation, whence the name. There were three classes —(a) funeral, (b) for the Hours of the Office, (c) for the Mass. Between the body of the *clamor* and its Verse an acclamation was added— 'Deo gratias, Kyrie eleison'—which is the essential part of the *clamor*.

7. The *Trenos*, a name derived from the Threnody or Lamentations of Jeremiah; replacing the *Psallendum* on some Lenten weekdays. The *Trenos* always began with the verse 'Quis dabit capiti meo'[1] and consisted of several phrases from Jeremiah, and sometimes from the Book of Job. It is of later date than the other chants, and the melody of the first strophe after the introduction is used for all the other verses.

8. On the last days of Holy Week a *Canticum* or special kind of *Psallendum* is used; its melody is similar to that of the *Trenos*.

9. The *Laudes*, corresponding to the Roman Alleluia, was sung after the epistle or gospel. The last syllable of 'alleluia' is much more florid than the Roman counterpart. The word *Lauda* now used at Toledo is not found in the oldest manuscripts.

10. The *Sacrificium*, corresponding to the Roman *Offertorium*, was an antiphon with several verses, surpassing in its musical development all the other chants of the Mass.

11. After the *Psallendum* were sung, on certain penitential days, the *Preces*, a series of supplications in short phrases. Their place in the Mozarabic Mass is comparable to that of the Roman sequences. The chant is ornate. The text of some of them has been published in the *Variae Preces* of Solesmes ('Attende Domine', 'Miserere et

[1] Jeremiah ix. 1.

parce', &c.). The musical study of the *Preces* of eleventh- to fourteenth-century manuscripts would yield very interesting results.

Ex. 32 (a)[1]
Preces

De-us, mi-se-re-re, De-us mi-se-re-re, o Je-su bo-ne, tu il-li par-ce. ℟. De-us mi-se-

-re - re.

Ex.32 (b)
(Octave higher)

De-us, mi-se-re-re, De-us mi-se-re-re, o Je-su bo-

-ne, tu il-li par-ce. De-us mi-se-re- - re.

(Lord, have mercy. Lord, have mercy. O good Jesu, do thou spare him, Lord, have mercy.)

12. 'Agios, Agios Dominus Deus' is a short simple piece sung by the whole choir after the *Sacrificium* and leading into the Sanctus.

13. *Ad pacem, Ad confractionem panis, Ad accedentes* are names given to the three antiphons, each with a verse as a rule, sung at the

Ex. 33 (a)[2]
Ad Confractionem panis

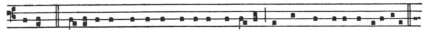

Gu-sta-te et videte quam su-a-vis est Dominus, Hallelujah, hallelujah, halle -

-lujah. ℣. Benedicam Dominum in omni tempore: semper laus ejus in ore meo.

℟. Hallelujah... ℣. Redimet Dominus animas servorum su-o-rum: et non delinquent

etc.

omnes qui sperant in e-o. ℟. Hallelujah.

[1] G. Prado, *El Canto mozárabe*, p. 74. [2] Ibid., p. 130.

Ex. 33 (b)

Gus - ta - te et vi - de - te quam suavis est Do - mi - nus,

Hal - le - lu - jah, hal - le - lu - jah, hal - le - - - lu - jah.

Be - ne - di - cam Do - mi - num in om - ni tempo - re:

Semper laus e - jus in o - re me - o. ℟. Hal - le - lu - jah.   etc.

℣. Red - i - met Do - mi - nus a - ni - mas ser - vo - rum su - o - rum:

et non delinquent o - mnes qui sperant in e - o. ℟. Hal - le - lu - jah.   etc.

(Taste and see how sweet the Lord is, alleluia. I will bless the Lord at all time:
his praise shall ever be in my mouth. The Lord shall redeem the souls of his
servants: and all they that hope in him shall not be destitute.)

corresponding acts of the liturgy—the kiss of peace, the breaking of
the bread, and the communion of the faithful. The melodies are
simple and not unlike the Roman *Communio*.

14. 'Credimus in unum Deum.' No contemporary melody is given
in the manuscripts, though its singing was directed by the Third
Council of Toledo in 589. At the present time it is sung on Sundays
and some feast-days before the *fractio panis*.

Ex. 34 (a) [1]

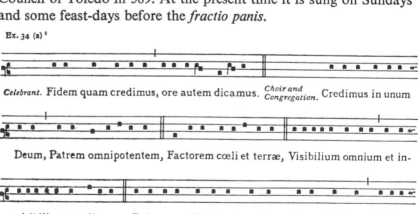

Celebrant. Fidem quam credimus, ore autem dicamus. *Choir and Congregation.* Credimus in unum

Deum, Patrem omnipotentem, Factorem cœli et terræ, Visibilium omnium et in-

-visibilium conditorem. Et in unum Dominum nostrum Jesum Christum, Filium

[1] G. Prado, *El Canto mozárabe*, p. 123.

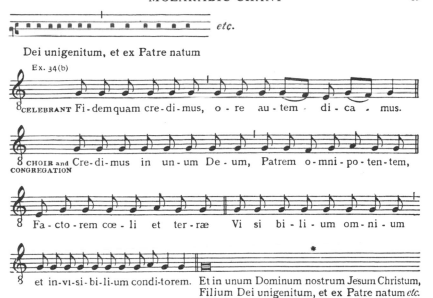

Dei unigenitum, et ex Patre natum

Ex. 34(b)

CELEBRANT Fi-dem quam cre-di-mus, o - re au - tem - di - ca - mus.

CHOIR and Cre-di-mus in un - um De - um, Patrem o - mni - po - ten-tem,
CONGREGATION

Fa - cto - rem cœ - li et ter-ræ Vi si bi - li - um om - ni - um

et in-vi-si-bi-li-um condi-torem. Et in unum Dominum nostrum Jesum Christum,
Filium Dei unigenitum, et ex Patre natum *etc.*

(The faith which we believe, let us declare with the mouth. We believe in one God, the Father almighty, maker of heaven and earth, creator of all things visible and invisible. And in one Lord Jesus Christ, the only begotten Son of God, begotten of the Father . . .)

(*b*) The Office. At the beginning of Vespers are sung two antiphons of exuberant and florid character, called *vesperum* and *sonum* respectively; under these antiphons several verses are sung as a rule. The remaining antiphons are less florid, but more so than the Gregorian. At the end of Lauds is sung the *sonum* as at Vespers, and a *psallendum*—the Gradual from the Mass—but without its verse.[1] Though the use of hymns is distinctive of early Spanish worship, as of Irish, their tunes are rarely given in the manuscripts. The hymn 'Alleluia, piis edite laudibus' is the oldest hymn with a refrain so far known. More than 200 hymns are known to have been sung in the Visigothic Mozarabic liturgy; about 80 are of extraneous origin.

(v) *Character of the Original Music.* It is quite likely that the manuscripts have preserved for us the entire liturgical music of the old Church of Toledo: but so far as we can see the variants of the churches of Tarragona and Seville have not been preserved. How much more, if any, has gone we have no means of knowing. At the present time the Mozarabic melodies remain untranslatable. At the time they were

[1] The antiphon 'In pace', in the Mozarabic and Gregorian versions, is recorded in *The History of Music in Sound*, ii, side 3.

beginning to be disused, diastematic notation (see p. 109) was just coming into use; but the copyists did not trouble to transcribe the music in the newer notation, so that while we can interpret an individual neum we are ignorant of both pitch and interval. We have about 21 melodies more or less authentic, and in them we can see elements of dramatization and of congregational singing. Thus in the *Pater noster* the Amen is sung by the people at the end of every phrase. But we can see from the manuscripts that the prolixity and exuberance of some of the melodies were in no way behind the Ambrosian. For example, on Ascension Day the antiphon *Ad accedentes* has for its verse the single word Alleluia, sung on 163 notes:[1] on Lady Day the fifth verse of the *Sacrificium* is also Alleluia, and has over 200 notes:[2] others have 250 and 300 notes.

Dramatic and congregational singing can be seen in the *preces*, *miserationes*, and *abecedaria*. These last are chants in which verses begin with the succeeding letters of the alphabet; this is a practice known to Hebrew psalm-writers and Latin hymn-writers alike, an example of the latter being 'A solis ortus cardine', written under the title of *Paean alphabeticus de Christo* by Sedulius (see p. 81) and incorporated into the Mozarabic and Gregorian rites, though not into the Ambrosian.[3] Sequences are not unknown in the Mozarabic rite: these *preces* and *miserationes* might almost be thought of as forerunners of the sequence. There are few tropes, in the ordinary sense (see Chapter V), but many of the formulas are found with glossed and paraphrased texts, e.g. some of the prayers and prefaces. As to the ultimate origin of the Spanish rite, Duchesne affirmed simply that it was Gallican. But Dom Cagin, Dom Cabrol, Dom Ferretti, and Cardinal Schuster all believe that it came partly from Jerusalem and Antioch, by way of Rome. Eastern and Byzantine influence can be seen in its forms and in the musical notation; in the liturgy can be detected also African, monastic, Ambrosian, and Gallican influences.

(vi) *Abolition of the Liturgy*. After the Moorish invasion the province of Tarragona separated from that of Toledo and linked itself to Narbonne, thus acquiring much of the monastic culture of Southern France. As an immediate result of this, Roman liturgy and Gregorian chant began to penetrate Catalonia as early as the Carolingian epoch.[4] Thanks to the introduction of the Roman liturgy and

---

[1] Antiphoner of Leon, fo. 201.
[2] Ibid., fo. 61ᵛ.
[3] W. H. Frere, Historical Introduction to *Hymns Ancient and Modern* (London, 1909), p. 71.
[4] Cf. H. Anglès, *La Música a Catalunya fins al segle XIII* (Barcelona, 1935).

to its close relation with St. Martial of Limoges, St. Peter of Moissac and other French monasteries, Catalonia very soon came to use both tropes and sequences. The monks of Ripoll also developed a diastematic type of notation, evolved from the Mozarabic and similar to the Aquitanian, as early as the beginning of the tenth century. The difficulties met with by Alexander II (1064–73) and Gregory VII (1073–85) in their efforts to substitute the *Lex Romana* for the Mozarabic rite are matters of historical record. In spite of the fact that Alexander II had approved the Mozarabic *Liber Ordinum*, Missal and Antiphoner presented to him by the Spanish bishops in 1065, Gregory VII returned to the attack and obtained the suppression of the ancient and venerable rite: the *Lex Romana* entered Aragon in 1071, and by 1076 had found its way into Castile and Leon.

The abolition of the Mozarabic liturgy took place just at the very time when diastematic notation was spreading rapidly through all the Churches of the West. It is an unexplained mystery why the Mozarabic musicians and cantors of the six parishes of Toledo allowed to keep the traditional chant, and of the exempt monasteries, did not take the trouble to transcribe the chant into diastematic notation, which could be easily read. The immediate result was the total loss of the key by which alone the treasure-chest of the ancient Spanish music could be unlocked. As we have seen, the neumatic manuscripts themselves were fortunately preserved. But when Cardinal Francisco de Cisneros tried to reform and revive the ancient Mozarabic liturgy, published the Missal (1500) and the Breviary (1502), and founded the famous Mozarabic Chapel in Toledo Cathedral, the musicians of Castile had no knowledge of how to transcribe a single note of the ancient melodies. Except for some of the recitative parts of the Mass, the music of which would have been preserved by oral tradition, the musical side of the reform of Cisneros has very little scientific value. The 'Explanationes ac dilucidationes' of the Mozarabic chant, prefixed to the *Missa Gothica seu Mozarabica* of Bishop Fabian y Duero (Angelopolis, 1770) and the explanations of Hieronymus Romero de Avila, choirmaster of Toledo, in the *Breviarium Gothicum* of Cardinal Lorenzana (1775) are of no academic importance. Mass is still celebrated today according to the Mozarabic rite in the Cathedral of Toledo, but no longer in Salamanca. There is room for improvement in the dignity of the chant, which might be gained by collecting much that is good and useful in the chant-books of Cisneros and others of various cathedrals in Castile.

IV

GREGORIAN CHANT

By Higini Anglès

MUSICAL VALUE AND PRINCIPAL FEATURES

IT is not so very long ago since plainsong was thought to have no interest for musicians who were not also ecclesiastics. Many writers on music did not even bother about its existence, as they thought it had no importance for musical history. Today, however, not only musicologists but also Romanists, orientalists, liturgists, hymnologists, and specialists in medieval history all think it worthy of their attention. This is only to be expected when we consider that historical investigations into the Latin liturgy have clearly established the fact that the Roman chant is coeval with the liturgy itself, that it came into existence along with the liturgy and developed with it, and even contributed largely to its formation. From the very earliest times of Christian worship ecclesiastical chant was designed for the glory of God and the edification of the faithful. This fact will help us to appreciate its characteristics.

There lies before us a magnificent musical repertory, the most spiritual ever created for the purpose of singing the divine praises. Its melody is unique in style; though diatonic and in free rhythm, it was always suited for the singing of liturgical texts in Latin, whether the text was taken directly from the Scriptures (above all the Psalms) or derived either from the writings of the Fathers or the Scriptures themselves. Some texts were taken from the Acts of the Martyrs. The melodies are as suitable for prose as for poetry of more or less popular form. Modern musicologists look upon this chant with special veneration: it is the most artistic, and the only one (except Byzantine, Ambrosian, and Mozarabic) that has been preserved in Europe from the past. As for the chants and dances of pagan Rome we only know the bare fact of their historical existence,[1] for up to this time no single specimen of this vocal or instrumental music has been discovered. In its melody Gregorian chant is always vivacious and technically perfect, coming as it does from an age when formal poly-

---

[1] See vol. i, chap. x.

phony was as yet unknown, when people sang only their national folk melodies.

This point should be borne in mind, the more so when we consider that next to nothing is known of European popular song during the first thousand years of the Christian era (see p. 220), and that beneath the Gregorian repertory there lies a substratum of the most ancient religious and popular chant of both Eastern and Western derivation. Inspired artists took it up and adapted it for the needs of Christian worship. Musical historians revere these Gregorian melodies: in them they can see every kind of monodic music belonging to Eastern music, with its reminiscences of the Jewish Temple and synagogue on the one hand and the Church of Antioch and Jerusalem on the other— these representing the remotest sources of Roman chant: and at the same time they discern features of Western character, used in the Church from the earliest days, until now. These forms and qualities, which surpass anything comparable elsewhere, produce a character both universal and enduring, proof against the changes brought about by temporary fashions or varieties of race and nationality.

For musicologists the existence of Gregorian chant and the investigation of its musical treasures has a secret charm and a special interest. Its melodic material formed the basis of a great part of European sacred polyphony from the ninth to the eighteenth century: at the beginning of this period we find the *organa* (see Chap. VIII–X) and all through the later centuries both religious and secular motets. Historians have to remember that it was the Roman model which was the basis of many melodies used by the troubadours of Provence and the trouvères of northern France in the twelfth and thirteenth centuries and by the German Minnesingers, as well as those of the Italian *laudi* and the Galician-Portuguese *Cantigas de Santa María* in the thirteenth century, even though all these pieces were composed in mensural rhythm (see Chap. VII). Moreover it was plainsong which gave rise to those interesting forms of trope, conductus, and sequence, now the subject of so much literary and musical study. Another sphere in which these melodies are important is the study of instrumental music. When we examine organ music from the sixteenth to the eighteenth century, and the art of instrumental variation introduced by lutenists and viol-players[1] we get some idea of the effectiveness and the fertility of the Gregorian repertory. Even comparative musical ethnography is interested in the monodic chant of Christian worship, because many tunes traditional among nations both Eastern

---

[1] See vol. iii, chap. xii; vol. iv, chap. xi; and vol. vi, chap. iv and v.

and Western show traces and reminiscences of the venerable Latin chant, and are linked to it by melodic, modal, and even sometimes rhythmical, analogies.

FORMATION OF ROMAN LITURGICAL CHANT

In the fourth century the Edict of Milan (313), by which Constantine granted liberty to the Christian Church and its worship, resulted in the opening of the great basilicas: and the artistic development of the liturgical chant began at the same time. In the East as well as in the West the singing of psalms was still the central and essential part of divine worship. Clerics and layfolk, men, women, and children all took part in its execution. The same century saw the rise of monasticism, when communities of men and women vied with each other in their devotion to the chant. The singing and reciting of the psalter was their continual, official prayer. Towards the end of the same century the splendour of Christian worship received a mighty impulse from two illustrious leaders of the Western Church, St. Damasus in Rome and St. Ambrose in Milan.

In this century there appeared the *antiphonia* for two choirs, and in Syria, Nicaea, Palestine, Egypt, Arabia, and Constantinople it is found both at Mass and in the Office. This choral psalmody consisted of the singing of a psalm by alternating choruses, maintaining the same melody: it was a practice already used in Jewish worship under the name of antiphonal chant.[1] The word *antiphonos* occurs for the first time in the Christian era about the middle of the first century, when Philo in his *De vita contemplativa* described the religious practices of the Therapeutae and Therapeutides near Alexandria. In use from the earliest days of Christianity, antiphony developed in the course of the fourth century (see p. 6), and was a favourite practice with the Arians, according to St. John Chrysostom and the historian Sozomen. When condemning the Arian heresy, the Church did not abolish this way of singing: on the contrary, she encouraged it, only taking care that the texts sung were doctrinally orthodox. It is generally agreed that the chief centre of diffusion for the antiphonal chant was Antioch, and that it passed thence to the Western Church through the agency of St. Ambrose of Milan. St. Augustine speaks of it with deep emotion in the ninth book of his *Confessions*.

Boys, trained as lectors and cantors in special schools, often alternated in the chant with men and women: the *Ordo Romanus IX*, when speaking 'de gradibus Romanae Ecclesiae' states that 'in qualicunque

[1] See vol. i.

schola reperti fuerint pueri psallentes, tolluntur inde, et nutriuntur in schola cantorum et postea fiunt cubicularii'[1] (in whatever school shall be found boys who sing, they are fetched out and brought up in the singing-school, and later on become papal officials). Historical testimony can be adduced to show that a vigorous musical evolution took place in Rome from the fourth century onwards, though its phases cannot be exactly determined. Pope Damasus (366–84) held a synod in 374 and a council in 382 with the collaboration of Eastern bishops. During the last years of his pontificate he made use of the services of St. Jerome, the first expert in Eastern liturgy, as a secretary and adviser in liturgical matters. The *Liber Pontificalis* contains a copy of the letter (apocryphal) which St. Jerome addressed to St. Damasus, relating how this pontiff 'gave order to sing the psalms by day and by night in all the churches', though they had been introduced by Celestine I into the 'missa fidelium' as antiphonal chant before the lections. His reform is saturated with Eastern influence; it brought in the order of Jerusalem, enlivening it with the Roman spirit. It was simultaneously with this movement that St. Ambrose established a new order in liturgy and music in the Church at Milan (see p. 59).

Although we possess no musical manuscripts from that epoch, it has been clearly proved that the actual Gregorian repertory is not exclusively the work of the Western Church. There are many elements which originate in the East, notably those which refer to the actual forms of the chant. St. Ambrose introduced at Milan, in addition to the antiphony, the singing of hymns. These had been used first in Syria, Egypt, and Constantinople, and had spread thence all over the Western churches. Athanasius, Bishop of Alexandria, passed his second exile in Rome (340–3) surrounded by his monks: it was then that he brought monachism to the West. St. Hilary of Poitiers, when exiled in Asia Minor (356–60), became acquainted there with hymnody and transferred it to the Western Church, though apparently without success.

In the time of Celestine I (422–32) choral psalmody was introduced into the Mass (Introit, *Communio*) for items which hitherto had been sung by a cantor as solo psalmody. It was in his days also that the foundation of a *Schola cantorum* was brought about in Rome itself, as a model centre for the cultivation and composition of plainsong. Sixtus III (432–40) is another illustrious pontiff who played his part in the development by definitely entrusting to a religious community the care of the chant of the Office. Leo the Great (440–61) in his turn

---

[1] *Patrologia Latina,* lxxviii, 1003.

founded a monastery at St. John and St. Paul to maintain the chant in the papal basilica. The *Liber Pontificalis* describes him as 'vir eloquentissimus . . . cantilena praecipuus' (a very eloquent man, excellent in song); and by his order the liturgy followed the ecclesiastical year closely, after the model of the Church of Jerusalem. His *Sacramentarium* (book of liturgical prayers, lections, and chants), together with the *Sacramentarium Gelasianum*—this being the work of Pope Gelasius (492–6)—are the oldest books we know with a definitely liturgical character. The *Liber Pontificalis* also says that Gelasius 'fecit hymnos in modum beati Ambrosii' (wrote hymns in the manner of St. Ambrose) and that he arranged the 'praefationes et orationes' of the Sacramentary. The Graduals of the Vatican Library, MS. 5319 and the Archives of St. Peter, MS. F. 22, with the Antiphoner MS. B 79 in the latter collection and Brit. Mus. Add. 29988, may be regarded as the chief musical sources for pre-Gregorian Roman chant (often referred to as 'Old Latin' chant), though they also contain later compositions.[1]

PERFECTION OF GREGORIAN CHANT

It was during the pontificate of St. Gregory the Great (590–604) that the liturgical chant took its definite and typical form in the Catholic Church, and was known henceforth as Gregorian chant. The *Schola cantorum*, reorganized by this Pope, came to be the pillar and foundation of the Roman musical tradition. Though it has not been possible to prove absolutely that St. Gregory himself wrote new melodies or that he was actually a good musician and composer, sufficient evidence is available to support the assertion that in his time the pre-existing melodies were (either by his work or that of the Roman *Schola cantorum*) collected and chosen; and that they received a particular mark of unity when they were codified and fixed in his *Antiphonarium cento* with that exquisite artistic taste and noble restraint which the Roman Church knew how to use in combining the most heterogeneous elements. Attempts have been made (without sufficient historical foundation) to debase and disfigure the admirable work of St. Gregory, alleging the fact that Italy did not join in the poetical and literary movements either of his age or of later times. Protagonists of this destructive criticism perhaps do not fully realize how St. Gregory the Great devoted most of his energies to exterminating the remains of paganism and Arianism, and to closing the contro-

[1] See B. Stäblein, 'Zur Frühgeschichte des römischen Chorals', in *Report of the International Congress of Sacred Music* (Rome, 1950).

versies between Rome and Constantinople. His writings, very much in vogue during the Middle Ages, always had a practical purpose. The well-known hymnologist Clemens Blume[1] does not hesitate to affirm that in addition to his *Sacramentarium* and his work of reforming the Mass in its liturgical aspect he also wrote hymns.

From what has been said above it is obvious that many of the melodies called Gregorian must have been composed in epochs earlier than that of St. Gregory. A great number of them came from the East and were modified in Rome: others were composed in Italy itself. And in spite of its great age, the existing corpus reveals remarkable identity in all the various schools of Europe. Comparative musical ethnology will find there an almost virgin field for the study of international melodies. It is not accurate to speak of Gregorian 'dialects', for the varieties that may be found are utterly insignificant. An attempt was made in this direction by Peter Wagner in his theory of German Gregorian dialect, in spite of the fact that the few manuscripts which suggested the idea belonged to a rather late period. In the Proper of the Mass the manuscripts show great uniformity and accuracy: but in the chants of the Office and the Ordinary of the Mass there is greater variety, especially in the case of the latter, in which development was taking place all over Europe: moreover, almost every nation wanted to enrich its repertory by some contribution of its own.

It was quite natural that, in addition to the genuine Roman collection, every country should create for itself new melodies, or adapt and arrange the old ones, supplying them with new texts for the celebration of local feasts and saints. These melodies, sometimes displaying internally their national characteristics, yet preserved to a high degree that mark of impersonality and universality which distinguishes the reform of the great Pontiff. It must be remembered that during the seventh and eighth centuries there were several popes of Greek and Syro-Byzantine descent, and their influence made itself felt in the details of divine worship. During that period, if not in earlier, pre-Gregorian times, the responsories of Holy Week and the antiphons of the 'Hodie' class, of Eastern origin, were introduced. The blessing and procession of palms show Eastern influence. The Adoration of the Cross and the Greek-Latin *Trisagion* (see p. 76) are ceremonies of the Church of Jerusalem and survived after 614 in the Jacobite and Maronite rites of Syria. Towards the end of the fifth century, or early in the sixth, the *Trisagion* passed from Constantinople to Gaul and became part of the patrimony of the Gallican and Visigothic-Mozarabic liturgies. The

---

[1] See especially his *Unsere liturgischen Lieder* (Ratisbon, 1932), pp. 52 seq.

ceremony of the Adoration of the Cross was established in Rome by
Pope Sergius I (687–701), who was of Syrian ancestry.

It is interesting to notice the persistence of Greek chants for so
many centuries in Western Europe, and especially in Italy, a fact
which may be due to the Greek communities which went on living
there. There is a still more interesting detail, confirmed by the *Ordines
Romani*, testifying that even after the eleventh and twelfth centuries
the singing of the Greek epistle and sequences still alternated with the
Latin epistle and sequences at certain feasts and in the presence
of the Pope.[1] Ferretti[2] holds the view that the antiphons of the
Circumcision, Holy Cross, and the Nativity of the Blessed Virgin
Mary betray Byzantine style. In this connexion we quote from
Wellesz:

> The chants of the Churches of Jerusalem and Antioch, a great number of
> them going back to the Service of the Jewish Synagogue, were introduced
> in the West partly in the first centuries, when Mass was celebrated in Greek,
> partly in the second half of the fourth century in the time of Pope Damasus
> (366–84), partly in the last quarter of the seventh century under the Greek
> popes Agatho (678–81), Leo II (682–3), Benedict II (684–5), and Sergius I
> (687–701). They formed the basic element of Western chant in all its
> derivations and became fully assimilated, without losing their character-
> istics, in the process of adaptation to Latin words. Only the Roman rite,
> not as influential then as it was after the days of the Carolingian Renais-
> sance, transformed the chants by a continuous process of permeation by
> its own particular features.[3]

The Roman musicians, known to us from St. Gregory until the end
of the Roman school in the ninth century, are cantors, composers,
monks, and popes. Several pontiffs distinguished themselves by the
special interest they took in liturgical chant: for example, we know
that Honorius (625–38) instituted the chant of the litanies on Saturdays, on the way from St. Apollinaris to St. Peter, and that the whole
people took part 'cum hymnis et canticis'. The *Liber Pontificalis*,
speaking of Leo II (682–3), says that he knew Greek and Latin very
well, and that he was 'cantelena ac psalmodia praecipuus'.[4] Benedict II is known to have devoted himself to the chant from early youth.
It is quite certain that Sergius I (687–701), of Syrian ancestry, was
educated in the *Schola cantorum* in Rome; as he was studious and
efficient 'in officio cantelenae' (in the duty of singing), 'priori can-

---

[1] See further, Wellesz, *Eastern Elements in Western Chant* (Oxford, 1947).
[2] *Estetica Gregoriana* (Rome, 1934), i, p. 317 (French translation (Paris, 1938), i,
p. 291, n. 1.)
[3] Op. cit., p. 184.
[4] L. Duchesne, *Le Liber Pontificalis* (Paris, 1886), i, p. 359.

torum pro doctrina est traditus"[1] (he was entrusted to the director of the singers for teaching): and he ordered that clerks and people should sing the *Agnus Dei* in the Mass. Catalanus Maurianus and Virbonus, abbots of St. Peter, revised new editions of the chant for the newly established feasts. Hadrian I (772–95), who was skilled in music, sent Theodore and Benedict at the request of Charlemagne to France for the purpose of teaching the Gregorian chant: their first work was done at Rouen, Metz, and Soissons.

DIFFUSION AND DECAY

The speed with which the Roman chant spread over Europe in post-Gregorian times is amazing. Its progress was spurred on by the desire for musical and liturgical unification expressed by the Roman pontiffs of the period. The *Schola cantorum* in Rome also took great pains to send skilled cantors to the different countries of Europe, so that they could teach the liturgical melodies. In this matter one of the most favoured nations was England, and St. Gregory, when sending St. Augustine and his thirty-nine companions to this country in 596, made use of the missionaries to bring in the Roman liturgy and chant. The musical tradition of the Church in England can be followed up for some decades after the death of the Pontiff who had reformed it: and in 630 Canterbury already had a flourishing Gregorian school.

The arrival of John, the Precentor of St. Peter's, in England was an epoch-making event for the artistic tradition of this country. With the permission of Pope Agatho he assisted at a national council, and stayed for two years, teaching the chant in different parts of the country; after which he retired to the monastery of Wearmouth, to which clerics and monks went 'ad audiendum eum, qui cantandi erant periti'[2] (to hear him, they themselves being versed in the chant). Bede speaks of two English singers who had been instructed by disciples of St. Gregory: the date of one of them, the deacon James, is given as 625. By the Council of Cloveshoe (747) all the churches under its jurisdiction were obliged to sing plainchant in accordance with the antiphoner received from Rome. Egbert, archbishop of York (732–66), mentions the Antiphoner and Missal of St. Gregory, brought to England by St. Augustine and his missionaries. The Cathedral monastery of Worcester is famous for its classical tradition of Roman chant, dating from the time when the monastery of Corbie, near Amiens, sent over two cantors to teach liturgical chant after the

[1] Ibid., p. 371.
[2] Migne, *Patrologia Latina*, xcv. 199.

pattern of the Antiphoner sent them by Pope Eugenius II fifty years previously. These are some indications of the particularly fine state of religious music in England and Ireland from the seventh to the ninth century, when the school of St. Gall in Switzerland took over as heir of this glorious musical tradition.

In Germany plainsong was introduced by its great apostle St. Boniface, who came from Wessex. In France it was planted by the activity of Pepin (d. 768), to whom Pope Stephen had sent clerics to teach the French cantors the Roman chant. It is also on record that Simeon, Succentor of the Roman *Schola cantorum*, was one of the first masters of Gregorian chant at Rouen and elsewhere. Paul I (757–67) sent an Antiphoner and a Responsorial as presents to Pepin. Charlemagne continued his father's work of unification by spreading the Roman liturgy and chant in Gaul and Germany, partly perhaps from political reasons. His relations with Pope Hadrian in this matter are told by Amalar, John the Deacon, and the Monk of Angoulême. The centre of Gregorian music was Metz in Lorraine, which from the time of Bishop Chrodegang (about 753) until the twelfth century displayed great activity in the spread of the authentic Roman chant. In 825 Pope Eugenius II gave the monastery of Corbie some copies of the Antiphoner as reformed by Hadrian I (772–92), and in that monastery the Roman tradition was faithfully maintained. Another important centre, where a great number of most precious manuscripts have been preserved, was St. Gall. Documents still in existence prove that this centre was not a branch establishment of Rome, but a dependency of England, and still more of Ireland. The Irish influence upon St. Gall is attested as far back as the ninth century by Marcellus and Iso, and has been confirmed by modern studies.

From the ninth century onwards the Gregorian repertory was enriched by many new forms of a character more popular than that of the earlier ones, the hymns only excepted. Such are the sequences (possibly a French invention), the tropes and the liturgical drama. All these forms were cultivated at St. Gall, and more will be said of them in subsequent chapters (see chap. V and VI). Other famous schools in Germany were those of Reichenau, where the theorists Walafrid Strabo (d. 840), Berno (d. 1048), and Hermannus Contractus (d. 1054) lived and worked; Mainz; Fulda, which was under the direction of the abbot Rabanus Maurus (d. 822), a disciple of Alcuin; and Treves. In Normandy and France mention should be made of the schools of Rouen, Corbie, Chartres, Tours, Rheims, St. Peter of Moissac, and St. Martial of Limoges, the last being most famous for its metrical influence upon the poetry of the Provençal troubadours, and for its place in the history of early polyphony. In the several kingdoms of Spain the chant used until the invasion of the Moors was Visigothic (Mozarabic). In Aragon, Castile, and Leon this survived until the second half of the eleventh century, when the *Lex Romana* for chant and liturgy was introduced at the request of popes who were anxious to accomplish the liturgical unification of the European churches. In Catalonia, however, the Roman chant and liturgy had already been implanted in Carolingian times, and spread in the land *pari passu* with its recovery for Christendom.

The Gregorian repertory, as it has come down to us, is almost entirely anonymous work: we are seldom able to name an author. And it is in this very feature that the principal charm of the chant is contained. Among composers who are known may be cited Theodulph, bishop of Orleans (d. 821), author of the 'Gloria, laus et honor' for Palm Sunday: Notker Balbulus (d. 912), composer of various sequences: and Tuotilo (d. 914), author of many tropes. The use of the Gregorian chant as source-material for practical or theoretical work begins with Alcuin, Abbot of Tours (d. 804), who adapted the introit 'Invocabit' of the first Sunday in Lent to the 'Benedicta sit' of Trinity Sunday; Aurelian of Réomé (*c.* 850), Remigius of Auxerre (ninth century), Notker Labeo, Regino of Prüm (d. 915), Hucbald, a Flemish monk of St. Amand (d. 930), Odo of Cluny (d. 942), and others: and last of this group, Guido of Arezzo (d. about 1050), whose *Micrologus* was the foundation of medieval music-teaching.

It is interesting to notice how, at the very moment when musical notation had reached a state adequate to express the intervals of the melody in definite form, a long and dreary period opened, during which the liturgical chant decayed. The causes are manifold. On this point it is necessary to correct certain misconceptions often found in text-books on the history of Gregorian chant. The golden age of composition of the liturgical chant proper was from the fifth and sixth to the eighth century: but the classical period of the manuscripts preserved with neums was from the ninth to the eleventh or twelfth centuries. The melodies of the 'Ordinarium Missae' (with rare exceptions), and of the new forms of Gregorian chant with more or less strictly metrical texts, were also composed during the ninth to the twelfth (or thirteenth) centuries. Various causes contributed to the decline of the Gregorian chant; lack of understanding and interest, lack of education of the singers, lack of copyists familiar with the art of the neums, and so on. The very practice of tropes and sequences at the end of the ninth century led to melodic finesse and rhythmic complication. It would be absurd to attribute the decline in the first place to the practice of polyphony, for this had no notation capable of expressing measured rhythm until the end of the twelfth century: moreover, the decline was much worse in monasteries and cathedrals where medieval polyphony was hardly ever practised, whereas among the centres famous for their polyphony from the beginning of the twelfth century there were several equally notable for the preservation of pure Gregorian melody. With the invention of printing the late fifteenth century forms of mensural notation were most illogically adopted, especially for melodies with metrical texts; and these must have seriously hindered and bewildered good chanters. Melodic decay began at the very time that the staff made it possible to write intervals with complete exactitude and certainty. The appearance of the Medicean edition in 1614–15 marked the lowest point of decadence, which was to continue for three centuries or more, and the extinction of melodic purity within the range of traditional liturgical chant.

MODERN RESTORATION

Musicology as a formal and comparative science is of recent growth. The liturgical revival in the middle of the nineteenth century in France was initiated by Dom Guéranger and resulted in a restoration of Gregorian chant and the methodical study of its notation and its ancient manuscripts. Those who have dedicated their lives to the study and the modern interpretation of polyphony and non-Gregorian medieval monody will fully appreciate the difficulties and the numerous problems presented by ancient music when its oral tradition and authentic execution have been lost. The main difficulty lies in the fact that up to recent times this music was, to our tastes, simply dead. It had to be revived by applying modern science to ancient features.

Gregorian chant, in spite of its unbroken tradition in Latin liturgy for more than sixteen centuries, underwent a profound crisis at least 700 years ago. That is why its art had come to be regarded as dead music. Two things were necessary to wake it to new life: systematic and scientific study of the most reliable neumatic manuscripts, and the daily execution of the chant. Such practice could not be carried out by isolated scholars, guided only by the study of the more or less mysterious neums and therefore in danger of subjective interpretation without any true basis in aesthetic or liturgical feeling. On the contrary, this chant had to be put into practice by a religious community, the motto of whose spiritual life was the liturgy, whose chant was the chief work of each day, the *opus Dei*, as St. Benedict calls it. In short, the music had to be lived as well as studied.

The liturgical and Gregorian reform of the last century pursued from the beginning an ideal, and a purpose practical rather than theoretical; but even so the pioneers of the movement always tried to rest their chant upon foundations as sound as possible in respect of history, archaeology, science, and art. Above all it was necessary to seek out the authentic melody of the Roman chant in all its primitive purity, and in this point there is no denying the fact that the work of Dom Guéranger's community at Solesmes provides the securest authority for the accuracy of the restored Gregorian melodies. In spite of all this, to have succeeded in establishing the original version, free from later deteriorations, would be little or no help towards the practical performance of plainsong in church unless the method of an actual interpretation, worthy of the artists who created this music, were provided. Herein lies the second problem of the modern restoration of Gregorian chant. Even if artists of really refined taste set to work, an interpretation based only on subjective modern ideas would be of little use. There must be certain laws of interpretation, validly deduced from the magnificent art of those ancient composers. Medieval theorists were found lacking in clarity, consistency, and aesthetic principles, so that it was necessary to go back to the notation of the earliest manuscripts and to study the types of every school and country.

Now in Gregorian manuscripts of certain regions there are found signs and letters to facilitate the interpretation of the melodies. The school of Solesmes and its followers today interpret these signs and letters after a method which gives fine artistic results, while others render them in different styles. Among the latter there are many who, in the name of art and historical science, prefer to sacrifice aesthetics, and do not hesitate to interpret the melodies in a cold and arbitrary fashion, lacking that taste and religious feeling which are inseparable from the true spirit of the liturgy. This is the mensural interpretation, applied by some musicologists to the ancient melodies, and even to those intended to be solo parts, which are the most florid items in the Gregorian corpus (Antoine Dechevrens, Hugo Riemann, Oskar Fleischer, Georges Houdard, Dom Jules Jeannin of the older generation, and Ewald Jammers of the younger).[1] Another school prefers to follow the older tradition of Solesmes, associated with the name of the great pioneer Dom Pothier rather than with his brilliant successor

[1] See the bibliography on p. 409.

Dom Mocquereau; their system can be labelled 'oratorical' or
'accentualist'. Others again believe that these signs and letters date
from a period which belongs to a transitional second chapter rather
than the earliest and most primitive condition of the Gregorian chant,
and find in the present Vatican editions of the service books all they
need for an adequate interpretation.

Rhythmical notation (this title, invented by Dom Mocquereau, is
singularly unfortunate, since all neumatic notations are at the same
time rhythmical) has always been and still is a battlefield among
Gregorian scholars. Up to the present time there have been found six
notations which show particular rhythmical signs: from St. Gall,
Metz, Chartres, Nonantola, Aquitaine, and Benevento. The followers
of Solesmes are of opinion that some of the letters written above the
neums of St. Gall are rhythmic, others melodic: their opponents, of
course, contest this division. When we remember that musicologists
are not yet unanimous about the rhythmic interpretation of troubadour songs (see p. 225) and ancient instrumental music we must not
wonder at a diversity of opinion among Gregorianists who adhere to
the theory of free rhythm in Roman chant, the only theory really
suited to an artistic execution of the greater part of liturgical music.
There are other minor differences in interpretation which have no
great significance, for this music is suitable for skilled soloists as
well as for unrehearsed congregations, and treatment must vary
accordingly.

The modern restoration of Gregorian chant received its first
official sanction at the hands of Leo XIII, when he publicly acknow-
ledged the work of the French Benedictines in the Brief *Nos quidem*
of 17 May 1901; and it was confirmed by Pius X in his *Motu proprio*
of 1903.[1] As a result of these pronouncements the Roman liturgy is
now fortunate in possessing a set of chant-books better than it has
ever had before. Up to date there have been published the *Graduale
Romanum* (1907), the *Antiphonarium Diurnum* (1912, 1919), the
Officium Majoris Hebdomadae (1922), and the *Antiphonale Monasticum*
(1934). The *Matutinarium* or *Responsoriale* is almost finished, but the
Hymnarium and *Processionarium* still await preparation. It may be
said that the *Graduale* and the *Antiphonarium* of 1912 were the exclusive and personal work of Dom Pothier. Since that time the investigation and interpretation of neums has made considerable progress, so
that in due time we may see the appearance of a new critical edition

[1] Translated in N. Slonimsky, *Music since 1900* (London, 1938), pp. 523–9, and in
R. R. Terry, *The Music of the Roman Rite* (London, 1931), pp. 253–63.

of the *Graduale* already prepared by the monks of Solesmes as a private study.

SOURCES AND NOTATION

Neumatic manuscripts of the Gregorian chant have been preserved in rich abundance; and from a comparison of their numbers with those of the lyrical monody of the troubadours, and with those of ancient polyphony, it is evident that the richest collection of medieval music is that of the Roman liturgical chant. It is a surprising fact that the spread of the neums over the different nations of Europe had no influence whatever on the essential nature of religious music. Variation is seen only in the exterior details, where 'orthography' and musical spelling are modified. The neums, though they can be classified as the work of one school or another, never provide us with a 'particular national version'; they transmit the primitive chant with a melodic and even sometimes a rhythmic uniformity which is really astounding.

Most of the modern musicologists who have devoted themselves to the study of neumatic Gregorian manuscripts have been Benedictine monks; to mention a few names—Joseph Pothier, André Mocquereau, Jules Jeannin, Paolo Ferretti, Gregory Suñol, Lucien David, Dominic Johner, Ephrem Omlin, René-Jean Hesbert, Eugène Cardine. In addition to these Benedictines we must remember the distinguished names of H. M. Bannister, Peter Wagner, W. H. Frere, G. H. Palmer, Amedée Gastoué, Ewald Jammers, and others. The genuine tradition of Gregorian music, in spite of its uninterrupted use in the Catholic Church, had been lost for centuries. For its effective revival it was necessary to found a school which, in addition to research in the ancient neums, should devote itself to the daily performance of these venerable melodies and the study of artistic nuance in accordance with what could be discovered about the tradition from ancient writings. This school, which was able thus to combine theory and practice, was that of Solesmes, directed at present by Dom Joseph Gajard and his collaborators. It was planned by Dom Guéranger in 1833, actually begun by Dom Jausions in 1856, and continued by Dom Pothier and Dom Mocquereau, helped by the liturgical scholars Dom Cagin, Dom Cabrol, Dom Leclercq, Dom Morin, and others. The result of this work was the formation of an unrivalled collection of materials, and the publication of the *Paléographie musicale* from 1889 onwards. The Gregorian archives of Solesmes today are the richest of their kind in the whole world, containing some 850 manuscripts in photographic reproduction: some 200 from Italy, 130 from France, 25 from the Low Countries, 26 from Switzerland, 109 from England, 60 from Spain, and about 300 from Germany, Austria, and Czechoslovakia.[1]

The last word on the origin of the Latin neums has not yet been said, but some points are quite clear. It is now agreed on all hands that the Greek accents gave birth to the Latin neums in their primitive, embryonic state. The acute and grave accent are therefore regarded as the origin of the Latin neums. It is worth mention that almost up to the present day most scholars assumed that the oldest musical manuscript of the Gregorian corpus did not antedate the end of the eighth century, and that the primitive antiphoners contained nothing but the liturgical text: and it was held that there was no musical notation in Europe before that time, and that singers were therefore obliged to learn the Gregorian repertory by heart.

Such statements, resting on the illusive argument *a silentio*, arose from the fact that earlier musical manuscripts were unknown until recently. They were supported by a misinterpretation of the words of St. Isidore of Seville: 'Nisi enim ab homine memoria teneantur, soni pereunt, quia scribi non possunt'[2] (sounds are lost unless they are preserved in man's memory, as they cannot be written down). All the writer meant to say, however, was that though the musical notation of his time showed how many notes there were, it could not indicate their place on the staff or their intervals, still less their aesthetic interpretation: these details had to be retained in the memory. It is an historical fact that the Gregorian corpus was formed in the fifth and sixth centuries, and that it consists largely of pieces from a pre-Gregorian repertory. We may argue *a priori* that it would have been very difficult for St. Gregory to create this corpus, and perhaps still more difficult for him to undertake his reform, if there had not been a musical notation already in use in the Church. Further, it is hard to imagine that while the Eastern Church used musical notation (see Ex. 1, p. 4) it was lacking at Rome. The *Ordo Romanus I*, which describes the papal Mass in the time of St. Gregory, seems to hint at the existence of song-books in Rome when it explains the singing of the Epistle of the Mass; for it says that the subdeacon 'ascendit in ambonem et legit. Postquam legerit, cantor cum cantatorio ascendit et dicit Responsum' (goes up into the pulpit and reads: after he has

---

[1] The Institut für Musikforschung at Ratisbon has built up in recent years what promises to be a very remarkable collection of microfilms of Gregorian manuscripts.
[2] *Etymologiarum sive Originum libri XX*, ed. W. M. Lindsay (Oxford, 1911), III. xv. 2.

read, a singer goes up with a song-book and performs the Respon-sory). The same *Ordo* clearly distinguishes the *codex* with which the deacon sings the Gospel from the *cantatorium* also needed for the ser-vice, though in fact the oldest *cantatoria* we possess are without neums.

No definitive study of the age of the neums in the Roman Church has yet appeared. The following dates may throw some light upon this highly debateable question. In the first place, in one of the pro-logues to the Mozarabic *Antiphonarium* of Leon, written in the begin-ning of the tenth century, it is stated that the transcriber copied his antiphoner from another manuscript of King Wamba, who ascended the throne in 672. The same copyist describes the artistic decadence of Mozarabic chant when he says that the singers of his time were no longer able to read those neums, 'finitam habentes hanc artem prae-fulgidam' (having reached the end of this brilliant art). If Spanish singers at the beginning of the tenth century no longer knew how to read Mozarabic neums, it means that these were much older. Further-more, it is historically certain that the Mozarabians did not invent anything, but confined themselves to the copying and preservation of Visigothic neums. Nor would it have been possible to keep up by mere tradition the *melodiae longissimae* of Visigothic chant from the sixth and seventh to the ninth, tenth, and eleventh centuries, the time when these manuscripts were copied. There has in the past been some hesitation among musicologists in accepting this argument, on the ground that no musical manuscripts earlier than the end of the eighth century existed. The *Orationale* of Verona, however, which was copied at and for Tarragona at the beginning of the eighth century, contains neums in the margins of some of the pages, and these were written at the same time as the manuscript. Moreover, Dom Suñol discovered some Ambrosian neums in a palimpsest of the seventh century, and Dom Alban Dold of Beuron claims to have found Latin neums in a sixth-century palimpsest of St. Gall.[1] The Antiphonarium of Leon contains all the antiphons and other choir items of the *Orationale*, with neums. Dom Louis Brou,[2] comparing the Leon book with the Roman antiphoner of the eighth century, has shown that in the vocal pieces the text is identical, or nearly so, in both antiphoners. This shows that there was a common stock of chants to which the liturgists of Milan, Benevento, France, and Spain all had access. Possibly this common source is the ancient Roman liturgy.

[1] Cf. Dom G. Suñol, *Introduction à la Paléographie musicale grégorienne* (Paris, 1935).
[2] See his 'L'Antiphonaire wisigothique et l'antiphonaire grégorien au début du VIIIᵉ siècle' in *Report of the International Congress for Sacred Music* (Rome, 1950).

The first mention of musical signs in the Latin liturgy appears in the treatise *Liber de promissionibus*, the work of Quodvultdeus, who was born probably about 400 in Carthage and was a disciple of St. Augustine. He was made bishop of Carthage in or about 437, and when the Vandals took the city in 439 he had to emigrate to Campania, dying at Naples about 453. He says: 'Restat, ut arbitror, musicorum voluptas: habes organum ex diversis fistulis sanctorum apostolorum doctorumque omnium ecclesiarum, aptatum quibusdam accentibus: gravi, acuto et circumflexo, quod musicus ille Dei spiritus per Verbum tangit, implet et resonat'[1] (there remains, I think, the pleasure afforded by musicians: you have the organ with its different pipes of the holy apostles and doctors of all the churches, adapted for certain accents—grave, acute, and circumflex, which that musician the Spirit of God plays on, fills and causes to sound through the Word). We cannot affirm with certainty that this is an early reference to neums, though it looks very much like it: but at least it does not refer to alphabetical notation (see p. 4). The testimony of Quodvultdeus and of the *De musica* of St. Augustine, which was begun in Italy in 387 and finished in Carthage in 388, as well as other passages about the chant in Carthage, point to the existence of musical notation in the African Church from the beginning of the fifth century onwards. There are also traces of musical notation in the south of France about the middle of the same century. The Gregorian reform itself would hardly have been possible unless there had been some kind of musical notation known in Rome. As we have seen (p. 99) the second Council of Cloveshoe (747) and Egbert, archbishop of York (732–66), even mention an antiphoner which was sent to England by St. Gregory. This suggests a noted copy; for though the authentic text itself would have been of value in a purely mnemonic age, sufficient testimony has been brought forward already in this paragraph to make it more likely that this antiphoner had neums. In fact, the study of the existing neums seems to indicate that the 'cheironomic' (or oratorical) notation, written *in campo aperto* (in an open field, i.e. without landmarks) is of extreme antiquity. This notation only gives the number of the notes and their relative height, never indicating precisely their pitch or the intervals between them. For the interpretation of these neumatic manuscripts it is necessary to compare them with later ones on the staff. Attention also has to be paid to the system used in each case: some manuscripts follow the Gregorian method; some display neums with fixed inter-

---

[1] Migne, *Patrologia Latina*, li. 856.

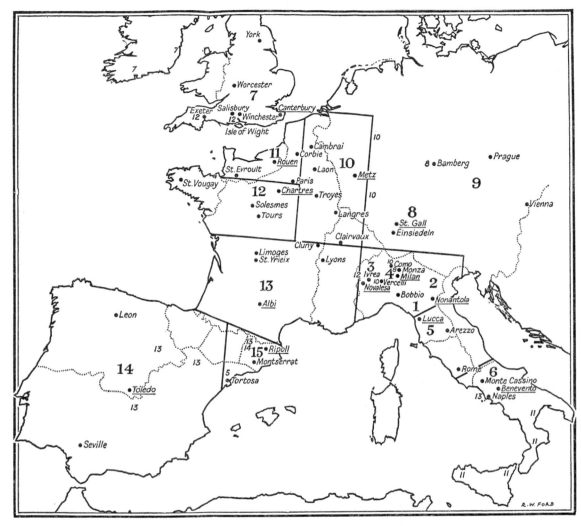

FAMILIES OF NEUMATIC NOTATIONS

1. North-Italian
    (2. Nonantolese; 3. Novalesan; 4. Milanese)
5. (Central) Italian
6. Beneventan
7. Anglo-Saxon
8. St. Gall
9. German

10. Messine
11. French (Norman)
12. Chartres
13. Aquitanian
14. Visigothic or Mozarabic
15. Catalonian

vals; others are interspersed with the so-called 'Romanian' letters, which give general indications of direction (e.g. *a* = *altius*, higher, *i* = *inferius*, lower) as well as suggestions for rhythmical interpretation (e.g. *c* = *celeriter*, quickly); and others contain passages with known melodic formulae.

Peter Wagner held a theory which has not yet been sufficiently elucidated: this was that 'diastematic' notation, which indicates the actual height of the notes, is older than cheironomic. The diastematic system followed an imaginary horizontal line around (or perhaps above) which the neums were arranged. Examples of this are found as far back as the ninth century, and by the tenth century it had become common practice. It would seem that the system originated in southern Italy, very possibly at Benevento, though manuscripts of English origin exist even older than the Beneventan. By the end of the tenth century the imaginary line became a real one. The line, drawn without ink ('dry-point') at the beginning of the eleventh century, was later on traced in red: it then meant *f*. The upper *c'* was indicated by a yellow line. In French, English, and Italian manuscripts *c'* is sometimes found in green, and in French manuscripts *f* also. Not very long afterwards letters, which we know as clefs (lit. 'keys'), appeared at the beginning of the lines, making the colour of the lines superfluous; but coloured lines continued in Italy until the end of the twelfth century and are found even later in England and Germany.

In order to give the reader a general view of the diffusion of the neums in the different scriptoria of Italy, England, the Low Countries, Switzerland, Germany, France, and Spain, we give here a map drawn up by Dom Suñol and reproduced in his *Introduction à la Paléographie musicale grégorienne* (Paris, 1935).

MELODIC TYPES AND TONALITY

We have now reached the most interesting and attractive part of our subject, which helps us to understand the musical and artistic value of the Gregorian chant. The artists of the Middle Ages, with their innate feeling for form, worried little about its rationalistic background, the logic of its aesthetics or the philosophy of its beauty. Nor did the medieval theorists pay any attention to these problems, being concerned only with the practice of the art which they knew as part of their daily life and occupation. Johannes de Grocheo (*c.* 1300) was the first, so far as we know, to use in his exposition of the secular monodies of the time sentences and phrases which might be regarded as the forerunners of those used in modern musical aesthetics (see pp. 223, 228). Medieval theorists who write about plainsong never trouble to essay artistic analysis of the different parts of the chant: still less are they interested in giving a scientific description of its forms. Theorists and cantors copied the *tonalia* (the opening cues of liturgical melodies), which were used in every country and school and are most informative for the study of both modality and melody. They merely classified the melodies, and in so doing followed a purely practical, not a scientific, method, dividing the antiphons and a few other chants into groups according to their respective modality and the liturgical order of the texts. Expressions in the old treatises about the character or flavour of any one mode, or phrases of approbation, have as a rule a value which is purely educational, devotional or mystical.

So far no legacy from the ancient composers has been found to tell us anything about their rules or practices in setting melodies to texts. Yet we can perceive that Western composers seem to have followed the same principles and rules as their Byzantine fellow-artists. Ferretti, in his *Estetica Gregoriana*,[1] studied exhaustively the characteristics of every melodic form of liturgical chant, and divided the melodies into three classes: original melodies, type melodies, and melodies formed on the method which he calls *centonique*, that is to say a mosaic of formulas. The first type is used for one text only, emphasizing some typical character of the feast or of the place which it occupies in the liturgy: for example, the antiphons of the Introits, in which this type occurs repeatedly. The second class may be called 'prototypes', for their melody was typical and distinctive, and so dear to the old composers that it served as a kind of model applicable to different texts, even if they had an entirely different sense. This type predominates in the antiphons of the Office. In the third group *cento* or patchwork melodies are composed out of various fragments (melodic formulas) of pre-existing tunes, logically fitted together into a pattern, after the fashion of a mosaic pavement or a patchwork quilt.

The Gregorian texts were not written in classical but in ecclesiastical Latin, with the established *cursus* as used from the end of the fifth century to the middle of the seventh, making the declamation regular and melodious. The Gregorian composers paid full attention to the stress of the word: they did not give it a strong dynamic prominence, but a melodic one. In Gregorian chant three styles can be recognized:

[1] Rome, 1934, pp. 95 ff.: French edition, *Esthétique grégorienne* (Paris, 1938), pp. 86 ff.

(*a*) Syllabic—one syllable for each note, occasionally two, three, or even four—occurring in many antiphons and in parts of the Ordinary of the Mass, especially in the *Credo*: (*b*) Neumatic or semi-syllabic— two, three, or four notes for one syllable—found in other parts of the Ordinary and in the Introit and *Communio* of the Proper of the Mass: (*c*) Melismatic, comprising the very rich and florid melodies typical of the solo chants, as seen in the Gradual, Tract, Alleluia, and Offertory of the Mass and the Responsories of the Office.

The tonality of the Gregorian melodies is grounded on the system of the *oktoechos* (the eight ecclesiastical modes). The question of the modality of troubadour melodies (see p. 229) is one of the most difficult and complicated problems of medieval non-Gregorian monody: but the problem is still more difficult in the sphere of the Roman chant. It is enough to say that the idea of classification according to the *oktoechos* is no older than the eighth or ninth century, though the Byzantine *oktoechos* goes back to Severus, who was the Monophysite Patriarch of Antioch from 512 to 519; so that there is no possibility of a theoretical system preceding the composition of the Gregorian melodies. On the contrary, the system was constructed in order to codify and classify melodies which had been written and collected centuries earlier. Still more thorny is the problem when we remember that many chants may have been modified according to the new theoretical system, losing in the process some of their characteristics. We are therefore not surprised to find that the classification of preexisting melodies according to the modes is not always consistent, a fact which can be verified from the actual *tonalia* as well as from the internal evidence of many of the actual melodies in the liturgical books. As Wellesz has said, 'the problem of modes is one of the most contradictory in the history of early medieval music':[1] the more so when we take into consideration the results of recent investigation of Byzantine music. In the face of all this we can well understand the insuperable difficulties in the way of writing suitable and well-written harmonies for the accompaniment of these ancient melodies. The system of the eight modes, as given in the oldest theoretical writings on the subject (eighth to eleventh centuries) runs as follows:

	Final	Range	Dominant
I. *Protus authenticus*	d	d–d'	a
II. „ *plagalis*	d	A–a	f
III. *Deuterus authenticus*	e	e–e'	c'
IV. „ *plagalis*	e	B–b	a

[1] *Eastern Elements in Western Chant*, p. 30.

	Final	Range	Dominant
V. *Tritus authenticus*	f	f–f′	c′
VI. „ *plagalis*	f	c–c′	a
VII. *Tetrardus authenticus*	g	g–g′	d′
VIII. „ *plagalis*	g	d–d′	c′

MUSICAL FORMS

The study of musical forms is a rather recent branch of the science of Gregorian chant, and has prospects of considerable developments with useful and perhaps surprising results. At the present moment we can name three great scholars who have distinguished themselves by research in this direction: Peter Wagner of Fribourg, Switzerland, Abbot Paolo Ferretti of Rome, and Dominic Johner of Beuron Abbey, Germany. We may summarize briefly the results of Johner's work, as he incorporates that of the other two: our summary is based more or less upon his book *Wort und Ton im Choral* (Leipzig, 1940). One thing stands out as evident: that the composers were not inventors of new musical forms apt for divine worship, but that the liturgy itself fixed the different types. The forms had to fit themselves to the various classes of officials who took part in public worship: the celebrant, the deacons, the soloist, the choir, and finally, the congregation. Before writing a new melody or adapting an old one, a composer had to consider not so much the contents of the text to be set as the place it was to occupy in the liturgy. The theme of his chants was always the glory of God and the edification of the faithful: and this implies that the chants had to be always religious in character, prayerful, suitable for the emotion which the liturgy wished to call forth and develop at that particular point. For these reasons the chant had to be monodic, vocal, and free from anything suggesting instrumental style. This is the explanation of the fact that the text 'Justus ut palma florebit', for instance, appears to a different melody each time when sung as Introit, Gradual, Alleluia, and Offertory: and also of the fact that the same melody can be applied to several texts when they are liturgically identical.

We may notice that in the liturgy some chants are associated with movement, others with rest: that is to say, chants sung while the officiants are moving, processional chants such as Introit and *Communio*, and chants which presuppose quiet and contemplation on the part of the officiants as well as the congregation, such as Gradual, Alleluia, and Sequence. Another division, of great significance, is into prose (Ordinary and Proper of the Mass, antiphons and responds of the Office) and poetry (hymns, sequences, tropes, &c.). Since psalmody is the very core and soul of public worship, psalmodic chant was a dominating factor influencing, directly or indirectly, the musical forms applied to a prose text for public worship. It will be necessary, therefore, to go into some detail about psalmody in its various forms, because it gave birth to the recitative, antiphonal, and responsorial style of the Mass and Office.

The psalm verse is divided into two parts (hemistichs). From the very beginning the music tended to mark this binary division of the literary text, trying to preserve the natural stress of the words without paying much heed to the contents of the text itself. We must consider liturgical psalmody in five different classes: (i) the simple psalmody of the Office; (ii) the antiphonal psalmody of the Mass; (iii) the psalmody of the Invitatory—Psalm 94, 'Venite exsultemus', always sung at the opening of Matins; (iv) the greater responds of Matins; (v) the tracts. The psalmodic origin of all these forms can be ascertained from the *incipit*, the tenor or reciting note (*tuba*), the medial cadence at the end of the first half-verse, and the final cadence at the end of the second half-verse, as in this example of simple psalmody:

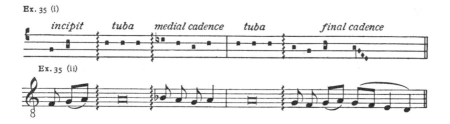

Ex. 35 (i)

Ex. 35 (ii)

Among the different styles found in psalmody we have to distinguish (*a*) the liturgical recitative—several syllables, words, phrases, or even whole sentences sung on the same note. This note was originally B or A, followed by a note one tone lower: in the course of time this rose to C, and the reciting note was then a semitone lower. The liturgical recitatives of the ancient tones of the collect, epistle, and gospel have a special charm: but a sublime point of art is reached in the Preface, the *Pater noster* of the Mass, the *Te Deum*, the *Exsultet*, the Litany of the Saints, the Passion chant of Holy Week, and such pieces. These melodic recitatives were known all over Europe and are particularly characteristic of the old Latin liturgies. While the Eastern Church, in its impressive dialogues between celebrant, deacon, sub-deacon, and choir, always used a recitative florid in melody and cadence, the Western Church, more restrained and conscious of its artistic resources, composed melodies of unequalled beauty.[1] Leo IV, in a letter to Abbot Honorius (c. 850), speaks of a 'traditio canendi legendique' (a tradition of singing and reading) which St. Gregory had given to the Church: most unfortunately no detail of it has come down to us.

Next comes (b) the antiphonal style. From the fourth century, or earlier, psalmody is combined with the antiphon and is sung as an alternating chant between two choirs, sometimes at the octave. In this respect it will be useful to examine (1) the simple antiphons of the Office, the most ancient form of which is represented by the Alleluia antiphons, in which the word Alleluia is repeated from three to nine times. For the text of the other antiphons Rome for a long time confined itself to the Bible, especially to the Psalter, and to the Acts of the Martyrs (sixth century). The antiphons to the *Magnificat* and *Benedictus* are usually taken from the Gospels. In the melodies of these antiphons the form used is that which we have described above as mosaic or patchwork; and they are, as may be expected, very numerous, the ordinary or secular Antiphoner containing 1,230, the monastic 1,183. Some antiphons are purely syllabic, others melismatic: some follow the parallelism of the text by dividing into two parts, others into three or four. Though written in all the eight modes, the eighth and the first predominate. Some are even written in a combination of two modes, such as the first and the third. The antiphons of the *Magnificat* and *Benedictus* are more florid than the rest, being comparable in this respect to the antiphons which are used in the Mass:[2]

Ex. 36 (a) [3]

Veni sponsa Christi, accipe coronam, quam tibi Dominus præparavit in æternum.

Ex. 36 (b)

Ve - ni spon - sa Chri - sti, ac - ci - pe co - ro - nam,

quam ti - bi Do - mi - nus   præ - pa - ra - vit in æ - ter - num.

[1] An example of liturgical recitative is recorded in *The History of Music in Sound* (H.M.V.), ii, side 4.

[2] An example of antiphonal psalmody is recorded in *The History of Music in Sound*, ii, side 4.   [3] *Antiphonale Vaticanum*, p. [56].

(Come, thou bride of Christ, receive the crown which the Lord hath prepared for thee in eternity.)

Ex. 37 (a)[1]

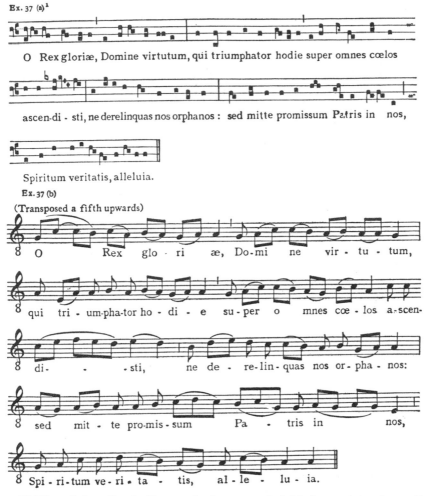

O Rex gloriæ, Domine virtutum, qui triumphator hodie super omnes cœlos

ascen-di - sti, ne derelinquas nos orphanos : sed mitte promissum Patris in nos,

Spiritum veritatis, alleluia.

Ex. 37 (b)

(Transposed a fifth upwards)

O   Rex   glo - ri   æ, Do-mi   ne   vir - tu - tum,

qui   tri - um-pha-tor ho - di - e   su - per   o   mnes cœ - los a-scen-

di- - sti,   ne de - re-lin-quas nos or-pha - nos:

sed   mit - te pro-mis-sum   Pa - tris in   nos,

Spi - ri-tum ve - ri - ta - tis,   al - le - lu - ia.

(O King of glory, Lord of hosts, who hast ascended this day as victor above all the heavens, leave us not as orphans: but send to us him who was promised by the Father, the Spirit of truth, alleluia.)

(2) The antiphons which are used in the Mass are the Introit and the *Communio*. They differ from those of the Office in being as a rule neumatic. They are unlike those of the Office in that they are as florid on an ordinary day as on great festivals. The melodies of these Mass antiphons are not adapted to other texts in the pure Gregorian corpus, as is the case with those of the Office: when an instance of this

---

[1] Ibid., p. 423.

occurs it is definitely post-classical and not always very fortunate, as may be seen in the case of the *Communio* 'Factus est repente' of Whitsunday, adapted in the thirteenth century to the 'Quotiescumque' of Corpus Christi. In the Introit the first and third modes are the most frequent, in the *Communio* (the shortest chant of the Mass) the first and eighth:

[1] *Graduale Vaticanum*, p. 61.

nem no - stram? Ad-hæ - sit in ter - ra ven - ter

no - ster: ex - sur - ge, Do - mi - ne, ad - ju - va nos,

et li - be - ra nos. *Ps.* De-us au - ri-bus

nos - tris au - di - vi - mus: pa - tres no-stri an-nun-ti -

a - - - ve - runt no - bis. Glo - ri - a Pa - tri... *etc.*

E u o u a e.

(Arise, O Lord, why sleepest thou? Arise, and turn us not away at the last: why
turnest thou thy face away and forgettest our misery? Our belly has cleaved to
the ground: arise, O Lord, help us and deliver us. *Psalm.* O God, we have heard
with our ears: our fathers have told us. Glory be to the Father . . .)

Ex. 39 (a)[1]

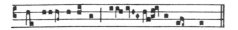

Vox in Rama audita est, plo-ra-tus et ululatus: Rachel plo-rans filios su-os, no-lu-

-it con - so-la-ri, qui - a non sunt.

Ex.39 (b)

Vox in Ra - ma au-di - ta est, plo - ra - tus et u -

-lu - la - tus: Ra - chel plo - rans fi - li - os

----

[1] Ibid., p. 39.

su - os, no - lu - it con - so - la - ri,

qui - - - - - a non sunt.

(A voice was heard in Rama mourning and weeping; Rachel mourning for her children would not be comforted, because they were not.)

Ex. 40 (a)

Communio

Videns Dominus flentes sorores Lazari ad monumentum, lacrimatus est coram

Judæis, et clamabat: Laza-re, veni foras: et prod-i-it ligatis manibus et pedibus,

qui fu-e-rat quatridu-a-nus mor-tu - us.

Ex. 40 (b)

Vi - dens Do - mi - nus flen-tes so - ro - res La - za - ri ad mo - nu -

-men - tum, la-cri-ma-tus est co-ram Ju-dæ-is et cla-ma-bat:

La-za - re, ve-ni fo-ras: et prod - i - it li-ga-tis ma -

-ni-bus et pe - di-bus, qui fu - e - rat qua-tri-du -

-a - nus mor - tu - - - us.

(When the Lord saw the sisters of Lazarus weeping at the tomb he wept before the Jews, and cried out: 'Lazarus, come forth!' And he who had been four days dead came forth, bound hand and foot.)

[1] *Graduale Vaticanum*, p. 127.

(c) The Tract. The word stands for *cantus tractus*, a melody sung without interruption from beginning to end, in other words, a psalm sung by the soloist without any refrain from the choir. The Tract has a special interest for historians of music, being the most ancient solo melody of the Mass. According to the researches of Peter Wagner the melismata of its cadences are not of Western origin. This system of melismatic *interpunctio* is still used by the Eastern Church, and its origins must be sought in the solo psalmody of the Synagogue, the same being true of the melodies of the Gradual and Alleluia. There are only a few Tract melodies and they are interchangeable; all are of the second and eighth modes, of which the latter is the more joyful and is used for shorter psalms.[1] There are other Tracts, called *responsoria gradualia* in the ancient books, such as 'Haec dies' in Easter week, consisting of sundry verses from Psalm 117. These Gradual responds are perhaps the most ancient.

(d) The responsorial class. Here the form is *ABA*, for the respond implies an answer or refrain: in the liturgy it always follows a lection, with which it provides an agreeable contrast. The responsorial chants of the Mass—Gradual, Alleluia, and Offertory—also follow lections (*Credo* is a later insertion between Gospel and Offertory). In the rites of Easter Eve and Ember Saturdays we see the Alleluia also immediately preceded by a lection; and this is always the case with the responsorial chants of the Office. The responds, which date from the fifth century or earlier, have florid melodies with occasional short syllabic passages. Some of them are built up on the *centonique* or mosaic method, others are composed on the 'prototype' systems.

1. We may take first the Gradual. The respond of the Mass was called the Gradual because it was sung at the *gradus* or step of the pulpit from which the Gospel was sung afterwards. St. Leo and St. Augustine both tell us that in old times a whole psalm was sung, into which the people inserted a refrain. But from the fifth century onwards the melody of the psalm as well as its refrain became melismatic, and after the repetition of the first part by the chorus one verse only was sung, to which the choir repeated the first part. From the ninth century onwards (according to some, from the twelfth) the repetition of the first part was discontinued, and the responsorial form of the Gradual was lost, though the Vatican edition of 1907 allows it, and it is desirable when the sense of the words demands it, as on the feast of St. John Baptist. The melody of the Gradual verse, though

---

[1] The Tract 'Domine, non secundum' is recorded in *The History of Music in Sound*, ii, side 6.

florid, retains the essential form of simple psalmody with its *incipit*, medial recitation and cadence, and final recitation and cadence, being thus reminiscent of synagogue psalmody. The most usual mode is the fifth:

Ex. 41(a)[1]

Christus factus est pro no- bis obe- di-ens us- que ad mor-tem, mor-

tem au-tem   cru-cis.   ℣. Propter quod et Deus   ex-alta-vit

illum,   et de-dit illi   no- men,

quod est super o-mne no- men.

Ex. 41 (b)

Chri - stus fac - tus est pro no - - - - - bis

o - be - - - - di - ens us - - -

que ad   mor - tem, mor - tem au - tem

cru - cis.

℣. Propter quod et   De - us ex - al - ta - vit il - lum,

[1] *Graduale Vaticanum*, p. 169.

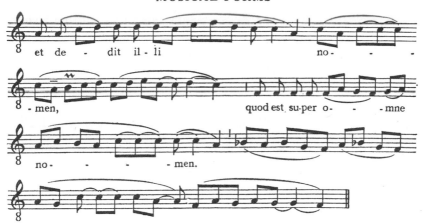

et de - dit il - li no - - -

- men, quod est su-per o - - -mne

no - - - men.

(Christ became obedient for us, even unto death, and that the death of the cross. Wherefore also God hath exalted him, and given unto him a name which is above every name.)

Seventy out of the 160 contained in the *Graduale Vaticanum* are in this mode, while the eighth is used only three times. The chorus part is subdued in comparison with the solo verse, which is vivacious and extended in range: both parts usually end on the same final.[1] Graduals of the second mode have a special construction.

2. The Respond of the Office. Here we have to distinguish between the 'Short Respond' and the 'prolix' or 'Greater Respond'. The text of the former is usually short, and its syllabic melody lies between the recitative and the antiphonal style. In the secular Antiphoner it is used only in the Lesser Hours, in the monastic at Vespers and Lauds alone. The melody of the Greater Respond takes the form ABA^1 distributed as follows: chorus A, verse B, chorus A' (which is usually shorter than A). In actual practice responds have only one verse, though 'Aspiciens a longe' and 'Libera me' have kept several verses. They are written mostly in the eighth, first, and seventh modes, and are not quite so florid as the Graduals:

Ex. 42 (a)[2]

Tenebræ factæ sunt dum crucifixissent Jesum Ju - dæ - i : et cir-ca

ho-ram no - nam excla-ma-vit Je - sus vo - ce ma- gna: De - us

[1] The Gradual 'Protector noster' is recorded in *The History of Music in Sound*, ii, side 5.   [2] *Officium majoris Hebdomadae*, p. 378.

me - us, ut quid me de-re-li-qui - sti?* Et inclinato ca - pi-te, e-mi-sit

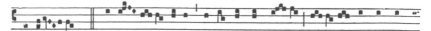

spi-ri - tum. ℣. Ex-cla-mans Jesus vo-ce magna, a - it : Pa - ter, in manus

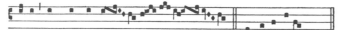

tuas commendo spi - ri-tum me - um. * Et inclinato....*etc.*
(*as far as* spiritum.)

Ex. 42 (b)

Te - ne - bræ fa - ctæ sunt   dum cru-ci-fi -

-xis - sent Je - sum Ju - - - -dæ - - - i:

et   cir - ca   ho - ram   no - - -nam

ex - cla - ma - vit   Je - - -sus

vo - - -ce   ma - - -gna:

De - us me - us,   ut   quid me de-re - -

-li - qui - sti?   et in-cli-na-to   ca - pi-te,

Fine

e-mi - sit   spi-ri - - -tum.

Ex-cla - mans   Je - sus vo - ce   ma - gna

a - it: Pa - ter, in ma-nus tu - as

D.S.

commendo spi - ri - tum me - um.

(Darkness fell when the Jews had crucified Jesus: and about the ninth hour Jesus cried out with a loud voice: 'My God, why hast thou forsaken me?' And having bowed his head, he gave up the ghost. Jesus crying with a loud voice, said: 'Father, into thy hands I commend my spirit.')

3. The Alleluia and its verse. The Alleluia came into the Christian Church from the Temple and the Synagogue, and was in general use from the earliest times both in East and West. It was originally sung throughout the year, but Pope Damasus restricted it at Rome to the fifty days from Easter to Pentecost, and St. Gregory suppressed it for the season from Septuagesima till Easter. The melody of the Alleluia had already been much embellished by the sixth century; in Rome it had a distinctly oriental character. It has been said that in the beginning the chanting of the Alleluia in the Mass consisted in singing the word 'Alleluia' with its wordless *jubilus*, and that later on, in the time of St. Gregory (others say in the ninth century), there was added the text of a verse, the better to impress on the mind the *melodiae longissimae*. But that does not correspond to the historical fact that in Rome even in ancient times, at least until the end of the fourth century, the Alleluia was sung in the psalmody of the Mass as a responsorial chant. The soloist sang a verse, and the people or the choir responded with the refrain 'Alleluia'. Now it is true that in the old manuscripts the Alleluia with the *jubilus* is copied without text (*sequelae*) and that in other manuscripts the verse of the psalm is not always uniform; but that does not mean that in ancient times they did not always add in the Mass a verse of the psalms sung by the soloist.[1] In old times the choice of the melody was left to the singer. For the most part the melodies are original, and the *centonique* method is not employed, though the 'prototype' is sometimes found.

Melodically it was the most artistic part of the Mass, but it is less florid than the chant of the Eastern, Ambrosian, or Mozarabic liturgies. Though it continued to be a solo chant, it acquired a responsorial form. Unlike the Gradual, it is frequently in the first or eighth modes; the fifth and sixth are very seldom used. In most of the Alleluias the

[1] Cf. J. A. Jungmann, *Missarum Solemnia*, i (3rd ed., Vienna, 1952), pp. 548 ff.

jubilus, or florid coda of the melody, is repeated at the end of the verse. The classical form is *ABA.* In others the *jubilus* does not correspond to the coda of the verse. According to Peter Wagner this 'archaic structure' is very old, and comes from an age when a balanced sense of symmetry was lacking. The Alleluias of the three Masses of Christmas are characteristic specimens: like the Tracts, they are in the second and eighth modes. Sometimes the melody of the verse has no connexion with that of the Alleluia: in other cases the Alleluia and its *jubilus* form the melodic base of the verse (as on All Saints' Day). In others, the verse has a psalmodic structure, as is the case with some typical Alleluias of the second mode—'Hic est discipulus', 'Vidimus stellam', and others; in others again, the same melody appears in 'prototype' style with different texts, e.g. 'Dum complerentur', 'Dilexit Andream', 'Justus ut palma'.

Ex. 43 (a)[1]

¹ *Graduale Vaticanum,* p. 203. Another Alleluia is recorded in *The History of Music in Sound,* ii, side 5.

- - - - - - - tus   est

Chri- - -stus.

(Alleluia. Christ our Passover is sacrificed for us.)

4. The Offertory and its verses. From the fourth century onwards the Offertory was an antiphonal chant in the sense of a simple antiphon inserted between the verses of a psalm, sung while the faithful carried their offerings to the altar. Some old manuscripts call it 'antiphona ad offerendum' or 'antiphona ad offertorium'. This antiphon is like those of the Introit and *Communio* in both character and structure. In Gregorian manuscripts the Offertory has already taken the form of a solo respond with a chorus and one, two, or three verses for a soloist, between which the choir sang either the whole or only the last phrase of the refrain. In this form it comes nearer to the style of solo chant (Tract, Gradual, Alleluia) than do the Introit and *Communio*. Later on the florid character of the verse made its influence felt upon the chorus part. For many centuries the Offertory in the Roman rite has been sung without a verse, keeping the antiphon only (the single exception is in the Requiem Mass). As a rule it is in florid style, though there may be syllabic passages. The eighth, fourth, first, and second modes are the most frequent. The text of the Offertory and its place in the liturgy sometimes induced composers to write descriptive melodies such as 'Stetit angelus' and 'Jubilate Deo omnis terra'. Some offertories have the unusual feature of a repetition of text, unique in the Gregorian repertory: the reason for this is not at all clear. Possibly it may be a relic from the days when the antiphon actually was a refrain, kept through some confusion of mind on the part of early copyists.

Ex. 44 (a)[1]

A-   ve Mari-   a, gra-   ti-a ple-na, Do-

mi-nus te-   cum: be-ne-di- cta tu   in mu- li- e- ri- bus,

[1] *Graduale Vaticanum*, p. 21.

et be-ne-di- ctus   fru - ctus ven-   tris   tu- i.

Ex. 44 (b)

A-   -ve   Ma ri - - -

.   - a,   gra-   -ti - a ple - na,

Do-

-mi - nus te -   -cum: be - ne - di -

-cta   tu   in mu -   li - e - ri - bus,

et be - ne -   di   -   ctus   fru -   -ctus

ven -   - tris   tu - i.

(Hail, Mary, full of grace, the Lord is with thee, blessed art thou among women, and blessed is the fruit of thy womb.)

To complete this analysis of the prose texts of the Gregorian corpus a few remarks must be added about the Ordinary of the Mass. Here we have invariable texts, a circumstance which made it possible for a congregation to take part. From the ninth and tenth centuries the appearance of tropes led to the composition of new melodies. *Kyrie eleison* had been used in pagan rites in honour of the Sun-god, and the Roman Church took it over from the East. *Christe eleison* was introduced by St. Gregory. Musically speaking there are three main forms:

(*a*) The simplest form: Kyrie A A A, Christe B B B, Kyrie A A A (*Graduale Vaticanum*, II, V, XI, XVIII).

(*b*) Kyrie A A A, Christe B B B, Kyrie C C C (*Graduale Vaticanum*, IX, for example, and several others).

(c) Kyrie A B A, Christe C D C, Kyrie E F E' (*Graduale Vaticanum*, III, VI, IX, X, I–VI ad lib.).[1]

Many of those in group (*b*) amplify the ninth *Kyrie* in the same fashion as group (*c*). There are thirty-one settings in the *Graduale*, and this number could be increased considerably. Group (*c*) is the latest of the three, but even so its oldest specimens date back to the tenth century. The earliest version of the *Gloria in excelsis* in Greek dates from the fifth century: in Latin the oldest is that of the so-called 'Antiphonary of Bangor' in the seventh century. It was always sung in Latin from the ninth century onwards, and has been part of the Roman rite from the sixth century. The music is mostly syllabic and is not so melismatic as the *Kyrie*. The oldest melody is that in Mass XV, which has a psalmodic recitation like that of the *Te Deum*. It may be worth notice that thirteen of the melodies given in the *Graduale* are in the plagal modes and only five in the authentic. The *Credo* was introduced into the Roman liturgy by Benedict VIII (d. 1024). The Gregorian music never dramatizes it, and displays a psalmodic form with *incipit*, reciting note, and cadence. Tropes were not used for the *Credo*: two examples[2] do, in fact, exist, but they were not sung liturgically.

The *Sanctus* (which is followed by the *Benedictus*) is of apostolic origin and comes from the Synagogue. The character of its music lies between that of the *Kyrie* and the *Gloria*. The oldest melody, that given in Mass XVIII,[3] is a continuation of the chant of the Preface. Most of the melodies are in the plagal modes. *Agnus Dei* was introduced into the liturgy by Pope Sergius I (d. 701): the triple form has been in use from the eleventh century. There are four forms of the music—A A A (the oldest type: in Masses I, V, VI, XVIII); A B A (in Masses II, IV, VIII, X, XII, XVI); A A B (Mass VII); and A B C (in Mass XI). The compositions used for many melodies of the Ordinary carry us, of course, far beyond the Golden Age of Gregorian music into what has been called its Silver Age (*c.* 1000–1325). They introduce us to the subject of the following chapter, where we shall see the results of the spread of tropes, more especially in relation to the most illustrious member of that family, the sequence.

[1] *Kyrie* IV ad lib. is recorded in *The History of Music in Sound*, ii, side 7.
[2] H. Villetard, *Office de Pierre de Corbeil* (1907), pp. 140, 172.
[3] Recorded in *The History of Music in Sound*, ii, side 4.

V

TROPE, SEQUENCE, AND CONDUCTUS

By Jacques Handschin

TERMINOLOGY

BEFORE embarking on the history of trope and sequence we must
agree on their definition. There is already general agreement about the
mutual relationship of the two, but unfortunately this does not extend
farther. The sequence is a subdivision of the trope: it is the trope connected with the Alleluia of the Mass—or, more precisely, the trope
added to the Alleluia when it is repeated after its verse. Since the
sequence became particularly prominent, the term 'trope', which
properly includes sequence, is also used, in a more restricted sense,
to indicate any kind of trope which is not a sequence. So far the
terminology is not in dispute. The controversy begins when we ask
what we mean by 'trope' (and consequently by 'sequence').

Léon Gautier, in his masterly book *Les Tropes* (1886), defined the
trope as 'l'interpolation d'un texte liturgique'. The objection to this
definition is that the trope is a musical phenomenon: it is, in fact, a
melodic interpolation, which supplied the framework for a literary
or poetic interpolation. Hence the melismatic, as well as the syllabic,
form of the melody has to be regarded as a trope, and this interpretation agrees exactly with the original terminology. The reasons
why Gautier defined the trope as the interpolation of a text were
first, that he was mainly interested in the literary side of the problem,
and secondly, that in the Middle Ages the melismatic form of trope
came to be superseded by the syllabic. An argument in favour of our
definition is that the word *tropus* originally meant a melody and not
a poem. In the early history of the trope, before the syllabic form was
used, the usual term is *melodia*, and *tropus* is evidently equivalent to
this. Since the word is Greek,[1] it is a natural temptation to assume
that the whole material of these added melodies was borrowed from
Byzantine music. But there are numerous objections to this assumption. It is simpler to suppose that the Western musicians, in adopting
the word *tropus*, were following a familiar practice—the practice

---

[1] τρόπος means properly a 'turn', and hence a figure in rhetoric or music.

of using a more impressive Greek word instead of the normal Latin.

The question now arises, how we are to distinguish these added melismata from others which occur normally in liturgical melodies. The answer is to be found in the nature of the Gregorian repertory. From the eighth century this was propagated in a fairly uniform version, which was imposed by the authority of the Church. The additions which we are considering can be distinguished from the official repertory, since they do not recur constantly but only in certain manuscripts, or else they are relegated to the end of the manuscript as an appendix. Whereas the liturgical chant was prescribed, the trope was an optional addition to the liturgy and merely tolerated by the Church. In consequence the melismata of the Gradual and Tract, as well as the normal Alleluia melismata, do not fall into the category of tropes. A further point concerns the term 'sequence'. Just as 'trope' indicates both the melismatic and the syllabic forms of the added melodies, so 'sequence' (*sequentia*) indicates the addition to the Alleluia in both forms. The term *sequela*, however, has sometimes been reserved for the addition to the already melismatic Alleluia,[1] and it is convenient to use it in that sense. The etymology of *sequentia* has been explained in two ways: either it is a melody following another chant (Latin *sequor*), or it is a melody regarded as a sequence or succession of notes.

There remains the term 'prose' (*prosa*), which is often found, particularly in France. This evidently refers only to the syllabic form of the melodies and derives from the fact that the texts set to the melodies were of necessity in prose, since in the early history of the trope the rule was to set one syllable to each note of a given melody. With this reservation, 'prose' is a general term, which includes the syllabic form of the sequence and of the other categories of interpolated melody. We may therefore use the word 'prose' whenever we wish to emphasize that we are speaking of the syllabic forms. Its diminutive *prosula* was largely used in the Middle Ages to indicate the syllabic form of the addition to the Responsory. It is difficult, however, to be strictly logical. There are proses which are not tropes—that is to say, melismata occurring in the normal liturgical chant which have been provided with a syllabic text, e.g. in the Gradual, the Alleluia, and the Offertory, with their verses.[2] The application of the term 'trope'

---

[1] See Hughes, *Anglo-French Sequelae* (London, 1934), p. 4.

[2] The Offertory verses are no longer in use—they were, in fact, abandoned in the Middle Ages—but they can be found in the *Offertoriale* edited by C. Ott (1935).

to proses which are not tropes is due to the later evolution which resulted in the disappearance of the melismatic trope, and this is the explanation of Gautier's terminology.

ORIGINS

The melodies added to the Gregorian chant, in the form in which it spread through Europe from the eighth century, had their proto-types in Ambrosian, Gallican, and Mozarabic chant, as well as in the older Roman chant. These earlier additions differ from the tropes in being purely melismatic. There appears also to be some difference of style between the 'historical' trope and its predecessors, but to appre-ciate this we should need a more substantial knowledge of Gallican and early Roman chant than we actually possess. The historical difference which we need to keep in mind is that in the older tradition these melodic developments were regarded as part of the singers' natural function and were not singled out for special attention; whereas in the later practice, represented by the word *tropus*, they were more clearly distinguished from the established repertory, and the difference between these optional embellishments and the prescribed melodies was more strongly marked. It is clear that by this time the liturgical repertory had attained a high degree of fixity.

Within the ecclesiastical chant there were certain places where, by an early tradition, free invention could take the form of expanding a single syllable by the addition of a melisma. This was the case in the Gallican as well as the Ambrosian and Mozarabic chant, and even in the Roman in its pre-Carolingian form. The Alleluia of the Mass—or more precisely, the repetition of the Alleluia after its verse—pro-vided such an opportunity; and it was here that the sequence grew up. An opportunity was also afforded by the repetition of the main part of the Responsory after its verse—or, more exactly, the end of this re-petition was another of the places where the trope developed. To speak of mere improvisation in this connexion would, however, be misleading, since the two cases quoted concern choral, not solo, sing-ing; and hence the parallel often drawn between such treatment and the melismata of Byzantine music or the Coptic Alleluia is not exact. None the less, these melismata preserve some elements of freedom: melodic invention can expand here unfettered by obligations imposed by the text. For the same reason this was rather the sphere of the musician than of the liturgist; and, so far as we can tell, there was also more freedom in the use of the church modes than in the rest of the

plainsong repertory—less submission, in fact, to the modal formulas
which were employed in antiphons and responsories.

In general these long melismatic additions were used mainly at the
great festivals, such as Easter, Christmas, or the commemoration of
the patron of a particular church. The use of these embellishments
was thus comparable to the application of polyphony to the traditional church melodies (see p. 361).

PROTOTYPES IN AMBROSIAN CHANT

We must first consider the use of these melismata in Ambrosian
chant, since this is probably the oldest type of ecclesiastical chant
preserved in the West. In the oldest extant Ambrosian antiphonary,
written in the twelfth century, we find in the supplement some
Alleluia melodies.[1] The first two evidently belong to the Alleluia verse
'Praeveniamus', which is several times mentioned but not included
in the manuscript (we must remember that the manuscript is incomplete and contains only the winter part of the ecclesiastical year). Yet
we find this verse in the *Antiphonale Missarum juxta ritum sanctae
ecclesiae Mediolanensis* (1935)[2] as the first of the Alleluias for Sundays; it is followed by the first of our melodies, while the Alleluia
which precedes the verse is shorter but still related to both the
melodiae. Both melodies, as given in the *Paléographie musicale*,[3] are
related to each other, the second still being longer than the first. Each
has the same beginning and the same close (we must, of course, add
the last twenty-two notes of the first melody to the second, this kind
of abbreviated notation being a common feature in manuscripts).
The first *melodiae* consist of five parts (this division, indicated in the
manuscripts, is preferable to that used in the *Antiphonale Missarum*),
each of which ends on *g*; and these in turn may be subdivided. If we
represent the five parts by Roman numerals and the subdivisions by
letters, we get the following scheme:

$$I = a, b\ c$$
$$II = d, e$$
$$III = f, g \text{ (ending like e), } g$$
$$IV = h, g' \text{ (in substance a transposition), } e'$$
$$V = i, k \text{ (ending like e or g), } l$$

The *melodiae primae* run as follows:[4]

---

[1] *Paléographie musicale*, vi, p. 321.
[2] p. 292.   [3] Loc. cit.
[4] *Paléographie musicale*, vi, p. 321 and v, p. 268. The notation of the examples in this
chapter is non-mensural, unless the contrary is stated. The quavers represent only
melodic values, and their combination in groups corresponds to the ligatures in the
original.

Ex. 45

We may say that the melody is in the eighth mode (*tetrardus plagalis*), since the final is *g* and the compass rather *d–d'* than *g–g'*. The *melodiae secundae*, on the other hand, range from *c* to *g'*, embracing the whole compass of the authentic and plagal *tetrardus* (seventh and eighth modes). As we shall see, this is a feature common to these melodies and to sequences.

In the same appendix there are two melismatic Alleluias marked 'de Venite', which are nearly identical. If we look at the *Antiphonale Missarum*[1] we find the Alleluia 'Venite exsultemus' as the second Alleluia for Sundays; here the Alleluia following the verse is the same as one of our melodies, while the Alleluia preceding the verse again bears resemblances to them but is shorter. In the manuscript there follows an Alleluia marked 'de Dominus regnavit'. This appears in the *Antiphonale Missarum*[2] after the third of the Alleluia verses for Sundays, but in a somewhat extended form, while the Alleluia before the verse is approximately the same in abbreviated form. We may therefore conclude that the appendix to the manuscript was intended to contain the longer Alleluias (those following the verses) for all the

[1] *Paléographie musicale*, v, p. 293.   [2] Ibid., p. 294.

Sunday Alleluias, but not the verses themselves nor the Alleluias preceding them; it corresponded, in fact, to what was later called a 'troper'. In theory an Alleluia melody of this kind could be linked up not only with the verse to which it primarily belonged but also with other verses. In the three cases which have been cited the Alleluia melodies are not in fact combined with any other verses; but there are examples where this occurs. For instance, both the initial and the final Alleluia of the verse 'Justorum animae'[1] are applied to many different verses. Of these the majority have practically the same melody as the verse 'Justorum animae', but there are also verses with other melodies—for example, the verse 'Venite et audite'.[2] We may note that the initial and final Alleluias of the verse 'Justorum animae' are in what is termed in Gregorian chant the first and second modes respectively, while the verse is in the second mode. On the other hand, the verse melody with which these Alleluias are most often connected is in the sixth mode, with a cadence on c (a fourth beneath the final f); but at the end we have a typical formula in the first or second mode which reintroduces the Alleluia, and the same formula occurs also at the end of the verse melody, which is in the second mode.

If we look again at the 'Praeveniamus' Alleluia, which belongs primarily to the verse 'Praeveniamus', we shall find a still more curious fact: the 'Melodiae de Praeveniamus primae et secundae' are also quoted in the manuscript as an addition to the Epiphany Responsory 'Ecce completa sunt omnia',[3] where the verse is followed by the *repetenda* (the repetition of the second half of the main part of the Responsory), indicated only by the initial words 'Hic est'. Evidently the *melodiae* are supposed to be adapted to the end of the *repetenda*—the words 'bene complacui', or rather one of these syllables. In the *Liber vesperalis juxta ritum sanctae ecclesiae Mediolanensis* (1939)[4] the *repetenda*, indicated by the words 'Hic est', is accordingly followed by the ending 'in quo bene complacui', with our *melodiae primae* placed on the syllable '-ne'; but the ending is preceded by the rubric 'ad libitum', indicating that it could be sung in the shorter form which preceded the verse. It will be remembered that the 'Melodiae primae de Praeveniamus' are in the eighth mode,[5] while the Responsory is in the fifth and sixth modes (the *tritus authenticus* and *plagalis* combined), ending on f. For this reason the end of the *melodiae* has been changed to end also on f; but we cannot be certain

[1] Ibid., p. 357.   [2] Ibid., p. 487.
[3] Ibid. vi, pp. 125–6.
[4] Ibid., pp. 148–9.
[5] So also in *Antiphonale Missarum*, pp. 292–3.

whether this was the result of the editor having been too scrupulous about tonal unity, or whether he actually discovered the adaptation in a manuscript—liturgical editions intended for practical use have no *apparatus criticus*. The 'Melodiae primae de Praeveniamus', therefore, are offered as an optional addition to the Responsory; but we must not exclude the possibility that both *melodiae* were sung after the Responsory.[1]

There is yet another case where two *melodiae* follow a Responsory, and this time they are noted in full. In the Christmas Responsory 'Congratulamini mihi'[2] the *repetenda* is followed by 'Melodiae Dom.' and 'Secundae Dom.' (The meaning of the abbreviation is unknown; but the Responsory occurs in a thirteenth-century manuscript with the rubric 'melodiae propriae',[3] which would suggest that the melisma originally belongs here.) Here the melismata occur on 'de-', the sixth syllable from the end of the Responsory.

It is a remarkable fact that the *melodiae* have been analysed in the manuscript itself. The component parts of the first *melodiae* are numbered, in the hand of the principal copyist, I I II III II III IV V I, while those of the second are numbered I II III IV V III IV V III IV VI VII VIII IX X; finally, we have a section marked 'vel de primis',[4] identical with I of the first *melodiae*, which would mean that I of the first *melodiae* can take the place of X of the second.[5] Thus the repetition of I of the first *melodiae* unites the first and second in a kind of higher unity. If this interpretation is correct, the double system would be:

$$a\ a\ \overbrace{b\ c}\ \overbrace{b\ c}\ d\ e\ a$$
$$f\ g\ \overbrace{h\ i\ k}\ \overbrace{h\ i\ k}\ \overbrace{h\ i\ l}\ m\ n\ o\ a.$$

It will be noticed that not only the opening group *a*, but also the pair *b c* and the triple group *h i k* are doubled, the latter even tripled, if we consider *l* as a substitute for *k*, and *h i l* as representing a modified repetition of *h i k*. Furthermore, *f* is similar to *h* (in its beginning), *e* to *l* (to a greater extent), *e* to *n* (in its beginning), and there is a marked similarity between *g* and *k*, and between *i* and *m*.

There are other places in the same manuscript where the *melodiae* are analysed in this way. Those of the Advent Responsory 'Sperent in te'[6] have the following scheme: I, II, III, *tractus* (this seems to

---

[1] As indicated in *Paléographie musicale*, vi, p. 126.
[2] Ibid., p. 61.
[3] M. Magistretti, *Manuale Ambrosianum* (1905), ii, p. 57.
[4] Not, as in *Paléographie musicale*, vi, 'prima de primis'; cf. ibid. v, p. 53.
[5] According to *Paléographie musicale* it would have to be added to X of the second.
[6] Ibid. vi, p. 22.

imply a special form of melodic phrase), IV, III, *tractus*, IV, III; those of the Advent Responsory 'Laetetur cor'[1] are: I, I, II, II, III, IV, *tractus*, V, *tractus*, V, *tractus*, IV, *tractus*, V, VI, IV; those of the Annunciation Responsory 'Tollite portas':[2] I I II II III I II III. The Advent Responsory 'Aspiciens'[3] is also accompanied by *melodiae primae* and *secundae*, the former being I II III IV V III IV V III IV (with an unnumbered final part reintroducing the end of the Responsory) and the latter I II III II IV II III II IV II III II (with a final section as in the *melodiae primae*).

Repetition of single parts often occurs—a feature characteristic of the sequence—but we also find groups of parts repeated, and this occurs also in a special type of sequence (see p. 137). These long melismata, where music develops in its own right, represent the very summit of musical architecture. There are also other melodic affinities besides those indicated by the Roman numerals: sometimes one part appears as a variation of another; very often parts are connected by the same ending, and sometimes by the same beginning—formal details which reappear in the sequence. There is also a tendency to adapt the inserted melody to the strictly liturgical one: it is particularly the beginning and the ending of the melisma that are related to the plainsong melody, and this also reminds us of the sequence and trope.

The two remaining cases where melismata are analysed by numerals in the manuscript are not Responsories but chants of the Mass. They are the *Psalmellus* 'Benedictus Dominus'[4], whose verse contains a melisma analysed as I II III IV V VI, and the Offertory 'Benedixisti',[5] where the melisma of the verse has the form (I), II, III, *tractus*, III, III.

The Alleluia of the Mass, the Responsory of the Office, the Offertory and the *Psalmellus* in the Mass (the last corresponding to the Roman Gradual) are the categories of Ambrosian chant which preserve these melismata. If we examine them in greater detail we note the following points: (1) The place where the long melisma occurs in the Alleluia is in the repetition of the Alleluia after the verse; the Alleluia preceding the verse is in general a shorter form of the same melodic pattern. In Roman use, on the other hand—or at any rate in later Roman use—the Alleluia preceding the verse and its subsequent repetition are identical and generally shorter than in Ambrosian use, which we may be certain is older in this respect: but the 'sequence' added to the

---

[1] Ibid., pp. 29–30.   [2] Ibid., p. 41.   [3] Ibid., p. 13.
[4] Ibid., p. 122.   [5] Ibid., pp. 23–24.

Gregorian Alleluia has precisely the same position as the final Alleluia in the Ambrosian chant. (2) In Responsories it is also, in most cases, the repetition of the main part after the verse—or, more exactly, the end of the main part in the repetition—which has the long melisma, though sometimes this occurs on a syllable of the verse. In Gregorian chant, however, the repetition after the verse is normally not extended; if it is extended, it is a 'trope'. (3) In the Offertory the long melisma is generally connected with one syllable of the verse, though in some cases it occurs at the end of the main part of the Offertory—not, however, as in Responsories, in the repetition after the verse, but in the part preceding the verse; more curious still, where the melisma occurs in the part preceding the verse there is no repetition: in all the large repertory of Offertories in the *Antiphonale Missarum* there is only one exception, 'Vidi speciosam',[1] which is treated like a Responsory, with the melisma in the repetition of the end of the main part. In the Gregorian Offertory, too, the principal melisma is regularly found in one of the verses; it is, however, a constant, not an optional, feature, and therefore, if provided with a syllabic text, would be a *prosula* without being a trope. (4) In the *Psalmellus* the long melisma is placed on one syllable of the verse. The Gradual of Gregorian chant, which corresponds to the *Psalmellus*, also has melismata, but they are included in the normal form of the Gradual or its verse and hence, if provided with text, are further examples of *prosulae* rather than tropes.

This survey helps us to answer the question whether these melismata are to be regarded as choral music or solo song. They are intended for the choir, in so far as they are included in the repetition of the main part of a Responsory, or the *repetenda* after the verse—or again in the Alleluia; but they are also solo song, in so far as they are included in the verse. This is, at any rate, a reasonable assumption, in view of what we know of the distribution of these forms of ecclesiastical chant between soloists and choir. The distinction, however, must not be exaggerated. The difference between choir and soloist was less then than it is now, since the choir, or *schola cantorum*, consisted of a few trained singers (to which a boys' choir could be added), while the solo parts were sometimes sung by two singers.

PROTOTYPES AT NONANTOLA

We may now turn to an interesting document first published in 1891,[2] of which the following is a transcription (with Roman numerals added):

---

[1] *Antiphonale Missarum*, p. 388.   [2] *Paléographie musicale*, ii, pl. 16.

All the parts of the melody are repeated, except the first and last—an arrangement similar to the sequence. The prevalent cadence ($f\,g\,g$ or $c\,d\,d$) is also one that is usual in sequences, but apart from this the melodic style is not that of the classical sequence. III is practically identical with IV, and IX is similar to X, with the result that we have something like quadruple repetition instead of double: quadruple repetition is often used in the secular counterpart of the sequence, the *lai* (see p. 247). We also note that X and XI are like II and VII transposed, and that the final part corresponds to the second half of X.

To ascertain the liturgical function of this melody we must consult its source. It occurs in a twelfth-century manuscript (fo. 11ᵛ) preserved in the monastery of Nonantola, which contains only the responsorial and solo songs of the Mass—Graduals, Alleluias, and Tracts: it is a *cantatorium*. This Alleluia takes the place of the Alleluia repetition after the verse 'Video caelos' for St. Stephen's day. The verse and the preceding Alleluia correspond to the Gregorian form published in the *Editio Vaticana*, but the melisma of the initial Alleluia is omitted and the final melisma of the verse is shortened (though they should probably be completed). Apart from this melody the manuscript is Gregorian, though there are also several *prosulae* obtained by providing Gregorian melismata with new texts. We can only explain the anomaly presented by this particular Alleluia by supposing that the manuscript (or its original, if it was written at Nonantola) was intended for a church dedicated to St. Stephen—probably the one at Bologna—and that devotion to a patron saint was the reason for preserving an obsolete rite.

If we are looking for evidence of added melismata in Gallican chant we must not forget the *manicantiones* (presumably 'songs of early morning', i.e. chants of Matins) mentioned in the eighteenth canon of the second Council of Tours (*c.* 570), as well as by Aimoin.[1] It is probable that by *manicantiones* is meant the Responsory adorned with a long melisma, or the melisma itself.[2] The question whether actual examples of such melismata survive must remain doubtful. A possible instance is an Alleluia in an Ambrosian manuscript[3] described as 'Alleluia Francigena', i.e. an Alleluia of French origin— which would indicate that exchanges took place from one country to another; yet it is not certain that this melody belonged to the Gallican repertory. There are also the melismata of a St. Denis Responsory:[4] these, however, are to be identified with the *neuma triplex* mentioned by Amalar (see p. 142), which is preserved in various versions, and for this reason we cannot be certain that they are not of Roman origin. Two further examples about which we cannot feel any certainty are (1) the 'Alleluia, Cantate domino canticum novum, quia mirabilia fecit dominus', which sometimes occurs in old manuscripts in a longer form than usual;[5] and (2) the 'Alleluia, Caeli enarrant' which occurs in the Einsiedeln manuscript 121,[6] not only in the normal form on p. 360 but also in an enlarged form on p. 361.[7] In both these examples the difference between the longer and the 'normal' form concerns only the verse; but it is quite possible that this presupposes also a more developed form of the Alleluia which follows the verse and which may have been omitted in conformity with the Gregorian rule of repeating the Alleluia after the verse in the same form as before it. There is evidence that added melismata

[1] *De gestis regum Francorum*, iii. 80. See A. Gastoué, *Histoire du chant liturgique à Paris*, i (1904), pp. 35–37 and *Revue du chant grégorien* (1938), pp. 146–7, and cf. my article in *Schweizer Musikbuch* (1939), pp. 21–24.

[2] I agree with Gastoué that these melismata may have been sung by boys; but we must distinguish them from the *versus puerorum* which occur, e.g. in Paris, Bibl. Nat. 15182, since these are versicles independent of the Responsory verse.

[3] Reproduced in *Schweizer Musikbuch* (1939), p. 46.

[4] Paris, Bibl. Nat. lat. 17296; reproduced in *Schweizer Musikbuch* (1939), pp. 46–49.

[5] e.g. St. Gall, 359, p. 129 (reproduced in *Paléographie musicale*, 2nd ser., ii) and Paris, Bibl. Nat. 903, fo. 124 (ibid. xiii).

[6] *Paléographie musicale*, iv.

[7] For a discussion of these two examples see Dom Pothier in *Revue du chant grégorien*, xx (1911–12), p. 40, and xxi (1912–13), pp. 97–101, and Dom Johner in *Musica Sacra*, xlv (1912), pp. 189–90.

were also used in Mozarabic chant; but none of them appear to have been preserved in a notation that is clearly decipherable.

ROMAN PROTOTYPES

In the Roman chant the situation was very much the same, until the Roman repertory received the fixed form which, from the eighth century, was disseminated throughout Europe and imposed on different countries, after which additions of the kind we are considering were definitely classified as tropes. We have a piece of literary evidence which suggests that added melismata were in use before this period. In the first Roman *Ordo*, a ceremonial designed for the papal service and probably written in the eighth century (though it is generally considered to contain older material), we read that in the Easter Day vespers an Alleluia is sung with three psalm verses, after which an Alleluia is sung again with *melodiae* by the boys.[1] The place occupied by the melisma and its designation are clearly the same as in the Ambrosian rite. In the second *Ordo Romanus*, which is of the late ninth century,[2] the phrase 'sequitur jubilatio quam sequentiam vocant' (here follows the jubilation which is called the 'sequence') follows the reference to the Alleluia of the Mass in the older editions, but it was omitted in the version published in *Patrologia Latina*.[3] The reason given by the editor for this omission is that the passage does not occur in Amalar's *Eclogae*[4] and that sequences did not appear before Notker. The *Eclogae*, however, are only a short extract, and the word *sequentia*, as used in the *Ordo*, is not to be taken in the sense assumed by the editor. The same term is also used in one of the oldest Gregorian antiphonaries for the Mass, written probably in the late eighth century but without musical notation. Here we have a list of 25 Alleluia verses, six of which are marked 'cum sequentia'[5]—a rubric which must refer to the Alleluia repetition after the verse. It is true that this manuscript belongs to the period when the Roman chant was being spread throughout Europe as a model, but it is still possible that remnants of an older use are preserved in it.

There is one very problematical case—that of certain twelfth- and thirteenth-century manuscripts which are undoubtedly of Roman origin but are quite independent in their melodic style. Dom Andoyer[6] considers the melodic version preserved here to be pre-Gregorian, i.e.

[1] *Patrologia Latina*, lxxviii. 965.
[2] See M. Andrieu, *Les Ordines Romani du haut Moyen Âge* (Louvain, 1948), ii, p. 215.
[3] *Patrologia Latina*, lxxviii. 971.   [4] Ibid. cv. 1315.
[5] Cf. Dom Hesbert, *Antiphonale missarum sextuplex* (1935), p. 199.
[6] In *Revue du chant grégorien*, xx (1911–12), pp. 69 ff. and 107 ff.

earlier than the end of the sixth century, but it is not even certain that it is earlier than the period when the definitive version of the Roman chant began to be circulated. All that we can say for certain at present is that these manuscripts preserve melodies which appear in some respects rather 'modern' but at the same time they bear testimony to old liturgical practices. In Vatican, lat. 5319, for example, the Alleluia after the verse is frequently a more developed form of the version preceding it: examples are the 'Alleluia Pascha', with second verse 'Epulemur' (fo. 84), and the Alleluias with Greek text 'O kyrios ebasileusen' (fo. 85^v) and 'Oty theos' (fo. 97).[1]

GENERAL HISTORICAL SITUATION (*c*. 800)

In order to understand the conditions in which the trope and sequence arose we must consider the general history of ecclesiastical chant in the time of Charlemagne (771–814). Charlemagne, following in the footsteps of his father Pepin, was anxious to have the liturgy and ecclesiastical chant in his kingdom moulded into conformity with those in Rome. His coronation as emperor, performed by Leo III in Rome in 800, gave religious sanction to his ideal of universal monarchy, and this ideal implied uniformity in ecclesiastical matters. From its alliance with the Carolingian monarchy the Papacy gained a new impulse to enforce liturgical and musical uniformity throughout the Western Church; its earlier practice had been more liberal, as we can see from a letter of Gregory I to his representative in England, in which he allowed him to take over liturgical practices wherever he found them suitable. Charlemagne's desire for uniformity had its fulfilment mainly in France, where the Gallican liturgy and Gallican chant had hitherto prevailed, though in actual fact the Roman rite itself took over certain elements of both. In Spain the Mozarabic rite and Mozarabic chant were not superseded by the Roman until the eleventh century, while in Milan the Ambrosian rite survived the move for uniformity and has continued down to the present day (see pp. 62, 64). In England conformity with the Roman use had been achieved even before the Carolingian era. England had experienced two phases of missionary activity—the first from Ireland, bringing the Celtic rite, which was closely related to the Gallican, and the second from Rome, which conflicted to some extent with the first and brought the country into an increasingly closer connexion with the see of Rome.

[1] Facsimile of the last of these in H. M. Bannister, *Monumenti Vaticani di paleografia musicale latina* (1918), pl. 81*a*.

The musical history of western Europe at this period has its centre of gravity in Charlemagne's empire, and particularly in France. The consequence of the change just mentioned was that ecclesiastical chant was in future regulated by the Gregorian antiphonary. Indeed the liturgical chant books preserved in different countries after the end of the ninth century show a remarkable unity of melodic tradition, particularly in the Mass. From that time the repertory of liturgical chant could admit additions only in the shape of offices required for new feasts or commemorations. The logical result would have been the throttling of all creative effort in the field of church music; but that could hardly be accepted in an age so devoted to music. An outlet for musical invention was therefore found within the liturgy, and a compromise was agreed on with the ecclesiastical authorities: hence the trope and the sequence—an optional addition which was merely tolerated by the Church and remained distinct from the official Roman chant.

We have a valuable account of the trope and sequence in the first half of the ninth century from the famous liturgist Amalar of Metz. He was, of course, an advocate of Roman chant: he had composed his own antiphonary, using elements taken from a Roman antiphonary preserved at Corbie and another at Metz, where the Roman chant had been introduced as early as the eighth century, and adding ingredients to be found in neither of them. There is still no absolute fixity at this stage, but the general plan is definitely Roman, though Amalar also refers to some Gallican practices which had persisted. He mentions the interpolations which we are discussing only as melismata, but among them are some which were later on provided with texts. For these melismata he uses the words *melodiae*, *sequentia*, and *neuma*, but not *tropus*. We may say that his conception represents an intermediate stage: he neither treats the melodies merely as a concern of the singers nor singles them out as a special category.

In referring to the Alleluia of the Mass Amalar speaks of 'haec jubilatio quam sequentiam vocant' (this jubilation which is called the 'sequence').[1] We may remember that this expression occurred also in the second *Ordo Romanus*.[2] Again, when speaking of the vespers for Easter Day in Rome Amalar says that the Alleluia is sung 'cum omni supplemento et excellentia versuum et sequentiarum' (richly supplemented and adorned with verses and sequences).[3] In another passage, which has also frequently been quoted, he speaks of

---

[1] *Patrologia Latina*, cv. 1123.
[2] Ordo V in Andrieu's enumeration (see p. 139).   [3] *Patrologia Latina*, cv. 1295.

the Responsory for St. John the Evangelist's day, 'In medio ecclesiae'.[1]
He says that, unlike other Responsories, a triple *neuma* is sung here,
and also that the verse and the *Gloria patri* are prolonged by a *neuma*.[2]
The term *neuma*, here used for the first time for a melisma, properly
means melody (or an element of melody).[3] Amalar adds that 'modern'
singers have transferred these melismata to the Christmas Responsory
'Descendit'. It is easily understood that singers in general preferred
to have a Responsory lavishly ornamented for Christmas rather than
for St. John the Evangelist. In actual fact manuscripts where these
melismata are added to 'Descendit' are numerous, whereas those
which have them attached to 'In medio' are scarce. This transference
of a melisma from one Responsory to another recalls Ambrosian
practice.

It is important to notice that Amalar does not refer to a recent
practice, though his words have sometimes been interpreted in this
sense. The words 'in novissimo responsorio' which he applies to
'In medio' do not mean that it was a recent Responsory but that it
was the last in the cycle of Responsories belonging to the Nocturns of
St. John. It was not the composers of the melismata who were
'modern' but the singers who transferred them from one Responsory
to another. It is not the application of melismatic decoration as such
which Amalar finds unusual but the fact that the melisma adapted to
the close of the Responsory is threefold and, secondly, that the verse
is decorated in the same way. He says that this treatment was applied
to 'In medio' by musicians of an earlier generation ('a prioribus').
From another passage[4] we may draw the conclusion that Amalar
even had in mind melismata embellishing the Introit of the Mass.
He contrasts with the Introit the *Kyrie* which follows it, as a song of
humiliation—a humiliation necessary to singers elated by the 'magnificent composition of *melodiae*'.

The *triplex neuma* described by Amalar often occurs with syllabic
text. It has been published from different sources by Dom Pothier[5]
and Peter Wagner[6] in its association with the Responsory 'Descendit'.
The version which follows is taken from one of the few manuscripts
where it is preserved in its original association with the Responsory
'In medio':

[1] *Patrologia Latina*, cv. 1273–5.
[2] The *Gloria patri* was sometimes added to responsories as a second verse, sung to the
same melody as the first.
[3] It is not certain whether this word is to be derived from νεῦμα = sign, nod, or
πνεῦμα (*pneuma*) = spirit, breath.   [4] *Patrologia Latina*, cv. 1113–14.
[5] *Revue du chant grégorien*, xi (1902–3), pp. 65–66.
[6] *Einführung in die gregorianischen Melodien*, iii (1921), pp. 347–8.

Ex. 47[1]

In me- di - o

ec - cle-

si - æ   a   pe - ru-

it   os

e - jus et im - ple - vit   e - um

do - mi - nus   spi - ri - tu sa - pi - en - ti - æ et

in - tel-

lec - - tus.

(*Versus*) Ci - ba-

vit   il - lum pa - ne

vi - tæ et   in - tel - lec - tus et   a - qua sa - pi - en - ti - æ

sa - lu - ta - ris po - - ta - vit il - - lum

[1] Laon 263, fo. 102 (probably late twelfth century). The text has been emended from fo. 110ᵛ, where an incomplete version of the same *triplex neuma* is associated with another Responsory for the Holy Innocents, 'Centum quadraginta'. Certain transpositions in the third melisma have also been corrected from Paris, Bibl. Nat. lat. 17296,

Ex. 47 contd.

*) Written a fourth higher.
**) Written a fifth higher.

fo. 35ᵛ. The version printed here cannot, however, be regarded as a critical edition of the text. In every case the flat affects only the note to which it is prefixed.

(In the midst of the church the Lord opened his mouth and filled him with the spirit of wisdom and of understanding. He fed him with the bread of life and of understanding, and gave him to drink the water of saving wisdom, and the Lord filled him with the spirit of wisdom and of understanding. Glory be to the Father and to the Son and to the Holy Ghost, as it was in the beginning, is now, and ever shall be, world without end, Amen. In the midst of the church . . ., &c.)

If we compare this version with those printed by Dom Pothier and Wagner we shall find that what is here the first melisma corresponds to the second in their versions, and vice versa, while the third *neuma* of our version is nearer to Pothier's text than to Wagner's. The present version is, in fact, unique, in that it includes not only the triple *neuma* but also other melismata in the main part of the Responsory.[1] The melismatic beginning of the verse, however, and the *Gloria* agree with Amalar's description, though the verse which he quotes is different.[2] The manuscript is also unique in that the third *neuma* is marked with the rubric 'Qui septem', for which no explanation seems to be forthcoming. Dom Pothier suggests the following method of performance: Principal section—solo, repeated by the choir with the insertion of the first melisma; verse—solo; principal section (or only the second half of it)—choir, with insertion of the second melisma; *Gloria Patri*—solo; principal section, with insertion of the third melisma—choir.

The transference of melismata from one Responsory to another, which, as we have seen, recalls Ambrosian practice, raises the question whether the inserted melody fits one Responsory as well as another. In this case, at any rate, both Responsories mentioned by Amalar are in the first mode, and this applies also to the Responsory 'Centum', with which the melismata are associated in the Laon manuscript. It may be added that the same triple *neuma* occurs in a St. Denis manuscript of the twelfth century with three different Responsories: 'Post passionem' (in the first mode) for the patron of the church, 'Descendit', and 'In medio'.[3] In the first two cases the three melismata are practically the same as in the Laon manuscript, but in the reverse order; in the third case we have only one melisma (the first in the other versions in this manuscript), which appears in syllabic form as well as melismatic.

The age of Amalar—the early ninth century—was one when the

---

[1] Cf. the versions reproduced in *Processionale Monasticum* (1893), pp. 226 and 227.

[2] It is included in the second version in *Processionale Monasticum*, p. 227. The verses of Responsories were often interchanged.

[3] Paris, Bibl. Nat. lat. 17296, fo. 229ᵛ, 21, 36. The first of these is printed in *Schweizer Musikbuch* (1939), pp. 46–49.

art of church singing was at its height.[1] We are told, for example, by Agobard of Lyons,[2] who was opposed to Amalar, that most of the singers, from childhood to old age, spent all their time exercising themselves in their art, to the neglect of their spiritual education: they were arrogant about the great number of songs they had learned, whereas in olden days they had been content with biblical texts and their natural skill in singing and so preferred frequently to repeat the same things rather than to burden themselves with endless and super-fluous novelties (it is not clear whether he is referring to texts or melodies, since he was equally insistent on textual purity and opposed to luxury in music). It was Agobard's view that there should be a single universal form of praying, reading, and singing—an ideal which soon came to be realized in large measure; this, he thought, could easily be learned by gifted youths without any hindrance to their spiritual education. Even Amalar, who was more tolerant in his attitude to non-biblical texts and assigned a mystical meaning to the richness of music, represented mainly by melismata, declares that stupid singers are delighted by the mere sound of their singing, with-out understanding its spiritual meaning, and boast of the magnificent composition of their *melodiae*.[3] We get the impression that an over-whelming richness of melodic invention flowed into church song at this period—at the very time when unity was ordered by the authori-ties. This seems at first sight paradoxical, since richness meant variety; it is more than probable, however, that a good deal of the influx con-sisted of musical material which later appeared in the guise of the syllabic trope and the sequence.

ADAPTATION OF TEXTS

We have now reached the point where this interpolated musical material came to be provided with a text whose syllables corresponded to the individual notes and whose content had naturally to be in con-formity with the words of the original plainsong. As time went on the purely melismatic interpolations were superseded more and more by those bearing a text, and consequently a sequence or trope came to mean what it means today—not a melismatic song but one with a definite text. In other words, the melodies become a part of hymnody. Considering the tremendous development of hymnody in the Eastern Church (see pp. 16–32) we may be surprised to find that in the West— apart from the Ambrosian hymns, which are very modest representa-

---

[1] Cf. H. F. Muller in *Zeitschrift für romanische Philologie*, xliv (1924), pp. 556 ff.
[2] *Patrologia Latina*, civ. 338.   [3] Ibid. cv. 1274.

tives of it—hymnody was limited to the syllabic adaptation of words to melismata. We must remember, however, that in the West, more than in the East, the ecclesiastical authorities were suspicious, for reasons of dogma, of new poetical texts,[1] and for that reason the new creative movement could enter the Church only in the form of musical interpolations; the poetry fitted to these interpolations was governed by a strict relationship to the liturgical texts, which for the most part were biblical, so that nothing comparable to Eastern hymnody was ever achieved. There were also considerations of language: Latin was not a national language in the West, as Greek or Syrian was in the East.

Since it was the rule that the text added to a melisma must be syllabic, it could not be metrical or in any regular rhythm: a group of syllables forming one or more words had to fit a group of notes forming a musical phrase. The author's task was no easier than if he had to conform to some regular rhythm. Rhyme, of course, was not yet used, but assonance was employed, not only at the end of a phrase but also in the middle.[2]

The question is, when the interpolated melodies first appeared in this new form, with a text adapted to the notes. H. F. Muller[3] thinks that Agobard was alluding to tropes of this kind. But the examples he has in mind are Responsories and Antiphons where the text, though not biblical, is liturgical, since it forms part of the antiphonary. The earliest reliable evidence we have of the adaptation of new texts to melismata concerns the sequence, i.e. the addition to the Alleluia. The famous treatise known as *Musica Enchiriadis*[4] quotes the beginning of a sequence of an archaic type as an example of organum (see p. 278), i.e. the melody is used as the *vox principalis*, to which a *vox organalis* is added; and in one of the manuscripts containing this treatise the whole sequence is included.[5] Further evidence is provided by Hucbald (d. 930), a monk of St. Amand (see p. 276), who in his treatise *De harmonica institutione*[6] mentions a sequence of the normal type. This brings us to the celebrated *proœmium* of Notker of St. Gall, who, like Hucbald, was born *c.* 840 and died in 912. This

[1] Cf. H. F. Muller, loc. cit.
[2] Cf. *Philologus*, lxxxvi (1930), pp. 62–67.
[3] Op. cit., p. 560.
[4] M. Gerbert, *Scriptores Ecclesiastici de Musica* (1784), i, pp. 152–73.
[5] Cf. *Zeitschrift für Musikwissenschaft*, xii (1929–30), p. 11. For the possibility that Johannes Scotus Eriugena refers to *Musica Enchiriadis* in 867 see *Deutsche Vierteljahrsschrift für Literaturwissenschaft und Geistesgeschichte*, v (1927), p. 321, and J. Handschin, *Musikgeschichte im Überblick* (1948), pp. 153–5. Cf., however, *infra*, p. 273.
[6] Gerbert, op. cit., i, p. 113; cf. *Zeitschrift für Musikwissenschaft*, xiii (1930–1), pp. 116–17.

proœmium, written in 884 or 885, is properly the preface to Notker's collection of sequences.[1]

The story which Notker tells is as follows. When he was a young man he had to take part in singing the 'longissimae melodiae' (the continuation shows that Alleluia melodies are referred to), but it was difficult for him to fix these melodies in his memory. Then a monk from the monastery of Jumièges, recently laid waste by the Normans, came to St. Gall with an antiphonary in which (probably in the appendix) some 'verses' were put below the *sequentiae*. Notker was delighted with the idea, but not with its execution; dissatisfied with the quality of the poetry, he began to write his own. (The destruction of Jumièges, we may note, is dated by historians as 862 or 851.) The authenticity of this document has been much disputed, both by those who claim Notker as the inventor of the sequence and by those who assign him an insignificant role in its history. There is, however, no reason to doubt its veracity, all the more since it makes no extravagant claims for its author.[2] We may therefore assume that from the middle of the ninth century sequences, and perhaps tropes as well, were known in both forms—with and without words.

HISTORICAL POSITION OF THE TROPE AND THE SEQUENCE

As we have seen, the music which was the foundation of this new art was already finding its way into the liturgy in the time of Amalar. Since music was highly valued at this period, we must suppose that this type of music was in accordance with the taste of the times. It was an independent music, not subject to the rule of words. That is equally true of the melismatic additions to Ambrosian and Gallican chant, so far as we have been able to observe them. Yet a comparison of the old and the new reveals certain differences of style: the new melodies are more vivid, less ornamental, and sometimes remarkably impressive. As early as Amalar we have evidence of music which was self-contained; and Agobard, speaking of the danger that such music would swamp the liturgy, quotes passages from St. Jerome directed against 'theatrical art'.[3] We must therefore conclude that the influx came largely from the secular music of the period, which would other-

[1] Cf. W. von den Steinen, *Notker der Dichter* (Berne, 1948), i, pp. 154–63, 504–7; ii, pp. 8–11.

[2] For a résumé of my arguments for accepting it as genuine see *Zeitschrift für Musikwissenschaft*, xii (1929–30), p. 12. Cf. also the decree of the Council of Cloveshoe in 747, which prescribed that the priests ought not to sing in the manner of secular poets and tragedians but must restrict themselves to the simple ecclesiastical melody, to biblical texts, and to the Roman use (A. W. Haddan and W. Stubbs, *Councils and Ecclesiastical Documents*, iii (1871), pp. 366–8). [3] *Patrologia Latina*, civ. 334–5.

wise have left no traces—or perhaps it would be more correct to say that the church musicians worked on the same lines as their secular colleagues. In the field of secular music instrumental music played a large part; and with this the music of sequences and tropes must have had at least some affinity. It is significant that a chronicler of St. Gall tells us that Tuotilo, Notker's contemporary, invented the melodies of his tropes on the *rotta* (a passage which has been wrongly interpreted as implying instrumental accompaniment); and we know how strong were the links between the medieval sequence and the secular *lai* and the instrumental *estampie* (see pp. 248–9).

It is impossible here to discuss all these questions in detail—the relation between the old melismata and the new melodies, the possibility of the survival of remnants of Ambrosian and Gallican interpolations, the extent to which the old melismata were inspired by secular music, and the question whether there was a continuous tradition of instrumental music from the ancient world right down to the Carolingian age.[1] Mention must be made, however, of the theory that the sequence was nothing but the pre-Gregorian Alleluia, 'curtailed' by Gregory I at the end of the sixth century and now restored. In actual fact the word 'amputavimus' used by Gregory in his letter to John, Bishop of Syracuse, refers not to the melodies but to the liturgical use of the Alleluia.[2] In spite of this a connexion must have existed between the sequence and the pre-Carolingian melisma.

A further question is the relation between the tropes and the Gregorian chant to which they were attached. This relationship was governed by the law of melodic 'harmony', or appropriate succession; but it would need a special investigation to make clear in detail exactly how this 'harmony' was realized in practice. To summarize, we may say that the relation of a trope to the Gregorian chant may vary between two extremes: in one case the interpolated material is so nearly related that it gives the impression of being a variation on the Gregorian chant; in the other, which seems to be more typical, the material is independent, but its beginning and ending are adapted to the Gregorian melody (cf. p. 135). Once the trope and sequence appeared with texts, the possibility of transferring a trope to a different Gregorian chant disappeared, and every trope was attached to a definite melody; only the sequence preserved a large measure of freedom in its association with the Alleluia verse.

[1] For a reference in Martianus Capella, which seems to point to the *estampie* form, see *Zeitschrift für Musikwissenschaft*, xii (1929–30), p. 6, and *Philologus*, lxxxvi (1930), p. 61.
[2] Cf., among others, A. Gastoué, *Les Origines du chant romain* (1907), p. 103, and E. Wellesz, *Eastern Elements in Western Chant* (Boston, 1947), pp. 175–85.

As this interpolated material is now more distinct from the strictly liturgical, its position in the liturgy is more clearly defined: it is an embellishment tolerated but not prescribed by the Church—a compromise between ecclesiastical law and creative freedom which was unnecessary in the Eastern Church. Since it was not obligatory, the repertory could differ in different countries: there is, in fact, a clear distinction between the French (or West Frankish) and the German (or East Frankish) repertory of sequences and tropes. There is also a further variety resulting from the resources available, which would naturally be more abundant in a cathedral or large monastery than in a smaller church.

The literary history of the tropes, though it presents interesting problems, also lies outside the scope of this chapter. It is mainly the relation of this new Latin poetry to Eastern hymnody which has aroused discussion. It is hardly possible that the former should have been largely dependent upon the latter: for the earliest sequence-writers, if acquainted with Greek, were primarily Latins. Yet the literary content of this Latin poetry does reveal the influence of Greek hymnody, and this is scarcely surprising, since the East was far ahead of the West in theological studies and many of the hymns of the Eastern Church are remarkably profound. The theological writings of the East from which these ideas were borrowed were to a large extent translated into Latin. The Latin poets, in spite of their ignorance of Greek, were also fond of using Greek words as representing a superior world of ideas, and in consequence it is not unusual to find Greek words occurring in the texts of tropes and sequences.

In trying to determine the 'origins' of the sequence and trope, we must distinguish between the musical and the literary side of the problem. The former seems to be more important than the latter, since the terms 'trope' and 'sequence' belong equally, as we have seen, to the melismatic and the textual forms of these liturgical interpolations. Another distinction depends on whether we have in view predecessors of the trope and sequence in the field of ecclesiastical chant, or in that of secular song, or of instrumental music. The first are predecessors in a more direct way than the rest, and therefore special attention has been paid to them above. As to instrumental music, reference has already been made to Martianus Capella (see note 1 on previous page) who seems to know of a parallel to the *estampie*—the instrumental form which was, like the sequence, constructed according to the principal of binary repetition but distinguished the sections forming a pair by different endings.

We must also, however, glance at the field of secular song. There are two pieces of evidence which have sometimes been quoted by historians of literature but are also relevant here. One is that of the Byzantine historian Priscus who, when at the court of Attila (d. 453), saw 'two barbarians' reciting 'composed songs'.[1] The other is supplied by the Anglo-Saxon poem *Widsith*, from the late seventh century, in which we are told that the author with a companion sang to the harp in the presence of their chief.[2] If we ask what was the poetic and musical form of these songs, it is difficult to avoid the assumption that they were performed alternately by both singers and, therefore, probably subjected to the scheme of 'progressive binary repetition'. Thus the history of the *lai* may extend back to the epoch of the great European migrations. There is further evidence of a form of old Irish poetry which was not strophic but governed by binary correspondence and called 'rhetoric';[3] in this case also it seems likely that there was not only poetic but melodic correspondence, although there is no question of alternation of singers. With this we have to compare the *Hisperica famina*, compiled in Latin by Irish rhetoricians in the sixth or seventh century, in which every line is divided into two corresponding sections.[4]

Turning back to the ecclesiastical sphere, we have to mention the *Oratio Moucani* contained in an eighth-century manuscript from the north of England.[5] This poem has been analysed by the great latinist W. Meyer in his posthumous materials preserved in the University Library at Göttingen, from which it appears that it is composed of pairs of lines (or verses), each pair being characterized by assonance

---

[1] Cf. *Historici graeci minores*, ed. Dindorf, i, p. 317.

[2] See the edition by K. Malone (1936), pp. 87–88.

[3] See E. Windisch in *Revue celtique*, v (1881–3), pp. 389 and 478, and his *Kurzgefasste irische Grammatik* (1879), p. 120. According to R. Thurneysen, *Die irische Helden- und Königssage* (1921), pp. 18 and 54 ff., this form is mainly applied to verse sections inserted into old prose legends.

[4] See the edition by F. J. H. Jenkinson (1908). The principle of this correspondence seems rather artificial: the first half of the line ends with the adjective belonging to the substantive situated at the close of the second half, and often there is still another adjective in the first half which belongs to a substantive in the second half, which produces a double assonance, e.g.:

Aligera placoreum / reboat curia concentum.

It is true that the equality of syllable numbers is not observed and we may doubt whether this literature was meant to be sung. Yet there may have existed parallels to this poetry, which were intended to be sung. Cambridge, Gonville and Caius College, MS. 418, from the thirteenth or fourteenth century, contains, among grammatical treatises and conductus-like poetry, some poems which are similar to the *Hisperica famina* in their strange phraseology, if not in their construction, and which may have been sung (fo. 114ᵛ: 'O barridae bardae', fo. 115: 'O paraphonistae almiphoni').

[5] Brit. Mus., Royal 2 A XX, fo. 42 ff.

and approximate equality of the number of syllables. This was probably intended to be sung. The fact that the whole poem consists of
nine larger sections, and that within these there appear some references
to the biblical canticles, seem to point to the influence of the Byzantine *kanon* (see p. 23). There is also the biography of St. Caesarius
(470–542), bishop of Arles, in which the term 'prose' is already
applied to a category of song. According to his biographer Caesarius
compelled the people to pray ('oraret'—or possibly 'pararet', i.e. 'to
prepare') psalms and hymns, and he induced them to sing with high
and melodious voice, in the manner of clergymen, proses and antiphons, alternately in Greek and in Latin.[1] If 'prose' is here meant
to be something distinct from 'antiphon', it can refer only to religious
poetry, and the alternation of Greek and (equivalent) Latin phrases
probably involved binary repetition.

Finally, the eminent Anglo-Saxon scholar and bishop Aldhelm
(d. 709) may be mentioned. According to William of Malmesbury[2]
he was skilled in the art of native poetry and song and put this to a
spiritual use: since the uncivilized people hurried home at once after
the Mass, he awaited them on their way back, singing like a native
singer (probably with the harp) and, by inserting sacred words into
his song, not only won their favour but induced them to piety. This
may have been some kind of Anglo-Saxon trope or paraphrase,
related to a liturgical text.

EARLY SOURCES

One or two examples may be given of the earliest sources in which
we find either the melodies alone, or the melodies with text, or the
text by itself. First there is the manuscript Autun 24 (28), which,
though its principal contents are not musical, includes on fo. 64 some
added melodic material connected with the Alleluia: (1) the Alleluia
verse 'Ego sum pastor'; (2) an Alleluia with a melisma which is the
sequence melody known as 'De profundis'; (3) another with the rubric
'Ostende', corresponding to the melody known as 'Ostende minor';
(4) another with the rubric 'Fulgida', very similar to the melody
known as 'Dulce lignum'; (5) another with the rubric 'Hieronyma',
occurring also in other sources as 'Frigdola'; (6) another with the
rubric 'Sirena', occurring elsewhere as 'Mater' or 'Musa'. On
palaeographical grounds these entries must be assigned to the ninth

[1] Quoted by M. Gerbert, *De cantu et musica sacra*, i (1774), p. 39. It is true that Gerbert
(p. 340) thinks that this has nothing to do with the prose of later times, but that is a little
exaggerated.
[2] *De gestis pontificum Anglorum*, ed. N. E. S. A. Hamilton (London, 1870), p. 336.

century. It is interesting to note that at this early stage the melodies
already have names, and that these names, which may vary, have a
secular flavour; it is therefore wrong to assume that the practice of
giving names to melodies dates from Notker's collection.

Another interesting source—the Antiphonary of Charles the Bald
(840–77)—has been described, rather casually, by Gastoué.[1] It is a
manuscript containing the chants of the Mass as well as those of the
Office, but without musical notation. Some pages which had been
left blank were used in the tenth century for writing in sequences.
These appear in three different forms: (1) on fo. 24 there is the end of
a sequence written normally, with neums above the text; (2) on fo.
29–30 there are others represented only by melismata; (3) in the same
place there is also a third form which at first sight appears strange
but occurs also elsewhere, e.g. at Winchester: only certain parts of
the melody are provided with text, and as these sections of text are
common to different sequence texts set to the same melody, we may
regard them as a nucleus of sequence poetry.[2]

The manuscript Paris, Bibl. Nat. lat. 1154, written in the ninth
century at St. Martial at Limoges, contains on fo. 142^v–3 as a later
addition (though possibly still ninth century) the St. Martial sequence
'Concelebremus'.[3] The manuscript Munich clm. 14843, to which
attention has been drawn by *Analecta Hymnica*, comes from Toul
in eastern France and was written in the ninth century; although it
has no neums, it is important in that it contains not only sequences
but tropes to the Introit, *Communio*, and *Gloria*, and also proses to
the 'Gregorian' Alleluia (cf. p. 129).

Manuscripts from the German-speaking region, on the other hand,
seem to be not earlier than the tenth century, the oldest of them being
apparently Vienna 1609 (probably from St. Gall) and British Museum
Add. 19768 (from Mainz). As is well known, the monastery of St.
Gall was particularly prominent in the East Frankish region:[4] the
chapter library still preserves a large number of beautifully written
manuscripts, including sequences and tropes, dating from the tenth
and eleventh centuries.

The Aquitanian manuscripts are noted in diastematic or 'heighted'

[1] *Le Graduel et l'Antiphonaire romains* (1913), pp. 105 ff.
[2] Texts of this kind are printed in *Analecta Hymnica Medii Aevi*, xlix (1906), nos.
515–30. There is, however, no justification for the editor's applying to them the term
'versus ad sequentias', borrowed from Notker's *proœmium*.
[3] Cf. *Zeitschrift für Musikwissenschaft*, xiii (1930–1), pp. 122–3. For a discussion of
two sequences of an archaic type preserved in the same manuscript (fo. 129^v and 130^v),
but without musical notation, v. loc. cit., pp. 113 ff.
[4] Cf. *Schweizerische Musikzeitung* (1945), pp. 243 ff.

neums, but this is not the case with the St. Gall manuscripts and those from the German-speaking region in general. The use of an approximate notation does not mean, as has sometimes been supposed, that the singers sang only approximate intervals; but it does mean that the Aquitanian manuscripts are more useful for the purpose of study. One interesting detail is that the texts of sequence melodies often have the neums not above the words but added in the margin.

The art of sequences and tropes spread relatively early to England and Spain, while Italy is represented by a manuscript (without neums) written probably as early as the end of the ninth century (Verona 90). None of these countries, however, produced in this field such a large and characteristic repertory as the West Frankish region, represented mainly by St. Martial at Limoges, and the East Frankish, represented mainly by St. Gall. In England the main centre where this art was cultivated seems to have been Winchester—the source of two tropers of the eleventh century (Cambridge, Corpus Christi College, 473, and Oxford, Bodleian, Bodley 775),[1] the former of which is also a monument of early polyphony (see p. 280). It appears that this art was brought to England from Northern France,[2] though tropes and sequences may have had some remote predecessors in England and elsewhere, as we have seen.

AN EXAMPLE OF THE SEQUENCE

As an example of a sequence melody we may take one which is preserved both at St. Gall and also at St. Martial, though with variants in the melody and a different text; in the St. Gall repertory the text is 'Hanc concordi', for St. Stephen (probably by Notker himself), at St. Martial it is 'Epiphaniam domino', for Epiphany:

Ex. 48 [3]

[Measured]

8 I Hanc con - cor - di   fa-mu-la - tu   co - la - mus sol-lem-ni - ta - tem

8 II (a) Auc - to - ris il - li - us   e - xem-plo doc - ti be - ni - gno
  (b) Pro per - se - cu-to - rum   pre - can - tis frau - de su - o - rum.

[1] See W. H. Frere, *The Winchester Troper* (1894).
[2] For a full discussion see *The Journal of Theological Studies*, xxxvii (1936), pp. 34 ff., 156 ff.
[3] The melody is based on the version given by C. A. Moberg, *Über die schwedischen Sequenzen* (Upsala, 1927), nos. 15b and 15a—a version established with the help of

III (a) O Ste-pha-ne, sig-ni-fer re-gis summe bo-ni, nos e-xau-di,
(b) Pro-fi-cu-e qui es pro tu-is e-xau-di-tus i-ni-mi-cis.

IV (a) Paulus tu-is pre-ci-bus, Ste-pha-ne, te quondam perse-cu-tus Christo cre-dit
(b) Et tecum tri-pu-di-at in re-gno, cui nul-lus perse-cu-tor ap-pro-pin-quat.

V (a) Nos pro-in-de, nos supplices ad te claman-tes et pre-ci-bus te pulsan-tes,
(b) O-ra-ti-o san-ctis-si-ma nos tu-a semper con-ci-li-et De-o nos-tro.

VI (a) Te Petrus Christi mi-nistrum statu-it, tu Pe-tro normam credendi astru-is,
(b) Te si-bi Christus de-le-git, Stephane, per quem fi-de-les su-os cor-ro-bo-ret,

ad dex-tram sum-mi pa-tris os-ten-den-do, quem plebs furens cru-ci-fi-xit.
se ti-bi in-ter ro-ta-tus sax-o-rum so-la-ti-o ma-ni-fes-tans.

VII Nunc in-ter in-cli-tas mar-ty-rum pur-pu-ras co-ru-scas co-ro-na-tus.

* The manuscripts with staff notation have *c* instead of *b*.

(I. Let us in united service celebrate this holy day,

II. Taught by the propitious example of the first martyr, who prayed for the wickedness of his persecutors.

III. O Stephen, standard-bearer of the King most high, hearken to us, thou our benefactor, whose prayers for thy enemies were granted.

IV. Through thy prayers, Stephen, Paul who once persecuted thee believes in Christ and with thee exults in the kingdom, to which no persecutor can come nigh.

V. So may we, thy suppliants, crying to thee and imploring thee in our prayers, always be reconciled to God through thy most holy petition.

VI. Peter made thee the servant of Christ, thou dost offer Peter the pattern of faith, by showing at the right hand of the Father him whom the raging mob did

several manuscripts with staff notation. The modifications introduced here are derived from a study of the following sources:

(1) 'Hanc concordi': St. Gall 376, p. 323; 378, p. 161; 380, p. 130; 381, p. 342; 382, p. 98; 484, p. 259 (melody without text). With these have been compared St. Gall 376, p. 379; 378, p. 239; 380, p. 199; 381, 435; 382, p. 152. The last of these has another St. Gall sequence with the same melody, 'Petre summe'. For the text of 'Hanc concordi' see *Analecta Hymnica*, liii, p. 345, of 'Petre summe', ibid., p. 336.

(2) 'Epiphaniam domino': Paris, Bibl. Nat. lat. 1118, fos. 165–6 (with text) and fo. 134ᵛ (melody only). Text in *Analecta Hymnica*, liii, p. 47.

For a discussion of the relation between the two versions see *Zeitschrift für Musikwissenschaft*, xvii (1934–5), p. 247. 'Hanc concordi' has been previously published in *Schweizer Musikbuch* (1939), pp. 49–50.

crucify. Christ chose thee, Stephen, to strengthen his faithful servants, showing himself to thee as a consolation amid the whirling of the stones.

VII. Now crowned thou dost shine in glory among the noble army of martyrs.)

Ex. 49

[Measured]

I E - pi - pha - ni - am Do - mi - no ca - na - mus glo - ri - o - sam,

qua pro-lem De - i ve - re ma - gi a - do - rant; II (a) Im - men - sam

Chal-dæ - i cui - us Per - sæ - que ve - ne - ran - tur po - ten - ti - am,

(b) Quem cunc - ti pro - phe - tæ præ - ci - ne - re ven - tu - rum gen - tes

ad sal - van - das. III (a) Cu - jus ma - jes - tas i - ta est in - cli - na - ta,

ut as - su - me - ret ser - vi for - mam, (b) An - te sæ - cu - la qui

De - us et tem - po - ra, ho - mo fa - ctus est in Ma - ri - a.

IV (a) Ba - la - am de quo va - ti - ci - nans, e - xi - bit ex Ja - cob

ru - ti - lans, in-quit, stel - la, (b) Et con-frin-get du - cum ag - mi - na

re - gi - o - nis Mo - ab max - i - ma po - ten - ti - a.

V (a) Hu - ic ma - gi mu - ne - ra de - fe - runt præ - cla - ra: au - rum,

si - mul thus et myrrh - am; (b) Thu - re De - um præ - di - cant, au - ro

Ex. 49 contd.

re - gem mag - num, ho-mi-nem mor - ta-lem myrrh-a. VI (a) In som-nis

hos mo-net an-ge-lus, ne re-de-ant ad re-gem com-mo-tum

propter reg - na. (b) Pa - ve-bat e - te-nim ni-mi-um re - gem na-tum,

ve-rens a - mit-te-re regni ju - ra. VII (a) Ma-gi stel-la si - bi mi-can-te

præ-vi - a per-gunt a - la-cres i - ti - ne-ra, pa-tri-am

quæ e-os du-ce-bat ad pro-pri-am, lin-quen-tes He-ro-dis man-da-ta;

(b) Qui per-cul-sus cor-de ni-mi-a præ i - ra ex-tem - plo mandat

e - lu-di-a ma-gi-ca non lin-qui ta-li-ter im-pu-ni-ta, sed mox

pri-va-ri e-os vi - ta. VIII (a) Omnis nunc ca-ter - va tin-nu-lum jun-gat

lau-di-bus or - ga-ni neu-ma, (b) My - sti-ce of-fer-ens re-gi re-gum,

Chri - sto, mu - ne - ra pre-ti - o - sa, IX Po-scens, ut per or - bem

re-gna om-ni - a pro - te-gat in sæc-[u] - la sem-pi - ter - na.

(I. Let us sing to the Lord his glorious Epiphany, at which time the wise men truly adore the offspring of God;

II. Whose measureless power the Chaldeans and Persians worship, whom all the prophets foretold would come to save the Gentiles.

III. He so abased his majesty that he took upon him the form of a servant; he who before all ages was God became man in Mary's womb.

IV. Balaam, prophesying of him, said: 'From Jacob there shall come forth a blazing star and shall break the armies of the leaders of the kingdom of Moab by its mighty power.'

V. To him the wise men offer precious gifts: gold, incense, and myrrh; by incense they signify God, by gold the great King, by myrrh the man of mortal flesh.

VI. In dreams an angel warns them not to return to the king, who fears for his kingdom. For he was terrified that a great king had been born, fearing to lose his royal jurisdiction.

VII. The wise men quickly set forth on their journey, the star shining before them, which led them to their own country; they paid no heed to Herod's commands. He, smitten to the heart, in his great anger straightway ordains that the wise men's trickery should not remain unpunished, but that they shall presently die.

VIII. Now let the whole assembly sing praise to the ringing melody of the organ, offering to Christ, the King of kings, precious gifts with mystic meaning,

IX. Asking that he shall protect all the nations of the earth for ever and ever.)

It is known that the initial and final sections of the sequence, i.e. those which lie outside the series of twofold repetitions, were sung by the whole choir, while the rest was sung by each half of the choir alternately. The rhythm given here appears to be indicated in the manuscripts, though this is obviously too complicated a question to be discussed in detail here. It is, however, interesting to note that the differentiation of longs and shorts disappears in later manuscripts. It may very well lie at the very root of the sequence and trope, as it appears in old manuscripts from St. Martial as well as from St. Gall; the practice has even been extended to Gregorian chant in manuscripts from these monasteries and elsewhere.[1]

MUSIC AND TEXT

Before we leave the older type of sequence we must consider for a moment the relation between text and melody. As a general rule there is no doubt of the priority of the melody, but this did not prevent the poet from expanding or compressing it, or modifying its structure, in the interests of his text. A poet working under these conditions was bound, in fact, to possess musical feeling and judgement—a require-

[1] Two observations, however, must be made concerning this puzzling subject: (1) we cannot claim *a priori* that all the versions of one melody must have the same rhythm; (2) as far as text rhythm is concerned, two tendencies seem to be involved and even to conflict with each other, one to connect the long note with the word accent and the other, to set it to the final syllable of the word. The distinction of longs and shorts is, of course, not always quite clear; and it is indicated by different means in the St. Gall and the Aquitanian manuscripts.

ment which was hardly a limitation at a time when music and singing
played such an important part in general education. There are, however, some sequence texts which are largely metrical, in which case it
is improbable that the melody existed before the words; the examples
are mainly sequences of the 'archaic' type mentioned on p. 153, n. 3.[1]

The strict connexion that existed between a trope and a particular
Gregorian chant has been mentioned. It is remarkable, however, that
some remnants of the older practice of transferring a single trope
melody to different chants survived late into the Middle Ages, at a
time when the normal evolution of trope and sequence had followed
new paths and was already in decline, owing to the overwhelming
pressure of polyphony. An example is the manuscript Laon 263,
probably dating from the late twelfth century. As we have seen
(p. 145), the triple melisma which, according to Amalar, belonged to
the Responsory 'In medio' and was transferred to 'Descendit', is
found in this manuscript in connexion with 'In medio' but also with
'Centum quadraginta', and where it is associated with 'In medio'
the third melisma has the enigmatic rubric 'Qui septem'. The same
manuscript also provides evidence of the transference of melismata
from Alleluias to Responsories—a practice which recalls Ambrosian
usage (see p. 133). On fo. 93ᵛ, for example, there is a long melisma
added to the Responsory 'Lapides torrentes', for St. Stephen, and
this is to a large extent identical with a sequence melody; it bears the
rubric 'Angelica', an alternative name for a melody which is more
often known as 'Romana'. On fo. 94ᵛ there is a melisma belonging
to another Responsory for St. Stephen, 'Patefactae sunt', which has
the rubric 'Gloriosa'. It is in fact the melody of the sequence 'Gloriosa
adest dies';[2] it is followed by a *prosula* of normal length, probably as
an alternative.[3]

We find survivals of the old practice even later.[4] An early fourteenth-
century treatise entitled *Speculum musicae*, by Jacobus of Liége, quotes
eight melismata, one for each church tone and each one sung to the
word 'Amen'.[5] We are told[6] that they might be sung at great feasts
or whenever the choir liked to extend their singing, either at the end

---

[1] Cf. *Zeitschrift für Musikwissenschaft*, xiii (1930–1), p. 115 (to which should be added
that not only the beginning is metrical).

[2] *Analecta Hymnica*, vii, p. 213.

[3] This remarkable manuscript also contains on fo. 57ᵛ the sequence 'Petre summe'
(otherwise almost exclusively preserved in Italian and German manuscripts) with the
title 'Pictarica' (i.e. from Poitiers or Poitou).

[4] Cf. P. Wagner, *Einführung in die gregorianischen Melodien*, iii (1921), pp. 345 ff.

[5] C. E. H. de Coussemaker, *Scriptorum de musica medii aevi nova series* (Paris,
1864–76), ii, pp. 339, 342, 347, 351, 354, 357, 362, 365.   [6] Ibid., p. 339.

of an Antiphon or a Responsory (probably the proper place) or a sequence. The melodies do not appear to be very old; but the practice they represent is very ancient. Some scholars have cited as further instances melodic formulas like 'Noeoane'[1]—mnemonics intended to illustrate the qualities of the individual modes—and particularly the modes as exhibited in the melodies of antiphons. It is true that these formulas were sometimes sung as an addition to the Antiphon; but they were in reality simply illustrations of the mode, and they may even have been historically the predecessors of the Antiphon. For there is evidence to suggest that, before the Antiphon as we know it existed, melismatic formulas characteristic of the given mode were sung in connexion with verses of the psalms. Cassian, writing about 420, refers to psalms 'prolonged by the melodies of antiphons',[2] though in another passage[3] he uses the word 'antiphon' as the equivalent of the Greek ἀντίφωνον, which is also not what we mean by Antiphon. In an anonymous story told of the abbot Silvanus there is a question of singing psalms with or without echoi, a word which properly signifies 'mode' but must probably be taken here to indicate a melody (or melisma) characteristic of a mode.[4] In another story referring to the abbot Pambo[5] the singing of echoi is censured as a characteristic of a luxurious way of performing the Office—probably the psalmody is meant.[6]

CHANGES OF STYLE

Among the five sequences[7] which survived the general prohibition decreed by the Council of Trent, and are still included in the service books of the Roman church, is the famous 'Victimae paschali'. It dates from the first half of the eleventh century and represents the transition between the style previously discussed and that associated with the name of Adam de St. Victor. Both words and music are too well known to need reproduction.[8] The characteristics of this transi-

[1] Cf. Wagner, op. cit. iii (1921), pp. 320–1, and P. Lucas Kunz, 'Ursprung und textliche Bedeutung der Tonartsilbe Noeane, Noeagis', in *Kirchenmusikalisches Jahrbuch*, xxx (1935), pp. 5–22.

[2] *De Coenobiorum Institutis*, ii, p. 2.   [3] Ibid. ii, p. 8.

[4] Silvanus lived in the fourth century, but the date of the story is not known. J. Quasten, followed by E. Werner, has erroneously taken it as part of a Syrian text written *c*. 515.

[5] Gerbert, *Scriptores Ecclesiastici de Musica*, i, pp. 2–4.

[6] Pambo lived in the fourth century, but here again the date of the story appears to be unknown.

[7] Including the 'Stabat Mater', which was not readmitted until the eighteenth century.

[8] For a full discussion see J. Handschin, 'Gesungene Apologetik', in *Miscellanea liturgica in honorem L. C. Mohlberg = Bibliotheca Ephemerides liturgicae*, xxiii (1949), pp. 75 ff.

tional style will be seen presently. We may, however, mention here that the priority of melody over text is no longer so common as it was in the preceding period; indeed, in many cases melody and text were the work of the same person and came to birth simultaneously.

The new style became definitely established in the late eleventh century. So far as the text is concerned, the distinguishing characteristics have been defined in *Analecta Hymnica*. The words are in regular verse form: there is a marked tendency to alternate accented and unaccented syllables, as well as to equalize the length of the lines, and the ends of the lines are distinguished by rhyme. We now have rhythmical poetry in the modern sense, with the rhythm determined by accent, in contrast to classical poetry governed by the quantity of the syllables—a form which by this time had become an artificial literary exercise. The verse, or strophe, assumes a more regular shape, the typical form consisting of two sets of three lines each. As in the old sequence, the two halves of the verse correspond to each other both in regard to the structure of the text and in melody. The verses do not differ so widely as in the old sequence, and often verses of similar construction follow each other. But the essential feature of sequence form is preserved, since the consecutive verses have different melodies, each composed of two analogous halves, and hence the musical form is not strophic.

It has been suggested that this new form is due to the influence of the hymn. But apart from the fact that the hymn is entirely strophic, its favourite rhythm is iambic, whereas the new sequence is trochaic. In fact the trochaic line of fifteen syllables ($-\cup-\cup-\cup-\cup\,|-\cup-\cup-\cup-$) may be regarded as the ancestor of the rhythm of the new sequence. The first half of this line may be doubled, giving three shorter lines (8+8+7, the typical form of one-half of the verse) or tripled (8+8+8+7), and so on. This fifteen-syllable trochaic rhythm had been used formerly in the type of songs called 'rhythms', i.e. pieces of sacred or secular character which had no place in the liturgy.[1] In the transitional type of sequence, as illustrated by 'Victimae paschali', we find either rhyme or the tendency to regular verse form, or even elements of both.

The new style is also reflected in the music, though here the change is not so easy to define. In general the melodies are more 'trivial' in character than the older ones: they often approach to some extent what is commonly termed 'major tonality' but is more properly

---

[1] A collection of ancient 'rhythms' is in the St. Martial manuscript Paris, Bibl. Nat. lat. 1154, mentioned on p. 153.

described as the *c* mode. Sometimes we have a succession of two thirds which conveys the suggestion of a common chord; melodic 'sequences' (in the modern sense) appear; and the rule by which each note of the melody has only one syllable is no longer strictly observed. By this time it was clearly not a question of writing a text for a pre-existent melody: indeed, sequences of this type were not sung as melismata, i.e. without words. The melodies were composed with a particular text in view—or at least a particular structure; but they may still have been related in idiom to the instrumental music of the period. The following example of the new type of sequence was probably composed by Adam of St. Victor, who lived in the first half of the twelfth century and was, if not the first, the outstanding representative of this style:

Ex. 50[1]

[1] After E. Misset and P. Aubry, *Les Proses d'Adam de St. Victor* (Paris, 1900), p. 302. The transcription is, of course, not measured.

ro - sa pa - ti - en - ti - æ, nar - dus o - do - ri - fe - ra.
sin - gu - la - re li - li - um, Chri - stus ex te pro - di - it.

V (a) Tu cæ - les - tis pa - ra - di - sus, Li - ba - nus - que non in - ci - sus,
(b) Tu es thro - nus Sa - lo - mo - nis, cu - i nul - lus par in thro - nis

va - po - rans dul - ce - di - nem; tu can - do - ris et de - co - ris,
ar - te vel ma - te - ri - a; e - bur can - dens ca - sti - ta - tis,

tu dul - co - ris et o - do - ris ha - bes ple - ni - tu - di - nem.
au - rum ful - vum ca - ri - ta - tis præ - si - gnant my - ste - ri - a.

VI Pal - mam præ - fers sin - gu - la - rem, nec in ter - ris ha - bens pa - rem,

nec in cæ - li cu - ri - a; laus hu - ma - ni ge - ne - ris,

vir - tu - tum præ ce - te - ris ha - bes pri - vi - le - gi - a.

VII (a) Sol lu - na lu - ci - di - or et lu - na si - de - ri - bus:
(b) Lux e - clip - sim ne - sci - ens vir - gi - nis est ca - sti - tas,

sic Ma - ri - a di - gni - or cre - a - tu - ris om - ni - bus;
ar - dor in - de - fi - ci - ens im - mor - ta - lis ca - ri - tas.

VIII (a) Sal - ve, ma - ter pi - e - ta - tis et to - ti - us tri - ni - ta - tis
(b) Ver - bi ta - men in - car - na - ti spe - ci - a - le ma - jes - ta - ti

no - bi - le tri - cli - ni - um, IX (a) O Ma - ri - a, stel - la ma - ris,
præ - pa - rans hos - pi - ti - um. (b) In su - pre - mo si - ta po - li,

di - gni - ta - te sin - gu - la - ris, su - per om - nes or - di - na - ris
nos com - men - da tu - æ pro - li, ne ter - ro - res si - ve do - li

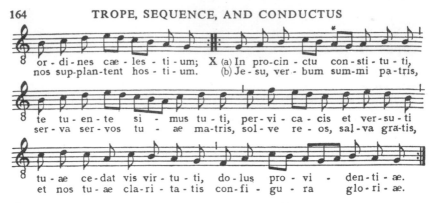

or - di - nes cae - les - ti - um; X (a) In pro-cin - ctu con - sti - tu - ti,
nos sup-plan-tent hos - ti - um.   (b) Je - su, ver - bum sum-mi pa-tris,

te tu - en - te si - mus tu - ti, per-vi - ca - cis et ver-su - ti
ser - va ser - vos tu - ae ma-tris, sol - ve re - os, sal -va gra-tis,

tu - ae ce - dat vis vir - tu - ti, do - lus pro - vi - den - ti - ae.
et nos tu - ae cla-ri - ta - tis con-fi - gu - ra glo - ri - ae.

*) The second note of this ligature is written as a liquescent note in (a).
**) The second note of this ligature is written as a liquescent note in (b).

(1. Hail, mother of our Saviour, chosen vessel, vessel of honour, vessel of heavenly grace, vessel foreseen from the beginning of time, noble vessel, vessel fashioned by the hand of wisdom!

II. Hail, holy mother of the Word, flower from the thorn, without any thorn, flower that art the glory of the thicket! We who are the thicket, we are stained with blood from the thorn of sin, but thou knowest no thorn.

III. Gate that art closed, spring that waterest the gardens, chamber where rich ointments and fards are preserved, exceeding in fragrance the cinnamon plant, myrrh, incense, and balsam.

IV. Hail, glory of virgins, that restorest life to men, thou that bringest forth salvation, myrtle of temperance, rose of patience, fragrant nard! Thou the lowly valley, the unploughed land that brings forth fruit, the flower of the field, the unmatched lily of the valleys, Christ came forth from thee.

V. Thou the heavenly paradise, the frankincense that knows not the knife, giving forth sweet fragrance; thou hast the fullness of beauty and glory, of sweetness and fair odour. Thou art the throne of Solomon, with which no throne can compare for skill or substance; the bright ivory of chastity, the red gold of charity prefigure mysteries.

VI. Thou alone dost bear the palm, there is none like thee on the earth or in the courts of Heaven; the glory of the human race, thou hast the prize of virtue before all others.

VII. The sun is brighter than the moon, and the moon than the stars; so Mary is more worthy than all creatures. The light that knows no eclipse is the virgin's chastity, the heat that never fails is immortal charity.

VIII. Hail, mother of piety and noble entertainment of the whole Trinity, yet preparing a special guest-chamber for the majesty of the Word incarnate!

IX. O Mary, star of the sea, alone in dignity, first in honour above all the citizens of Heaven; where thou standest at the summit of heavens, commend us to thy Son, that neither the threats nor the guile of our enemies may overthrow us.

X. Standing in battle array, let us be safe under thy protection, let the force of the stubborn and deceitful man yield to thy virtue, his guile to thy providence. Jesu, Word of the heavenly Father, save the servants of thy mother, absolve the guilty, bring free salvation, and fashion us after the brightness of thy glory.)

It will be noticed that the only verses which are not divided into two symmetrical halves are III and VI; but they repeat each other, though they are separated by IV and V.

TROPES OF THE FIRST PERIOD

The sequence, by reason of its extended form and a certain independence which it shows towards the Gregorian Alleluia, is the most remarkable of the tropes; yet it is only one species. We turn now to the trope in its narrower sense, excluding the sequence; and even here there are many subdivisions. One of these, the Responsory trope, inserted at the end of the repetition of the Responsory, is related to the sequence and, like it, can be traced back to the earliest stage of trope composition. Its typical form, like that of the sequence, is governed by progressive repetition—*aa bb cc*, &c.—but it is in general much less extended. Like the sequence the Responsory trope or the *prosula* is an appendix, sung by the choir. The other types of trope are not, as a rule, all in one piece but consist of sections inserted in different places in the plainsong, so that plainsong and trope occur alternately. The musician's task—and the poet's—is therefore more specialized than in the sequence and the Responsory trope: each section of the trope has to harmonize with the plainsong which precedes and follows it. Even so the melodic character of the trope sections may very well be different from that of the Gregorian chant, and the 'harmony' between the two may imply some degree of contrast.

There are two main categories: (1) tropes added to the antiphonal forms of plainsong, chiefly within the Mass—Introits, Communions, and Offertories; some of these are merely introductions; (2) tropes added to parts of the Ordinary of the Mass—*Gloria, Sanctus, Agnus,* and, very rarely, *Credo*. One feature is common to both these categories: the troped plainsong is not intended for a soloist or for responsorial singing but is performed by the choir, and consequently the trope itself is solo music. There is also a special category to be mentioned—the tropes to the Epistle, in which the Bible text is interspersed with a sort of commentary; in this case both the liturgical text and the trope are sung by a soloist.

There is a clear distinction, based on historical principles, between the tropes to antiphonal chants and those for the Ordinary of the Mass. The antiphonal chants were a very ancient part of the Gregorian repertory, and so the tropes were in marked contrast to them; whereas the music of the Ordinary acquired its elaborate form much later—after Gregory I, or even after the diffusion of the Roman chant in the eighth century, when tropes were already in existence. In the latter case, therefore, the plainsong and the trope are very near to each other in time, in fact they may be said to belong to the same stratum. The Ordinary is not represented in the Gregorian antiphonary as propagated in the eighth century, and this may indicate that its melodies were considered to be the province of trained singers. We know that the music of the Ordinary had been sung by all the clergy and even the whole congregation before it became the preserve of the *schola cantorum*. In the Middle Ages the Ordinary had its place as an appendix to the Gradual; it represented a repertory of available melodies, but its position was different from that of the troper, since its texts were obligatory.

The tropes to the *Kyrie*, the 'Ite missa est' and the 'Benedicamus Domino' may also be considered as tropes of the Ordinary. They differ, however, from the other tropes of this class in that there is no simple melodic version to which the tropes can be added; there is only a melodic version which may or may not have the text of a trope, and though the melisma may be repeated in syllabic form with words, or vice versa, there is no question of combining heterogeneous material. There is some resemblance to those proses which are not tropes, though in this case the melisma and the new text are practically contemporary.

Within the two main categories of trope—those for the antiphonal chants and those belonging to the Ordinary—we find that the melismatic form occurs in the earlier period as well as the syllabic; but it disappears more quickly than it does in the case of the sequence. For the sake of completeness mention should also be made of a form which is really a prose without being a trope—the Gregorian melisma provided with a syllabic text. Examples of this are to be found mainly in the Gradual, the Alleluia, and the Offertory; melismata which are treated in this way are found more often in the verse than in the main part of the chant.

Our first example is an Introit trope found in a Nonantola troper of the eleventh century,[1] as well as in other sources.[2] It must be admitted that it is a special type, which foreshadows the tropes of the second period: the introductory section, preceding the first section of the plainsong, is in verse form (the rhythm is iambic as in the Ambrosian hymn); it is unlikely, therefore, that this section uses a pre-existent melody without words—indeed, introductory sections of this kind never occur in melismatic form. The version of this trope in the manuscripts other than the Nonantola troper is longer and may

---

[1] Bologna Univ. 2824, fo. 30.
[2] Vienna 1609, fo. 4ᵛ; St. Gall 484, p. 36; 381, p. 212, &c.

well be the original form; unfortunately the Nonantola troper is the only manuscript written in carefully heighted (diastematic) neums, so that this is the version which must be chosen for reproduction, as far as it goes. The notation in the other manuscripts shows at any rate that they have the same melody as ours; it also differentiates between longs and shorts—more clearly in the later sections of the trope than in the introduction. For this reason a rhythmical interpretation has been given to the later sections, though it must be remembered that the rhythmical interpretation of neums is still debatable. The plainsong sections not found in the manuscript are taken from other sources and are marked with square brackets.

Ex. 51[1]

Di-lec-tus is-te Do-mi-ni Jo-han-nes est a - pos-to-lus,Scriptis cu-jus et
mo-ni-tis Pol-let de-cus ec - cle-si - æ. *In me - di - o·*
ec-cle-si-æ a - pe-ru-it os e - jus, Os tu-um, in-qui-ens, a-pe-ri
me-que ipsum il-lud pro certo sci-as im-ple-re.
Et im-ple - vit e - um Do-mi-nus (etc.)

(John is that beloved apostle of the Lord, by whose writings and counsel the glory of the church prevails. In the midst of the church [the Lord] opened his mouth, saying: 'Open thy mouth, and be sure that I am filling it.' And the Lord filled him . . ., &c.)

The way in which the symmetrical introduction, the decorated psalmody of the Introit and the concise melody of the succeeding section of the trope harmonize with each other is remarkable. In the manuscripts other than the Nonantola troper the sections of the trope, except the introduction, are followed by melismata reproducing the same melody in the same rhythm.[2]

The next example is a *Gloria* trope from the same manuscript:[3]

[1] The small melisma after the word 'ecclesiae' is very indistinct in the manuscript; it may have had a different shape.

[2] The text of the introduction is printed in *Analecta Hymnica*, xlix, p. 32.

[3] Bologna Univ. 2824, fo. 3.

Ex. 52

Glo-ri - a   in ex-cel-sis De - o, Quem ci-ves cæ-les-tes sanctum clamantes

lau-de fre-quen-tant; *Et in ter-ra pax ho- mi- ni-bus bo-næ vo-lun-ta-tis,*

Quam mi - ni-stri Do-mi - ni ver-bo in-car-na-to ter-re-nis promi-se-rant.

Lau-damus te, Lau-di-bus cujus as-tra ma-tu-tî-na in-sistunt. *Be-ne - di-ci-mus te,*

Per quem o-mne sa-crum et be-ne-dic-ti - o con-ce-di-tur at-que au-ge-tur.

A - do - ra-mus te, O - mni - po-tens a-do-ran-de, co-len - de, tre-men - de,

ve-ne-ran-de. *Glo-ri-fi- camus te,* Ut   creatura creantem, plasma plasmantem,

fi-gu-lum figmentum. *Gra-ti-as a-gi-mus ti - [bi propter magnam gloriam tuam,*

Hymnum majes-ta - ti, gra-ti-as au-tem pi-e-ta-ti fe-ren-tes, *Do-mi-ne*

De-us, rex cœlestis, De-us pa-ter omni-potens, Do-mi-ne] fi-li u-ni - ge - ni-te

Je - su Christe al-tis-si-me, Quem, quisquis adorat in   spi-ri-tu et ve-ri-ta-te,

o - por-tet o - ra - re. *Do-mi-ne [De-us, agnus De-i, fi-li-us pa-tris,*

Qui tol-lis pec-ca-ta mundi, mi - se-re - re no-bis, Qui tol-lis pec-ca-ta mun-di,

su-sci-pe de-pre-ca-ti-o-nem no-stram, Qui se-des ad dex-te-ram pa-tris,

mi-se-re-re nó-bis, Quo-ni-am tu so-lus sanctus, Tu so-lus Do-mi-nus,

Tu so-lus al-tis-si-mus, Je-su Chri-ste, Qui ve-ni-sti, Je-su Chri-ste,

et pre-ti-o-so san-gui-ne tu-o nos re-de-mi-sti. Cum sancto spi-ri-tu

in glo-ri-a De-i pa - - tris, A - - men.

(*Glory to God in the highest*, to whom the citizens of Heaven, crying 'Holy',
sing their praises; *and on earth peace to men of good will*, which the angels of God
had promised to those on earth when the Word was made flesh. *We praise thee*,
whose praises the morning stars sing together. *We bless thee*, through whom every
holy thing and every blessing is granted and increased. *We worship thee*, omnipotent, worthy of worship, adoration, awe, and veneration. *We glorify thee*, as
the creature glorifies its creator, the mould the moulder, the pot the potter. *We
give thanks to thee for thy great glory*, offering a hymn to thy majesty, thanks to
thy piety, *O Lord God, heavenly King, God the Father almighty. Lord, the only begotten Son, Jesus Christ most high*, to whom every man should pray who worships
thee in spirit and in truth. *O Lord God, lamb of God, Son of the Father, that takest
away the sins of the world, have mercy upon us, thou that takest away the sins of
the world, receive our prayer, thou that sittest at the right hand of the Father, have
mercy upon us. For thou only art holy, thou only art the Lord, thou only art the
most high, Jesus Christ,* who didst come, Jesus Christ, and redeem us with thy
precious blood. *With the Holy Ghost in the glory of God the Father, Amen.*)

The words 'Jesu Christe altissime' are probably to be taken as the
end of the preceding plainsong rather than as the opening of a section
of the trope. This assumption is supported by the version given in two
St. Gall manuscripts,[1] as well as by the fact that the word 'altissime'
often occurs in Glorias as the only addition. In the St. Gall manuscripts the trope is written in rhythmical neums, and here, too, every
section of the trope appears twice, first with words and then as a
melisma. Another version, also rhythmical but more extended and
without melismata is in a manuscript at Paris.[2] In this composition
the sections of the trope are not in marked contrast to the plainsong,

[1] St. Gall 484, p. 232; 381, p. 306.
[2] Bibl. Nat. 1118, fo. 4ᵛ. Facsimile of fo. 5 in Dom Jeannin, 'Nuove osservazioni sulla
ritmica gregoriana', in *Santa Cecilia* (1930).

but at the same time they add great variety. The plainsong melody is written in the *e* mode in the *Editio Vaticana*,[1] but as this would not suit the trope we must suppose that it was assigned to the *a* mode, at any rate where the trope was first sung.

Since this trope occurs in some of the oldest tropers from Aquitaine, German Switzerland, and Italy, it would be interesting to compare the different versions. Here we must be content with the opening of the version in the Paris manuscript. The disposition of intervals, both of the plainsong and of the sections of the trope, is different, while the melody is evidently the same. The mode cannot be exactly determined, since there is no clef and no *custos* (or 'direct') at the end of the lines. There is, however, a fair probability that it is the *a* mode:

Ex. 53

Glo-ri - a in ex-cel-sis De - o, Quem ci-ves cæ-lestes sanctum cla-man-tes

lau - de fre-quen-tant; *Et in ter-ra pax ho - mi - ni - bus bo-næ volun-ta-tis* (etc.)

The transposition of the melodic framework from *a c d* to *a b c* is very curious. Not only is there an exchange between major and minor second and between major and minor third, but also between minor third and major second. This might appear at first sight to be an argument in favour of the theory that in the first period of plainsong singers were not concerned with the exact value of intervals but only with ascent and descent.[2] Yet the fact that the mode could vary and that a melodic sequence could give equal satisfaction in different modal settings does not mean that there was no clear perception of the difference between the modes, any more than the adaptation of a melody to a different rhythmical scheme meant that the medieval musician was indifferent to rhythm. Which of these modal versions was the earlier it is not yet possible to say.[3] As for the rhythm, our example shows that *cantus fractus* (measured music) was applied to the Ordinary of the Mass before the late Middle Ages. We can take it as certain that the short horizontal stroke and the point in this specimen of Aquitanian notation signify long and short notes respectively,

---

[1] *Gloria* No. 15.
[2] Cf. *Acta Musicologica*, xv (1943), p. 22.
[3] These melodic styles have been distinguished, in a very provisional way, as 'Germanic' and 'Romanic', or 'pentatonic' and 'heptatonic'.

though in a number of cases doubts may arise, since the horizontal stroke is very like a point; an exact determination of the note values would involve a comparative study of several manuscripts.

The relation between text and music in the tropes of this first period was probably the same as in the sequence, except for introductory sections in verse form of the kind mentioned above. Introductory sections written in hexameters, even complete tropes in hexameters, are often found—more often, in fact, than metrical sequences.

TROPES OF THE SECOND PERIOD

The tropes of the second period show the same tendency to use regular rhythmical verse as the sequences; but the principle is not so easily applied, since regular rhythm and rhyme have little scope within the narrow limits of the short passages that alternate with the plainsong. The new development is found mainly in the *Sanctus* and *Agnus* tropes, where the insertions occurred at fixed points and had room to expand. The sections of the trope in these cases often take the form of strophes, separated by the plainsong sections.[1] Another method is sometimes applied to tropes of this period—the mosaic method, or *méthode centonique*[2] (cf. p. 110). Here the sections of the trope—both words and music—are quotations from other sources (antiphons, sequences, &c.), and the author has to exercise his ingenuity as poet and musician in finding a suitable extract and, if necessary, adapting it. This method is naturally more suitable for cases where the interpolations are short, as in the *Gloria*.

THE CONDUCTUS

The new style of poetry which came into existence in the late eleventh century was not restricted to the trope, where there were limitations of space, or to the sequence, where it was subject to the law of progressive repetition. There was a strong tendency towards independent creative invention, both in music and in poetry, and it is even possible that this found scope in other forms earlier than the trope and sequence. In this new style there is an intimate connexion between rhythmical verse and music. We find the same connexion in the field of secular music, for instance, in the songs of the troubadours (see p. 225); indeed it is impossible to say for certain whether it first appeared within the orbit of the church or outside it. The oldest preserved specimens of rhythmical verse set to music are the 'rhythms' which preceded the sequence (see p. 161), in which the trochaic line

[1] See *Analecta Hymnica*, xlvii (1905).
[2] See H. Villetard, *L'Office de Pierre de Corbeil* (1907), pp. 119–25.

of fifteen syllables played a predominant role, the rhythm being governed in the Ancient World by quantity and in the Middle Ages by accent. It is perhaps surprising that these 'rhythms', though older than the early sequences, actually bear a closer relation to the later ones. It is evident, however, that the influx of the melodic material which formed the basis of the 'classical' sequence retarded the development of the older form, and hence there was a break in what would otherwise have been the continuous evolution of a 'normal' relationship between words and music. By the end of the eleventh century the old relationship comes into its own, and we have the new type of song, illustrated by the new sequence, the new trope, and the conductus. The difference between this new art and its remote predecessor is that now the use of rhyme creates a new formal harmony, and the verse forms, including the forms of the individual strophes, are more varied.

The name 'conductus', given to this new independent art of song, properly means a song for escorting—in particular, a song for a ceremonial procession.[1] The occasion for it might arise in the liturgy whenever an official moved from one place to another to perform a liturgical function, e.g. when the deacon or subdeacon carried the Gospels or the Epistles to the reading-desk at Mass. At Matins the reader had first to ask the priest's benediction, for which there was a fixed formula, and in this case the conductus often ends with an invitation to ask for the benediction. The general benediction given by the celebrant at Matins was also frequently preceded by a conductus. Thus the word also has the meaning of an introduction to some liturgical function. There is obviously an analogy between the conductus and the trope, since both were embellishments which were optional; the difference is that the trope was connected with a particular Gregorian chant, while the conductus was associated with a liturgical function.

An introduction of this kind was also prefixed to the 'Benedicamus Domino' sung at the end of Vespers and Lauds, and this, too, came to be known as 'conductus', though it did not have this name from the beginning. In this case the text had to end with a formula anticipating the 'Benedicamus' which followed. This formal obligation, however, was more and more disregarded, and in consequence a conductus could be transferred from one liturgical function to another, provided its text referred to the same feast. Hence 'conductus' came to signify generally a song with a text in verse form,

[1] Cf. L. Ellinwood, in the *Musical Quarterly*, xxvii (1941), pp. 169–70.

used in the liturgy as a transition to a particular function or to precede the end of the service. The word was also employed in secular
music, but it preserved its solemn associations and was never used,
for example, of a love-song.[1] It occurs also in the twelfth-century
Daniel play from Beauvais (see p. 214) for the ceremonial entries
of the characters.[2]

The form of the conductus is strophic, i.e. the text consists of verses
which have the same structure. As a rule these strophes also have the
same music; but in some cases there is new music for every strophe,
while in others we find the system of progressive repetition used in
the sequence. The difference between the old 'rhythm' and the conductus is not only that the verse forms and the strophes are now more
varied but also that the music is much more elaborate: long melismata
are used which form a splendid contrast to the purely syllabic sections.
Equally important is the fact that the conductus became a polyphonic
form as early as the beginning of the twelfth century, within the so-
called 'St. Martial school', and developed still further in the work
of the 'Notre Dame school' about 1200 (see pp. 326–37). In fact
the melismatic element reaches its height in the polyphonic form.

The following example of a monodic conductus occurs in some of
the St. Martial manuscripts and in another from Beauvais; the transcription follows one of the former:[3]

Ex. 54

a) Ex   A - dæ   vi - ti -   - o   Nos - tra   re -
b) De - i   et   ho - mi -   - nis Per   Chris - tum

-demp - ti -   o Tra-xit pri- mor -
do - mi -   - num Fac-ta con-cor -

---

[1] For a fuller discussion see J. Handschin, 'Notizen über die Notre Dame-Conductus',
in *Bericht über den musikwissenschaftlichen Kongress zu Leipzig* (1925), pp. 209 ff.;
Ellinwood, loc. cit., pp. 165 ff., and *Die Musik in Geschichte und Gegenwart*, s.v. *Conductus*.

[2] J. Handschin, op. cit., p. 211. The right explanation of the word 'conductus', though
not the explanation of its wider use, was given as early as 1853 by J. L. d'Ortigue in his
Dictionnaire du plain-chant, but it was not generally accepted and was even forgotten.
The Latin *conductus* has a forerunner in the Byzantine *apelatikos* (see J. Handschin,
Das Zeremonienwerk Kaiser Konstantins und die sangbare Dichtung, 1943), but the
analogy extends only to the function, not to the form. The manuscript Schaffhausen 108
contains one of the Latin *lais* in the so-called 'Cambridge song-book' (no. 12 in K.
Strecker, *Die Cambridger Lieder*, 1926), with the title 'Conductus Pythagoricus'. This
is an early example of the wider use of the word 'conductus', since the manuscript
appears to date from c. 1100.

[3] Paris, Bibl. Nat. lat. 1139 (c. 1100), fo. 35–35ᵛ, where two strophes are written with
neums.

di-a,   E - - ja, Gau-de-at ec-cle-si-a
di-a.

Fi-de-li-um; Vir-go   ma-ter   fi-li-um, Hu-mil-li-mum

Re-demp-to - rem, Virgo manens e-didit, Quod ac-ci-dit Præter   mo - rem.

1) This melisma has the form $a\widehat{f}\ \widehat{ge}fdc$ in the second strophe.

2) This melisma has slightly different forms in the second strophe.

3) This note may have been intended as a. In Paris, Bibl. Nat. lat. 3549, where this conductus is written on fo. 165 in staff notation but without key signature, the descending passage is $d\ c\ a\ f\ d$.

4) In the second strophe the melody is: $f\ e\ f\ a$, in Bibl. Nat. lat. 3549: $f\ a\ g\ a$.

5) In the second strophe the final note is d; in 3549 this line runs as follows: $f\ g\ a\ b\ c\ a\ f$.

6) In the second strophe this line is as follows: $f\ e\ g\ \widehat{fe}dc$.

(From Adam's sin came the beginning of our redemption. God and man are reconciled through Christ the Lord. Eja, let the church of the faithful rejoice; a virgin mother has borne a son, redeemer most lowly, and remains a virgin—an unwonted occurrence.)

The form of the strophe, which is very elaborate, may be roughly represented as *A A B*.[1] Section *B* itself contains an element of binary division, since 'redemptorem' corresponds to 'praeter morem'. 'Eja' was clearly intended by the poet as a three-syllable word (in fact, as a separate line), while the composer took it as two syllables. Examples of the simpler type of conductus may be found in the office for New Year's day edited by Villetard.[2] One of them is the so-called *Prose de l'âne*, which has often been quoted:

Ex. 55[3]

O - ri-en-tis par-ti-bus Ad-ven-ta-vit a-si-nus, Pulcher et for-tis-si-mus,

Sar-ci-nis ap-tis-si-mus. *Hez, sir as-ne, hez!*

[1] Cf. H. Spanke, 'St. Martial-Studien', in *Zeitschrift für französische Sprache und Literatur*, liv (1930–1), p. 291.

[2] H. Villetard, *L'Office de Pierre de Corbeil* (1907).

[3] Op. cit., p. 130. For a three-part setting of this melody and translation of the text *v. infra*, pp. 321–2.

VI

LITURGICAL DRAMA

By W. L. SMOLDON

GENERAL HISTORY

Much has been written on the subject of medieval church drama, an art which perforce had to develop from the most elementary beginnings, since the Dark Ages had obliterated almost all knowledge of the classical stage. Between the tenth and thirteenth centuries a large number of these religious dramas were composed, the work of the only learned society of the time—the clerics of the medieval church—and regularly performed in church precincts. These compositions are recognized as being of great importance in the history of drama, for they mark its rebirth in western Europe. They also have considerable musical significance. The medieval world was as conscious as classical Greece of the power of music to reinforce drama. But whereas the melodies of Aeschylus and his fellow dramatists have perished beyond recovery,[1] it is still possible to recapture the music to which the liturgical dramas were sung. The more dramatic moments were usually reserved for solo voices and were in swift-moving recitative: but impressive choral climaxes were not lacking. This art flourished throughout the Middle Ages and must have established a strong tradition of performance.

The texts were in Latin, prose and verse, with later occasional excursions into the vernacular. These texts have been competently dealt with by scholars, and such works as E. K. Chambers's *The Medieval Stage* and Karl Young's *The Drama of the Medieval Church* sum up all there is to be said on the literary side. Only in comparatively modern times, however, has a full investigation of the music been possible. In most of the earlier manuscripts and some of the later ones the settings, which were at first in the style of Gregorian chant, are written in neums, and the correct interpretation of this notation often involves the collation of many sources. In 1861 Édouard de Coussemaker published his *Drames liturgiques du moyen âge*— transcriptions into what was then modern plainsong notation of

---

[1] The only surviving fragment consists of a few lines of Euripides' *Orestes* with musical notation (see vol. i, chap. ix).

twenty-two examples of various types. He did not attempt the more difficult neumatic notations. But, great pioneer though he was, his works in general suffered from the fact that Gregorian musical palaeography was in its earliest stages. Owing to lack of opportunities for adequate comparison the transcriptions are marred by a number of errors and misreading of clefs. The examples in this chapter, which are reproduced in plainsong notation, are based on new transcriptions from the original manuscripts.

It will be useful here to define 'liturgical drama' in more detail. The first simple compositions to which this term could be applied were closely connected with Divine Service, and arose from a brief dialogue sung before the Easter Mass, one of the free compositions known as 'tropes' which in early medieval times had begun to invade many parts of the liturgy (see pp. 128 ff.). By an evolution which will presently be described this became the 'Easter Sepulchre' music-drama, the three Marys at the empty tomb receiving the news of the Resurrection from the angel. This drama expanded as the other events of Easter Day were added. The whole Easter season was eventually drawn upon. Another series dealt with the 'Journey to Emmaus', while, extending in the other direction, some few attempts were made to represent the Passion and other related events in one single continuous performance. All these works were performed within the church. The Christmas season developed dramatically in imitation. 'The Shepherds at the Manger' and, more important, 'The Journey of the Magi' were the first subjects. Further extension introduced Herod and his court and the episode of the Slaughter of the Innocents. Again there were attempts to create a comprehensive drama, a Christmas play. At this point it may be mentioned in connexion with the early Byzantine Church that certain hymns associated with the Nativity and with Good Friday contain passages which were sung by soloists, representing, for example, the Narrator, Joseph, and Mary (see p. 22). But there is no sign that real dramatic impersonation was attempted, and these efforts never passed the 'semi-dramatic' stage. There is no link between them and the Easter and Christmas dramas of the West, which sprang from a primitive but original beginning, and developed by a progressive evolution.

Before either the Easter or Christmas themes had reached their full expansion the dramatization of other subjects from the Old and New Testaments had begun, e.g. 'The Raising of Lazarus', 'The Conversion of St. Paul', 'Joseph and His Brethren', and 'Daniel'. The legends of the Saints, particularly those dealing with St. Nicholas, were drawn upon, and that most persistent of all medieval preoccupations, the Last Judgement. Many of the later compositions were of considerable dimensions, calling for many participants and plainly needing every available inch of ecclesiastical space. The rubrics indicate considerable resource in the use of properties, costumes, and general *mise-en-scène*. Many of these dramas must have included scenes of brilliant pageantry. The music indicated no more than a single vocal line.[1] Probably the earliest performances consisted merely of unaccompanied monody; but it would be unwise to be dogmatic in the matter, for harmony was certainly being employed in Church services by the eleventh century. There is evidence that musical instruments were used in the larger works. Performances of these music dramas continued in the various countries of western Europe into the sixteenth century; but long before that time drama in general had refused to be bound by ecclesiastical restriction and had overflowed to the world outside, where its secular development began. It shed most of its music in doing so, and thus passes beyond the scope of our subject.

THE EASTER SEPULCHRE DRAMA

(i) *First Stage.* One of the results of the revival of culture in the reign of Charlemagne was the new splendour which appeared in Church architecture, interiors, vestments, and details of ritual. A misguided enthusiasm, however, was shown in the increased practice of allowing additions to various parts of the authorized liturgy in the form of tropes. They served to expand, explain, or comment upon the established texts—anonymous 'free compositions' representing local tastes but liable, if they became popular, to travel widely. The Easter Mass trope, the expansion of which we are to trace, consisted of three sentences placed before the Introit. The rubrics given in some manuscripts show definitely that it was sung in dialogue form. There is no direct authority in the Gospel account for the actual wording, which therefore represents free composition. In translation it would read as follows:

(*Angel*) Whom seek ye in the sepulchre, O followers of Christ?
(*Marys*) Jesus of Nazareth who was crucified, O celestial ones.
(*Angel*) He is not here; he is risen as he foretold; go, announce that he is risen from the sepulchre.

---

[1] For a unique exception see p. 189.

From the two opening Latin words it is usually referred to as the 'Quem quaeritis' trope. Its original home is still a matter of doubt. As the important ecclesiastical centres of Limoges and St. Gall can both show a tenth-century example in a very simple form, these may dispute the claim. The following is the St. Gall version, accompanied by a transcription of the original neums in plainsong notation:

Ex. 56 (i)[1]

Ex. 56 (ii)

The last word, 'Resurrexi', marks the beginning of the Introit proper to the Mass.

Below are two lines from the Limoges Troper, again with transcription. Obviously it is the same tune, only slightly varied. The neums above the text are of the 'Aquitaine' type and unlike the St. Gall neums are 'heighted' to show the approximate rise and fall of the melody:

'QUEM QUAERTIS' TROPE

(Piacenza, Bibl. Capit. MS. 65, fo. 235.) Eleventh or twelfth century

Ex. 57 (i)[1]

Quem quæ-ri-tis in se-pul-chro, o Chri-sti-co-læ? Je-sum Na-za-re-num cru-

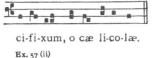

ci-fi-xum, o cæ li-co-læ.

Ex. 57 (ii)

(Transposed)

Quem quæ - ri - tis in se-pul - chro, o Chri-sti - co - læ?

Je - sum Na-za-re-num cru-ci-fi - xum, o cæ - li - co-læ.

This particular trope is itself 'troped', i.e. further sentences, in the nature of commentaries, are added to it, both before and after. In spite of being thus more elaborate than the St. Gall version the manuscript is of slightly earlier date.

Scores of examples of the 'Quem quaeritis' trope are in existence, belonging to a number of European countries. Only the slightest variations of the original dialogue text are found, and the setting never strays far from the original melody. The changes are characteristic, however, and often serve to place a version. Different ecclesiastical centres added to the dialogue in different ways, preceding and concluding it with suitable liturgical antiphons, or newly composed sentences. But while the dialogue remained attached to the Mass there is no sign of any attempt at impersonation. This occurred some time in the second half of the tenth century, when the little composition was moved to Easter Matins. This accorded well with the Gospel account of the women coming 'very early in the morning', and being placed at the end of the service gave a much better chance of expansion. Almost invariably the *incipit* 'Te Deum' is found at the conclusion of a dramatized version. This refers to the last canticle of Matins and so fixes the position of the new composition. Surviving rubrics tell us that three clerics are required to robe and hood themselves as women and to move towards an improvised sepulchre at or near the altar, where they encounter another representing an angel, who questions them, hears their reply, and dismisses them with news

[1] Paris, Bibl. Nat. lat. 1240, fo. 30ᵛ (*c.* 930).

of the Resurrection. Sometimes two angels are employed. The movements and gestures of the participants, and often their tone of voice,
are detailed in the accompanying rubrics.

Probably the earliest surviving document which shows the 'Quem
quaeritis' dialogue as true drama performed at Easter Matins is an
English one.[1] This is the Winchester Troper, an Anglo-Saxon service
book dating from about 980. It gives neums above the words but very
few directions. Fortunately these can be supplemented by a very full
account of such a performance, detailed (but without music) in the
Regularis Concordia, a 'Customary' for the Benedictine order in
England issued by Ethelwold, Bishop of Winchester, and slightly
anterior to the Troper. The only difference is the omission of one of
the antiphons found in the Troper version. Careful details are given
as to how the scene shall be prepared and how the three shall advance.
After the usual dialogue the Marys' rejoicing is expressed in a familiar
liturgical piece: 'Alleluia, resurrexit Dominus hodie'. The angel then
invites them to inspect the tomb; again, an antiphon is employed:

Ex. 58 (i)

Ve-ni-te et vi-de-te lo-cum u-bi po-si-tus e-rat Do-mi-nus, al-le-lu-ia, al-le-lu-ia.

Ex. 58 (ii)

(Come and see the place where the Lord was laid, alleluia, alleluia.)

The second dismissal is secured by a further antiphon:

Ex. 59 (i)

Ci-to e-un-tes, di-ci-te di-sci-pu-lis qui-a sur-re-xit Do-mi-nus.

[1] Oxford, Bodleian, Bodl. 775, fo. 17–17[v]. Recorded in *The History of Music in Sound*
(H.M.V.), ii, side 8.

Ex. 59 (ii)

Ci - to e - un - tes, di - ci - te di - sci - pu - lis qui - a sur -

-re - xit Do - mi - nus.

(Go quickly; tell the disciples that the Lord has risen.)

and the whole rounded off by the Marys singing in chorus yet another familiar liturgical piece:

Ex. 60 (i)

Sur-re-xit Do-mi-nus de se-pul-chro, qui pro no-bis pe-pen-dit in li-gno, al-le-lu-ia.

Ex. 60 (ii)

Sur - re - xit 'Do - mi - nus de se - pul - chro, qui pro no - bis

pe - pen-dit in li - gno, al - le - lu - ia.

(The Lord has risen from the sepulchre, who for us was hung upon the cross, alleluia.)

Here is our earliest surviving music-drama, with costumes, proper-ties, and careful directions as to action and gesture.[1] It does not follow, however, that the dialogue was first dramatized in England. It prob-ably had a Continental origin: the music of the Winchester Troper version seems to have close affinities with that of Limoges. It is a small beginning, with original composition displayed only in the dialogue, but the process of accretion began immediately. Sentences were added which varied from country to country and centre to centre, but were sometimes original, with original music. A successful innovation was taken up widely. This type of single-scene *Visitatio Sepulchri*[2] seems to have become immensely popular and to have been

---

[1] Cf. W. L. Smoldon, 'The Easter Sepulchre Drama', in *Music and Letters*, xxvii (1946), pp. 1–17, where there is a transcription of the whole of the Winchester Troper version and a full translation of the account in the *Regularis Concordia*.

[2] This is the term used in many medieval manuscripts to describe all types of Easter Sepulchre drama.

performed in churches all over Europe throughout the Middle Ages. Though further scenes were added, the more elaborate forms did not displace the single-scene type, since in many churches the latter was probably found to be the most convenient. Many versions are even more primitive than the Winchester example, consisting merely of the dialogue and a concluding antiphon. The 'Venite et videte' and 'Cito euntes'—the recall and second dismissal—were, however, usual additions, and further antiphons and original sentences were added to these. The display of the grave-clothes produced a new composition, beginning 'Cernitis, o socii' (See, O friends). Additions to the beginning included sentences for the Marys to sing as they approached the sepulchre. One of these was 'Ad monumentum venimus' (We are come to the tomb) of which both words and music were original. Another, 'Quis revolvet nobis lapidem?' (Who will roll away the stone for us?), was adapted from an antiphon. Proses were also used as introductions, sung by the Marys or the chorus. An unusual introduction is found in a German version from Bamberg, beginning:

Ex. 61 (i) [1]

1. Ad tu-mu-lum ve-ne-re ge-men-tes, A.
2. Et se-cum a - ro-ma-ta por-tan-tes, A.

Ex. 61 (ii)

1. Ad   tu-mu-lum ve-ne-re ge - men - tes,   A.
2. Et   se-cum a - ro-ma-ta por - tan - tes, A.

(To the tomb came they mourning, and bringing with them spices.)

A curious feature is the vocalized echo of the melody of each line.

Perhaps the best of the not very enterprising single-scene versions is one found in a Madrid manuscript of the twelfth century,[2] but representing a French use adapted for Norman-ruled Sicily. It includes several original touches which seem to show an independent mind at work, both in text and music. But the most considerable addition to the single-scene form was the adaptation of the sequence 'Victimae paschali'. This famous eleventh-century composition still remains in the modern Roman liturgy. The melody is a fine broad tune arranged, almost throughout, on the principle of one syllable to

---

[1] Bamberg, Staatsbibl. 22, fo. 128 (twelfth to thirteenth century).
[2] Madrid, Bibl. Nac. C. 132, fo. 102ᵛ–103 (twelfth century).

a note. The first part is lyrical—a call to all Christians to praise the Paschal Victim, but later the lines are in dialogue form. The question 'Tell us, Mary, what thou sawest on thy way?' can be presumed to be put by the disciples and therefore could be sung by the choir impersonating them. Mary's reply makes it evident that she is returning from the tomb with the assurance of the angel and the evidence of the grave-clothes. The sequence ends with a triumphant chorus. It is not surprising that early in the twelfth century it was incorporated into many versions of the *Visitatio Sepulchri* with excellent dramatic results. In some cases, Mary Magdalen sang the first reflective part, but other arrangers preferred to omit it and proceed directly to the section containing the dramatic question and answer. A final new feature of the single-scene type consisted of a completely new dialogue, though plainly modelled on the old. It is found for the first time in an eleventh- or early twelfth-century manuscript from Einsiedeln.[1] After this date German versions tended to use it in preference to the original dialogue, which, however, still held its own elsewhere. The new composition remains remarkably consistent wherever found. The example below is taken from a fifteenth-century manuscript from Klosterneuburg:

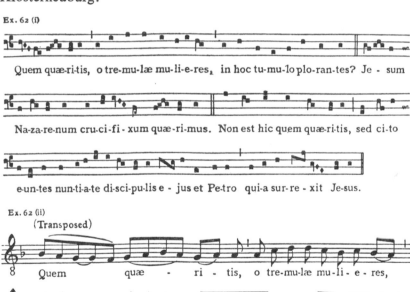

Ex. 62 (i)

Quem quæ-ri-tis, o tre-mu-læ mu-li-e-res, in hoc tu-mu-lo plo-ran-tes? Je - sum

Na-za-re-num cru-ci-fi - xum quæ-ri-mus. Non est hic quem quæ-ri-tis, sed ci-to

e-un-tes nun-ti-a-te di-sci-pu-lis e - jus et Pe-tro qui-a sur-re - xit Je-sus.

Ex. 62 (ii)
(Transposed)

Quem   quæ - ri - tis, o tre-mu-læ mu-li- e - res,

in hoc tu-mu-lo plo-ran-tes?   Je   -   sum Na-za - re - num cru-

¹ Einsiedeln, Stiftsbibl. 366, pp. 55–56.
² Klosterneuburg, Stiftsbibl. 629, fo. 103ᵛ–105.

-ci - fi - xum quæ - ri - mus. Non est hic quem quæ-ri - tis,

sed ci - to e - un - tes nun-ti - a - te di - sci - pu - lis

e - jus et Pe -tro qui- a sur - re - xit Je - sus.

(ii) *Second Stage*. Another group of Easter Sepulchre dramas is termed 'second stage', since a further dramatic episode has been added. Peter and John appear on the scene, the playwrights having recalled the fourth verse of John xx: 'So they ran both together; and the other disciple did outrun Peter, and came first to the Sepulchre.' The rubrics indicate that this was done in dumb-show, two clerics appropriately attired (Peter in red and John in white, according to one version), racing the length of the building, and one of them groping within the 'sepulchre' for the abandoned grave-clothes.[1] A setting of the appropriate verse was already in existence as an antiphon, 'Currebant duo simul', and in a large number of versions this was sung by the choir as the action took place. There is one quaint instance of the apostles first singing the antiphon themselves, and then proceeding to suit the action to the words. In some versions writers were content with the dumb-show. The best of them combine it satisfactorily with the 'Victimae paschali' dialogue, since Mary's report gives a logical reason for the race.

The 'second stage' versions are all German (using the revised 'Quem quaeritis' dialogue), with one exception, and this is far ahead of the others in finish and originality. It is the so-called 'Dublin play', surviving in two fourteenth-century manuscripts, one still in Dublin and one in the Bodleian Library.[2] The opening scene is much extended by a series of laments for the Marys. It should be remarked that closely similar material is found in an earlier *Visitatio* belonging to the monastery of Fleury (see next page). But there is much else that seems unique: there are generous details as to costumes and acting,

---

[1] These 'properties' were left over from the two ancient liturgical ceremonies—the Burying and Raising of the Cross, carried out on Good Friday and Easter Day respectively. The symbolism is obvious, but the actions remained symbolic and never became dramatic. The texts and music of the ceremonies were drawn wholly from the liturgy. They were carried out in many places without any sign of a succeeding sepulchre drama.

[2] Dublin, Archbishop Marsh's Library, Z. 4. 2. 20, fo. 59–61; Oxford, Bodleian, Rawl. liturg. d 4, fo. 130–132.

and the race is combined with 'Victimae paschali' for an effective conclusion.

(iii) *Third Stage*. Dramas which make use of the 'Scene of the Risen Christ' are usually termed 'third stage'. The material employed is drawn from SS. Matthew, Mark, and John, who relate, each in his own way, the meeting of Christ, after His resurrection, with one or more of the Marys. These varying details account in part for the variety of treatment which the episode receives in the couple of dozen or so extant 'third-stage' versions. What seems to be a prototype is found in a twelfth-century manuscript from Spain.[1] It is a disordered and badly written text and the music is not complete, but it is an important historical document. Besides the scene of Mary Magdalen's recognition of the supposed gardener, with the dramatic 'Maria', 'Rabboni' dialogue, there is an encounter between the Marys and the *Mercator*—the first appearance of the famous 'Merchant Scene', in which the women bargain for the purchase of spices. Several centres developed the idea along different lines. Rouen has a number of almost identical versions which omit the race and the 'Victimae paschali' conclusion, carrying through the whole drama in straightforward and plain fashion, but with some very individual music. A fourteenth-century group from Prague is similarly independent and direct, but uses both the race and the sequence. It opens with a rudimentary 'Merchant Scene'. The rubrics direct that the Marys shall accept the spices from an *unguentarius*. He is here a silent figure, no doubt at first merely a church servitor. In more developed versions he is given a singing part and debates with the Marys. Later still in dramatic history he becomes a comic character.

Probably the most artistic of the Easter Sepulchre music-dramas comes from the famous 'Fleury play-book'.[2] This manuscript, written in the thirteenth century in the monastery of St. Benoît-sur-Loire at Fleury, contains ten music-dramas, representing all the important types. Nearly all show a high standard of originality both in text and music. The latter is clearly noted on four lines throughout. The *Visitatio*[3] shows a tendency, common to the whole of the liturgical drama from the twelfth century onward, towards an increasing amount of versification. Sometimes stanzas were newly composed; sometimes familiar and established prose passages were turned into verse. This versification had its effect on the music, bringing about a greater shapeliness and sense of form in the melodies, but at times

[1] Vich, Museo 111, fo. 58ᵛ–62. [2] Orleans, Bibl. de la Ville 201.
[3] Ibid., pp. 220–5.

blunting the dramatic results. The more striking situations, however, such as Mary's recognition of the Gardener, remained in prose. In the Fleury example nearly thirty lines of verse occupy the Marys in their journey to the Sepulchre, including a lament, beginning:

Ex. 63 (i)

Heu, pi-us pas-tor oc-ci-dit, quem cul-pa nul-la in-fe-cit.   O   res plan-gen-da.

Ex. 63 (ii)

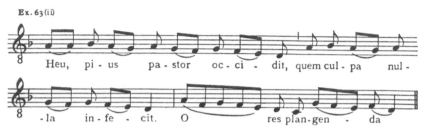

Heu, pi - us   pa - stor   oc - ci - dit, quem cul - pa   nul -
- la   in - fe - cit.   O   res plan-gen - da

(Alas, the Good Shepherd is slain, whom no guilt stained. O mournful event!)

The remaining examples of the 'third stage'—all German and belonging to the thirteenth and fourteenth centuries—represent variations of one general plan. Versification, mainly in ten-syllable lines, is even more marked. The core is the revised 'Quem quaeritis' dialogue (with some familiar succeeding antiphons), but the remaining dramatic situations are met by six groups of verses, found with some variations and omissions in each of the dramas. These stanzas deal with (1) the lament of the Marys, (2) the prayer of the Marys and the decision to buy ointment, (3) the buying of the ointment ('Merchant Scene'), (4) the lament of Mary Magdalen at the Sepulchre, (5) Christ's words to Mary Magdalen, (6) Mary's announcement to the disciples and the other Marys.[1] To each of these groups was attached a particular stanza-melody. These melodies, with some degree of variation, were used by all the versions. In general they are rather more ornamental and thus probably less effective dramatically than any before met, e.g. in the scene between Mary and the risen Christ (Cividale version):

---

[1] Some of the manuscripts containing these are as follows: Einsiedeln 300, Klosterneuburg 574, Munich 4660a, Rheinau 18, Nuremberg 22923, Cividale C1, Engelberg 314, Prague Univ. Lib. VI G. 3b. They probably all derived from a prototype, composed perhaps at Klosterneuburg.

Ex. 64 (i)

Mu - li - er, quid plo - - - ras?

Ex. 64 (ii)

Mu - - - li - er, quid plo - - - - - - ras?

(Woman, why weepest thou?)

Besides the rhyming verse-forms the German dramas made new use of Gospel texts, especially in the scene of the risen Christ. Here special musical composition is found often peculiar to the particular drama. Several liturgical texts are also used, but the liturgical music is usually discarded in favour of fresh settings. 'Sancte Deus, sancte fortis' is an example. The race and 'Victimae paschali' conclusion are usually included.

Four examples of the Sepulchre drama are extant which include further incidents. They are all much longer than anything we have yet met and comprise two German and two French manuscripts, belonging respectively to Klosterneuburg, Benediktbeuern, Tours, and Origny-Sainte-Benoîte.[1] The last-named, while containing some novelties, owes its bulk mainly to the expansion of certain familiar versified scenes. In the other three we encounter Pilate and his soldiers, the Tours example including the incident of doubting Thomas. The first of the German versions was written at the famous Klosterneuburg monastery early in the thirteenth century, and probably represents a great amount of fresh invention. Several of the groups of stanzas of the ten-syllable type, and several of the melodies, make their first appearance, chronologically, in this manuscript. Unfortunately, the text is greatly disordered, with repetitions and obvious displacements; over seventy lines represent a recopying of part of the text, and much music is omitted. What there is, is in a difficult neumatic notation. The same is true of the thirteenth-century example from Benediktbeuern, which is part of the collection known as *Carmina Burana* (see also pp. 194, 204, 222). It appears to be merely a first half, and much of the text and music has been drawn from the Klosterneuburg version, with improvement in the borrowing. There is also some new material. In both dramas there are incidents concerning

[1] Klosterneuburg, Stiftsbibl. 574, fo. 142ᵛ–144ᵛ (thirteenth century); Munich, Staatsbibl. lat. 4660a, fol. v–viᵛ (thirteenth century); Tours, Bibl. de la Ville 927, fol. 1–8ᵛ (thirteenth century); St. Quentin, Bibl. de la Ville 86, pp. 609–25 (fourteenth century).

Pilate, the chief priests, and the soldiers who are detailed to guard the Sepulchre. When the latter march round the Sepulchre each in turn sings a verse, and there is a Germanized refrain-chorus, 'Schowa propter insidias', to what seems an original melody. In the Klosterneuburg drama we obtain a brief glimpse of the 'Harrowing of Hell' theme. Christ is represented as breaking down the infernal gates, confounding Satan, and being acclaimed by the ransomed spirits. The fragments of music are liturgical.

From the nunnery of Origny-Sainte-Benoîte comes the fourteenth-century St. Quentin drama, a beautiful manuscript with clearly written notation on four lines.[1] The rubrics are in French throughout, as are the Merchant Scene and the dialogue of the angel and the Magdalen. Both these lengthy episodes are in verse. The Merchant Scene begins with a free translation of the Group 2 verses (see p. 186). The music is the usual setting, repeated for no less than sixteen uniform verses. After completing their purchase the Marys apparently make a convert of *li marchans*, and then invite him to accompany them on their journey. A long and similar 'stanza' scene between the angel and Mary Magdalen is set to an unfamiliar melody. For the rest, apart from a few short new verses and new tunes, the drama follows familiar paths, including a 'Victimae paschali' conclusion.

Our last example, found in the thirteenth-century Tours manuscript, is the longest version of the *Visitatio Sepulchri* extant. The setting is written in square notation on four lines.[2] It is not a good example of the Easter Sepulchre type. It appears to be a very careless copy of an unwieldy compilation, in which are included texts and music from a number of older sources. Some passages can be paralleled in Vich 111, Madrid 132, the Fleury drama, and elsewhere. It may be that some of the apparently new verses and melodies which occur have come from sources which have not survived. The text contains a number of obvious blunders and misplacements. Inaccuracies are apparent also in the writing down of the music. Some pages are missing from the middle; these contained, probably, the Christ-Magdalen scene and the race to the tomb. At least a page is missing at the beginning, the first verses being those of Pilate, addressing the soldiers who are to guard the tomb. These take their posts and are struck to earth by the angel. The Merchant Scene is familiar. Much of it is from Vich 111, almost without alteration. From the same source Tours has also borrowed the term *mercator juvenis* and from

[1] Printed in Coussemaker, *Drames liturgiques du moyen âge* (Paris, 1861), pp. 256–79.
[2] Ibid., pp. 21–48.

the hint created a part for *alius mercator*, who assists in the bargaining. Here is the first sign of the 'apprentice' who was later in medieval drama to become a comic figure. Much material that follows can also be found in the Fleury and Dublin versions. The succeeding scene at the Sepulchre is frankly a jumble and contains some unnecessary repetition. The 'Quem quaeritis' section has apparently been lifted from Madrid 132 or some similar source, followed by material which seems to be original.

A long Magdalen lament follows, found nowhere else, and the setting is worthy of note by reason of its construction. The text is written in irregular verse-form and merges finally into the well-known medieval prose, 'O quam magno dies ista celebranda gaudio', to its usual setting. It then becomes apparent that the music of the rest of the verses has been founded on this tune, anticipating and foreshadowing its appearance—an interesting and unusual device. Then come passages founded on material from the Fleury and Rouen versions, including a momentary appearance of Jesus, which appears to be misplaced. At the end of this scene comes the break in the manuscript. When it resumes, Peter is questioning Mary Magdalen, the music, strangely enough, belonging to 'O quam magno'. Later, Jesus enters to his disciples and the scene of the incredulity of Thomas begins. This particular incident is usually found in the type of Easter season drama known as *Peregrinus* (the scene of the journey to Emmaus). Most of the material of this part of the Tours version can be paralleled in examples of French origin, of earlier date than the Tours manuscript. The drama then ends conventionally enough with the usual adaptation of 'Victimae paschali'.

Lastly, some mention must be made of the 'Shrewsbury Fragments', an English manuscript still preserved in the library of Shrewsbury School.[1] It consists not of a single Church play, but a single actor's part, complete with cues, for three of them—the *Visitatio Sepulchri*, the *Peregrinus*, and the *Pastores* (the Shepherds at the Manger). These dramas may have been concerned with the diocese of Lichfield in the thirteenth or fourteenth century. The actor is the third of the Marys and the Shepherds, and Cleopas of the *Peregrinus*. While there are Latin passages in the texts which are familiar, the plays show a traditional stage, and consist largely of verses in the vernacular, a northern English dialect. The Easter play has very little music, and this in 'measured' notation, the passages ('Jam, jam, ecce' and 'Quis revolvet') apparently being sung in three-part harmony.

[1] Shrewsbury School Library, vi (Mus. iii. 42), fo. 38–42ᵛ

PEREGRINUS PLAYS

The *Peregrinus* dramas previously referred to seem to have been in existence by the twelfth century as separate compositions. The surviving examples, little more than half a dozen but all complete with musical settings, show some variety of construction; but neither in dramatic achievement nor in vogue can they compare with the longer examples of the *Visitatio Sepulchri*. They deal in the main with the journey to Emmaus (Luke xxiv. 13–32). A few versions include the appearance of Christ to the eleven at Jerusalem (Luke xxiv. 33–39) and his encounter with Thomas (John xx. 24–29). It will be remembered that the original dialogue of the *Visitatio Sepulchri* had to be invented, together with many further details of speech and incident. In the case of *Peregrinus* a great deal of the dialogue and narrative were ready and waiting in the Vulgate texts. Moreover, many of the sentences were already employed in the Easter services as antiphons. The result of this is a certain formality of construction. In spite of this general conclusion, we find occasional versifications of the Gospel accounts and some free composition in the musical settings. Most of the versions seem to have been performed on Easter Monday evening, during the elaborate three-fold Vespers which were sung on that day in medieval times and included much processional movement.

The simplest of them is found in a fourteenth-century breviary from Saintes.[1] As its single scene contains dialogue found in all the other versions, it may well be given in some detail. At the opening the two disciples are represented as saying: 'Tertia dies est quo haec facta sunt' (today is the third day since these things were done), adapted from Luke xxiv. 21. *Dominus* then appears, asking them what they are discussing so sorrowfully (v. 17). Not recognizing him, Cleopas inquires: 'Art thou only a stranger (*peregrinus*) in Jerusalem, and hast not known the things which are come to pass there in these days?' (v. 18). The question and reply of verse 19 follow directly, succeeded by Jesus's reproach: 'O fools, and slow of heart to believe' (v. 25). In the Vulgate text there is now the narrative which reads in translation: 'And they drew nigh unto the village whither they went: and he made as though he would have gone further. But they constrained him' (vv. 28, 29). The rubrics make it plain that this is acted in dumb-show, but at this point we have also the chorus singing a liturgical setting of these words. All the music so far, with the exception of the 'Tertia dies' setting, is liturgical, every sentence being an official antiphon. The opening dialogue is here given:[2]

[1] Paris, Bibl. Nat. lat. 16309, fo. 604–5.   [2] Cf. *Paléographie musicale*, II. i, p. 233.

Ex. 65 (i)

Qui sunt hi ser-mo-nes quos con-fer-tis ad in-vi-cem am-bu-lan-tes et es-tis tris-tes,

al-le-lu-ia. Tu so-lus pe-re-gri-nus es in Je-ru-sa-lem, et non co-gno-vi-sti quæ

fa-cta sunt in il-la his di-e-bus, al-le-lu-ia. Quæ? De Je-su Na-za-re-no, qui fu-it

vir pro-phe-ta, po-tens in o-pe-ra et ser-mo-ne coram De-o et o-mni po-pu-lo,

al-le-lu-ia.

Ex. 65(ii)

Qui sunt hi ser - mo-nes quos con-fer - tis ad in-vi-cem

am-bu - lan-tes et es-tis tri-stes, al - le - lu - ia.

Tu so-lus pe-re-gri-nus es in Je - ru-sa-lem, et non co - gno-vi-sti

quæ fa-cta sunt in il - la his di-e - bus, al - le-lu-ia.

Quæ? De Je - su Na - za - re - no, qui fu-it vir

pro-phe - ta, po - tens in o - pe - ra et ser - mo - ne

co-ram De-o et o-mni po-pu-lo, al - le - lu - ia.

(What are these communications that ye have one to another, as ye walk, and are sad, alleluia? Art thou only a stranger in Jerusalem, and hast not known the things which are come to pass there in these days, alleluia? What things? Concerning Jesus of Nazareth, which was a prophet mighty in deed and word before God and all the people, alleluia.)

But the sentences in which the disciples invite the stranger to stay with them at the inn are found neither in the Vulgate nor in the service books. Both words and music seem to represent free composition. Again the chorus intervenes. Verse 30, describing the blessing and breaking of the bread, is sung in its antiphon form, while the action takes place in dumb-show. A rubric then directs that Jesus shall vanish from sight. The astonishment of the disciples is expressed partly by the antiphon 'Did not our hearts burn within us' (v. 32), partly by newly invented phrases. A liberty is now taken with the Gospel account. Jesus reappears at the same spot and reassures the two in phrases from verses 36 and 39. Liturgical music was available for these words, but in this case a new setting seems to have been invented. Finally, the disciples sing the familiar antiphon 'Surrexit Dominus de sepulchro'.

This version has been given in some detail since it fairly illustrates the technique of these dramas. In all there is a proportion of antiphon material. A thirteenth-century example from Munich,[1] consisting of the Emmaus scene and the incredulity of Thomas, actually draws the whole of its material, words and music, from the service books. In the more ambitious versions there is a much greater proportion of originality and a certain amount of versification. A thirteenth-century single-scene example from Rouen[2] cathedral is of interest, mainly for its generous rubrics. The gestures and movements of the actors are carefully described. The disciples have purses and staves, while Jesus wears an alb and holds a cross. Mary Magdalen is also represented, clad 'in modum mulieris'. The dwelling at Emmaus is a special construction erected in the nave, containing a table. Jesus and the two disciples enter by two different doors at the west end of the church, and their path to the structure represents the road to Emmaus. Space does not permit attention to other versions, several of which are more satisfactory dramatically and musically.[3] We shall deal in detail only with the *Peregrinus* from the famous Fleury play-book.[4] The first meeting in Jerusalem is here a separate episode, Thomas's

[1] Munich, Staatsbibl. lat. 4660a, fo. vii–vii ᵛ.
[2] Rouen, Bibl. de la Ville 222, fo. 43ᵛ–45.
[3] For example, a twelfth-century text from Beauvais (Paris, Bibl. Nat., nouv. acq. lat. 1064, fo. 8–11ᵛ).
[4] Orléans, Bibl. de la Ville 201, pp. 225–30 (thirteenth century).

incredulity and confession having a scene to itself. There is much new textual material, but only two versified sections, both original. Some of the prose contributions, verses from the Vulgate, are already liturgical antiphons, but Fleury displays its independent spirit in the musical settings, which, after the first few sentences, either go their own way or have their own individual twist.

Details of the *mise-en-scène* are copious and picturesque. The two disciples and Thomas have cloak-like garments, hats, and staves. The Emmaus setting is elaborate. Seats and a table are provided, with an uncut loaf, three wafers, and cup of wine. Water is brought for the washing of hands. *Dominus* has three changes of costume. He is at first barefooted, with palm and script. At Jerusalem, appearing to the eleven, he carries a golden cross and wears a white vestment with a red cope. His feet and hands are marked with red. In the final meeting, after eight days, he has in addition a crown of gold, and holds a gospel book in his left hand. We have already noted that the famous fifteenth-century manuscript, the 'Shrewsbury Fragments', contains some lines of a lost English *Peregrinus* (see p. 189). A few verses in the disordered twelfth-century manuscript Vich 111 seem also to refer to a *Peregrinus* section. That the drama was also played in Italy seems apparent from the description of it in a thirteenth-century *ordinarium* from Padua.

PASSION PLAYS

One part of the Easter season has so far remained untouched, that containing the Passion, the greatest dramatic subject of all. Yet within the medieval Church, comparatively infrequent use was made of the theme by clerical playwrights, and nothing has survived which dates before the beginning of the thirteenth century. In spite of semi-dramatic incidents in the ceremonies of Holy Week, such as the deposition and raising of the Cross or the *mandatum* (the foot-washing), the core of the Passion play would seem to be the various *planctus* or laments—extra-liturgical compositions represented as being sung by one or another of the mourners at the foot of the Cross. We have already seen the employment of such metrical laments in the Easter dramas. The earliest of both types date from the twelfth century. Although some of the most famous of the *planctus* of the Passion are solo stanzas, spoken by the Virgin Mary, yet there are a number in dialogue form, the speakers being most frequently Mary and St. John. With impersonation, dramatic dialogue, and setting, these compositions became true music-dramas, and were sung most frequently at the Good Friday ceremonial of the Adoration of the Cross.

The most extensive surviving example is contained in a fourteenth-century processional from Cividale.[1] Mary is the dominant figure, but there are four other singing parts. There is also an angel and the figure of Christ on the Cross. In the manuscript the *planctus* is incomplete, there being 125 surviving lines, together with a four-line musical setting. The striking feature of the composition is the wealth of stage directions. There are nearly eighty of them, laying down details of action such as would satisfy the most painstaking of producers. These *planctus* could hardly claim to bear the same relationship to the Passion dramas as the 'Quem quaeritis' dialogue does to those of the Resurrection, but in the few medieval Latin Passions which exist the laments occupy a central position. No doubt the composition of the play was a result of a direct desire to dramatize the Crucifixion story. But the clerical playwrights, as a body, do not seem to have been drawn to the task. Perhaps the central rite of the Mass seemed to them to commemorate sufficiently the greatest moment of the liturgical year.

There are only two complete texts of this type of Passion drama, both found in the famous thirteenth-century *Carmina Burana* manuscript (see also pp. 187 and 222). The first[2] is relatively brief, and is crudely put together by direct borrowings from the Vulgate, both for the dialogue and for directions. The other example[3] is much more ambitious and is of considerable dimensions. One imagines that it would be difficult to accommodate in any liturgical service, and there is no proof that it was performed within a church at all. Since it contains a good deal of vernacular German verse it may represent a transitional stage towards the secular drama. It is in the general liturgical style, however, and contains a proportion of choruses from the service books which would be performed by a clerical choir. Several different 'stations' are called for, to localize such places as the house of Simon, the Mount of Olives, the house of Pilate, and the place of the Crucifixion. Many incidents are included: the calling of Peter and Andrew, the career and repentance of Mary Magdalen, the raising of Lazarus, the Last Supper, the betrayal and trial of Jesus, and the Crucifixion. Again much of the dialogue is drawn from the Vulgate. This is much more extensive, however; a proportion is

---

[1] Cividale, Museo Archeologico, C1, fo. 74–76ᵛ.
[2] Munich, Staatsbibl. lat. 4660a, fo. iiiᵛ–ivᵛ.
[3] Ibid. 4660, fo. 107–112ᵛ.

in metrical form, and there is much other original versification, including the stanzas in the vernacular. The musical notation is unfortunately German neums written *in campo aperto* (see p. 108), giving no indication of the pitch of the notes. When liturgical pieces are not involved the music appears to represent free composition not found elsewhere. A striking feature is the introduction of *Diabolus* and *Angelus*, representing the evil and good influences that sway Mary Magdalen. This is the first appearance of figures prominent in later medieval drama. The Crucifixion scene consists very largely of the *planctus* of the Virgin Mary and St. John in Latin and German verse. On the whole the drama gives the impression of being a compilation, a patchwork of scenes which may previously have had independent existence.

We might well expect that the stories both of the Ascension and of Pentecost would have inspired numerous early medieval playwrights. But there is little sign of any such development. In spite of the attachment to the Ascension Day Mass of a trope with dramatic possibilities, 'Quem creditis super astra ascendisse?', one example alone of an Ascension drama has survived.[1] Text and music, however, are drawn wholly from the liturgy. There appears to have been some stage device by which an image of Christ was drawn up to the curtained roof. As for Whit-Sunday, though we have significant actions such as the descent from the roof of a dove, wafers, drops of water, or even burning tow, none of these actions passed beyond the symbolic stage.

CHRISTMAS PLAYS

Turning to the Christmas season, we find a dramatic evolution similar to that of Easter. Once again a dramatic trope is the germ of the development; once again the details of the Vulgate text are added to by free invention as to dialogue and situation. The starting-points are (*a*) Luke ii. 7–20, which details the birth of Christ and the visit of the shepherds, and (*b*) a trope of the Introit of the third Mass of Christmas Day, which suggests a dialogue and recalls the scene of the shepherds at the manger.[2] In translation the latter runs:

'Whom seek ye at the manger, O shepherds? Say!'

'Christ the Saviour, the infant Lord wrapped in swaddling clothes, according to the words of the Angel.'

'The child is here with Mary his mother, of whom long ago the prophet

---

[1] Munich, Staatsbibl. lat. 9469, fo. 72ᵛ–73ᵛ (a fourteenth-century *ordinarium* from Mosburg).

[2] Paris, Bibl. Nat. lat. 887, fo. 9ᵛ (a Limoges troper of the eleventh century). A number of eleventh-century tropers show the same version.

Isaiah spoke, prophesying: "Behold a virgin shall conceive and bear a son'":
and now as ye go forth say that he is born.'

'Alleluia! Now do we know truly that Christ is born into the world; of
whom let all sing, saying with the prophet:

'*Puer natus est nobis*[1] (unto us a child is born).'

The dramatic possibilities of the text are obvious, as is its close similarity of construction to the 'Quem quaeritis in sepulchro' trope. The
relative dates of the earliest appearances of the tropes make it certain
that the Christmas trope is the debtor. Once again we have a single
act of composition. Words and music are found almost unchanged
in various eleventh-century tropers of France and Italy. (Other countries do not favour the dialogue in trope form.) The setting, unlike
the words, does not seem to owe anything to the Easter music. The
first two sentences with their melodies are here transcribed from the
Limoges troper:

Ex. 66 (i)

Quem quæ-ri-tis in præ-se-pe,   pa-sto-res, di-ci-te.   Sal-va-to-rem Chri-stum

Do - mi-num, in-fan-tem pan-nis in-vo-lu-tum, se-cun-dum ser-mo-nem an-ge-li-cum.

Ex. 66 (ii)

Quem quæ- ri - tis in præ-se - pe,   pa - sto-res, di-ci - te.

Sal-va - to - rem Christum Do   -   mi - num, in -   fan-tem pan-nis

in - vo - lu - tum, se - cun-dum ser - mo - nem an -   ge-li-cum.

As in the case of its Easter model, the dialogue in its trope form
seems to have no actual dramatic intent. But the desire for such development resulted similarly in a transference to Matins, generally
after the conclusion of the service. This was in any case a natural
position, since once again the incidents related occurred early in the
morning. When impersonation begins we discover that the questioners
of the shepherds are the midwives (*obstetrices*), in attendance at the

[1] The first words of the Introit of the Mass.

manger, a tradition dating from the second century. The necessary property, the *praesepe* or crib, is located behind the altar, usually complete with figures of Virgin and Child, and thus, by the eleventh century, another music-drama, the *Officium Pastorum*, was in being. Some expansion quickly followed, and though there are but few extant examples of the drama, the most extensive, a thirteenth-century version from Rouen,[1] is an attractive composition. There are five shepherds, dressed in amices and tunics, and bearing staves. As they enter the choir a solo 'Angel', high up under the roof, sings 'Nolite timere' (Luke ii. 10–12). This is followed by an angelic chorus, 'Gloria in excelsis'. The music in each case seems to be specially composed. As the shepherds advance towards the curtained crib, behind the main altar, they sing an original composition, based on verses 14–15, beginning:

Ex. 67 (i)

Pax in ter-ris nun-ti-a-tur, in ex-cel-sis glo-ri-a.

Ex. 67 (ii)

Pax in ter-ris nun - ti - a-tur, in ex - cel - sis glo-ri - a.

(Peace is proclaimed on earth, and glory in the highest.)

and continuing for five verses. The arpeggio on 'nuntiatur' and the 'cadence' in the major scale on 'gloria' have a curiously modern ring. The scene at the crib when the midwives draw aside the curtains consists mainly of the trope dialogue with its usual music. There is one modification: the setting of the first four words of the midwives' question is not the usual Christmas tune, but the notes of 'Quem quaeritis in sepulchro?' The spell of the older melody prevails for this brief time, and then the usual setting is resumed.

Next, the shepherds kneel to Mary and sing another new composition, beginning 'Salve virgo singularis'. The drama concludes with the last sentence of the trope, but in the Midnight Mass which follows the shepherds 'rule the choir'—that is to say, they start the Introit, and sing the verse of the Gradual. In Lauds, which follows, there occurs the relevant antiphon 'Quem vidistis, pastores, dicite'. This is rendered so dramatically between the priest and the shepherds as almost to constitute another part of the play. Repeated several

[1] Paris, Bibl. Nat. lat. 904, fo. 11ᵛ–14.

times, it gives the impression of the shepherds being questioned on their return by various people. This idea is used dramatically in some of the plays which expand the story of the Christmas season. In spite of the effectiveness of the Rouen example the *Officium Pastorum* had no important separate existence. As a subject it appears to have been neglected in favour of the later events of the Twelve Days. The figures of the *Magi* and Herod seemed to offer more scope. The Christmas crib, however, has survived to modern times, not as the background for a liturgical drama but as a silent object of religious devotion. Epiphany, rather than Christmas Day, saw the greatest dramatic activity of the season. There developed the plays of the *Magi*, the Wise Men, who followed the star from the East, who encountered Herod, and who brought their gifts to the manger at Bethlehem. The medieval playwrights are not agreed on a consistent name for these dramas. We have such terms as *Officium Stellae, Officium Regum Trium,* and in the longer ones, where Herod begins to be the outstanding figure, *Ordo ad representandum Herodem.* Ample material for such drama was provided by the second chapter of St. Matthew, verses 1–12, and verse 16. Christian tradition, influenced perhaps by Psalm lxxii. 10, gave them the status of kings, three in number, of Tharsis, Arabia, and Saba. In accordance with the Gospel account, they bore gifts of gold, frankincense, and myrrh. The most elementary dramas of the *Magi* are actually found within the liturgy. A Limoges text (probably twelfth-century)[1] shows the Three Kings, crowned, robed in silk, and bearing their gifts in gilt vessels, taking an appropriate part in the Offertory of the Epiphany Mass. They are guided to the altar by a star-shaped candelabrum hanging from the roof, and capable of being moved by means of cords. This property is present in all *Magi* dramas, thus justifying the frequently used title, *Officium Stellae.* Although the *Magi* are greeted by an angel and act their parts, texts and music are of liturgical origin. This dramatic use of the Epiphany oblation was undoubtedly a custom common to other centres, and is possibly the germ of the fully developed *Officium Stellae.*

The simplest form of the real drama can be seen in a Rouen version from thi teenth- and fourteenth-century manuscripts.[2] Though still loosely linked with the Mass this example shows a large amount of original dialogue, which, together with its music, is present in all

---

[1] Cf. Martène, *De Antiquis Ecclesiae Ritibus,* iii, p. 44.

[2] Paris, Bibl. Nat. lat. 904, fo. 28ᵛ–30. More detailed rubrics are found in Rouen, Bibl. de la Ville 384, fo. 38ᵛ–39 (fourteenth century), which lacks musical notation.

other extant *Officium Stellae* dramas, however much new material these may acquire. In this version we have, in fact, the core of the whole *Magi* series. As the most advanced of the dramas were probably in existence by the end of the eleventh century at the latest, the Rouen manuscripts may not represent the most primitive form; but it seems possible that there was a prototype made of much the same material. The Rouen action takes place between Terce and Mass. The three, robed and crowned, each with an attendant bearing the gifts, enter from different directions and meet before the altar. Pointing to the star, the first sings:

Stel - la ful-go-re ni-mi-o ru-ti-lat.

(The star shines with exceeding great light.)

The others reply in turn: 'Quae regem regum natum demonstrat' (which showeth that the King of Kings is born), and 'Quem venturum olim prophetiae signaverant' (whose advent prophecies foretold in ancient days), to music similar in style. These sentences are no doubt suggested by an antiphon of Lauds, but the wording and the music are probably original. Afterwards the *Magi* greet each other with the kiss of peace and sing of their intention to seek the Child and offer gifts.

The three then move into the nave, following the star, while liturgical responsories, relevant to their journey, are sung by the choir. Another star is suspended over the 'Altar of the Holy Cross', by which is located the curtained *praesepe* with the figures of Mother and Child. As they approach, the *Magi* sing another new composition, beginning: 'Ecce stella in oriente praevisa iterum praecedit nos' (lo, the star seen aforetime in the East goes before us again). Two clergy in dalmatics standing by the altar then question them. The *Magi* reply, announcing their identities. The other two, who represent the midwives, although this is not directly stated, draw aside the curtains. The Kings bow themselves to the earth and greet the child, while each in turn offers his gift:

Ex. 69 (i)

Primus: Sús-ci-pe, Rex, au-rum.   *Secundus:* Tol-le thus, tu ve-re De-us.

Tertius: Myr-rham, si-gnum se-pul-tu-ræ.

Ex. 69 (ii)

8 PRIMUS: Sus-ci-pe, Rex, au - rum.   8 SECUNDUS: Tolle thus, tu ve- re De - us.

8 TERTIUS: Myr - rham, signum se-pul - tu-ræ.

(Accept gold, O King. Receive incense, thou very God. Myrrh, the sign of burial.)

The dialogue is plainly modelled on the shepherds' visit to the crib. It is, however, an entirely new composition, as is the last section—the triple offering. They then fall asleep, but are awakened by a boy dressed as an angel, who tells them to return by another road, lest they bring harm to the 'King'. This is suggested by Matt. ii. 12, but is quite an independent composition. As they retire the chorus sings an appropriate liturgical responsory. In the Mass which follows, the Kings, like the shepherds before them, 'rule the choir', and during the Offertory again bring gifts.

The material quoted above, with only minor variation, is reproduced in every *Officium Stellae* drama which has survived. These are barely a dozen in number, but they happen to show stages of growth which may well represent something like the historical development. The first and most important progress is the appearance of Herod, the most picturesque figure of medieval drama, who questions the *Magi* at his court. Subsequent additions expand this scene. Herod acquires courtiers, and sends emissaries to the *Magi*. He confers with his scribes, and with a military attendant who tells him of the flight of the *Magi*, 'warned of God in a dream', and advises the massacre of the Innocents. Meanwhile Herod is seen developing towards the blustering furious tyrant of tradition, who in the Guild Plays was directed to 'rage on the pageant and in the street', to the admiration of every village Bottom. A further expansion links the *Magi* with the shepherds, whom they meet returning from the manger.

Finally the *Officium Pastorum* itself is used as a prelude. A further addition will be spoken of in its place.

One striking feature of these *Magi* dramas is the large amount of free invention that is displayed at each stage. The Vulgate narrative and ideas from Epiphany antiphons are used to shape dialogue, but the wording, and certainly the music, represent free composition. Versification is found, but not in undue proportion. Liturgical antiphons and hymns are used very sparingly. It is noticeable that once a dialogue and its music have been invented for a certain scene, they are taken over and used with minor alteration and rearrangement in the more extended versions. One gains the impression, however, of a fair amount of variety and independence of treatment: every version has dialogue features peculiar to itself.

A somewhat bleak drama of the eleventh century from Nevers,[1] performed at Matins, shows the briefest presentation of Herod. He appears abruptly after the *Magi* have introduced themselves with the words and music of the Rouen drama, and sings:

Ex. 70 (i)

Re-gem quem quæ-ri-tis na-tum es-se quo si-gno di-di-ci-stis? Si il-lum re-gna-re

cre-di-tis, di-ci-te no-bis.

Ex. 70 (ii)

Re - gem quem quæ - ri - tis na-tum   es - se quo si-gno di- di-

-ci -- stis? Si il - lum re-gna - re   cre - di -tis, di-ci-te   no - bis.'

(By what sign have ye learned that the King ye seek is born? If ye believe that he reigneth, tell us.)

This question, the *Magi's* reply, and the King's instructions that they shall seek the child and bring him word, are the basis of the court scene of all subsequent versions. All this is free composition. Herod disappears as abruptly as he came, and the encounter at the manger follows the exact terms of Rouen, with the acts of oblation. The little drama closes with the angelic warning. We assume that the *Magi* will

[1] Paris, Bibl. Mazarine 1708, fo. 81ʳ.

'depart another way'. Between the Nevers example and a version from Compiègne,[1] also of the eleventh century, there may be an evolution- ary gap, for in the latter Herod's court suddenly comes to life, and the drama is considerably extended. A *nuntius* questions the *Magi* and reports to Herod. Several of these newly composed sentences go into the pool, as it were, for later use. The *Magi*-Herod encounter is very close to that of Nevers. Then occurs another new scene which also becomes common property, in which Herod tells his courtiers to summon the scribes, who appear and relate prophecies concerning the Coming. Herod sends the *Magi* away with sentences already en- countered, but they sing newly composed verses on their way to the manger. Here the usual scene occurs, in the usual terms. The action then returns to Herod's court, where a messenger warns him:'Delu- sus es, Domine; magi viam redierunt aliam' (Sire, thou art deceived; the *Magi* have returned by another way)—an invention of the play- wright. *Armiger* then makes his cruel suggestion, to which Herod assents. An antiphon ('Suffer little children') sung by an angel con- cludes the drama, which has shown a great deal of original material.

Only brief reference need be made to a number of versions which further expand the Herod episode. The court rather than the crib is becoming the centre of interest. Some outstanding points may be mentioned. In a Strasbourg manuscript[2] we encounter a verse clearly imitated from Virgil, while another of Herod's sentences comes direct from Sallust.[3] A Rouen example[4] shows two of the *Magi* replying to Herod in a gibberish intended to represent an outlandish tongue. We also meet Archelaus, Herod's son, for the first time, and see the drama concluded with a flourishing of swords. A version from Bilsen[5] in Belgium has three separate messengers, one of them in his eagerness to report calling out: 'Rex, rex, rex'—a delightfully vivid touch. The *Magi* are greeted very curtly, and unlike their treatment in other versions, where they are sometimes given seats and a ceremonial kiss, they are here dragged off to prison. Altogether this version livens the dramatic note considerably. A fine treatment of the subject in the Fleury play-book[6] shows a good deal of the originality we have come to expect. A useful feature is its wealth of rubrics. The star is mobile, travelling overhead from the

[1] Paris, Bibl. Nat. lat. 16819, fo. 49–49ᵛ.
[2] London, Brit. Mus., Add. 23922, fo. 8ᵛ–11 (thirteenth century).
[3] Cf. Young, *Drama of the Medieval Church*, ii, pp. 67–68.
[4] Montpellier, Bibl. Univ., H. 304, fo. 41ᵛ–42ᵛ (twelfth century).
[5] Brussels, Bibl. des Bollandistes 299, fo. 179ᵛ–180ᵛ (twelfth century).
[6] Orleans, Bibl. de la Ville 201, pp. 205–14 (thirteenth century).

main altar to the door of the choir, to Herod's throne in the nave, and finally to the crib at another door. There are several descriptions of costume, and the scribes are bearded. Herod has several bursts of rage, while the emotions of other characters are also described, such as the initial fear and subsequent cheerful confidence of the shepherds. We may assume similar conditions in the performance of other versions, less happily supplied with directions. At the conclusion of an eleventh-century version from Freising,[1] after the threat to the Innocents has been made, there occurs a procession of children singing in chorus. This episode is significant in view of a further development soon to be discussed. The drama is a full-length one, and its date indicates how early the *Officium Stellae* was brought to full maturity. Altogether, the series must be regarded as a successful phase of the liturgical music-drama. A high proportion of the texts and music represent free composition; there is an interesting variety of dramatic action, and, especially in the case of Herod, characterization is definitely being attempted.

St. Matthew's account, which inspired the dramas just discussed, would inevitably suggest the addition of the episode of the slaughter of the Innocents. As it happens, there are but few surviving examples of a dramatization of this. One only, contained in a thirteenth-century service book from Laon,[2] is actually linked with the *Officium Stellae*. A better example can be found in the Fleury play-book,[3] where it exists as an independent composition. It is clearly a sequel to the *Magi* drama of the same manuscript, which purposely omits the scene of Herod's rage. It opens with a procession of boys, headed by a lamb bearing a cross (or more probably, by a banner bearing that device): the music is liturgical. The Holy Family are warned by an angel and depart to Egypt. Herod now enters, and lines occur which have been met with in the Freising and Strasbourg manuscripts. *Armiger* greets Herod and tells him of the flight of the *Magi*. Herod's emotion is such that he is about to commit suicide. At this moment the children appear again, singing what seems an original composition, and Herod's rage is diverted to them. On the suggestion of *Armiger*, in terms already met with in *Magi* versions, the massacre is ordered. A new feature, however, is the attempted intervention of a number of mothers. An angel also sings a passage, without preventing the slaughter. Then comes a *Lamentatio Rachelis*,

---

[1] Munich, Staatsbibl. lat. 6264*a*, fo. 1.
[2] Laon, Bibl. de la Ville 263, fo. 149–151.
[3] Orleans, Bibl. de la Ville 201, pp. 214–20.

with two *consolatrices*, who support her when she is about to fall.[1] This extensive scene, in verse, is an extraordinary patchwork: free composition, lines found also in the Freising version, and actually a tenth-century sequence of Notker's. It is skilfully unified, though, and the seams are not apparent. In unique fashion a 'happy ending' is contrived. The angel appears again, singing the antiphon 'Sinite parvulos' ('Suffer little children'), whereupon the victims are restored to life, rise and enter the choir singing a liturgical piece. Then in dumb-show Herod is dethroned, to be succeeded by Archelaus. Finally the angel summons back the Holy Family, to what is probably original music. An antiphon concludes the drama, which takes place apparently at Matins, though the actual day remains uncertain. In spite of a high proportion of borrowings we have here an attractive music-drama, with ample details of costume and action.

Some mention must be made of a piece of dramatic pageantry known as *Ordo Prophetarum*, the time and date of performance during the Twelve Days of Christmas varying in different places. This 'Procession of the Prophets' was a dramatization of a section of a famous sixth-century sermon (erroneously ascribed to St. Augustine) in which the preacher calls on various Biblical personages— Moses, Isaiah, David, Jeremiah, and a number more—for utterances concerning the coming of Christ. Even pagan witnesses, Virgil and the Sibyl, are cited. The dramatic possibilities of the *Ordo Prophetarum* were obvious, but the resultant metrical adaptations were few in number and of no great interest from either a dramatic or a musical point of view.

We have found that three of the Christmas themes—those of the Shepherds, the *Magi*, and the Innocents—tend to fuse into single compositions. This tendency towards unwieldiness, which we have already seen in the Easter group, must at times have strained the resources of ecclesiastical space, time, and patience. It is not surprising to find that further combination seems to be confined to one famous example, the so-called 'Christmas Play' from the *Carmina Burana*, dating from the thirteenth century.[2] This drama may be the product of the monastery, or perhaps one of the efforts of the goliards, the wandering scholars, who contributed other compositions to the collection. It displays a great deal of theological and classical learning, frequently to the detriment of its dramatic elements. It is altogether

---

[1] The mourning Rachel as a dramatic subject is found as early as the eleventh century. (Cf. Paris, Bibl. Nat. lat. 1139, fol. 32ᵛ–33.) Her *planctus* has the precedent of a wealth of similar laments of the Virgin.

[2] Munich, Staatsbibl. lat. 4660, fo. 99–104ᵛ.

so long and unwieldy as to raise doubts whether it could be performed at all in the church precincts. It consists almost wholly of Latin verses, certainly showing the influence of previous material, but in themselves original and competent. There are also a few sentences from the Vulgate and some liturgical antiphons. With the exception of a few lines, it has musical notation throughout; but this is in the form of German neums, without heightening. As the text is unique, there is no possibility of making a transcription in staff notation. All that is apparent is that the long stanzas are set strophically, with a great deal of repetition of phrase, as in the case of other dramas from Benediktbeuern: for example, the two opening stanzas sung by 'Augustine' are both attached to the same tune, whose form is *A B A B C D C D*.

The work begins with a variation of the *Ordo Prophetarum*, in which the prophets appear in support of Augustine as opposed to *Archisynagogus* and the Jews. The main action includes the Annunciation, the Nativity, the appearance of the *Magi*, and then the familiar events at Herod's court, including the Slaying of the Innocents. We have also the Flight to Egypt and the Death of Herod. This last drama of the Christmas season exceeds all the others in stature, and with its careful details of costume, setting, and grouping, must have been an impressive pageant. But its prolix technique compares unfavourably with that of the shorter versions. In these, the brief prose sentences with their recitative-like settings, and the rapid dramatic action, seem much more likely to have produced satisfactory results on the stage.

SUNDRY RELIGIOUS PLAYS

The remaining extant medieval dramas which could fairly be described as both 'liturgical' and 'musical' are not very large in number. They deal with New and Old Testament themes, legends of the saints, and the Last Judgement. During the later Middle Ages the authors of vernacular drama, no longer in close contact with the Church service and no longer attempting musical settings, produced an astonishing number of plays in all these categories. We are only concerned here with the Latin music-dramas, which in the main precede them. Of these no less than six owe their preservation to the Fleury play-book (see p. 185). One New Testament drama deals with the Raising of Lazarus,[1] keeping close to the account of St. John, but using as a preliminary scene the incident of the anointing of Jesus's feet by Mary at the house of Simon the Pharisee. As the action takes place in various localities—the house of Simon, Galilee, Bethany, and

[1] Orleans, Bibl. de la Ville 201, pp. 233–43.

the tomb of Lazarus—these are represented by various parts of the church. The rubrics are generous, and describe actions and emotions in some detail. A concluding *Te Deum* seems to place the drama at Matins, but the day, and even the season, are uncertain.

A disappointing feature of the drama is that, apart from an opening prose sung by the disciples, all the characters express themselves in verses that are identical in structure throughout. These are dignified and competent, but certainly handicap the realism of what might have been a striking composition. Added to this, apart from the prose, the music throughout is that of the first stanza, with a few occasional variations of cadence. The pattern and the music of the whole composition, then, is apparent in the following extract:

Ex. 71 (i)

(Vouchsafe to declare thy power through the vileness of my flesh, grant us the joy desired, and deign to enter our lodging.)

Another working of the same subject is found in a remarkable manuscript of the twelfth century.[1] At last we have the name of a playwright of these times, Hilarius, a wandering scholar, a pupil of

---

[1] Paris, Bibl. Nat. lat. 11331, fo. 9–10ᵛ.

Abelard, and the author of two other dramas in the same manuscript, later to be noted. Hilarius and his goliard companions undoubtedly acted these plays themselves. They are wholly in verse, very competent, and varied rhythmically in accordance with the emotional demands. It is all the more to be regretted that no musical setting is given, although there is no doubt that everything was sung.

Another New Testament subject treated in the Fleury play-book is the Conversion of St. Paul,[1] probably performed on the feast day of the saint, and (to judge by the *Te Deum* at the close) probably at Matins. Once again the rubrics are very generous. A large area is apparently needed, for on one side is the station which represents Jerusalem, with *sedes* (seats) for the High Priest and Saul with his soldiers. On the other side is Damascus, and between, in quaint realism, the bed of the reclining Ananias, awaiting the vision. A further interesting rubric concerns the lowering of Saul in a basket, 'quasi a muro' (as though from a wall). There are elaborate directions at every stage of the story, which follows the course of the narrative of Acts ix fairly closely, with some few minor improvised expansions. The text, wholly in verse, is disappointingly uniform and dull; no rhythmic variation breaks its steady monotony. The music, however, shows greater variety, going almost to the opposite extreme from that of 'The Raising of Lazarus'. True, the first two verses sung by Saul, are to the same melody, beginning:

Ex. 72 (i)

Pro-pa-la-re vo-bis non va-le-o quam in-gen-ti mi-hi sint o-di-o...

Ex.72 (ii)

Pro - pa - la   re vo - bis non   va - le - o   quam in - gen ·

-ti mi - hi sint   o - di - o...

(I cannot reveal to you how extremely odious [the Christians] are to me.)

But new tunes are employed for each of almost all the other verses. The few similarities which occur may be fortuitous. The result in general is an impression of shapelessness.

The cult of St. Nicholas, one of the most popular saints of medieval times, is represented in the Fleury manuscript by three plays. The first,

[1] Orleans, Bibl. de la Ville 201, pp. 230–3.

most appropriately, deals with his care for three wandering clerks
(he was in particular the patron saint of scholars). The brief drama of
'The Three Clerks'[1] begins without rubrication. Each speaks an even,
four-line, rhyming verse. From the first two we learn that they are in
need of shelter for the night; then the third clerk calls attention to an
old man who may provide it. After *Senex* has refused them, they
appeal to his wife, who intercedes in their favour. They are immediately shown to a bed, and the old man and his wife plot to rob them.
The wife, a primitive Lady Macbeth, urges an extra precaution. The
guests are murdered. A stranger promptly appears, none other than
St. Nicholas himself, also asking for shelter. Again it is the wife who
decides that he shall be admitted. He calls for food, and when difficulties are raised, remarks grimly that they have fresh meat in plenty.
Recognizing the saint, the couple beg for mercy. St. Nicholas calls on
them to repent, and, uttering a prayer over the dead bodies, recalls
the clerks to life.

The rapidity of the action and a certain amount of characterization
in the case of the husband and wife may redeem the regular monotony
of the stanzas. The music is not much help in this respect. With the
exception of St. Nicholas's prayer, all the verses are set to a single
tune of *A A B C* pattern, a Dorian melody of great beauty repeated
with minor variations well over a dozen times. One stanza is given
here:

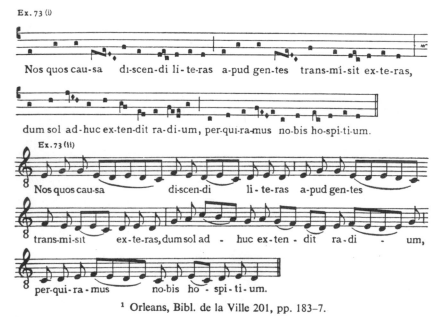

Ex. 73 (i)

Nos quos cau-sa   di-scen-di li-te-ras a-pud gen-tes   trans-mi-sit ex-te-ras,

dum sol ad-huc ex-ten-dit ra-di-um, per-qui-ra-mus no-bis ho-spi-ti-um.

Ex. 73 (ii)

Nos quos cau-sa   di-scen-di   li-te-ras a-pud gen-tes

trans-mi-sit   ex-te-ras, dum sol ad - huc ex-ten - dit ra-di - um,

per-qui-ra - mus   no-bis ho - spi-ti-um.

[1] Orleans, Bibl. de la Ville 201, pp. 183–7.

(Let us, who have travelled to foreign peoples to learn letters, seek a lodging for ourselves while it is still daylight.)

Very different in literary style is the second miracle of the Saint, found at Fleury.[1] The 'Image of St. Nicholas' tells of a Jew who, going on a journey, leaves his treasure to the protection of a figure of the Saint which he possesses, doing so with a certain amount of trepidation and incredulity. In his absence three robbers carry away the prize. The rightful owner returns, bewails his loss and promises the image a beating. Nicholas, whether or no influenced by this threat, appears to the robbers and commands restoration. In spite of the saintly displeasure two of them hesitate, but the third persuades them. Duly converted, the Jew rejoices at some length. The following and supporting chorus proves to be the Introit of the Mass for the Feast of St. Nicholas. The story is told in verses which have metrical variety. This is reflected in the setting. The Jew's long opening soliloquy is divided into two parts musically, each with a single tune. There is a great deal more melodic variety in the scene of the robbery. When the Jew returns, his first dismay is pictured thus:

Ex. 74 (i)

Vah!   pe-ri-i,   ni-hil est re-li-qui mi-hi,   cur es-se cœ-pi?

Ex. 74 (ii)

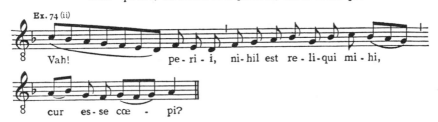

Vah!   pe - ri - i,   ni- hil est re - li-qui mi - hi,

cur   es- se cœ   -   pi?

(Woe! I am undone. Nothing is left to me. Why was I born?)

Altogether the drama is quite interesting musically, and deserves fuller attention than can be given here. An independent working of the legend by Hilarius[2] contains even more subtle variation of rhythm in the stanzas. Once again the absence of musical notation must be deplored.

The Fleury manuscript contains another St. Nicholas play, 'The Son of Getron'.[3] A striking feature of the composition is the unusual range of time and place. At one point it is made clear by one of the

[1] Ibid., pp. 188–96. See *Kirchenmusikalisches Jahrbuch*, li (1967), p. 12.
[2] Paris, Bibl. Nat. lat. 11331, fo. 11–12.
[3] Loc. cit., pp. 196–205.

speakers that a year is supposed to have elapsed. Events occur at the court of the pagan conqueror Marmorinus; at the home of Getron and Euphrosina in the Christian City of Excoranda; at the church of St. Nicholas in the city; and in the city streets. The rubrics also call for the scene of a banquet at the king's court, and a meal for the poor and the clerics at Euphrosina's house. In spite of this ambitious stage-setting, the use of a concluding antiphon of St. Nicholas's Day points to a church performance, probably at Lauds.

The usual story of the legend is followed faithfully. It deals with the captivity of the youthful Adeodatus at the court of the heathen conqueror Marmorinus, and his miraculous restoration to his parents through the agency of St. Nicholas. The text consists almost wholly of ten-syllable quatrains, but the musical device is interesting. All the main characters, or groups—the king, each of the two parents, the boy, the king's attendants, and the citizens—have tunes for their own special use, but when Adeodatus expresses his longing for home he does so, for a single verse, to his mother's music. The following is the king's melody:

Ex. 75 (i)

(To Apollo who rules over all, let there always be praise, and to you who have made so many countries subject and tributary to me, let thanks be given.)

The tune deserves attention, not only for its tonality, its form, its general shapeliness and beauty, but for the appoggiatura-like passage ('mihi tot patrias'), which has nothing Gregorian about it. Many of these strophic melodies seem indistinguishable from those of the trouvères.

The last drama of the Fleury play-book to be considered is 'The Three Daughters'.[1] This is also concerned with St. Nicholas and, to judge by the concluding antiphon, may have been performed at Lauds or Vespers on the Saint's day. The versification shows considerable skill, but in the main consists of ten-syllable quatrains with a short additional refrain line. The story concerns a father who, having fallen into poverty, is enabled to marry off his three daughters through successive and anonymous gifts of gold. In the end St. Nicholas is found to be the donor. The settings of the opening laments of father and daughters are almost identical. Then the father continues with a new and very striking melody:

Ex. 76 (i)

(You, my daughters, are my precious pledge, the only wealth of an indigent father and a comfort to my unhappiness; have regard then at last for my misfortune. Woe is me.)

The rest of the music, up to the concluding antiphon chorus, consists of over thirty repetitions of this tune or part of it, since it is used by all the characters in turn.

In the later Middle Ages a certain amount of dramatic ceremony

[1] Loc. cit., pp. 176–82.

attached itself to the various feasts of the Virgin Mary. Impersonation
is met with in all these, though in the main the atmosphere is liturgical.
The most remarkable example is the 'Presentation' drama organized
by Philippe de Mezières (1326–1405), crusader and scholar, and performed at Avignon before Mass on the feast-day in 1395. A full text
of the *Ordo* has survived.[1] There is no music given, and it cannot be
ascertained with certainty how much of the dialogue was actually
sung. The details of the stage-setting, however, are the fullest in
liturgical drama, and recall a brilliant spectacle. A point of interest
is that the cast included two musicians, and the action was accompanied by instrumental music.

The most impressive of Church dramas dealing with the Last
Judgement is undoubtedly the twelfth-century 'Antichrist' from
Tegernsee,[2] comprising over 400 lines of Latin verse, and ranging
in its action through all the kingdoms of the world. Armies march
and fight; cities are overwhelmed; prophets are murdered; finally,
thunder from heaven slays the Usurper. Wide spaces, brilliant
pageantry, and considerable stage resources were obviously called for
in this ambitious work, which was written during the reign of the
Emperor Frederick Barbarossa and probably performed before him.
Though the parts were undoubtedly sung, no musical notation is
given except for the one liturgical responsory found in the text.

The great interest taken by later medieval drama in the theme of
the Last Judgement is foreshadowed in the famous *Sponsus* contained
in the twelfth- or thirteenth-century troper from Limoges,[3] previously
mentioned (see p. 204, n. 1). The text has been much studied, as it
is an early example of the invasion of the vernacular, here a dialect
of Angoulême. Some verses are wholly Latin, some wholly French,
others Latin with a French refrain. The text is generally held to be
disordered. It is perhaps founded on a Latin original. Rubrics are
scanty. The action is founded on the parable of the Ten Virgins as told
in Matt. xxv. 1–13. There is an opening chorus, twenty Latin lines,
whose musical form could be described roughly as being *A B A C*.
Then Gabriel utters a warning, four verses in French with the refrain:

Ex. 77 (i)

Gai-re noi dor-met! Ai-sel e - spos que vos hor a-ten-det.

---

[1] Paris, Bibl. Nat. lat. 17330, fo. 18–24.
[2] Munich, Staatsbibl. lat. 19411, pp.6–15.   [3] Paris, Bibl. Nat. lat. 1139, fo. 53–55ᵛ.

Gai-re noi dor-met! Ai-sel   e - spos   que vos hor a - ten-det.

(Beware lest you sleep! The bridegroom awaits you outside!)

The form of the new melody used here is, in the first verse, *A B A B C D A B*, but this is a good deal modified in the other stanzas. The alternating sets of verses for *fatuae* and *prudentes* are in Latin, with a French refrain, used by both:

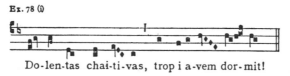

Do-len-tas chai-ti-vas, trop i a-vem dor-mit!

Do - len - tas   chai-ti - vas, trop i a-vem   dor - mit!

(Unfortunate wretches are we, we have slept there too long!)

The music of the *fatuae* is consistent throughout, the form being simply *A A A B C* (*C* = refrain). The *prudentes*, however, use two different melodies for their two sets of verses. When the *mercatores* refuse the request for oil they do so to the tune of the *fatuae*. The last verse of the composition is the pronouncement of *Christus*, striking a harsher note than in the parable, and consigning the *fatuae* to hell. Then follows an unusual rubric: 'Modo accipiant eas Daemones, et praecipitentur in infernum' (now let the devils receive them, and let them be thrown into hell). This is probably the first appearance in Church drama of the devils who were so popular on the later medieval stage.

THE DANIEL PLAYS

There are only a few surviving examples of the liturgical drama which deal with Old Testament subjects. Two of them, 'Esau and Jacob',[1] and 'Joseph and his Brethren',[2] are found incomplete in form and scantily supplied with neums. The rubrics, however, give interesting stage details. The other two are more satisfactory. Each of them

[1] Vorau, Chorherrenstift 223. The volume itself is a fifteenth-century book of sermons. The text mentioned above was found on an older sheet of vellum pasted to the cover.
[2] Laon, Bibl. de la Ville 263, fo. 151–153ᵛ (thirteenth century).

has the Book of Daniel for its theme. The verses show a high standard of scholarship and metrical variety. The dramas are skilfully constructed, and must have made brilliant and impressive spectacles. Only one of them preserves its music. The manuscripts are both of the twelfth century, the first a product of the scholar Hilarius,[1] the other a communal effort of the cathedral school of Beauvais.[2] Both versions follow the Bible story fairly faithfully, but both add the later apocryphical episode of the miraculous visit of Habakkuk, guided by an angel, to the imprisoned Daniel. A further addition is the concluding pronouncement by the prophet, found in both versions, in which he foretells the coming of Christ. Except for one brief phrase the two dramas represent two independent literary workings; but some link there must have been, for they develop the theme along closely similar lines. As Beauvais possesses a clearly written musical setting on a four-line staff, we may leave its companion and consider it alone in detail.

The drama was probably performed at Matins on 1 January, the day which also saw the 'Feast of Fools'. Indeed, Darius's cry 'O hez' seems to echo the bray of the ass from the office of misrule. That 'Daniel' was a spectacle of great splendour cannot be doubted, and in many ways it is a fitting example with which to round off our review of the liturgical drama. It is clear that a large number of performers were needed. Both Belshazzar and Darius seem to have a following of princes and soldiers. Belshazzar's queen enters and retires escorted by her own followers. The 'golden and silver vessels that were taken out of the Temple' were no doubt richly furnished by the treasury of the great Cathedral. Some device was employed to call forth the prophetic words 'Mane, Thechel, Phares'. The defeat and slaying of Belshazzar by Darius and his forces was apparently represented in action, as was the scene of Daniel's ordeal, where an angel threatens the lions with a sword. Again, the followers of the two kings were not merely 'supers', but claimed long stretches of the text for their exultant choruses in praise of their leaders.

As for the music, no use is made of the effective device that we have encountered, of attaching one tune to one particular character. Instead, we have a wealth of melodies—nearly fifty in all. There is one striking repetition; time and again the King, whether Belshazzar

---

[1] Paris, Bibl. Nat. lat. 11331, fo. 12ᵛ–16. Owing to the entry on various parts of the text of the names 'Hilarius', 'Jordanus', 'Simon', and 'Hugo', it has been inferred that Hilarius shared his task with some of his scholar-companions. There is no doubt that everything was sung, but once again he has omitted the musical setting.

[2] London, Brit. Mus. Egerton 2615, fo. 95–108.

or Darius, is greeted with the phrase 'Rex, in aeternum vive!' (O King, live for ever). This is always to the same setting; otherwise, though a melody may be repeated for a number of times in one section, another speaker usually means another tune. Occasionally these are continuous, i.e. with a new melodic curve for each line of the text; but normally clear-cut patterns are found: *A B* repeated; *A B C D* repeated; *A B C C*; *A B A C*; or even complications like *A A B C B D D B C B*. A great deal of the melody is in the direct style of the sequence, with one syllable to a note as a general rule. This is particularly true of the big choruses, which have a fine momentum and power in consequence. More reflective moments give occasionally a more florid style.

We now turn to the action. After what may have been a brief solo introduction, beginning:

Ad honorem tui, Christe,
Danielis ludus iste,[1]

Belshazzar the king makes his entry, while the assembled company sing a chorus of nine verses, each to the same fine five-phrase tune, which summarizes the action of the piece. The first verse is given:

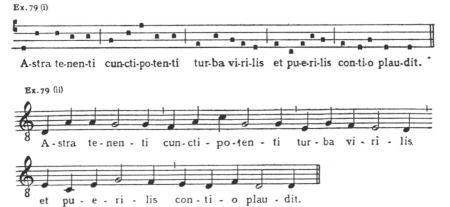

Ex. 79 (i)

A-stra te-nen-ti cun-cti-po-ten-ti tur-ba vi-ri-lis et pu-e-ri-lis con-ti-o plau-dit.

Ex. 79 (ii)

A-stra te-nen-ti cun-cti-po-ten-ti tur-ba vi-ri-lis,

et pu-e-ri-lis con-ti-o plau-dit.

(To him who holds the stars, the omnipotent, the congregation of men and choir of boys give praise.)

The drama proper then begins. The King ascends his throne amid the applause of his satraps, and then calls for the Temple vessels for use at the feast. Again comes the turbulent chorus to a new 'sequence' tune, beginning:

[1] In thy honour, O Christ, this play of Daniel [was written at Beauvais].

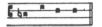

Ju-bi-le-mus re-gi no-stro ma-gno ac po-ten-ti; Re-so-ne-mus lau-de di-gna vo-ce

com-pe-ten-ti.

Ju - bi - le - mus re - gi no - stro ma - gno ac po - ten - ti;

Re - so - ne - mus lau - de di - gna vo - ce com - pe- ten - ti.

(Let us rejoice in our great and mighty king. Let us cry aloud his praiseworthy acts in a fitting voice.)

As the text indicates, it is probable that the sounds of musical instruments were heard in this scene. This full-throated chorus continues for four more verses. As the tumult ends there comes the dramatic moment of the appearance of 'fingers of man's hand', writing on the wall.

Urgently the King calls for his wise men and asks for an explanation. They reply in repetitive musical phrases which seem exactly to suit the expression of their bewilderment. Then comes a messenger of the Queen and finally the Queen herself, advising that the aid of Daniel should be sought. At the King's command the lords summon Daniel, in a strange mixture of tongues:

Ex. 81 (i)

Vir pro-phé-ta De - i Da-ni-el, vien al Roi.

Ex. 81 (ii)

Vir pro- phe-ta   De -   - i Da-ni-el, vien   al   Roi.

(Thou man, Daniel the prophet of God, come to the King.)

For the next few verses we have a brief invasion of the vernacular, the messengers using the French refrain 'Cestui manda li Rois par nos' (these are the commands of the King by us), but the text soon returns wholly to Latin. Daniel's long exposition, thirty lines of verse, is once more set in 'sequence' style, suited to a rapid recitative. On its conclusion the King, true to his word, orders that he shall be richly rewarded. The Queen then retires to another ringing chorus, seven repetitions of a two-phrase melody. The precious vessels are presented to Daniel, seated in honour near the King, and the scene closes with several stanzas in his praise.

Whether these characters now withdraw is not clear, but the interest is suddenly switched to King Darius and his lords. The latter, led by a 'citharist', sing a long and vigorous chorus, beginning:

Ex. 82 (i)

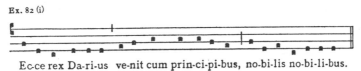

Ec-ce rex Da-ri-us ve-nit cum prin-ci-pi-bus, no-bi-lis no-bi-li-bus.

Ex. 82 (ii)

Ec - ce rex Da-ri - us ve - nit cum prin-ci - pi-bus, no - bi-lis no-bi - li-bus.

(Lo, King Darius comes with his satraps, a prince among princes.)

rising to a really splendid climax at its conclusion. From the evidence which we have of the use of every conceivable kind of medieval musical instrument at church festivals, from harps and viols to trumpets and drums, it is difficult to think that Beauvais did not make full musical use of such a moment as this:

Ex. 83 (i)

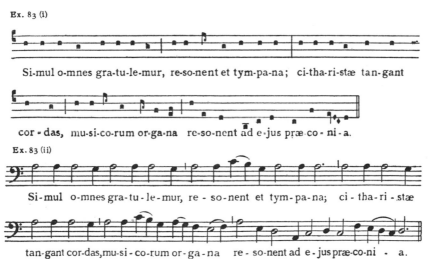

Si-mul o-mnes gra-tu-le-mur, re-so-nent et tym-pa-na; ci-tha-ri-stæ tan-gant

cor - das, mu-si-co-rum or-ga-na re-so-nent ad e-jus præ co - ni - a.

Ex. 83 (ii)

Si-mul o-mnes gra-tu - le - mur, re - so-nent et tym-pa-na; ci - tha-ri - stæ

tan-gant cor-das, mu-si - co-rum or-ga-na   re - so-nent ad e - jus præ-co-ni - a.

(Let us all with one accord wish him joy; let the drums sound; let the harp players touch their strings; let the instruments of music sound in his praise.)

The tune itself is one of great beauty.

Then follows a dumb-show, the defeat and death of Belshazzar and the establishment of Darius, hailed in his turn with 'Rex, in aeternum vive!' Further verses show messengers greeting Daniel and summoning him before the new ruler, who confirms him in his honours. Daniel retires to his own home and 'adores his God'. Then come the plotters to the King, and (to another fine tune) beg for the proclamation of the decree that shall trap the prophet. This is done, and Daniel is haled before Darius. The King is no Herod, and he replies to them uneasily:

Ex. 84 (i)

Nun-quam vo-bis con-ce-da-tur   quod vir san-ctus sic per-da-tur.

Ex. 84 (ii)

Nun-quam vo - bis con-ce - da-tur   quod vir san - ctus sic per-da-tur.

(Be it never conceded to you that a holy man should thus be destroyed.)

But he is reminded of the *lex Parthorum et Medorum* and reluctantly condemns the prophet to the lions.[1] In fairness to Daniel's accusers it should be recorded that after his delivery they show a proper repentance, and proclaim their remorse in an eight-line chorus.

In the den Daniel is defended by an angel, sings a very melodious prayer, and is fed by the prophet Habakkuk, who, with a laden basket, is 'translated' by another angel from his own harvest fields for that purpose. Rather drastically, to judge by the rubric, 'Tunc Angelus, apprehendens eum capillo capitis sui, ducet ad lacum . . .'.[2]

The King, having left his throne and come to the prison, rejoices to see that Daniel is yet alive, learns from him how he has been saved, and then consigns the plotters to the fate they had intended for the prophet. Finally, he proclaims the omnipotence of Daniel's God. Then follows Daniel's prophecy, beginning:

[1] Daniel's lament is recorded in *The History of Music in Sound*, ii, side 8.
[2] 'Then the angel, seizing him by the hair of his head, will take him to the pit'

Ex. 85 (i)

Ec-ce ve-nit   san-ctus il-le, san-cto-rum san-ctis-si-mus.

Ex. 85 (ii)

Ec-ce ve-nit   san-ctus il - le,   san-cto - rum san-ctis - si-mus.

(Lo, that holy man cometh, most holy among the holy.)

and the drama is rounded off by an angel singing the hymn, 'Nuntium vobis fero de supernis' (I bring you tidings from the highest), the only liturgical piece in the whole composition, other than the *Te Deum* which follows. Here, surely, we have most of the ingredients for a medieval opera.

A brief reference must be made here to Terence's celebrated imitator, the learned German nun, Roswitha, who in the tenth century had at Gandersheim studied the Roman author, and remained torn between fascination and pious deprecation. The result was that she herself produced six plays in Latin prose avowedly modelled on the form of that master, but without imitating his metres or the 'worldly licence' of his plots. Her own themes celebrated Christian chastity and the constancy of the martyrs, but whether the plays, brief expositions of traditional legends, were acted in any way even in her own nunnery is still a matter of controversy. It is even doubtful whether in those times the normal methods by which the classical stage would have presented a Terence play were really understood. Estimates of the real value of Roswitha's dramatic experiments vary widely,[1] but the conclusion that they were almost wholly unknown until their rediscovery in the early sixteenth century has yet to be shaken. What to the present writer seem exaggerated claims have been made in late years as to the part they may have played in the development of drama. It may be true that they 'fairly cry out for performance', but until they can show themselves linked to an evolutionary development such as the liturgical drama can claim, with records and details of production, these extraordinary plays must remain an interesting side-issue.

[1] See *Speculum*, Oct. 1945, for an interesting article by Edwin H. Zeydel on Roswitha. The writer leans to the view that the plays were probably performed in the lifetime of the authoress, but admits the absence of proof. The article provides a useful and up-to-date bibliography on the subject. Karl Young, op. cit., i, pp. 2–6, has a scholarly review of the question, and concludes that Roswitha's work had no influence on the development of drama.

VII

MEDIEVAL SONG

By J. A. WESTRUP

LATIN SECULAR SONGS

THE materials for a study of medieval song are not so complete as
we could wish. From the time of Charlemagne (768–814) up to the
thirteenth century we have a considerable amount of Latin poetry, in
which scansion by accent, as in the hymns of the Church, replaces the
scansion by quantity of classical verse. Much of this is vivacious and
often licentious in character, and has in consequence been attributed to the *clerici vagantes*, or travelling scholars, who wandered
over Europe in the eleventh and twelfth centuries before the practice
of residence at a university became established. While there are no
grounds for such a precise attribution, it is undeniable that the popular style of many of these pieces reflects the careless habits and the
natural optimism of the young. The music, however, remains very
largely a closed book; the majority of melodies are noted in neums
and in default of certain transcription must remain buried in the
manuscripts. The same is true of the laments, or *planctus*, on the
deaths of kings, queens, and princes, and other pieces of official or
public character, some of which seem to be as early as the seventh
century,[1] and the settings of verses by Horace, Juvenal, Virgil, and
others. Among the official pieces the tenth-century song in honour
of Otto III (983–1002)[2] is interesting as an early example of a secular
song modelled on the plan of the sequence. It consists of six stanzas
of different lengths and in different rhythms: it is not clear how these
were sung to the melody known as the *modus Ottinc*, which is mentioned in the first stanza.

Two early melodies survive the obstacle of notation. One is a setting
of Horace, *Odes*, iv. 11, 'Est mihi nonum',[3] where the tune is recog-

---

[1] Seventh-century laments survive in the tenth-century manuscript Madrid, Bibl.
Nac. 10029; facsimiles in H. Anglès, *El Còdex musical de Las Huelgas* (Barcelona, 1931),
i, p. 26. A ninth-century lament on Charlemagne and other pieces are in the tenth-century
manuscript Paris, Bibl. Nat. lat. 1154; facsimiles in C. E. H. de Coussemaker, *Histoire
de l'harmonie au moyen âge* (Paris, 1852), pls. i and ii.

[2] Text (without music) in K. Breul, *The Cambridge Songs* (Cambridge, 1915), p. 49;
music of the *modus Ottinc* in Coussemaker, op. cit., pl. viii, no. 1.

[3] Montpellier, 425; facsimile in Coussemaker, op. cit., pl. x.

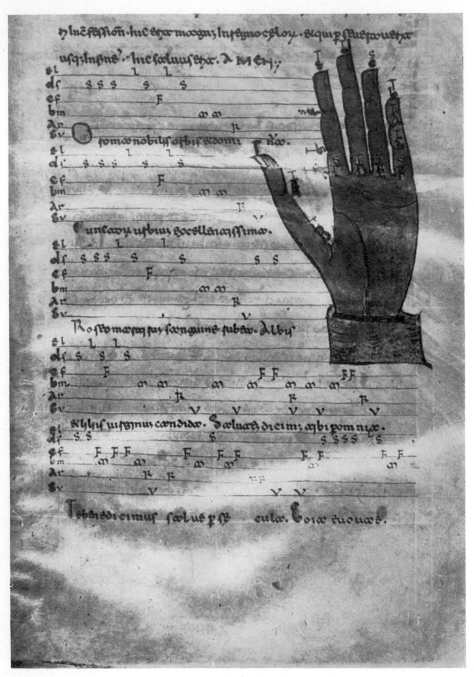

'O ROMA NOBILIS'

(Monte Cassino, MS. q. 318, fo. 291.) Twelfth century

nizable as that of the hymn 'Ut queant laxis'. The other is a love-song addressed to a boy, 'O admirabile Veneris idolum', which appears to have been written in Verona, possibly in the tenth century. We have three sources for the tune. In the Cambridge song-book it is noted in neums;[1] in a manuscript at the Vatican[2] the words 'O admirabile Veneris idolum' appear on the same page as the pilgrim song 'O Roma nobilis', which is in the same rhythm and is provided with a melody in heighted neums; while in a manuscript preserved at Monte Cassino[3] 'O Roma nobilis' occurs by itself with the same melody exactly noted in solmization letters. The last two of these sources agree in all essentials. Both end with an ornamented cadence which appears in a simpler form in the neumatic notation of the Cambridge song-book. A comparison of the three sources makes possible the following transcription of the Cambridge version:

Ex. 86[4]

O ad - mi - ra - bi - le   Ve - ne - ris i - do - lum,
Cu - jus ma - te - ri - æ   ni - hil est fri - vo - lum,
Ar - chos te pro - te - gat   qui stel - las et po - lum
Fe - cit et ma - ri - a   con - di - dit et so - lum.

Fu - ris in - ge - ni - o   non sen - ti - as   do - lum,   Clo -

-tho te di - li - gat   Quæ ba - ju - lat   co - lum.

(O lovely image of Venus, in whom there is no blemish, may the Lord who made the stars and the heavens and fashioned the seas and the earth protect thee; may no thievish cunning ever come nigh thee, and may Clotho who bears the distaff love thee.)

The rhythm of the words is dactylic, but a trochaic interpretation seems to suit the tune better. The melody, it will be noted, is in the major mode, of which we shall find plenty of examples in troubadour and trouvère songs.

The Latin secular songs of the Middle Ages are not wholly frivolous. A large number of them, without being specifically religious,

[1] Cambridge, Univ. Lib. Gg. v, 35, fo. 441ᵛ; facsimile in Breul, op. cit., facing p. 22.
[2] Vatican, 3327; facsimile in L. Traube, 'O Roma nobilis', in *Abhandlungen der philosophisch-philologischen Classe der königlich Bayerischen Akademie der Wissenschaften*, xix, 2 (1891), pp. 299–309.
[3] Monte Cassino, Q 318, fo. 291; printed in J. Wolf, *Handbuch der Notationskunde*, i (Leipzig, 1913), p. 58.
[4] Recorded in *The History of Music in Sound* (H.M.V.), ii, side 9.

express moral sentiments; others make satirical reference to the circumstances of the time, such as the song on the exile of St. Thomas à Becket (d. 1170) beginning 'In Rama sonat gemitus'[1] or the verses 'Bulla fulminante',[2] in which Philippe the Chancellor of Paris (d. 1236) seems to refer to the conflict between the Church and the Sorbonne. The thirteenth-century anthology known as *Carmina Burana*[3] (see also pp. 187, 194, 204) contains a large number of poems of this kind, some of which survive elsewhere with melodies in staff notation. No valid distinction can be made between the religious and secular Latin songs of this period; the same types of melody, the same forms occur in both. There is also a close connexion with songs in the vernacular.[4]

CHANSONS DE GESTE

We had to admit a dearth of musical material in the case of the goliard songs. The same is true of the French *chansons de geste*, epic poems in the vernacular celebrating the deeds of men of old, which were recited to music by the *jongleurs*, or travelling minstrels. The word *jongleur* is an altered form of *jogler* (later *jougleur*), which has given us the English 'juggler', and is derived from the Latin *joculator*, a jester. The *jongleur* was in fact more than a minstrel; he was an entertainer. He could sing and play, and do acrobatic feats; he could juggle with knives and put a performing bear through his paces. He was at home in the castle and on the high road; he would take part in the celebration of a court wedding or relieve the tedium of pilgrimage. He might also be attached to a noble family as a resident performer. A master of his modest craft, he was much valued in an age when newspapers and the music-hall were unknown. He might be frowned on by the Church, but he brought gaiety into men's lives. The tunes to which he recited the *chansons de geste* have practically all disappeared. One fragment appears to belong to Thomas de Bailleul's *Bataille d'Annezin*;[5] another, attached to a coarse parody,

---

[1] Text and melody in Wolfenbüttel, 677 (Helmstedt, 628), fo. 168ᵛ; facsimile in J. H. Baxter, *An Old St. Andrews Music Book* (London and Paris, 1931).

[2] Text and melody in London, Brit. Mus. Egerton 274, fo. 33ᵛ; printed by F. Gennrich in *Zeitschrift für Musikwissenschaft*, xi (1928–9), pp. 326–30. The melody also forms part of the three-part *conductus* 'Dic Christi veritas', of which several versions are printed by Gennrich, loc. cit.

[3] Munich, Staatsbibl. lat. 4660. References to other sources with staff notation are in the still incomplete edition of the text by A. Hilka and O. Schumann, 3 vols. (Heidelberg, 1930–41); cf. W. Lipphardt in *Archiv für Musikwissenschaft*, xii (1955), pp. 122–42.

[4] See pp. 243, 248, 262.

[5] London, Brit. Mus. Royal 20 A. xvii, fo. 177; printed in F. Gennrich, *Der musikalische Vortrag der altfranzösischen Chansons de geste* (Halle, 1923), p. 15.

is quoted in Adam de la Hale's pastoral play, *Li Gieus de Robin et de Marion* (see pp. 232–3):

Ex. 87[1]

Au - di - gier, dist Raim - ber - ge, bou - se vous di.

('Audigier', said Raimberge, 'I say cowdung to you.')

These fragments are very short, and modern taste might find it intolerable to hear a long poem recited to a constant repetition. The listener's interest, however, would be directed to the narrative, not to the tune to which it was sung. The music serves a practical purpose; at the same time it has something of the character of primitive incantation, a form of magic which survives still in the repeated supplications of the litany. The lack of examples is obviously due to the fact that there was no need to write them down; but the method of performance is confirmed by the treatise written about 1300 by Johannes de Grocheo,[2] who seems to have been a lecturer in Paris. He describes the *chanson de geste* as made up of a number of lines with the same rhyme, each of which is to be sung to the same tune,[3] and mentions incidentally that in some *chansons de geste* the poem ends with a line having a different rhyme[4]—a description which strictly applies not to a complete poem but to individual sections. The subject-matter of these poems, he says, includes not only such things as the story of Charlemagne but also the lives of the saints. He recommends that the *chansons de geste* should be sung to old people and workers while they are resting from toil; the recital of the hardships endured by others will make it easier for them to bear their own.[5] Two religious epics of the kind mentioned by Johannes de Grocheo survive with music—one a life of St. Léger, the other the story of the Passion— but they are noted in neums.[6] The best illustration we have of Johannes de Grocheo's description is not a *chanson de geste* but the *chante-fable* 'C'est d'Aucassin et de Nicolete',[7] in which prose

[1] Aix-en-Provence, Bibl. Méjanes 572 (499); printed in Gennrich, op. cit., p. 13.

[2] Printed by J. Wolf in *Sammelbände der internationalen Musikgesellschaft*, i (1899–1900), pp. 69–130. A number of corrections are supplied by H. Müller, op. cit., iv (1902–3), pp. 361–8. New edition by E. Rohloff (Leipzig, 1943).

[3] 'Idem etiam cantus debet in omnibus versibus reiterari' (Wolf, op. cit., p. 94).

[4] 'In aliquo tamen cantu clauditur per versum ab aliis consonantia discordantem' (ibid.).

[5] Op. cit., pp. 90–91.

[6] Clermont-Ferrand, 240, fos. 110 and 159ᵛ; facsimiles in G. Paris, *Album de la Société des anciens textes français* (Paris, 1875), pls. 3 and 8.

[7] Paris, Bibl. Nat. fr. 2168 (thirteenth century); facsimile edition by F. W. Bourdillo (Oxford, 1896).

narrative alternates with song. Here each verse-section consists of a number of lines of equal length, followed by a shorter line with a different rhyme. The ordinary lines are sung in pairs to a recurrent tune, the short line has its own melody and serves as a coda. The first section runs as follows:

Ex. 88

Qui vau-roit bons vers o - ir	Del de-port du viel an-tif,
De deux biax en-fans pe - tis,	Ni - cho-lete et Au-cas-sins,
Des grans pai-nes qu'il sou - fri	Et des prou-e-ces' qu'il fist
Por s'a-mie o le cler vis?	Dox est li cans, biax est li dis
Et cor-tois et bien a - sis,	Nus hom n'est si es-ba-his,
Tant do-lans ni en-tre - pris	De grant mal a-ma-la-dis,
Se il l'o-it ne soit ga - ris	Et de joi-e res-bau-dis,

Tant par est dou - ce.

(Who would hear some good verses of joy in former days, of two fair young children, Nicolette and Aucassin, of the great trials he endured for the sake of his lady with the bright face? The song is sweet and the tale is beautiful, courtly, and fitting. No man is so bewildered [by love], or grief-stricken, or distracted or ill from great affliction that he is not cured if he hears it, and cheered with joy, such is its sweetness.)

TROUBADOURS AND TROUVÈRES

(i) *Background.* The transformation of vulgar Latin into a vernacular had resulted in two related languages—the *langue d'oïl*, spoken in the north of France, the *langue d'oc*, spoken in the south. The second of these is commonly called Provençal, though it was spoken as far north as Limoges and Clermont-Ferrand. In this language a new art of lyric poetry, set to music, began to appear at the end of the eleventh century. It was the product of a feudal society which could spare time to cultivate the arts of peace and in which the prestige and refinement of women created a new race of courtiers—a society for whom Latin had become little more than the language of the clergy and scholars, remote from life and even unintelligible. The troubadours were not all of noble birth; some of them were born in humble circumstances and owed their position to patronage. But their art flourished in an aristocratic environment, in which the conceits of courtly love were tolerated and admired. The origins of this poetry are disputed; the work of the first troubadour of whom we have record—Guillaume of Aquitaine, Count of Poitiers (1071–1127)—

does not suggest the sudden efflorescence of a new art. A plausible case has been made for Arab influence, resulting not merely from contact with the Iberian peninsula but also from the crusades; but against this is urged the similarity of structure to be observed in Latin and Provençal songs. So far as the music is concerned, the argument in favour of Arab influence lacks foundation, since we have no specimens of Arab music; it is also unconvincing in face of the obvious influence of Gregorian chant and popular song.

Northern France was particularly the home of the *chanson de geste* (though the epic appears also in the south), but it could not resist the influence of the Provençal lyric. Contact may have come from the crusades or from the activities of travelling *jongleurs*. Patronage also played a part. Eleanor of Aquitaine, granddaughter of Guillaume and successively wife of Louis VII of France and Henry II of England, invited troubadours to her court in Normandy. The new art appears in the north in the latter half of the twelfth century. The poets of northern France were called trouvères. Like the troubadours in the south they were men who 'found out musical tunes and recited verses in writing'.[1] The generalization must, however, be accepted with reserve. There is no certainty that the poets always wrote their own tunes. Some of the poems in fact appear with different tunes in different manuscripts. There is a strong probability that some of the melodies were written by *jongleurs*, some of whom—for instance, Colin Muset—are known to have been composers as well as performers. We may also suspect that professional musicians were responsible for the elaborate manuscripts of the thirteenth and fourteenth centuries, in which the melodies of the troubadour and trouvère songs survive. A large number of songs have been preserved without any tunes; but we have something like 270 troubadour melodies and about 1,700 for the trouvères, and these, representing the work of the twelfth and thirteenth centuries, afford a substantial basis for study.

(ii) *Notation and Performance.* The notation of the majority of the songs is non-mensural: pitch is exactly indicated but not rhythm. Various interpretations of this notation have been advanced at different times. The one most generally accepted at the present day is due to the work of Pierre Aubry, Jean Beck, and Friedrich Ludwig. It assumes that the rhythm of the music is latent in the words, and

---

[1] The connexion of *trouvère* with *trouver*, 'to find' (as of *trobador* with *trobar*), is obvious, but the derivation of the word is not certain. A widely accepted conjecture is the Latin *tropus*, a song or tune (cf. p. 128).

that the music is to be transcribed in one or other of the rhythmic modes (see p. 318). The principal arguments for this interpretation may be summarized. (1) We have examples of songs in mensural notation, indicating clearly the trochaic, iambic, and dactylic modes, in the so-called Chansonnier Cangé.[1] (2) We have examples of polyphonic motets written in non-mensural notation in the same volume as troubadour and trouvère songs, e.g. in the so-called Manuscrit du Roi.[2] It is obvious that polyphonic music must be measured, and this is confirmed by the fact that some of these motets occur elsewhere in mensural notation. (3) Some of the songs were written for dancing. We are told, for instance, that the troubadour Rambaut de Vaqueiras wrote the well-known song 'Kalenda Maya'[3] on an *estampida*, or dance-tune, which the *jongleurs* had played on their *vièles*.[4] (4) Trouvère songs occur in motets written in mensural notation.

These arguments carry conviction. There is, however, something to be said on the other side. (1) The existence of examples in mensural notation does not prove conclusively that these songs were sung in regular rhythm when they were first composed. (2) Polyphonic music must be measured, undoubtedly. Mensural notation, in fact, became a necessity with the development of polyphonic writing. But it does not necessarily follow that monodies must be measured too. (3) The fact that songs for dancing are likely to be in regular rhythm does not prove that all the songs were measured. (4) The occurrence of monodies in motets does not prove that they were in regular rhythm when they were sung separately, since the same argument might be used to maintain that plainsong was in regular rhythm. It is also argued that the elaborate ligatures and ornamentation sometimes to be found in these songs are opposed to a strictly mensural interpretation. Two passages in Johannes de Grocheo bear on this question. In the first he distinguishes between 'simplex musica vel civilis, quam vulgarem musicam appellamus' (monodic or secular music, known as popular music) and 'musica composita vel regularis vel canonica, quam appellant musicam mensuratam' (music in parts or music composed according to rule, known as measured music). In the second he criticizes theorists who give the name 'musica immensurabilis' (music

[1] Paris, Bibl. Nat. fr. 846; edited with facsimile by J. Beck, 2 vols. (Paris and Philadelphia, 1927).

[2] Paris, Bibl. Nat. fr. 844; facsimile edited by J. and L. Beck (London and Philadelphia, 1938).

[3] Printed in P. Aubry, *Trouvères et troubadours* (Paris, 1909), p. 56, and G. Adler, *Handbuch der Musikgeschichte* (Berlin, 1930), p. 190.

[4] 'Aquesta 'stampida fo facha a las notas de la 'stampida quel joglar fasion en las violas' (Aubry, loc. cit.).

which cannot be measured) to music which is 'non ... praecise mensurata' (not exactly measured).[1]

These two passages, taken together, seem to provide a clue to
the problem. Polyphonic music is 'musica praecise mensurata', i.e.
strictly measured music, because any rubato in an individual part will
ruin the ensemble. Solo songs are also measured, in the sense that
they have a regular rhythmical foundation, but not necessarily in
the sense that they are performed in strict time. Folk-song provides
a good example. Traditional versions constantly exhibit irregular
rhythms which are quite obviously a performer's modification of a
regular original. The same is true of performances of unaccompanied
song by trained singers. A sensitive artist will not follow with mathematical exactitude the notation in front of him but will introduce such
rhythmical nuances as the text and the mood of the poem suggest.
It follows that no method of transcribing troubadour and trouvère
melodies will be faultless, because notation cannot precisely represent
performance. This may very well be the reason why in the majority
of the manuscripts no attempt is made to use mensural notation.
Songs which appear to be dactylic may equally well be represented
by ♩. ♪♩ or by ♩ ♪♪,[2] or alternatively the dactyls may be regarded as tribrachs (♪ ♪ ♪). The exact definition of detail which was
essential in polyphonic music in order to secure synchronization
between the parts is not only unnecessary in solo songs but may even
be inartistic. A change of mode, for instance, may be desirable in the
course of a song to avoid awkwardness. And even when we have
secured a reasonable transcription of a particular melody we still have
to remember that the manuscript source probably represents an oral
tradition and that this explains the existence of so many variants. The
transcriptions in this chapter, made in accordance with the rhythmic
modes, are to be regarded merely as the framework from which a
skilled singer will recreate a living art.

One further observation by Johannes de Grocheo must be mentioned here. In speaking of the various forms of 'musica civilis' or
'vulgaris' he says that the cantus coronatus 'ex omnibus longis et
perfectis efficitur'[3] (the cantus coronatus is made up entirely of long

[1] Wolf, op. cit., pp. 84–85.

[2] Cf. Robertus de Handlo on the mos lascivus: 'In hoc vero more denegamus omnem
brevem alteram et omnes brevium inaequalitates, quarum aequalitatem affirmamus.
Duae igitur breves inter duas longas positae in hoc more sunt aequales, ambae longae
imperfectae' (C. E. H. de Coussemaker, Scriptorum de musica medii aevi nova series
(Paris, 1864–76), i, p. 388; cf. p. 402). For an instrumental example see Ex. 181 (p. 338).

[3] Wolf, op. cit., p. 91. The cantus coronatus is defined as a song which is crowned by
experts for its excellence in poetry and music.

and perfect notes). This might be interpreted as a reference to non-mensural notation. Beck, however, regards it as indicating the spondaic mode, consisting of a sequence of long notes of equal length,[1] and hence transcribes a number of the songs in the Chansonnier Cangé in 4/4 time. It is by no means certain that this is justified. It is true that we have no grounds for asserting that troubadour and trouvère songs were necessarily in triple time. Triple time was necessary in polyphonic music because it provided the only convenient way of performing simultaneously different rhythmic modes. No such necessity occurs in monodies. An interpretation of the dactylic mode in duple time has, in fact, been suggested above. The objection to Beck's interpretation is rather that Johannes de Grocheo is not sufficiently precise. It is significant that when he is speaking of the plainsong forms he says that the *Gloria in excelsis* 'cantatur tractim et ex longis et perfectis ad modum cantus coronati' (is sung slowly and in long and perfect notes in the same way as the *cantus coronatus*).[2] This makes it clear that 'efficitur' in the previous quotation refers to the method of performance; but if we are to adopt Beck's interpretation we shall be forced to conclude that the *Gloria in excelsis* is also to be sung in slow 4/4 time. Johannes de Grocheo also says that the *cantilena rotunda* or *rotundellus* (rondeau) 'longo tractu cantatur velut cantus coronatus' (is sung slowly like the *cantus coronatus*).[3] It seems reasonable to suppose that what he says about the *cantus coronatus* refers simply to the speed at which it is sung. This is all the more likely since he does not discuss the details of mensuration at all until he has finished with *musica civilis* and is ready to deal with *musica praecise mensurata*. A slow speed would be natural for the *cantus coronatus*, because it had 'concordantiae pulchrae et ornate ordinatae' (pleasing intervals arranged in an elaborate sequence).[4] It was a dignified type of song, suitable for performance before kings and princes.[5]

We have no exact information about the method of performance. Miniatures of the time make it quite clear that instruments were employed, and this is confirmed by literary texts, e.g.:

Cil juglëor en piéz s'esturent,
S'ont vïelles et harpes prises,

---

[1] *Le Chansonnier Cangé*, ii, pp. 51–52.
[2] Wolf, op. cit., p. 125.
[3] Ibid., p. 92.
[4] Ibid., p. 120.
[5] 'Qui etiam a regibus et nobilibus solet componi et etiam coram regibus et principibus terrae decantari, ut eorum animos ad audaciam et fortitudinem, magnanimitatem et liberalitatem commoveat' (op. cit., p. 91).

Chançons, laiz, sons, vers, et reprises
Et de geste chanté nos ont.[1]

(The *jongleurs* stood up, took fiddles and harps, and sang to us songs, *lais*, tunes, verses, and refrains, and *chansons de geste*.)

There are examples of secular songs accompanied by a single instrumental line, but these are strictly two-part motets, in which a secular melody has been combined with a plainsong *canto fermo*,[2] and are not to be regarded as evidence for the type of accompaniment normally provided by the *jongleurs* for monodies. All that Johannes de Grocheo has to say on this subject is that a good performer can play any type of song on the *vièle* (fiddle) and that it was customary to play a coda to the *cantus coronatus* on this instrument.[3] This would suggest that the singer accompanied himself in unison and added a brief postlude. On the other hand, the use of plucked instruments may imply the playing of a chord as the prelude to a song or as an occasional background to a phrase. It is impossible to be more definite. It should be added that many of the instruments in use in the Middle Ages came from the East: Johannes de Grocheo, for example, mentions the Saracen guitar,[4] and we have references to Saracen horns and Saracen dances[5] side by side with Gascon and French songs. This fact has been used to support the argument for Arab influence in the songs of the troubadours and trouvères, but it is not conclusive in itself, any more than the French origin of the saxophone has determined the character of the music written for it.

(iii) *Tonality*. Both the tonality of the songs and their structure show a considerable variety. Subject as they were to the pervading influence of Gregorian chant, the troubadours naturally wrote melodies in the church modes. As an example we may take one of the four surviving melodies of Marcabru, one of the oldest of the troubadours, who flourished in the first half of the twelfth century. The text refers to a crusade against the Moors:

Ex. 89[a]

Pax in no-mi-ne   Do - mi - ni! Dist Ma - ca - bruns lou vers   del

[1] Huon de Mery, *Le Tornoiement de l'Antechrist*, 482–5. A number of other passages are quoted by T. Gérold, *La Musique au moyen âge* (Paris, 1932), chap. xx.

[2] e.g. 'A la clarté qi tout enlumina nostre grant tenebror', quoted by H. Besseler, *Die Musik des Mittelalters und der Renaissance* (Potsdam, 1931), p. 121.

[3] Wolf, op. cit., pp. 97, 122.   [4] Ibid., p. 96.

[5] 'Cors sarrazinois': Adenès li Rois, *Cléomadès*, 17,283, &c. 'Notes sarrasinoises': Jean Renart, *Galeran de Bretagne*, 1169. *Note* = Latin *nota*, defined by Johannes de Grocheo as a dance form (Wolf, op. cit., p. 98): cf. 'Dansses, notes et baleries' (Jehan Maillart, *Roman du Comte d'Anjou*, 14).

[6] Paris, Bibl. Nat. fr. 844, fo. 194ᵛ (Beck, fo. 186ᵛ). The manuscript has C♯ in the last bar, but it is difficult to believe that this can be correct.

son. Oi - as qu'eu dis: Que nos a fait per sa dou - cor Lou Seigno-

-ris ce - les - ti - aus Qu'il post per nos un la - va - dor, Que

for d'ou - tre - mar non fu taus, Et lai de - vers val Jo - sa-

-phat: Et d'ai - kel de cai vos co - nort.

(Peace in the name of the Lord! Marcabru has made the words of this song. Hear what I say: The Lord of Heaven, in his mercy, has made for us here a purifying place such as never was before, except beyond the sea towards the valley of Jehosophat; and with this one he now consoles you.)

In the following song by Gace Brulé (twelfth century) the rising fifth—a common formula—also shows unmistakably the influence of Gregorian chant:

Ex. 90[1]

Cil qui d'a-mors me con - seil - le Que je m'en doi - e par - tir

Ne sent pas que me res - veil - le Ne quel sont mei grie sos -

- pir. Pe - tit a sens et voi - di - e, Cil qui m'en vuet

chas - toi - er, N'en ainz n'a - ma en sa vi - e.

Cil fait bien ni - ce fo - li - e, Qui s'en - tre - met

del mes - tier Dont il ne se seit ai - dier.

[1] Paris, Bibl. Nat. fr. 20050, fo. 55; facsimile edition of this manuscript by P. Meyer and G. Raynaud (Paris, 1892).

(He who counsels me that I should part from love does not realize that he awakens me, nor what are my grievous sighs. He who wishes to reproach me has little sense or perception and has never loved in his life. Whoever meddles in a trade at which he is no good himself does a very stupid and foolish thing.)

The modal flavour of troubadour and trouvère melodies, however, is often modified, as here, by the use of accidentals. The sharp (represented by the sign now reserved for the natural) is used wherever a note has to be raised a semitone (e.g. B♭ to B♮, or C to C♯). The flat occurs not only as an accidental but also as a key-signature. How far accidentals are to be supplied when the copyists have not inserted them is a problem to which the existence of variants in different manuscripts affords, if not a complete solution, at least some guidance. No doubt the use of accidentals was a matter which individual singers often decided for themselves; it would be a mistake to assume a cast-iron tradition. The theorist known as Anonymus II gives two reasons for the use of *falsa musica*—necessity and melodic beauty—and cites trouvère songs as examples of the application of the second criterion.[1] Johannes de Grocheo also makes the point that one does not refer to the modes in discussing *musica vulgaris*, even if particular examples happen to be modal.[2] In fact a large number of the melodies are unmistakably in the modern major scale, e.g. the following song by Thibaut de Champagne (1201–53), one of the most important of the later trouvères, who became king of Navarre in 1234:

Ex. 91[3]

Tuit mi de - sir et tuit mi grief tor - ment Vien - nent de
Grant po-or ai pour ce que tou - te gent Qui ont ve -

la ou sont tuit mi pen - sé: mé Sont si sor - pris de bo -
- ü son gent cors a - ces -

-ne vo - len - té; Nes Dex l'ai - me, gel sai a es - ci -

- ent: Grant mer-veille est quant il en suef - fre tant.

[1] 'Fuit autem inventa falsa musica propter duas causas, scilicet causa necessitatis et causa pulchritudinis cantus per se. . . . Causa pulchritudinis, ut patet in cantinellis coronatis' (Coussemaker, op. cit., i, p. 312).

[2] 'Non enim per tonum cognoscimus cantum vulgarem, puta cantilenam, ductiam, stantipedem' (Wolf, op. cit., p. 115; cf. p. 114).

[3] Paris, Arsenal 5198, p. 51; facsimile edition of this manuscript by P. Aubry (Paris, 1910). Recorded in *The History of Music in Sound*, ii, side 10. The manuscript has 'mont' for 'sont' in bar 9.

(All my desire and all my bitter grief come from that source where all my thoughts are fixed. I fear greatly, since all who have seen her, who is fair and beauteous, are overcome by goodwill towards her. God himself loves her, I know it truly: it is a marvel when he suffers so much.)

It is very probable that this tonality betrays the influence of popular song and dance, just as the modal melodies owe something to Gregorian chant. This view is strengthened by the use of major tonality in songs of a popular character, e.g. this anonymous song, which begins with a slightly modal flavour but settles down into F major:

Au tans d'a-oust que fuil-le de bos-chet Chiet et ma-tist a pe-
-tit de ven-tet, Flours n'a du-ré-e, Ver-dure est pas-sé-e, Re-maint chant doi-
-sel. Blan-che ja-lé-e A la ma-ti-né-e S'a-pert ou pra-el.

(In August, when the leaf falls from the bush and dies with the slightest wind, the flower does not last, the verdure has gone, but the song of the birds remains. The white frost appears in the morning in the meadow.)

An even more vivid illustration is this dialogue with refrain from Adam de la Hale's *Li Gieus de Robin et de Marion*, which seems to have been written for the French court at Naples about 1285:

ROBIN
Ber-ge-ron-ne-te, douche baisse-le-te, Don-nés le moi vostre cha-pe-

MARION
-let, Don-nés le moi vostre cha-pe - let. Ro-bin, veux-tu que je le

ROBIN
me-che Seur ton chief par a-mou - re-te? O-il, et vous se-res m'a-mi -

-e-te, Vous a-ve-res ma chain-tu - re-te, M'au-mos-niere et mon

---

[1] Paris, Bibl. Nat. fr. 846, fo. 13[v]. Recorded in *The History of Music in Sound*, ii, side 9.
[2] Paris, Bibl. Nat. fr. 25566, fo. 41; facsimile in J. Wolf, *Musikalische Schrifttafeln* (Bückeburg and Leipzig, 1923), no. 4. The original notation is mensural. Recorded in *The History of Music in Sound*, ii, side 10.

fie - ma - let. *Ber-ge-ron-ne - te, douche baisse-le - te, Don-nés le*

MARION

moi vos-tre cha-pe - let. Vo - len - tiers,men douc a - mi - et.

(*Robin*: Sweet shepherdess, give me your garland. *Marion*: Robin, would you wish me to put it on your head as a token of love? *Robin*: Yes, you shall be my love and have my girdle, my purse, and my clasp. Sweet shepherdess, give me your garland. *Marion*: Willingly, my sweet love.)

It has often been supposed that the songs in *Li Gieus de Robin et de Marion* were popular melodies adapted by the author. This may be true of some of them, but there is no certainty that it is true of all. Melodies of a popular cast appear frequently in the works of the troubadours, side by side with others in which the elaborate ornamentation demands a skilled singer. In general the range of the songs is such as to make them suitable for singers with a modest compass. Melodies with a range of more than an octave occur—one exceptional piece extends over nearly two octaves[1]—but they are not frequent.

(iv) *Structure*. The structure of the songs varies from simple repetition to the most subtle symmetry. A piece like 'Le Tournoiement des Dames' by Huon d'Oisy (late twelfth century) has obvious affinities with the repeated formula of the *chanson de geste*:

Ex. 94[2]

En l'an que che - va - lier sont A - bau - bi, Ke d'ar-mes noi -
                                            Lez da - mez tour-

-ent ne font Li har-di, Le tour-noi - e - ment ple - vi,
-noi - er vont A Lai-gni.

La con-tes - se de Cres-pi Di - ent que sa - voir vou-dront Quel
Et ma da - me de Cou - ci Lez da-mez par tout le mont Pour-
                          Quant es prez ve - nu - ez sont, Ar-

li colp sont, Que pour e - les font Lour a - mi.
-cha - cier font, Qu'e - lez men - ront Chas - cune od li.
-mer se font, As - sam - bler vont De - vant Tor - chi.

[1] 'Bem pac d'ivern e d'estiu' by Peire Vidal, printed by T. Gérold, *La Musique du moyen âge*, pp. 178–9.

[2] Paris, Bibl. Nat. fr. 844, fo. 50 (Beck, fo. 47).

Y - o - lenz   de   Cail - li   Vait pre - mierz   as - sam-bler;
Mar - ge - ri - te   d'Oy- si   Muet a li   pour jous-ter;
A - misse au   corz har - di   Li vait son   fraim ha - per.

(In the year when the knights are weary of action and the bold accomplish no feat of arms, the ladies go tourneying to Laigni. The tournament being sworn, the Countess of Crespi and the Lady of Couci say that they want to know what the blows are like which their lovers strike for them. They summon the ladies throughout the world to bring all hither. When they have come into the field they let themselves be clad in armour and assemble before Torchi. Yolande de Cailli comes first into the lists, Marguerite d'Oysi hastens towards her to joust, Amisse the bold goes to snatch her bridle.)

There is an even greater economy of material in the following example by Conon de Bethune, a contemporary and relative of Huon d'Oisy:

Ex. 95[1]

L'autre ier a - vint en cel   au - tre pa - is   Cuns che - va - liers ot u -
Tant que la da - me fu   en son bon pris   Li a s'a-mour es - con-

- ne dame a - mé - e.   Puiz fu uns jours que le   li dit: A - mis,
-dite et ve - é - e.   Me-nez vous ai par pa - ro - le mainz dis;

Or   est   l'a - mour coun - eu - e   et   mous - tré - - e,

Dore   en   a - vant se - rai   a   vo   de - vis.

(The other day it happened in yonder foreign land that a knight loved a lady. As long as she was at the height of her worth she refused and denied him her love. Then came a day when she said to him: 'Friend, I have led you on by words for many a day; but now love is known and made manifest, from now on I shall be at your service.')

Allied to forms of this extremely simple type are the songs which indulge in the repetition of formulas, but with less rigidity, e.g. the following *chanson de croisade*, sung by a lady whose dear one is in Palestine, where the refrain repeats the opening melody of the verse. The author is Guiot de Dijon:

---

[1] Paris, Bibl. Nat. fr. 844, fo. 45 (Beck, fo. 42).

Ex. 96[1]

Chan-te - rai por mon co - rai-ge Que je vuil re-con-for-
-ter, Qu'a-vec - ques mon grant do - mai-ge Ne quier mo-rir
n'a-fo - ler; Quant de la ter - re sau - va-ge Ne voi mais nul
re-tor - ner, Ou cil est qui ras-so - ai - ge Mes maus
quant j'en oi par - ler. *Dex, quant cri - e - rons Ou - tré - e,*
Sir, ai - diez au pe - le - rin, Por cui sui es -
-po - an - té - e, Car fe - lon sunt Sar - ra - zin.

(I shall sing to cheer my heart, for fear lest I die of my great grief or go mad, when I see none return from that wild land where he is who brings comfort to my heart when I hear news of him. O God, when they cry 'Forward', help the pilgrim for whom I am so fearful, for the Saracens are evil.)

With this example, which uses repetition to achieve unity, we may contrast a melody which unfolds without any reliance on recurrent formulas—a song by the troubadour Albertet de Sisteron, who was the son of a *jongleur*:

Ex. 97[2]

Ha! me non. fai chantar foil - le ni flor, Ni chanz d'au-zel ni lou-
-sei - gnol en mai, Mais le meil - leur de tou - tes les meil - lors

[1] Paris, Bibl. Nat. fr. 846, fo. 28. Recorded in *The History of Music in Sound*, ii, side 10. Simpler versions of this tune occur in other manuscripts, e.g. Paris, Bibl. Nat. 844, fo. 174ᵛ (Beck, fo. 159ᵛ). From these sources the reading 'outrée' has been substituted above for the incorrect 'entrée' of the manuscript.
[2] Paris, Bibl. Nat. fr. 844, fo. 204 (Beck, fo. 196).

Et la gen-sors de la gen-sor qu'eu sai Mi fai chan-tar lou preis
que de li n'ai, Car per son preis dei je ben chan-con fai-re;
Si fe-rai eu, pos li ven a plai-ser, Car ren non fai fors que
lou son vo-ler, Tant es vail-lanz et sage et de-bon-ai-re.

(Ah! neither leaf nor flower, nor the song of bird or nightingale in May inspires my song, but the best of the best; and she who is fairer than the fairest I know makes me sing of the worth that I have from her: for her worth I must well compose a song. And thus must I do, since it is her pleasure, as I do nothing but what is her wish, so noble is she and wise and courtly.)

Melody of this type is described by Dante[1] as 'una oda continua usque ad ultimum progressive, hoc est sine iteratione modulationis cuiusquam et sine diesi' (a single melody continuing right up to the end, without any melodic repetition and without a division in the middle). More subtle in its melodic organization is the justly celebrated 'Quan vei l'aloete mover' by Bernard de Ventadour (twelfth century), which exists in several versions. Here one of the phrases occurs twice, but the total impression is one of continuous growth:

Ex. 98[2]

Quan vei l'a-lo-e-te mo-ver De joi ses a-les
contre al rai, Que s'ou-blide et lai-se ca-der
Per la dou-çor qu'el cor li vai, Hé! tan granz
en-vi-de m'en pren De ço qu'est si en-

[1] De vulgari eloquentia, ii. 10. 2.
[2] Paris, Bibl. Nat. fr. 844, fo. 190ᵛ (Beck, fo. 180ᵛ). Recorded in *The History of Music in Sound*, ii, side 9. The manuscript has 'moder' for 'mover' in bars 3–4.

-jau - si - on, Mi - ra - vill me q'eu n'ies del
sen Et cor de de - sir - rier non fon.

(When I see the lark in joy rise on its wings in the rays of the sun and then, oblivious, let itself fall, because of the gladness that fills its heart, such great envy comes upon me to see it so joyful, I wonder then that I do not rave and that my heart does not melt with desire.)

Here, too, the rise and fall of the melody shows the influence of Gregorian chant. The initial phrase recalls the opening of the *Kyrie eleison* of the Mass *Cum jubilo* (Vatican IX):

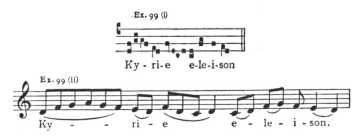

.Ex. 99 (i)

Ky - ri-e e-le-i-son

Ex. 99 (ii)

Ky - - ri - e e - le - i - son.

It is hardly surprising that this beautiful song was widely known. Dante paid it his tribute:

> Quale allodetta che in aere si spazia
> prima cantando, e poi tace contenta
> dell' ultima dolcezza che la sazia,
>
> tal mi sembiò l'imago della imprenta
> dell' eterno piacere, al cui disio
> ciascuna cosa, quale ell' è, diventa.[1]

The melody was also used for other texts, including the equally famous argument between the heart and the eye, 'Quisquis cordis et oculi Non sentit in se jurgia', by Philippe, the Chancellor of Paris.[2]

In addition to continuous melody Dante also describes other types involving various forms of subdivision.[3] The simplest of these, consisting of two *pedes* (feet) and a *cauda* (tail), may be represented by the formula *AAB*. The following song by Gace Brulé will serve as an illustration:

---

[1] *Paradiso*, xx. 73–78.
[2] Printed with variants (but without any reference to the original source of the melody) by F. Gennrich in *Zeitschrift für Musikwissenschaft*, xi (1928–9), p. 322.
[3] *De vulgari eloquentia*, ii. 10. 3–4.

R

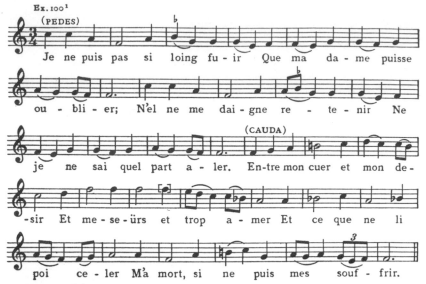

(I cannot flee so far that I can forget my lady. She will not deign to keep me and I do not know where to go. My heart and my desire and misfortunes and loving too much and what I cannot conceal from her have killed me, so that I can suffer no more.)

or this example by Bernard de Ventadour:

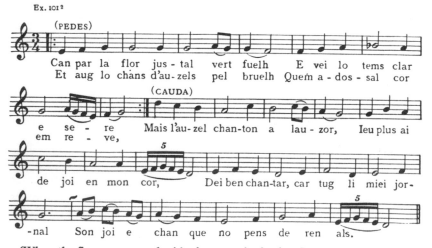

(When the flower appears beside the green leaf, when I see the weather bright and serene and hear in the wood the song of the birds which brings sweetness to

[1] Paris, Arsenal 5198, p. 87. The accidentals in the text and the emendation 'Et meseürs et' in bars 20–22 are supplied from Paris, Bibl. Nat. fr. 846, fo. 61ᵛ. Recorded in *The History of Music in Sound*, ii, side 9.

[2] Paris, Bibl. Nat. fr. 22543, fo. 56ᵛ; facsimile in C. Appel, *Bernart von Ventadorn* (Halle, 1915), pl. xxi.

my heart and pleases me, the more the birds sing to merit praise, the more joy I have in my heart and I must sing, as all my days are full of joy and song and I think of nothing else.)

A variant of this form is that in which the ending of the first *pes* is *overt* (open) while the second is *clos* (closed), as in dance tunes of the same period; in other words, the first of the two *pedes* ends with a half close, the second finishes on the tonic (see Exs. 90 and 91). Repetition is also found in the second half of the song, e.g. in this anonymous piece:

Ex. 102[1]

Qant li ro - si - gnols s'es - cri - e Qui nos des - duit de son chant,

Por ma be - le dolce a - mi - e Vois mon cuer ro - si - gno - lant.

Join - tes mains mer - ci li cri - e, Car on - ques rien n'a - mai tant,

Et bien sai s'e - le m'o - bli - e Que joi - e me va fi - nant.

(When the nightingale sings, who delights us with her song, my heart is singing like a nightingale for my fair and sweet lady. With joined hands I pray her for mercy, for I never loved anything so much, and I know well that if she forgets me my joy is at an end.)

Here the form is simply *AABB*. Similar examples are also found in which a coda is added to the double repetition—*AABBx*. In the following song by Gautier d'Épinal, one of the earliest trouvères (twelfth century), the second half of the melody is actually sung three times, the ending being *overt* the first and second times and *clos* the third (*AABBb*):

Ex. 103[2]

Se par for - ce de mer - ci Ne des - cent a -
En la moil - lour des loi - aus, Ja ne m'en ver -

-mors co - raux, De bien qui ne me soit max.
-rai sai - si Par lor douz co - man - de - ment

[1] Paris, Bibl. Nat. fr. 20050, fo. 39ᵛ.
[2] Ibid. fr. 846, fo. 130.

Mais se   pi - tiez   a - vec   aux   Me - is - sent en
Un pe - tit   d'es - for - ce - ment

lor po -   oir,   Lors por - roi - e   joie a -   voir.

(If by the power of mercy true love does not descend to the most loyal, never shall I see myself possessed of good which is not evil to me. But if pity with them at their gentle bidding were to put into their power a little coercion, then I could have joy.)

We find also various forms of *da capo*. In the following song, the authorship of which is disputed, part of the *pedes* is repeated at the end of the verse:

Ex. 104[1]

Quant li   lou - sei - gnolz jo - lis   Chan - te seur la   flour d'es -

-té,   Que naist   la rose   et li   lis   Et la   rou - sée

u   vert   pré,   Plainz de   bo - ne   vo - len - té   Chan - te -

-rai   con   fins a - mis.   Maiz de   tant sui   es - ba - hiz

Que j'ai   si   tres   haut pen - sé   Qu'a pain - nes iert

a - com - plis   Li ser - virs dont   j'a - tent   gré.

(When the joyous nightingale sings on the summer flowers, when the rose and the lily blossom and the dew appears in the green meadow, full of goodwill I shall sing as a true lover. But I am bewildered that I have set my thoughts so high that I may scarcely accomplish the service for which I expect favour.)

Our next example—a lively piece attributed by modern editors to the *jongleur* Colin Muset (early thirteenth century)—shows the melody of the *pedes* recurring in its entirety at the end of the song:

[1] Ibid. fr. 844, fo. 83 (Beck, fo. 73). Johannes de Grocheo (Wolf, op. cit., p. 91) cites 'Quant li roussignol', together with Thibaut de Champagne's 'Ausi com l'unicorne', as an example of the *cantus coronatus*. As more than one song, however, begins with these words (cf. Ex. 102) it is not certain to which he refers.

Ex. 105[1]

Quant je voi y-ver re-tor-ner Lors me vou-droi-e se-jor-ner,
Se je po-oie os-te tro-ver Lar-ge qui ne vou-sist con-ter,

Qu'e-ust porc et buef et mou-ton, Mas-larz, faisanz et ve-noi-son, Gras-

-ses ge-li-nes et cha-pons Et bons fro-ma-ges en gla-on.

(When I see winter return, then would I find lodging, if I could discover a generous host who would charge me nothing, who would have pork and beef and mutton, ducks, pheasants, and venison, fat hens and capons and good cheeses in baskets.)

(v) *Songs with Refrains.* These examples will give some idea of the varieties of structure to be found; to illustrate all the types of song-form would necessitate an anthology, since the troubadours and trouvères attached great significance to originality, even if it appeared only in minor details. A large number of songs have refrains. Two have been quoted above (see Exs. 93 and 96). The refrain may recur at the beginning (as in the *virelai*), in the middle, or at the end of successive verses, or within a single verse. It may consist of a single word, a series of conventional and virtually meaningless syllables, or an extended phrase. It is closely associated with dancing and clearly has a primitive origin. The leader has the more difficult task of remembering an extended text; the chorus has only to sing a recurrent phrase, the tune of which may also be borrowed from the soloist's melody. A well-known example of the dance-song with refrain is the Provençal *ballade* 'A l'entrade del tens clar'. More than one editor has suspected an error in the latter part of the song; and this supposition is confirmed by a three-part setting of the tune to the Latin words 'Veris ad imperia',[2] which shows that from bar 13 onwards the solo version is a tone too low. The mistake may have arisen because at the right pitch the melody requires both F♯ and C♯. The following is the emended text:

Ex. 106[3]

A l'en-tra-de del tens clar, E - y - a, Pir joi-e re-co-men-çar,

---

[1] Paris, Bibl. Nat. fr. 846, fo. 125ᵛ. Recorded in *The History of Music in Sound*, ii, side 9.

[2] Florence, Bibl. Laur. plut. xxix, 1, fo. 228ᵛ; printed by F. Gennrich, *Grundriss einer Formenlehre des mittelalterlichen Liedes* (Halle, 1932), p. 85.

[3] Paris, Bibl. Nat. fr. 20050, fo. 82ᵛ (with bars 13 to the end emended).

(When the fine weather comes, eya, to bring back joy again, eya, and to annoy the jealous, eya, I wish to show the Queen, for she is so much in love. Away, away, jealous ones, leave us to dance among ourselves, among ourselves.)

This exhibits both a simple refrain in the course of the verse and an extended one at the end. In the northern French *aube* (early morning song) 'Gaite de la tor' the refrain occurs only at the end, and the words are changed in the course of the song: there are altogether four versions of the words of the refrain—one for verses 1 and 2, a second for verses 3, 4, and 5, a third for verse 6, and a fourth for verse 7. This is the first verse:

(Watchman on the tower, look around the walls, and may God see you, for lords and ladies are now resting here, and thieves are prowling around. Hu and hu and hu and hu! I have seen one yonder beneath the hazel-bush. Hu and hu and hu and hu! I would very nearly have killed him.)

A song of this kind, like many of the songs that children sing at play,

---

[1] Paris, Bibl. Nat. fr. 20050, fo. 83.

invites mimed representation. A reconstruction of the song on these lines, with parts assigned to the lover's companion, the watcher, and the lover, has been suggested by Alfred Jeanroy and Joseph Bédier.[1] The refrain is in fact found in songs of very different character and is not confined to dance-songs. It occurs, for example, in a large number of *chansons de toile*, songs in which a lady is represented at her needle-work, while her heart sighs for love. The melody of the refrain is often a repetition of the end of the verse. The generic term *rotrouenge*, which occurs originally in northern France, has been applied to songs of this type[2]—on grounds which are hardly justified by the evidence. It is important to remember that in general it is the poetic text, rather than the melodic structure, that distinguishes songs with a refrain from those without them. Nor need we suppose that the primitive alternation of soloists and chorus, which is appropriate enough in dance-songs, was necessarily retained in all songs with a refrain. There is little justification for a chorus in the song where the lady sings of her absent crusader (Ex. 96). In such songs the refrain had become a poetic convention.

There is, however, one type of song with refrain, where the poetic and musical structures are closely allied. In the *rondeau* the refrain recurs within a single stanza and is set to a recurrent theme on which the whole setting is based. The number of lines in a *rondeau* was not fixed. A simple type had six lines, with half the refrain as the second line and the complete refrain at the end. Examples of this type occur in the *Roman de la Rose ou de Guillaume de Dole*,[3] and also among Latin *rondelli*, e.g.:

Ex. 108[4]

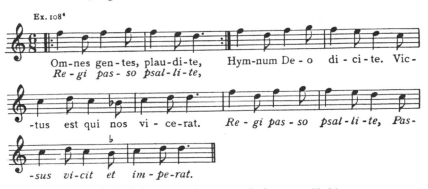

Om-nes gen-tes, plau-di-te,
Re - gi pas- so psal-li-te,

Hym-num De - o di - ci - te. Vic-

-tus est qui nos vi - ce-rat. Re - gi pas - so psal-li - te, Pas-

-sus vi-cit et im - pe-rat.

[1] Complete text in P. Aubry, *Trouvères et troubadours*, pp. 89–94.
[2] F. Gennrich, *Die altfranzösische Rotrouenge* (Halle, 1925).
[3] Printed in F. Gennrich, *Rondeaux, Virelais und Balladen* (Dresden, 1921, and Göttingen, 1927), i, pp. 3–10 (cf. ii, pp. 1–12).
[4] Florence, Bibl. Laur. plut. xxix, 1, fo. 465; printed in G. M. Dreves, *Analecta Hymnica Medii Aevi*, xxi (Leipzig, 1895), pp. 43 and 213.

(Clap your hands, all nations, sing praises to the King who has suffered, sing a hymn to God. He was conquered who had conquered us. Sing praises to the King who has suffered. He suffered and conquered and reigns.)

We may represent this by the formula *aAa'bAB*, where the capital letters indicate the refrain and the letters *A, a, a'* and *B, b* respectively stand for the same melodic phrases fitted to different words with the same rhyme. In the more elaborate type of *rondeau*, with eight or more lines, the refrain also occurs in full at the beginning, as in the *virelai*. The formula of the eight-line *rondeau*, which may be taken as the standard type, is thus *ABaAa'bAB*. A number of *rondeau* refrains were used in thirteenth-century motets, so that if the complete words are extant elsewhere it is possible to reconstruct the complete song. We may take as an example the *rondeau* 'Toute seule passerai le vert boscage', which is cited by Johannes de Grocheo as an example of what he calls the *cantilena rotunda* or *rotundellus*.[1] No complete text of this *rondeau* survives with music. But there is a thirteenth-century motet which begins:

Ex. 109[2]

A-mours qui vient par me-sa-[ge]

Tou-te sou-le pas-se-rai

Notum

with the words 'li vert boscage' and 'puis que compaignie n'ai' occurring later in the same part; and as the complete text of the words is available elsewhere:

> *Toute seule passerai le vert boscage,*
>   *Puis que compaignie n'ai;*
> Se j'ai perdu mon ami par mon outrage,
> *Toute seule passerai le vert boscage.*
> Je li ferai a savoir par un mesage
>   Que je li amenderai.
> *Toute seule passerai le vert boscage,*
>   *Puis que compaignie n'ai,*[3]

---

[1] Wolf, op. cit., p. 92. It is curious that Johannes de Grocheo's description of the form of the *rondeau* is inaccurate.

[2] Bamberg, Staatsbibl. Ed. iv. 6, fo. 58; facsimile in P. Aubry, *Cent Motets du XIIIe siècle* (Paris, 1908).

[3] Paris, Bibl. Nat. fr. 12786, fo. 78^v; printed in Gennrich, op. cit., i, p. 79. Gennrich

it is possible, by assembling this material, to reconstruct the complete melody:

Ex. 110

Tou - te seu - le pas - se-rai le vert bos-ca - ge Puis-que com-pai-

-gni - e n'ai; Se j'ai per - du mon a - mi par mon ou-tra - ge,
Tou - te seu - le pas-se -rai le vert bos-ca - ge,
Je li fe - rai a sa-voir par un me-sa - ge

Que je li a - men-de - rai. Tou - te seu - le pas - se-rai le

vert bos-ca - ge Puis-que com-pai-gni - e n'ai.

(All alone I shall pass through the green woodland, since I have none to bear me company. If I have lost my lover through my ill-doing, all alone I shall pass through the green woodland. I shall let him have a message saying that I will make him amends. All alone I shall pass through the green woodland, since I have none to bear me company.)

Johannes de Grocheo tells us that *rondeaux* were sung in Normandy by young people at great festivals.[1] This is confirmed by our sources, which are confined to northern France, with the single exception of Ex. 111, which is in Provençal. The text of the complete song is preserved as the *motetus* of a thirteenth-century motet.[2] It will be noticed that the musical form differs slightly from that given above, though the poetic structure remains the same:

Ex. 111[3]

Tuit cil qui sunt en - a - mou-rat Vie - gnent dan-çar, li

au - tre non! La re - gi-ne le com-men-dat! Tuit cil qui sunt en-

reconstructs the melody of the refrain from the opening three lines of the motet. I have preferred to use the music actually attached to the words of the refrain in the motet.

[1] 'Et hujusmodi cantilena versus occidentem puta in Normannia solet decantari a puellis et juvenibus in festis et magnis conviviis ad eorum decorationem' (Wolf, op. cit., pp. 92–93).

[2] Montpellier, Bibl. Univ., H. 196, fo. 219; facsimile in Y. Rokseth, *Polyphonies du XIIIe siècle* (Paris, 1936–9). In the last line the manuscript has 'avant' for 'dancar.'

[3] Recorded, with alternation of soloist and chorus, in *The History of Music in Sound*, ii, side 10.

-a - mou-rat. Que li ja - lous soi - ent fus-tat Fors

de la dan - ce d'un bas-ton. *Tuit cil qui sunt en -*

-a - mou-rat Vie - gnent dan - çar, li au - tre non!

(Let all those who are in love come and dance, the others not! The queen ordains it. All those who are in love! Let those who are jealous be driven with blows from the dance. Let all those who are in love come and dance, the others not!)

This melody was also used for a Latin text on the Assumption of the Virgin,[1] though the Latin words are not in *rondeau* form. More striking is the case of the *rondeau* 'En ma dame a mis mon cuer', the refrain of which, associated with these words in several motet collections,[2] was also used for a Latin *rondeau*, 'Veni, Sancte Spiritus'.[3] The popularity of the *rondeau* continued in the early fourteenth century. Several examples occur among the lyrical interpolations in the *Roman de Fauvel*.[4]

A very curious form of song with refrain is that in which each verse is followed by an entirely different refrain.[5] For instance, the song 'Ier main pensis chevauchai' by Baudes de le Kakerie[6] has eight verses, for which there are eight separate refrains, differing in words, rhythm, and melody. There may even be a constant refrain within the verse as well as the changing refrains at the end. This is the case with 'En mi mai, quant s'est la saisons partie' by Guillaume le Vinier.[7] There are five verses, each with its own final refrain, but in all the verses the second line—'Mal est enganez cil n'aimme mie'—is the same and, of course, set to the same melody. In a good many of these *chansons avec des refrains* the copyist has transcribed the music of the first refrain only, either because he did not know the others, or more probably because they were so well known that he thought notation unnecessary. They constitute, in fact, a series of familiar melodic tags

---

[1] Gennrich, op. cit. ii, p. 43.

[2] Ibid. ii, p. 96.

[3] London, Brit. Mus. Egerton 274, fo. 49; printed in Dreves, op. cit. xxi, p. 214. The French and Latin texts are printed together with the melody in G. Adler, *Handbuch der Musikgeschichte* (Berlin, 1930), p. 184.

[4] Printed in Gennrich, op. cit. i, pp. 290–306 (cf. ii, pp. 230–45).

[5] The refrains of the *chansons avec des refrains* are printed ibid. ii, pp. 255–91.

[6] Paris, Bibl. Nat. fr. 844, fo. 99ᵛ (Beck, fo. 172ᵛ).

[7] Ibid., fo. 108ᵛ (Beck, fo. 100ᵛ).

added to a normal strophic song. Listeners must have derived a certain amount of amusement from wondering what the singer was going to quote and from recognizing the quotation when it occurred. The choice was not entirely capricious, since the words of the refrain would relate to the verse, and the melody would have to follow logically on what had gone before.

(vi) *Lais*. There is an element here of popular music-making. We find also clear evidence of popular traditions in quite a different type of song—the *lai* or *descort*. This is made up of a number of verses (or sections) of varying structure, strung together to form a continuous whole. Since the metrical shape of the verses differs, there is also a difference in their musical setting. The effect of the whole is rhapsodical. In the earlier *lais* it is not uncommon to find one or more sections built on the same pattern and hence using the same melody; for example, in Ernoul le Vieux's 'Lai de l'Ancien et du Nouveau Testament',[1] which presents a concise summary of biblical history, there are only nine melodies, distributed among twenty-three sections. These simple examples are mostly anonymous. The *lais* by known trouvères and troubadours show a preference for the more sophisticated type, in which constant variety is a virtue. The melodic style of the *lais* is in general extremely simple. Whole sections are built up from the repetition of small melodic units, e.g. the first section of the 'Lai de l'ancien et du nouveau Testament':

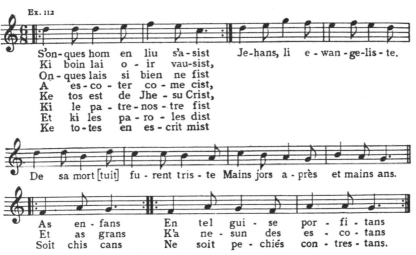

Ex. 112

S'on-ques hom en liu s'a-sist Je-hans, li e - wan -ge-lis - te.
Ki boin lai o - ir vau-sist,
On - ques lais si bien ne fist
A es-co - ter co - me cist,
Ke tos est de Jhe - su Crist,
Ki le pa - tre-nos -tre fist
Et ki les pa - ro - les dist
Ke to-tes en es - crit mist

De sa mort [tuit] fu - rent tris - te Mains jors a - près et mains ans.

As en - fans En tel gui - se por - fi - tans
Et as grans K'a ne - sun des es - co - tans
Soit chis cans Ne soit pe - chiés con - tres - tans.

(If ever a man sat down, who wished to hear a good lay, there was never one

[1] Paris, Bibl. Nat. fr. 12615, fo. 63ᵛ; printed in A. Jeanroy, L. Brandin, and P. Aubry, *Lais et descorts français du XIIIᵉ siècle* (Paris, 1901), pp. 113–20.

so good to hear as this, which is all about Jesus Christ, who made the Lord's Prayer and spoke all the words that John the evangelist has written down. All grieved over his death for many days and many years after. May this song be of use to young and old so that sin may not prevail against any of those who listen.)

and the same melodic formulas occur, with slight variations, in a number of different works. Among these formulas is one built on the notes of the major triad, which may be instrumental in origin. A similar formula occurs in one of the best-known of medieval dance-tunes;[1] we meet it also in popular hymns like 'Resonet in laudibus',[2] the tune of which is known to English choirs from its association with Neale's carol 'Christ was born on Christmas day'. The persistence of the formula in popular song may be illustrated by a very familiar example in current use—the nursery song 'Boys and girls come out to play', the melody of which would cause little surprise if it were discovered in a thirteenth-century manuscript.

Whether or not the *lai* is Celtic in origin, as has been suggested,[3] it clearly derives from an old tradition of minstrelsy in which persistent repetition similar to that of the *chanson de geste* is combined with the variety of structure to be found in the *puncta* (or contrasted sections) of dance-forms such as the *estampie*. The second phrase of the music to *Aucassin et Nicolete*, set to the even-numbered lines (see p. 224), occurs also in the anonymous 'Lai des Amants';[4] and although melodic identity is not to be stressed where the materials are so simple, the coincidence provides evidence of a close similarity of style. There is also a connexion with church music, not only in the use of a repeated formula but also in the rhapsodic structure, which may be compared with the diversity to be found in the early sequences. It is worth noting that the first verse of two different *lais*—the 'Lai des Hermins' and the 'Lai de la Pastourelle'[5]—is set to the music of the corresponding section of the sequence 'Ave gloriosa virginum regina', which exists also in a French translation as 'Virge glorieuse, pure, nete et monde'.[6] This process might also extend to a complete sequence. The well-known Christmas sequence 'Laetabundus' furnished the material for innumerable imitations and adaptations. These included a French translation, 'Hui enfantez', and an Anglo-Norman song in praise of beer, beginning:

[1] Oxford, Bodleian, Douce 139, fo. 5ᵛ; facsimile in H. E. Wooldridge, *Early English Harmony*, i (London, 1897), pl. 24. See p. 338.

[2] Printed in *Piae Cantiones* (1582), ed. G. R. Woodward (London, 1910), no. iii.

[3] Jeanroy, Brandin, and Aubry, op. cit., p. xv. Cf. also p. 151.

[4] Ibid., p. 123.

[5] Paris, Bibl. Nat. fr. 845, fo. 185ᵛ–6; printed in Jeanroy, Brandin, and Aubry, op. cit., pp. 147 and 139.

[6] J. Beck, *Die Melodien der Troubadours* (Strasbourg, 1908), pp. 76–79.

Or hi para:
La cerveyse nos chauntera.

Both these French texts retain in the form of Latin tags the verse endings of the original sequence—'Alleluia', 'Res miranda', and so on.[1] A further connexion between the *lai* and the sequence may be found in the secular Latin songs built on the same principle, some of which occur in the eleventh-century song-book at Cambridge (see p. 221). A connexion between the sequence and the dance is implied by Johannes de Grocheo, who says that the sequence is sung like the *ductia*, that the *ductia* is a brisk but serious song, sung by young men and girls, and that there is also a purely instrumental *ductia* for dancing, in which a regular beat is clearly marked.[2] It is significant, too, that the name *lai* was also given to purely instrumental pieces, e.g.:

Cil juglëor la ou il vunt,
Tuit lor vïeles traités unt,
Lais et sonnez vunt vïelant.[3]

(Everywhere the *jongleurs* go they use their fiddles, playing *lais* and tunes.)

Opposition to the view that all these forms are connected has been based partly on differences in detail and partly on too rigid a conception of the structure of the sequence. It is a mistake, however, to suppose that the acceptance of a connexion between sequence, *lai*, and dance necessarily implies the acceptance of a precise genealogy. It is much more likely that all three derive from a common ancestor. The principles of repetition and contrast play an important part in the dance music and songs of every century and it is hardly surprising

[1] F. Gennrich, 'Internationale mittelalterliche Melodien', in *Zeitschrift für Musik-wissenschaft*, xi (1928–9), pp. 273–8. Facsimile of 'Hui enfantez', from Paris, Bibl. Nat. fr. 2163, fo. 224, in P. Aubry, *Les plus anciens monuments de la musique française* (Paris, 1905), pl. vi.

[2] 'Sed sequentia cantatur ad modum ductiae, ut ea ducat et laetificet, ut laete recipiant verba novi testamenti puta sacrum evangelium, quod statim postea decantatur' (Wolf, op. cit., p. 126).
'Ductia vero est cantilena levis et velox in ascensu et descensu, quae in choris a juvenibus et puellis decantatur, sicut gallice: *Chi encor querez amoretes*. Haec enim ducit corda puellarum et juvenum et a vanitate removet et contra passionem, quae dicitur amor eroticus, valere dicitur' (ibid., p. 93; 'eroticus' is conjectured by Müller, op. cit., p. 366).
'Est autem ductia sonus illitteratus cum decenti percussione mensurata. Dico autem illitteratus, quia, licet in voce humana fieri possit et per figuras repraesentari, non tamen per litteras scribi potest, quia littera et dictamine caret. Sed cum recta percussione, eo quod ictus eam mensurant et motum facientis et excitant animum hominis ad ornate movendum secundum artem, quam ballare vocant, et ejus motum mensurant in ductiis et choreis' (ibid., p. 97).

[3] *Chronique de l'abbaye du Mont St. Michel*, quoted by Gennrich, *Grundriss einer Formenlehre des mittelalterlichen Liedes*, p. 160, n. 1. Several other references are quoted by Gérold, *La Musique au moyen âge*, pp. 296–8.

that the Middle Ages should have offered different manifestations of them.

Though the troubadours and trouvères were not normally composers of polyphonic music (Adam de la Hale is an exception), their art of song played an important part in the development of the motet in the thirteenth century. We have seen already that a large number of refrains were incorporated in motets. There are also a dozen or so examples of song melodies occurring in polyphonic music. It seems clear, however, that in several of these cases the song melody has actually been extracted from the motet.[1] The reason why the examples of complete trouvère songs incorporated in motets can be counted on the fingers of one hand is that the nature of the two forms was different. The symmetry of the song melody would impose a similar symmetry on the composer of the motet and would also create difficulties where the melody had to be harnessed to an existing tenor. The introduction of a short refrain did not present the same problem. Yet in spite of the fact that the song and the motet led an independent existence, the influence of trouvère song on the composers of polyphonic music is constantly in evidence. It provided a model of lyrical expression to which the contrapuntists were not slow to respond.

ENGLISH SONGS

The influence of the troubadours extended to England. This was not unnatural since in the second half of the twelfth century England was a part of the Angevin empire, which included Poitou, Guienne, and Gascony as a result of Henry II's marriage, before his accession, to Eleanor of Aquitaine, the divorced wife of Louis VII of France. Eleanor's patronage of the troubadours has already been mentioned; her son Richard Coeur-de-Lion himself practised the art. But the very fact of this close connexion was an obstacle to the growth of a purely native art of song. The literary language of England was Norman-French until the middle of the thirteenth century. In consequence only a mere handful of English songs with music survive. Among them is a French *lai*, accompanied by an English translation, which is preserved in a manuscript at the Guildhall, London.[2] It is the song of a prisoner who prays to be delivered. The first half of the second verse runs:

---

[1] For the evidence see F. Gennrich, 'Trouvèrelieder und Motettenrepertoire', in *Zeitschrift für Musikwissenschaft*, ix (1926–7), pp. 8–39, 65–85.

[2] *Liber de antiquis legibus*, fo. 160ᵛ; printed by F. Gennrich in *Zeitschrift für Musikwissenschaft*, xi (1928–9), p. 346.

Jhesu Crist, veirs Deu, veirs hom,
Prenge vus de mei pité,
Jetez mei de la prisun
U je sui a tort geté.

Jesu Crist, sod God, sod man,
Loverd, thu rew upon me,
Of prisun thar ich in am,
Bring me ut and makye fre.

Some of the wholly English songs seem to be imitations of liturgical music, for instance, the songs attributed to St. Godric,[1] who for sixty years lived as a hermit at Finchale on the Wear and died in 1170. The following may serve as an example of the few secular songs of the thirteenth century. The melody is constructed from a few simple formulas with two of the lines repeated; it is also remarkable for its adherence to movement by step:

Ex. 113[2]

World-es blis ne last no thro-we, Hit wit ant wend a -
-wey a - non. The leng-ur that hich hit i - kno-we, The
lasse hic find-e pris ther - on. For al hit is i -
-meynd wyd ka - re, Mid so-re-we ant wid u - vel fa - re, Ant
at the last-e poue-re ant ba-re Hit let mon wen hit
gin-net a - gon. Al the blis-se, this he - re ant
the - re Bi - lou-keth at hend-e wop ant mon.

[1] London, Brit. Mus. Royal 5. F. vii, fo. 85; facsimile in G. Saintsbury, *A History of English Prosody* (London, 1906), i, frontispiece. Printed by J. B. Trend in *Music and Letters*, ix (1928), pp. 120–3, with facsimile on p. 119.
[2] Oxford, Bodleian, Rawlinson G 18, fo. 105ᵛ; facsimile in Wooldridge, *Early English Harmony*, i, pl. 23. The notation is non-mensural. Recorded in *The History of Music in Sound*, ii, side 11.

(The world's joy lasts no time at all, it departs and fades away at once. The longer I know it, the less value I find in it. For it is all mixed with troubles, with sorrow and misfortune, and at the last, when it begins to pass away, it leaves a man poor and naked. All the joy, both here and there, is finally encompassed by weeping and lamentation.)

MINNESINGER

(i) *Notation and Structure*. In the German-speaking countries the art of the troubadours had quite a different effect. There an existing art of poetry in the vernacular received a stimulus from Provence and developed into a literature of song inspired by similar ideals yet faithful to its own traditions. There was, no doubt, a direct contact between Provence and Austria through the crusades, and patronage played its part here as elsewhere. Beatrice of Burgundy, who became the wife of the emperor Frederick Barbarossa in 1156, was a patron of the trouvère Guiot de Provins; and Barbarossa himself held an international festival at Mainz in 1184, which may well have contributed to a closer association. The earliest German Minnesinger, who originated in Austria and Bavaria, belong to the latter half of the twelfth century and the thirteenth century, and were thus contemporary with the trouvères of northern France. Like them they sang of chivalrous love (*Minne* in German, *amour courtois* in French), but put a rather different interpretation on the theme, preferring to express reverence for womanhood in general rather than passion for an individual. Like them they also composed religious and political verses. Like them, too, they linked poetry with music, the notation of which is generally non-mensural. The modal interpretation used for the melodies of the troubadours and trouvères can also be applied to the songs of the Minnesinger, though it must be admitted that the arguments for doing so rest on rather more slender foundations. The evidence of later examples in mensural notation suggests that duple time would often be appropriate. In any case the metrical structure of German verse is less rigid than that of the songs in French and Provençal, so that the need for freedom in interpretation is, if anything, even stronger.

We have seen that the type of verse described by Dante as consisting of two *pedes* and a *cauda*—in other words, the form *AAB*—occurs frequently in troubadour and trouvère songs in one shape or another. In German songs the *pedes* were known as *Stollen* (props), forming the *Aufgesang*, and the *cauda* as the *Abgesang*. A good example is one of the few surviving melodies of Walther von der

Vogelweide (*circa* 1170–1230), who though of noble birth travelled
for several years as a *fahrender Sänger* or *jongleur*:

Ex. 114[1]

Nu al - erst leb' ich mir   wer-de Sint myn sun-dich ouge er -
-sicht Das he - re lant und ouch die   er - de Dem man vil der
e - ren   gicht. Mir ist ge-schen als   ich je   bat: Ich byn
ko-men   an die   stat Da got me-n[i]s - li - chen   trat.

(Now at last life begins for me, since my sinful eyes behold the Holy Land, the
very soil which men hold in honour. My prayer is answered: I have come to the
land where God in human form set foot.)

It will be noticed that the *Abgesang* ends with part of the melody of
the *Stollen*—a parallel to the *da capo* type of trouvère song and not
uncommon in Minnesinger songs, where the complete melody of the
Stollen may recur as the latter part of the *Abgesang*, e.g. in this song
by Wizlaw von Rügen (d. 1325):

Ex. 115[2]

Ich par - re - re dich durch mi - ne tro - we, De dich
Her - tze-tru - te, sich min eyn - var vro - we Tzŭ al - ler
lep - lich sach vor mi - nen ou - - ghen. Wer mach vŭr-
ghŭ - te schin-bar un - de tou - - ghen.
-ghŭ - ten di - ne ghŭ - te Wen ghot der ghu - te

[1] From a fragment discovered in the State Archives, Münster; facsimile in *Sammelbände der internationalen Musikgesellschaft*, xii (1910–11), facing p. 500. The note E
in the last bar but one appears to be the correct reading, in spite of the discrepancy with
the *Stollen*.
[2] Jena, Universitäts-Bibl. MS., fo. 75; facsimile edition of this manuscript by K. K.
Müller (Jena, 1896). The manuscript has 'vrowen' for 'trowe' in bar 5 (first time), 'eyn
par' for 'eynvar' in bar 4 (second time), and 'untoughen' for 'unde toughen' in bars
9–11 (second time).

dich be - hů - te! Des be - darph ich wol, sol ich mich

ne - ren Vor di - ner min - ne diz mach ich swe - ren.

(I adore you with my loyalty, that saw you in all your charm before my eyes.
Dearest loved one, behold my pure joy in all your goodness evident and secret.
Who can reward your goodness, even though the good God may guard you!
That do I need, if I am to be unscathed by your love: that I can say on oath.)

Not all the songs, however, are as neatly contrived as this. In the
following song by the singer known as the Tannhäuser (thirteenth
century) the *Abgesang* is loosely constructed. There is no systematic
borrowing from the *Stollen*, but short phrases recur and are pieced
together in a new association. A melody of this kind vividly suggests
the methods of a singer accustomed to improvise:

Ex. 116[1]

(STOLLEN)

Ez ist hiute eyn wun - nych - li - cher tac. Nu phle - ge myn, der al - ler din - ge

wal - te, Daz ich myt sel - den mů - ze wesen Unde ich ge - bů - ze

my - ne gro - ze scul - de. Wente her mich wol ge - hel - fen mac, Al-

-so daz ich die se - le myn be - hal - te, Daz ich vůr sun - den

(ABGESANG)

sy ge - nesen Unde daz ich noch ir - wer - be go - tes hul - de. Nu

gebe her mich so ste - ten mut, Daz ez der lib vůr - die - ne so Daz

myr got dan - ken mů - ze, Daz myr daz en - de wer - de gůt Und

---

[1] Jena, Universitäts-Bibl. MS., fo. 42ᵛ. The manuscript has AG, instead of FE, for
'Nu phle-'.

ouch die se - le wer - de vro, Myn schei-den wer - de sů - ze. Daz

mich de hel - le gar vůr - ber Des hel - fe mir de[r]

rey - ne Unde vů - ge mich, des ich da ger, Daz mich die hœs - te

vreu - de sў ge - mey - ne. Also ich der ma - ge můz un-per, Daz

ich dort vriun - de vyn - de, Die my - ner kunf-te wer - den vro, Daz

ich ge - hey - zen můge eyn sel - den - ri - chez in - ge - syn - de.

(Today is a joyous day. May he who rules all things care for me, that I may be blessed and atone for my great guilt. For he is well able to help me, so that I may save my soul and be preserved from sin and may attain God's grace. Now may he grant me the steadfast mind that the body should merit, so that God may requite me and my end be good and my soul also joyful and my parting happy. That hell may spare me, may the pure one help me and grant me what I desire, that the highest joy may be my lot. May I be so parted from my kin that I may find friends yonder who will rejoice at my coming, that I may be called one of the blessed followers.)

These examples are in a simple melodic style. But there are others where provision has clearly been made for the virtuosity of a trained singer. The beginning of an anonymous spring song will serve as an example:

Ex. 117[1]

Ich   set - ze

mi - nen vuz An des sum - mers

[1] Berlin, Preuss. Staatsbibl. germ. 4⁰, 981; facsimile in J. Wolf, *Musikalische Schrifttafeln*, no. 21. For another example of elaboration see 'Ich warne dich' by Wizlaw von Rügen (Jena MS., fo. 77).

kle   Die   da

was   ghe - - - - stalt.

(I set my foot on the summer clover which was placed there.)

Here the modal interpretation must obviously be treated with a good deal of freedom. The setting of the word 'ich' at the beginning might be regarded as an instrumental introduction, in which case the singer could begin on the A immediately before 'setze'. But there is no reason why the melisma should not have been sung. Historians have been too ready to assume that any elaborate passage in medieval music must be 'instrumental' in style, forgetting the delight in florid vocal melody expressed in the plainsong *jubilus*.

(ii) *Influences*. The Minnesinger had before them the example of troubadour song; some of the earlier texts are actually modelled on Provençal or French originals, though in the absence of music it is not possible to assert categorically that they were intended to be sung to the same melodies.[1] But their music was also clearly influenced, like that of the troubadours, by the idioms of Gregorian chant and popular song. Ex. 114, for instance, shows a family resemblance to the well-known Easter sequence 'Victimae paschali laudes', and it would be possible to quote many more examples where a common ancestry is apparent. The influence of popular song is best seen in the songs composed by, or attributed to, Neidhart von Reuental (*circa* 1180–1250), which have the frank simplicity of traditional melody, e.g.:

Ex. 118[2]

Win-der wie ist   nu dein kraft Wor-den gar un - si - ge-haft,
Vor den wäl-den   auff der plan   Sicht man vol-kum - li-chen stan

Seyt der may - e   sei - nen schaft, Auff dir hat zu - sto - chen.
Liech-te plümb-lein wol-ge - than,   Der han ich ge - pro - chen.

[1] Conjectural adaptations have been made by F. Gennrich in *Zeitschrift für Musik-wissenschaft*, vii (1924–5), pp. 75–98.
[2] Berlin, Preuss. Staatsbibl. germ. 779, fo. 142; facsimile in *Denkmäler der Tonkunst in Österreich*, xxxvii (1), p. 4; printed with emendations, ibid., p. 32.

Gar be‑sun‑der Durch ein wun‑der Sol‑ches kun‑der Ich ver‑nam.
Man und fraw‑en Ir sult schawen In der aw‑en O‑ne scham.

Wie des lich‑ten may‑en schar Stet be‑clait in pur‑pur‑far!

Jun‑gen maidt,das ne‑met war, Blei‑bet un‑ver‑spro‑chen.

(Winter, how has your might lost its victory, since May has broken his lance upon you! Outside the forest on the meadow are to be seen standing in perfection fair and lovely flowers, some of which I plucked. I alone, through a marvel, learned such tidings. In the meadows you may behold men and ladies without shame. See how the gay throng of May stands arrayed in purple! Young maid, mark it well, remain unbetrothed.)

A particular connexion with troubadour and trouvère song is provided by the *Leich*. Like the *lai*, of which it is the German counterpart, it consists of a number of more or less independent sections loosely strung together. The extent to which the sections are independent varies, as with the *lai*. Sometimes the same melody does duty for more than one section, often melodic fragments are transferred from one section to another. The music is generally syllabic and simple in character; the ninth section of a *Leich* by Reinmar von Zweter (thirteenth century) will serve as an illustration:

Ex. 119[1]

Dy mynne ist gut, Dy sun‑den glut Und ir ge‑lust er‑le‑schen tut. Dy

a‑bir nach sun‑den wey‑chet mut, Der min‑ne sul wir wen‑ken.

(That love is good which quenches the fire of sin and lust. But that which turns toward sin, to that love we should be inconstant.)

A complete illustration would involve printing a complete *Leich*, and as most of them are of considerable length that is not practicable within the limits of this chapter. The principle of contrast, however, can be illustrated from the first two sections of a *Leich* by Frauenlob:

---

[1] Vienna, Nationalbibl. 2701, fo. 12; facsimile in *Denkmäler der Tonkunst in Österreich*, xx (2), p. 14.

Ex. 120[1]

[I]
Ey ich sach in dem tro - ne Ein jungfraw die was swan-ger, Sie
Sie wol - te sin en - bun - den Suss gie die al - ler-bes - te; Zwolff

trug ein wun-der-cro - ne In my - ner au - gen an - ger.
stei - ne zu der stun - den Koss in der kro-nen ves - te.

[II]
Nu merck-ent wie sie trü - ge Die ge-fü - ge Der na -
Sie tet auch waz sie sol - de, Ja die hol - de Trug den

tu - ren zu ge-nü - ge; Von dem sie was ge-bür - det, Den
blu-men [sam] ein tol - de; Meit, ob' ir mu - ter wûr-det Dez

sach sie vor ir sit - zen Mit wit - zen In si - ben luch -
lam - mes und der tu - ben, Den tru - ben Ir liess - ent uwer

-te - ren Und sach in doch ge-sund-ert In ei - nes lam-mes
swe - ren; Da - von mich nit en wund-ert Daz uch dy-sel - be

wy - se Uff sy - on dem ber-ge ge - hu - ren.
spy - se Kan [wol] zu der früchte ge - stu - ren.

(I saw on the throne a virgin, who was with child. She wore a wonderful crown in the pasture of my eyes. She wished to be delivered, so was she the best of womankind; at the same time twelve jewels I saw set fast in the crown.

Now note how fitly she bore, as nature demanded. She saw him who was her burden sitting before her, full of wisdom, under seven lights; and yet she saw him apart, like a lamb on the fair mount of Zion. She did even what she should, yea, the gracious one bore a flower like the crown of flowers. Maiden, though you became the mother of the lamb and the dove, you gave up your heaviness to the clusters of the vine; and so I do not wonder that the same food can help you to such fruitfulness.)

Frauenlob (praise of ladies) was the name given to Heinrich von Meissen (d. 1318), who was the last of the early Minnesinger. The old

[1] Munich, Staatsbibl. germ. 4997, fo. 19; facsimile in P. Runge, *Die Sangweisen der Colmarer Handschrift und die Liederhandschrift Donaueschingen* (Leipzig, 1896). Recorded in *The History of Music in Sound*, ii, side 11.

traditions continued to survive but the environment was different. We find isolated examples of Minnesinger of the old type, but the main activity passed into the hands of citizen guilds. The work of the later Minnesinger and the Meistersinger, however, lies outside the scope of this volume.

(iii) *Melodic Formulas.* The *Leich* resembles the *lai* in making use of a number of very simple melodic formulas. This is also true of a large number of strophic songs, though there are occasional examples of more elaborate treatment (see Ex. 117). A particularly common formula, with a pentatonic flavour, is one based on the following succession of notes:

This has obvious associations with Gregorian chant, e.g. from the Gradual for the Holy Innocents:

La-que-us

La - que - us

It was later adopted by the Meistersinger and serves as the opening of Heinrich Müglin's *langer Ton* (long tune):

Ge - ne - sis am neun und zwan-zig-sten uns be-richt.

(Chapter XXIX of *Genesis* tells us.)

which is familiar to us from Wagner's adaptation in *Die Meistersinger*. It also forms the opening phrase of the chorale 'Wachet auf'. It is not difficult to think of parallels in sea shanties and Hebridean songs. A variant of the same formula modifies the pentatonic

[1] J. C. Wagenseil, *Der Meister-Singer holdseligen Kunst Anfang, Fortübung, Nutzbarkeiten und Lehr-sätzen* (1697), facing p. 554 (an appendix to the same author's *De sacri Rom. Imperii libera civitate Noribergensi commentatio*); facsimile in H. Thompson, *Wagner und Wagenseil* (London, 1927).

structure by the addition of a passing note, e.g. in this song by 'Der Gutere':

(Before it lay a worthy knight.)

with which we may compare the trouvère song 'Qant li rossignols s'escrie' (Ex. 102) or the following example from the *Cantigas* of Alfonso el Sabio (see p. 261):

It occurs among the Italian *laudi spirituali* (see p. 266), e.g.:

(Holy and blessed Trinity.)

It is familiar to us today from the macaronic carol 'In dulci jubilo' and the *Kyrie eleison* of the *Missa de angelis* (Vatican VIII):

Formulas of this kind are part of the common stock of early psalmody and popular song.

SPANISH MONODY

The close relations—cultural, geographical, and political—between southern France and northern Spain made it natural that the influence of the troubadours should be felt there, all the more since the Spaniards were waging their own crusades against the infidels within the peninsula. A number of troubadours are known to have been welcomed at the courts of Aragon and Castile, and Spanish and Catalan

[1] Jena MS., fo. 38.
[2] H. Anglès, *La Música de las Cantigas de Santa María del Rey Alfonso el Sabio*, ii (Barcelona, 1943), no. 252.
[3] Cortona, 91, fo. 70; facsimile in F. Liuzzi, *La Lauda e i primordi della melodia italiana* (1935), i, p. 390.

poets in their turn wrote verses in Provençal.[1] The only secular poems, however, to survive with music are six love-songs in Galician-Portuguese by the early thirteenth-century Martin Codax, a *joglar* of Vigo.[2] The notation, like that of the troubadour and trouvère songs, is non-mensural but is capable of rhythmical interpretation. No. 5 will give an idea of the style of these simple ditties:

Ex. 128

Quan-tas sa - be - des a - mar a - mi - go,

Trei - des co - mi - g'a lo mar de Vi - go

E ban - nar nos e - mos nas on - das.

(All you who know how to love a lover, come with me to the sea at Vigo and we shall bathe in the waves.)

Comparisons have been drawn with the melodic idioms of Galician folk-song; but it is equally evident that the composer was familiar with Gregorian chant.

This little trickle of secular song is completely overshadowed by the magnificent collection of *Cantigas de Santa María* made by Alfonso X (brother-in-law of Edward I of England), who reigned over the united kingdoms of Castile and Leon from 1252 till his death in 1284. Alfonso, who won the surname 'el Sabio' (the learned), was a man of considerable intellectual attainments and extended a generous patronage to the troubadours, including Guiraut Riquier. The *Cantigas* are anonymous, but some of them may very well be by the king himself. Like the *Miracles de Notre Dame* by the trouvère Gautier de Coinci, they are concerned mainly with the relation of miracles performed by the Virgin. The majority of the verses are in a form similar to that of the French *virelai*, i.e. with a refrain (*estribillo*) at the beginning of each verse (*estrofa*) and at the end of the complete song, in other words before and after each verse. The tune of the refrain is often used for the second part of the verse, e.g.:

[1] See H. J. Chaytor, *The Troubadours* (Cambridge, 1912), pp. 109–26.

[2] Facsimile edition (with modifications) by P. Vindel, *Las siete canciones de amor* (Madrid, 1915). See also I. Pope, 'Mediaeval Latin Background of the Thirteenth-Century Galician Lyric', in *Speculum*, ix (1934), pp. 3–25. Of the seven songs in the manuscript only six have musical notation.

Ex. 129[1]

Ma-ra-vi-llo-sos Et pi-a-do-sos Et mui fre-mo-sos

Mi-ra-gres faz San-ta Ma-ri-a, A que nos gui-a,

Fine

Ben noit' e di-a, E nos da paz.   E d'est' un mi-ra-gre
Ma-dre de Deus, ma-ra-

vos con-tar que-ro Que en Fran-des a-ques-ta Vir-gen fez,
-vi-llos' et fe-ro Por hũ-a do-na que foi hũ-a vez

A sa ei-gre-ia, D'es-ta que se-ia Por nos, et vei-a-mo-la sa faz

D.C.

No pa-ra-y-so, U Deus dar qui-so Go-yo et ri-so a quen lle praz.

(Saint Mary, who guides us well night and day and who gives us peace, works
marvellous and compassionate and very beautiful miracles. And I wish to tell
you one marvellous and extraordinary miracle which the Virgin Mother of God
wrought in Flanders for a woman who one day went to her church—and may
she be for us and may we see her face in Paradise, where God has chosen to give
joy and pleasure to those in whom he is well pleased.)

A further resemblance to French song will be noticed here in the use of
overt and *clos* endings for the melody of the refrain. The *virelai* form
is found also in Latin songs in an early thirteenth-century manuscript
from the monastery of Ripoll, e.g.:

Ex. 130[2]

Ce - dit fri - gus hi - e - ma - le, Re - dit tem - pus

Fine

æs - ti - va - le, Ju - ven - tus lae - ta - tur.

[1] Escurial, T. j. 1, fo. 140; facsimile in E. López Chavarri, *Música Popular Española*
(Barcelona, 1927), pl. iii; printed in Anglès, op. cit., no. 139.
[2] Paris, Bibl. Nat. lat. 5132, fo. 108ᵛ; printed in H. Anglès, *El Còdex Musical de Las
Huelgas* (Barcelona, 1931), i, p. 55.

Ec - ce tem - pus est ver - na - le In - ter li - gna
Quo per li - gnum tri - um - pha - le,

nul - lum ta - le, Ge - nus ho - mi - num mor - ta - le

D.C.

Mor - te li - be - ra - tur.

(The winter cold departs, the summer returns, and youth rejoices. Lo, here is the spring-time, when through the victorious tree, a tree beyond compare, the mortal race of men is delivered from death.)

These resemblances make it unnecessary to assume that the *virelai* form as found in the *Cantigas* is simply an imitation of the Arab verse-form known as the *zajal*. The derivation of the music from Moorish origins, as we have seen in the case of troubadour songs, is purely a speculation, with no certain evidence to support it. The representation of Moorish instruments and players in miniatures accompanying the songs is not conclusive. Recent research suggests that the resemblances between Spanish and Arab music are for the most part not due to any specific influence resulting from the Moorish invasion, but derive from a much more remote origin common to all the Mediterranean peoples.[1] What is undeniable is that the monodies of the *Cantigas* often have a flavour which is unmistakably Spanish, just as the Minnesinger melodies are unmistakably Teutonic, e.g.:

Ex. 131[2]

Co-mo po-den per sas cul-pas os o - mes se-er con-trei-tos, As-si

Fine

po - den pel - a Vir - gen de-pois se - er sã - os fei - tos.

Ond' a - vẽ - o a un o - me por pe - ca-dos que fe - ze - ra,
Que foi to - llei-to dos nem-bros d'ũ-a do - or que ou - ve - ra,

---

[1] See M. Schneider, 'A propósito del influjo árabe', in *Anuario Musical*, i (Barcelona, 1946), pp. 31–141.

[2] Anglès, *La Música de las Cantigas*, ii, no. 166. Recorded in *The History of Music in Sound*, ii, side 12.

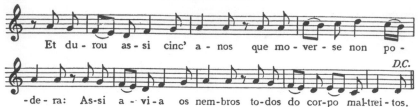

Et du - rou as - si cinc' a - nos   que mo - ver - se non po -

-de - ra: As-si a - vi - a os nem-bros to-dos do cor-po mal-trei - tos.

(As men may be crippled through their sins, so may they afterwards be made sound by the Virgin. Whereby it happened to a man through the sins that he had committed that he was paralysed in his limbs from a disease that he had, and so he could not move for five years: so were all the limbs of his body in pain.)

The rhythm of this song, as of Ex. 129, admits no dispute, since the notation of all three manuscripts is mensural. It is equally certain from the notation that a number of the songs are in duple time, e.g.:

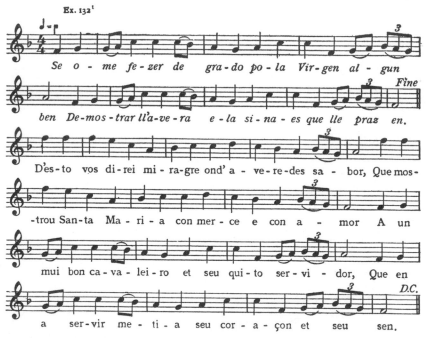

Ex. 132[1]

Se o - me fe - zer de gra-do po - la Vir-gen al - gun

ben De-mos - trar ll'a-ve - ra   e - la si - na - es que lle praz en.

D'es-to vos di - rei mi - ra-gre ond' a - ve-re-des sa - bor, Que mos-

-trou San-ta Ma - ri - a con mer - ce e con a - mor A un

mui bon ca - va - lei - ro et seu qui-to ser - vi - dor, Que en

a ser-vir me - ti - a seu cor - a - çon et seu sen.

(If a man will do freely some good thing for the Virgin, she will show him signs that she is pleased with him. I shall tell you a miracle about this by which you will be pleased, which Saint Mary wrought with compassion and love for a very good knight who was her freed servant, who pledged his heart and his mind to serve her.)

There are, however, cases where the literal interpretation of the notation results in irregular rhythms, involving, for instance, the interpolation of a bar of 4/4 time into a melody predominantly in 3/4. In

[1] Anglès, *La Música de las Cantigas*, ii, no. 207.

such cases we may either suppose that the notation exhibits local variations which are to be interpreted in such a way as to maintain a consistent rhythm, or we may follow Anglès in accepting it at its face
value. It is hardly necessary, however, to assert that the acceptance
of a literal interpretation entirely alters our conception of medieval
monody, or to insist on applying similar methods to the non-
mensural notation of troubadour songs. The irregular rhythms in
actual fact amount to little more than the equivalent of a singer's
rubato—a variation from strict time which in the transcription of
folk-songs has often resulted in the expansion or contraction of a
normal bar-length.

Tonality varies in the *Cantigas*, as in troubadour songs. Exs. 129 and
131 are modal, while Ex. 132 is in F major. There is also variety in the
melodic style. Songs like Ex. 132 suggest the influence of popular song,
whereas the following is more akin to the idioms of Gregorian chant:

(He who will serve the Virgin well can never fail. And about this I shall tell you
a great deed of a miracle which made a most beautiful tribute to the Mother of
the great King, truly as I found it written, if you will hear me.)

But, as we have seen already, the two categories are not exclusive; the
relationship between the idioms of the church and popular music-
making are too subtle to submit to rigid classification. An interesting
example of tonality helping to emphasize the structure of a melody
is the following, where the key changes for the first part of the *estrofa*.

[1] Ibid., no. 59. Recorded in *The History of Music in Sound*, ii, side 12.

The tritone (F to B, B♭ to E) is a characteristic feature both of the verse and of the refrain:

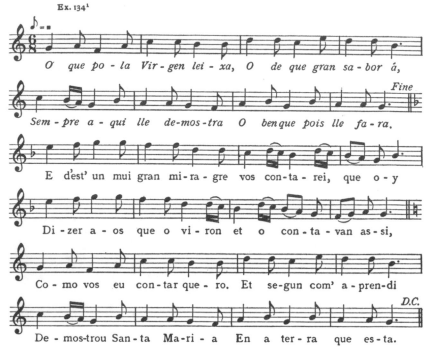

Ex. 134[1]

O' que po-la Vir-gen lei-xa, O de que gran sa-bor á,

Sem-pre a-qui lle de-mos-tra O ben que pois lle fa-ra. *Fine*

E d'est' un mui gran mi-ra-gre vos con-ta-rei, que o-y

Di-zer a-os que o vi-ron et o con-ta-van as-si,

Co-mo vos eu con-tar que-ro. Et se-gun com' a-pren-di

De-mos-trou San-ta Ma-ri-a En a ter-ra que es-ta. *D.C.*

(To the man who abandons that which gives him much pleasure the Virgin always shows here the good things she will do for him afterwards. And of this I shall tell you a great miracle which I heard of from those who saw it and who told it thus, as I will tell it to you. And as I heard it, Saint Mary showed it in the land where she is.)

LAUDI SPIRITUALI

In Italy and Sicily, as in Spain, the troubadours had considerable influence and were widely imitated,[2] but no examples of secular songs with music have survived. We possess, however, a considerable number of hymns in the vernacular, known as *laudi spirituali*, contained in anthologies dating from the late thirteenth and early fourteenth centuries. They were associated with the lay brotherhoods which had existed as early as the eleventh century. A particular impetus was given to the singing of these hymns by the outbreak of a popular religious movement in 1260. Northern Italy had been racked by cruel

[1] Escurial, T. j. 1, fo. 174ᵛ; facsimile in *Bulletin Hispanique*, xiii (1911), pl. xvii; printed in Anglès, op. cit., no. 124.
[2] Chaytor, op. cit., pp. 95–108.

and bloody wars between Frederick II and the Papacy. It was believed that the day of judgement was at hand. To propitiate a wrathful God the people of Umbria formed themselves into processions, practising flagellation as a penance and singing hymns as they went.[1] The movement was checked in the south of Italy, but in the north it spread beyond the Alps—to France, Austria, and Germany, and as far afield as Poland. A number of German *Geisslerlieder* (flagellants' songs) survive from the middle of the fourteenth century,[2] when the horrors of the Black Death added fuel to the penitential fervour.

The Italian hymns, which are in non-mensural notation, show equally the influence of Gregorian chant and secular song. St. Francis of Assisi (1182–1226), himself the author of a celebrated hymn, is said to have wished that his followers should sing the praise of God 'tamquam joculatores Dei' (like God's minstrels). Among the songs of the troubadours and trouvères also there occur a number of pieces of a religious character, notably the *Miracles de Notre Dame* by Gautier de Coinci. Various theories of rhythmical interpretation have been advanced. It has been suggested that the hymns should be sung in the free rhythm of plainsong, or again that they should be transcribed in a regular rhythm suggested by the words. The examples that follow are transcribed on the same principles as the melodies of the troubadours and trouvères. But here again the modern notation is not to be accepted as something that must be followed with mathematical precision; and since duple time is attested without any doubt in the *Cantigas* of Alfonso el Sabio we need not hesitate to use it as an alternative for the *laudi spirituali*. A particularly free interpretation must be allowed where the melodies show a good deal of elaboration. Indeed it is difficult to believe that these more elaborate melodies were ever sung by a company of penitents, particularly if they were walking in procession and engaged in flagellation. They demand the skill and judgement of the expert soloist.

The normal shape of the *laudi* is similar to that of the *Cantigas* and the French *virelais*; a refrain (*ripresa*) is followed by the verse (*stanza*), and that in turn is followed by a repetition of the refrain. Here, too, the melody of the refrain is often used, wholly or partially, for the latter part of the verse, or in the simplest type of song for the whole verse. In the following song, which is in the Mixolydian mode, the melody of the verse is heavily indebted to the refrain:

---

[1] For a vivid contemporary account see E. J. Dent, 'The Laudi Spirituali', in *Proceedings of the Musical Association*, xliii (1916–17), p. 65.

[2] See P. Runge, *Die Lieder und Melodien der Geissler des Jahres 1349* (Leipzig, 1900)

Ex. 135[1]

O di - vi - na vir - go, flo - re Au - lo - ri - ta d'o - gne au - lo - re. Tu se' flor Ke sem - pre gra - ne, Mol - ta gra - tia in te per - ma - ne; Tu por - tas - ti'l vi - no e pa - ne Ciò e'l no - stro re - demp - to - re.

(O heavenly Virgin, flower of every fragrance, thou art the flower that never fades, in thee is abundance of grace; thou didst bear the bread and wine, which is our Redeemer.)

Very similar in style is the opening phrase of the next example; but here the melody of the verse is entirely independent of the refrain. The style of the whole is also nearer to Gregorian chant than to popular song, and the melodic line is more freely decorated:

Ex. 136[2]

Spi - ri - to sanc - to glo - ri - o - so, So - vra noi sia gra - ti - o - so. Ké con gran dol - çor ve - ni - sti, La pen - te - cos - te tu con - pi - sti; Li di - sci - pu - li rin - pi - sti Del tuo a - mo - re gau - di - o - so.

[1] Cortona, 91, fo. 32ᵛ; facsimile in Liuzzi, op. cit. i, p. 314. Recorded in *The History of Music in Sound*, ii, side 12.
[2] Ibid., fo. 64ᵛ; facsimile in Liuzzi, op. cit. i, p. 380.

(Holy Spirit all glorious, let thy grace be upon us, thou that camest so gently; thou didst fulfil the Pentecost and didst fill the disciples with thy love and joy.)

Finally, we have an example where the music of the two lines of the refrain is telescoped to provide a melody for the last line of the verse. The tune as a whole is one of the noblest of the *laudi*, rising as it does to a dramatic climax in the second half of the verse:

(Let us lament that cruel kiss which made God crucified for us. The traitor Judas came; a kiss he gave and great pain. We kiss for love; for him it was the sign of suffering.

It is perhaps not extravagant to see in it one of the finest flowers of medieval song.

¹ Ibid., fo. 46ᵛ; facsimile in Liuzzi, op. cit. i, p. 344. Recorded in *The History of Music in Sound*, ii, side 12. Bar 15 has been emended by the omission of an otiose C.

VIII

THE BIRTH OF POLYPHONY
By Dom Anselm Hughes

EARLIEST REFERENCES

THE earliest stages of polyphony are obscure, not only from the scarcity of contemporary written material, but also because that limited amount of material has itself undergone different interpretations at the hands of scholars. This is not to be wondered at, for until the new art and science of composition had been in existence some little time we could hardly expect to find that the contemporary writers possessed a vocabulary of agreed technical terms by which they could explain exactly what they were discussing. Occasional references in very early days are taken by some scholars as suggestive evidence for an established practice of singing in two parts. But the interpretation of these passages is, and will perhaps remain, somewhat controversial. Some of them are not even ambiguous, as has often been suggested, but can be shown to refer quite certainly to monophonic music. It seems that there was a formal, almost scholastic, terminology in use from the time of Cassiodorus (479–575)[1] and St. Isidore of Seville (565–636) down to Aurelian of Réomé and Rémy of Auxerre in the ninth century, according to which *harmonia* was used of melody, and *symphonia* of consonant intervals (fourth, fifth, octave, eleventh, twelfth, fifteenth). *Musica organica* meant instrumental music, in particular wind music, as in Isidore,[2] who borrows his list of instruments from Cassiodorus;[3] *vox* was used to mean note as well as voice. No serious evidence has been adduced to show that Isidore himself was acquainted with harmony. Borrowing again from Cassiodorus,[4] he describes *symphonia* as a consonant interval, accurately sung or played, the opposite of *diaphonia* (dissonance).[5]

---

[1] These dates are given by Dom Justin McCann, *Saint Benedict* (London, 1938), p. 201.

[2] 'Secunda est divisio organica in his, quae spiritu reflante conpleta in sonum vocis animantur, ut sunt tubae, calami, fistulae, organa, pandoria, et his similia instrumenta' (*Etymologiarum sive Originum libri XX*, ed. W. M. Lindsay (Oxford, 1911), III. xxi. 1).

[3] *Institutiones*, ed. R. A. B. Mynors (Oxford, 1937), II. v. 6 (p. 144).

[4] Ibid. II. v. 7 (pp. 144–5).

[5] 'Symphonia est modulationis temperamentum ex gravi et acuto concordantibus sonis, sive in voce, sive in flatu, sive in pulsu. Per hanc quippe voces acutiores gravioresque concordant, ita ut quisquis ab ea dissonuerit, sensum auditus offendat. Cujus

This definition reappears in Aurelian;[1] but there is nothing to show that the definition of consonance and dissonance refers to simultaneous, rather than successive, sounds, until we come to the specific explanation given by Regino of Prüm (d. 915) in his *De harmonica institutione*.[2] The use of *diaphonia* in a purely melodic sense persisted even after polyphony was well established, e.g.:

Solus quidquid cantet vel legat, mediocriter inchoet, et tali voce ut sine strepitu perficiat . . . ac neumata dulci diaphonia symphoniace terminet, ut aedificentur audientes.[3]

(If one man is singing or reading alone, he should begin quietly and see that his voice is never unduly raised and that he ends his melody with agreeable and tuneful intervals, so that those who hear may be edified.)

The silence of Alcuin (*c.* 735–804) on the subject of polyphony is particularly noteworthy. If any one of this group of writers was likely to have mentioned it, it would have been this polymath, who not only knew about most things that were to be known in his day but also wrote freely about them. One of his works is actually entitled *De Musica*, but it contains no allusion whatever to polyphony.

The earliest claimant to deserve serious consideration is Aldhelm, bishop of Sherborne (640–709). Two passages are of sufficient importance to merit quotation here. The first runs as follows:

Discipulus. Unde ergo ista diversitas et veluti inconveniens diafonia nascatur, cum in praedictis X pedibus aequo divisionis exagio trutinatis, quasi quaedam organicae modulationis melodia, ita concors temporum armonia teneatur?[4]

This may be translated:

Student. How then would that disagreement—that awkward discordance, as it were—arise, seeing that in the aforesaid ten feet, in which the exact value of the syllables is calculated, the quantities all fit together, like the notes of a musical melody?

There is clearly no reference to polyphony here. Aldhelm is discussing

contraria est diaphonia, id est voces discrepantes vel dissonae' (*Etymologiarum* . . . *libri XX*, III. xx. 3).

[1] M. Gerbert, *Scriptores Ecclesiastici de Musica* (1784; facsimile edition, Graz, 1905), i, p. 34.

[2] 'Quotiens enim duae chordae intenduntur, et una ex his gravius, altera acutius resonat, simulque pulsae reddunt permixtum quodammodo et suavem sonum, duaeque voces in unum quasi conjunctae coalescunt, tunc fit ea quae dicitur consonantia' (ibid. i, p. 237).

[3] *Instituta Patrum de modo psallendi sive cantandi* (twelfth century); in Gerbert, op. cit. i, p. 7.

[4] *Monumenta Germaniae Historica, Auctores antiquissimi*, quarto series, xv (Berlin, 1919), p. 189.

prosody and merely refers to melody for the sake of illustration. Whether *organica modulatio* means instrumental music or not is immaterial.

The second passage runs:

Magister. . . . Consona vocis armonia psallentes concorditer cecinerunt Benedictus qui venit in nomine Domini. Cujus rei regulam nostra quoque mediocritas autentica veterum auctoritate subnixa in sacrosancta palmarum sollemnitate binis classibus canora voce concrepans et geminis concentibus Osanna persultans cum jocundae jubilationis melodia concelebrat.[1]

We may render this:

Master. . . . Chanting in voices blending happily together, they sang 'Benedictus qui venit in nomine Domini'. And we in our humble way, relying on the unquestioned authority of the men of old, observe the same practice with due solemnity: on the holy festival of Palm Sunday we divide into two groups, singing with melodious voices and crying out 'Hosanna' with two bodies of singers, in joyful and triumphant melody.

There is no word here to cause difficulty except perhaps *geminis*, which may at first sight suggest the later form known as gymel or *gemellus* (see p. 342), meaning song in parallel thirds. On the other hand, the solemnity of Palm Sunday is quite unique in the liturgical observance of western Europe, for on that day the choir divides as the procession reaches the church door, part going inside to sing the verses of 'Gloria laus et honor', while the rest stay outside to sing the refrains. This particular hymn is said to date from about 820, but the passage above suggests that the custom, perhaps to a different text, is older than the hymn 'Gloria laus'. And this ceremony would explain the reference to two groups and a double chant. Aldhelm actually uses the word *gemellus* in other places, without displaying any knowledge of the technical sense which the word acquired later —in the tenth or eleventh century at the very earliest.

If there were a series of quotations, all unmistakably referring to harmony, from Aldhelm down to the time of Hucbald in the tenth century, we might be inclined to admit these two passages of Aldhelm, and others[2] which might be adduced. It is indeed quite possible that new evidence will one day appear which would justify bringing Aldhelm into a stream of witnesses to the early existence of harmonized singing in the British Isles or elsewhere. But that possibility does not justify reading into early authors what they did not certainly

[1] *Monumenta Germaniae Historica, Auctores antiquissimi,* quarto series, xv (Berlin, 1919), p. 268.
[2] Cf. J. Handschin in *Zeitschrift für Musikwissenschaft,* viii (1925–6), pp. 321–41.

intend to say, nor in translating their terms in accordance with definitions which were not current until a century or more later.

The language of Johannes Scotus Eriugena (ninth century) is a further case in point. A passage from his writings has often been brought forward as evidence for singing in harmony, but when read in the light of the contemporary definitions of terms, such as those of Aurelian and Rémy, it does not appear to contain any certain reference to polyphonic music. The passage runs as follows:

Ut enim organicum melos ex diversis vocum qualitatibus et quantitatibus conficitur, dum viritim separatimque sentiuntur longe a se discrepantibus [intentionis et remissionis proportionibus segregatae], dum vero sibi invicem coaptantur secundum certas rationabilesque artis musicae regulas per singulos tropos naturalem quamdam dulcedinem reddentibus: ita universitatis concordia ex diversis naturae unius subdivisionibus a se invicem, dum singulariter inspiciuntur, dissonantibus juxta conditoris uniformem voluntatem coadunata est.[1]

This can, though with difficulty, be translated as it stands. But the words here enclosed in square brackets seriously affect the balance of the complete sentence and the author's argument; and as they have every appearance of being a gloss on 'discrepantibus', which they explain as 'separated by various degrees of pitch', they can be omitted, with consequent improvement in the sense. With this omission the translation will run:

Just as a melody consists of notes of different character and pitch, which show considerable disagreement when they are heard individually and separately, but provide a certain natural charm when they are arranged in succession, in one or other of the modes, in accordance with definite and reasoned principles of musical science; so the universe, in accordance with the uniform will of the creator, is welded into one harmonious whole from the different subdivisions of nature, which disagree with each other when they are examined individually.

The probability that this passage refers to melody is strengthened by the analogy, which is designed to illustrate the essential unity of the many component parts of the universe.

A greater difficulty than the obscurity of language in these early writers is the entire lack of any specimens of part-music from their period. Reference has already been made (see p. 90) to the indefinite character of notation before 950. If music existed in parts at that time there was no method of writing it down. Now throughout the period covered by this volume (to about 1315) actual music is of far greater value as evidence to historians of the art than the treatises,

---

[1] *De divisione naturae*, III. 6; Migne, *Patrologia Latina*, cxxii. 638.

some of which are nothing more than students' notes. 'It is necessary to note with M. Gastoué (*Origines du Chant romain*) that these
writings, in the form in which we possess them, are far from representing the oral teaching of the master, being in the majority of
cases nothing but the rough drafts of lectures, or even notes taken
down by students at the lectures: and every professor knows by
experience how reliable is the version of his work as it appears in the
students' notebooks.'[1]

We shall therefore be wise if we do not ascribe to the medieval
theorists a final scientific authority for which they establish no very
satisfactory claim. Sometimes their writings are interesting, but more
often they are very dull: in some places they are illuminating, but in
others they are more or less obscure. We cannot reprint the history
of medieval music from contemporary writers; we must compile our
own. And it seems better to compile it from observation of the music
itself than from any theories written about it, however contemporary
they may seem to be, and to use the theorists for an occasional side-
light, or as confirmatory rather than as primary evidence.

PROCESSES OF RECONSTRUCTION

The origins of harmony take us back beyond the true sphere of
history, to the border-line of prehistory, where reasoning is frequently inductive, not deductive; and where observed facts often
have to be replaced by mere guesswork. We can draw conclusions,
if we wish, from the present practice of primitive peoples; or we may
speculate about drone basses on early bagpipes or stringed instruments. All such useful investigations as these belong to the domain of
archaeology rather than to that of history, and they are quite valid
lines of inquiry; but they are not matters of contemporary record.
Our business now is not archaeological but historical: to survey and
make tentative maps of the borderland which separates the two
regions of monody and polyphony; to study the first recorded instances of, or references to, harmonized music; to enumerate what
is known to exist, to decipher, classify, and describe it, to set it in its
background; and last but not least, to sing it, play it, and listen to it.
Then, and not until then, we shall be entitled to indulge in speculations as to what may possibly or probably have gone before. The
actual facts of musical composition or performance must always
precede the description of them, and still more must they precede any
attempt to throw them into a theoretical form and to justify their

---

[1] Dom Augustin Gatard; *Plainchant* (London, 1921), p. 44.

existence by acoustic or aesthetic principles. 'Les théoriciens', remarks Combarieu,[1] 'se bornent souvent à codifier des idées qui leur
sont antérieures.'

We have now reached a period in which the difficulty of knowing
exactly what music was used, other than the church plainsong, begins
to fade; for as soon as we arrive at the middle of the tenth century
we find coming into existence a definite system of notation (to speak
more accurately, three competing systems) by which the actual music
can be preserved. Obviously the task of the progressive musician in
that period was to find or to devise some notation which should be
definite, which should express at the same time (a) accuracy of pitch
and of interval, (b) rhythm, and (c) actual time-duration. These three
steps were reached one by one, not all at once: first the interval, then
the rhythmic form (which will be considered in Chapter X under the
subject of 'modal notation'), and finally the definite time-value, the
representation of which is reached a century or so later than modal
notation, about 1250. Mensural notation of this kind is explained in
connexion with the motets and other forms discussed in Chapter XI.

THEORIES ABOUT THE ORIGIN OF HARMONY

When did harmonized music first come into being, and how?
These two questions are virtually inseparable: moreover, they are
practically unanswerable with any high degree of certainty, and for
that very reason they have always exercised an irresistible attraction
for the student of musical history. As to the first question, some
reasons have just been given to show that suggestions of evidence
earlier than the end of the ninth century can only be accepted with
the utmost caution. In forming an opinion as to the true answer it
will be necessary to take into selective account a number of answers
which have been proposed for the second question. These can be
divided into two classes, the prehistoric and the historic: that is to
say, those which predicate happenings which may have taken place
at any epoch, and those which rest upon features found at a more or
less definite date.

The first theory is based on acoustics. In the sounding of any note
there are present the overtones or upper partials, at a distance from
the fundamental note of 8, 12, 15, 17, &c., notes above. The distance
from the octave to the twelfth is a fifth, from the twelfth to the fifteenth is a fourth, from the fifteenth to the seventeenth is a third.
The instinct of singers, as of organ-builders with their mixtures,

[1] *Histoire de la musique* (Paris, 1913), i, p. 273.

cymbals and *fournitures*, may have been to fill in these upper partials to increase the brilliance and sonority of the sound. A second 'pre-historic' theory is stated, without very extended argument in support, by Joseph Yasser,[1] who holds that organum or primitive harmony (see next page) has always existed 'hand in hand with the use of the ecclesiastical scales'.[2] Others have seen in organum a finished product which implies centuries of growth behind it, though it would seem to the plain man exactly the opposite, a system clearly elementary and primitive. Machabey[3] rests his explanation upon the supposed natural difference between a tenor voice and a bass voice: to this we shall return later.

'Historical' theories, those which can be associated with definite periods in history, seem to be three in number. The first is associated with the name of Amédée Gastoué, and reminds us that the organ was introduced into France from Constantinople in the latter half of the eighth century and that the simultaneous sounding of different notes upon the organ by two players may be supposed to have evoked an imitation by singers. This theory is not only attractive but is also highly probable: but it is also provoking, for there is as yet no absolute evidence from which it can either be proved or disproved.[4] Another theory was propounded by the present writer in 1934,[5] drawn from a peculiar convention in the writing of *sequelae* (see p. 129) by which one of the musical phrases (which occur in pairs alternating between two bodies of singers or between solo and chorus) is very often repeated a fifth higher in the scale. From the repetition in sequence to a simultaneous performance of the melody in both pitches at once is a small step which results in parallel movement in fifths. The frequent occurrence of sequences and tropes among the examples of early harmony lends some support to this view. Finally, there is the opinion, already suggested, that the nature of the earliest examples of organum would lead us to date the first appearance of harmony in the late ninth century. These three 'historical' solutions are by no means mutually exclusive.

FIRST WRITTEN RECORDS

The earliest unmistakable reference to harmonized music appears to be in Hucbald's *De harmonica institutione*. Hucbald (d. 930), who

[1] *Medieval Quartal Harmony* (New York, 1938), pp. 68–82.
[2] G. Reese, *Music in the Middle Ages* (New York, 1940), p. 250.
[3] *Histoire et évolution des formes musicales du Ier au XVe siècle* (1928), p. 52.
[4] Reasons in support of this theory are advanced by W. Apel in *Speculum*, xxiii (1948), pp. 210–12.   [5] *Anglo-French Sequelae* (London, 1934), p. 13.

was a monk of St. Amand in Flanders, used a system of alphabetical notation sometimes called Boethian. Boethius (d. 524) was looked upon as the father of Christian musical theory, just as St. Ambrose was regarded as the father of the hymnody of the choir Office and Notker Balbulus of the sequence in Germany and Italy. If it is claimed that Boethius invented and taught this system, it is highly suspicious, to say the least, that no example of its use survives from the four or five intervening centuries. It will suffice to say here that Hucbald used a system like ours, except that his *a* was our *c*; and that a well-known plainsong manuscript, Montpellier H 159,[1] and the addition to Oxford, Bodleian, Bodl. 572, 'Ut tuo propitiatus',[2] used an alphabetical notation in which the notes were named as ours are but continued after *g* with *hik* instead of repeating *abc*. Hucbald's reference to simultaneous sounds is brief but convincing:

Consonantia . . . est duorum sonorum rata et concordabilis permixtio, quae non aliter constabit, nisi duo altrinsecus editi soni in unam simul modulationem conveniant, ut fit, cum virilis ac puerilis vox pariter sonuerit; vel etiam in eo, quod consuete organizationem vocant.[3]

(Consonance is the calculated and concordant combination of two notes, which will only occur if two notes of different pitch are combined to form a musical unity, as happens when a man and a boy sing the same tune, or in what is generally known as 'organizing'.)

It may be assumed that the term *organizatio* refers to the form of part-singing generally known as organum. The way in which it is introduced suggests that it was in origin a popular, not a technical, term;[4] and this would lend colour to the theory mentioned above, that the practice of organum, like the name, was derived from the instrument. Hucbald's language also suggests that the practice was already quite familiar.

For a precise description of organum we must turn to another treatise of the same period, the *Musica Enchiriadis*.[5] This was formerly attributed to Hucbald, but it is now, after proposals to ascribe it to other authors, reckoned as anonymous. The *Scholia Enchiriadis*[6] is, as its name implies, a commentary on the *Musica Enchiriadis*. Both

---

[1] Facsimile edition in *Paléographie musicale* (Solesmes, 1901–5), vols. vii and viii.
[2] Facsimile in H. E. Wooldridge, *Early English Harmony*, i (London, 1897), pl. 1.
[3] Gerbert, op. cit. i, p. 107.
[4] Cf. 'Haec namque est quam diaphoniam cantilenam, vel assuete organum, vocamus' (*Musica Enchiriadis*, Gerbert, op. cit. i, p. 165); 'qui canendi modus vulgariter organum dicitur' (John Cotton, *Musica*, Gerbert, op. cit. ii, p. 263).
[5] Ibid. i, pp. 152–73.
[6] Ibid., pp. 173–212.

works make use of a clumsy system of notation known as the Daseian, based upon the cutting up, reversal, and other maltreatments of Greek letters. Both the Daseian and the alphabetical systems failed to establish themselves. But the 'carefully-heighted' neums (see p. 109) maintained their ground, improved in accuracy and alignment, and finally developed into the staff-notation which we use today by stages which can be traced in detail. These stages we shall be able to observe at intervals in these pages up to the end of the third volume, when in the early sixteenth century the palaeography of music ceases with the advent of music-printing: and thenceforward all subsequent changes in the manner of noting music will be no more than typographical modifications, for the convenience sometimes of the printer or engraver, sometimes of the musician.

From the *Musica Enchiriadis* we learn about four types of organum: (1) in parallel fifths, with the plainchant melody on the top line; (2) in the same, with the higher voice or *vox principalis* doubled at the octave below and the lower voice or *vox organalis* doubled at the octave above, thus resulting in a four-part effect (see Ex. 138); (3) taking either the higher or the lower pair of these four voices and running on in parallel fourths, recognizing (but not solving) the difficulty of the tritone or augmented fourth which will occur between *f* and *b*; (4) a variant of this last method (generally known as 'free organum') in which the second voice may remain stationary for the lowest notes (see Ex. 139):

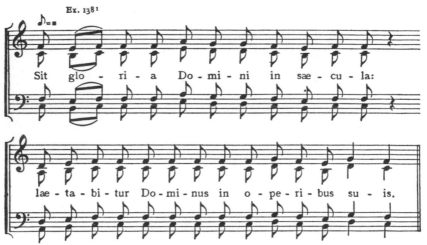

(May the glory of the Lord abide for ever: the Lord shall rejoice in his works.)

[1] Recorded in *The History of Music in Sound* (H.M.V.), ii, side 13.

Ex. 139

Rex cœ - li, Do - mi - ne   ma - ris un - di - so - ni,
Ti - ta - nis ni - ti - di   squa - li - di - que so - li,

Te hu - mi - les fa - mu - li,   mo - du - lis ve - ne - ran-do pi - is,
Se ju - be - as fla - gi - tant   va - ri - is li - be - ra - re ma-lis.

(King of heaven, Lord of the wave-sounding sea, of the shining sun and of
the dark earth, thy humble servants entreat thee, worshipping thee with pious
words, to free them—be it thy command—from their sundry ills.)[1]

That the earliest harmony was sometimes, if not always, antiphonal
is beyond doubt. Here is an apposite contemporary quotation, from
the account of the dedication of Ramsey Abbey in 991:

Cum dextera pars sonum melodum personaret inclytis vocibus, tum
sinistra jubilando organicis desudabat laudibus.[2]

(While the Decani side of the choir sang a melodious strain with excellent
voices, the Cantoris side laboured at organum parts in joyful songs of praise.)

GUIDO'S *MICROLOGUS*

There is a gap of a century or more after the *Musica Enchiriadis*
before we meet the next technical description of organum. This occurs
about 1040 in the treatise called *Micrologus* by Guido of Arezzo
(born *c.* 995).[3] Of Guido's importance in the history of notation there
will be something to say in the next chapter (see p. 290). In the matter
of harmony it is a little puzzling that there had been so little development since the *Musica Enchiriadis*. The explanation may be that
Guido was not keenly interested in this subject and so gave only a
summary account of it. Free instead of strict organum is clearly
recognized by him as the normal form, and where the organum is
strict it is to be at the fourth, not the fifth. This difference is perhaps
partly or wholly regional, for the earliest examples of harmony tend
to show that the fourth is more prevalent in Italy and the southern
parts of Europe, while in the Anglo-Norman and French areas the
fifth takes its place, and the third is not at all uncommon. The third

[1] From A. T. Davison and W. Apel, *Historical Anthology of Music* (Cambridge,
Mass., 1946), p. 243.
[2] Byrhtferth, *Vita S. Oswaldi*; in *The Historians of the Church of York and its Archbishops*, ed. James Raine (London, 1879–94), i, p. 464. The original has 'sinister' for
'sinistra'.
[3] For a full and recent discussion of Guido's work see J. Smits van Waesberghe in
Musica Disciplina, v (1951), p. 15.

occurred naturally in free organum where the lower voice remained
stationary (see Ex. 139), and Guido himself gives the following
example to show the agreeable effect of a passing major third in the
approach to a cadence:

Ex. 140

Ho-mo e - rat in Je - ru - sa - lem.   *or,*   Je - ru - sa - lem.

(There was a man in Jerusalem.)

His comment is: 'Ecce distinctio in deutero E, in qua ditoni occursus,
vel simplex vel intermissus, placet'[1] (here we have a cadential formula
in the second [plagal] mode [i.e. Mode IV], where it is satisfactory
to precede the unison with a major third, whether simple or delayed).

EARLY EXAMPLES OF POLYPHONY

The most substantial example of early polyphony outside the
theoretical treatises is the collection of 164 two-part organa known
as the Winchester Troper,[2] which dates from the early part of the
eleventh century. Its music is more or less concealed from us, since
the notation is neumatic, though with some indication of 'careful
height' in the neums. Attempts to transcribe some of the pieces in
staff-notation have not been very convincing. It is possible, however,
to recognize occasional instances of contrary motion, other than those
that arise normally where the voices come together at cadences. One
such occurs in the Alleluia with Greek text beginning 'Ymera agias-
mene':

Ex. 141

Conjectural

eth - ny

We can find in this remarkable Troper—confining ourselves to two-

---

[1] Gerbert, op. cit. ii, p. 23.
[2] Cambridge, Corpus Christi College, MS. 473. Edited with some facsimiles by W. H.
Frere for the Henry Bradshaw Society (London, 1894). Other facsimiles in Wooldridge,
Early English Harmony. Cf. J. Handschin in *The Journal of Theological Studies*, xxxvii
(1936), pp. 34, 156; E. Wellesz, *Eastern Elements in Western Chant* (Oxford, 1947),
pp. 192–201.

part music—no fewer than five Introit-tropes, twelve Kyries, eight settings of *Gloria in excelsis*, nineteen Tracts, fifty-six Alleluias, seven *Sequelae*, and fifty-seven Responds. It has been said more than once that the deciphering of the Winchester organa is the most pressing need in the investigation of early harmony; but until we can unearth a document in pitch-notation which contains a number of pieces identical with those in the Winchester Troper, the task appears hopeless.

There are a few other fragments or isolated specimens of two-part music from the eleventh century—namely, Chartres 109 and 130, Vatican 586 and 592, Paris, Bibl. Nat. lat. 11631 and 12596, Lucca 603.[1] The often-quoted *Kyrie* 'Cunctipotens' from Laon, now in the Ambrosiana at Milan,[2] is an example appended to a theoretical work and therefore lies outside the class of evidence now being considered. A complete list of known sources is given by Lincoln B. Spiess in *Speculum* for January 1947. The first item given there (Einsiedeln 121, p. 416) is not quite certainly polyphonic, and the last, 'Ut tuo propitiatus', does not in my opinion belong to this very early stage, despite its archaic alphabetical notation. 'Regi regum glorioso', from the Lucca manuscript,[3] is quite short, so that we can reproduce it complete. It gives us twenty-seven intervals only, of which eleven are octaves and unisons, eight are fourths, and four are fifths, while there is one sixth. The interval of the major third appears three times, in each case as a cadential approach to the unison in the way that Guido recommends: and in three places we see two notes of the upper voice against one of the lower:

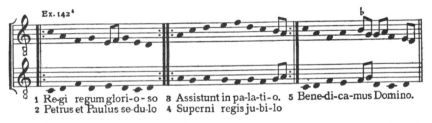

Ex. 142[4]

1 Re-gi regum glori-o-so 3 Assistunt in pa-la-ti-o. 5 Bene-di-ca-mus Domino.
2 Petrus et Paulus se-du-lo 4 Superni regis ju-bi-lo

(By the glorious King of Kings stand faithfully in his palace Peter and Paul: with triumph to the highest King let us bless the Lord.)

But we must wait for a notation which shows all the intervals with

---

[1] Details partly from J. Handschin in *Revue du chant grégorien*, xli (1937), p. 14.

[2] Printed in *Oxford History of Music*, 1st ed., i, p. 86; 2nd ed., i, p. 45.

[3] Transcription by R. Baralli, in *Rassegna Gregoriana*, xi (1912), col. 10; facsimile, ibid., cols. 5–6.

[4] Recorded in *The History of Music in Sound*, ii, side 13.

entire certainty before making any full inquiry into the relationship
between the individual voices, a matter of the highest importance in
the history of early harmony.[1]

Among the documents available for studying the intervals which
were actually sung in the eleventh century the most valuable is a leaf
from Chartres 109, reproduced and transcribed by H. M. Bannister
in *Revue grégorienne* for March 1911. It is the most valuable because
of its relative length, in contrast to the tiny scraps from which (the
Winchester Troper excepted) we have to obtain our knowledge of the
practical music of the age. We are less in danger of generalizing from
particulars or from isolated instances when we have, as here, reasonably certain indications of as many as 241 intervals:

Ex. 143[2]

[Soloists]
[Plainsong]
...mo - ri - tur: mors

(*)
il - li ul - tra

[Chorus in plainsong:-]
[upper voice indecipherable]
[Soloists]
(†)
non dominabitur. Al-le - lu - ia. Sur-re - xit Christus

qui cre - a - vit   o - mni - a:

[1] Cf. W. Apel, 'The importance of notation in solving problems of early music', in
American Musicological Society, Papers (1938), p. 51.
[2] Recorded in *The History of Music in Sound*, ii, side 13. The missing ends of the sen-

tences 'shall not have dominion' (*non dominabitur*) and 'on the human race' (*humano generi*) are not shown in the original: the fashion in all this music was for the final phrase to be caught up by the whole choir in unison, and it is reasonably supposed that the polyphonic part was performed by soloists only. This corresponds closely with the ordinary practice of the unison Gregorian chanting.

Di - cant   nunc   Ju - dae - i   quo - - mo - do

[End of the fragment]

mi - li-tes cus-to-di-en-tes se - pul - chrum per- di- [derunt regem, *etc.*]

(*)   Lower voice not written in MS, but evidently to be repeated
(†)   So in MS.
(‡)   Apparently so in MS, according to H.M. Bannister

(Christ being raised from the dead no more doth die: death on him no longer shall have dominion. Christ is risen, who created all things, and had compassion on the human race. Alleluia. The Angel of the Lord descended from heaven, and approaching rolled the stone and sat upon it. Praise the Lord who was crucified, and glorify him who was buried for you; adore him rising again from the dead. Let the Jews now say how the soldiers guarding the sepulchre lost the king . . . .)

In later analyses a distinction will have to be observed between accented and unaccented chords. This is necessary when a kind of dance-rhythm seems to predominate in the interludes, and when the idea of the passing-note, or passing-chord, is apparent. Frequent and definite information is given by the contemporary theorists on this distinction, and we shall find that unprepared discords on an unaccented beat are found as late as Dunstable (d. 1453). For the present, however, we shall probably be right to regard the composer of the harmony as proceeding note by note, without desiring to superimpose any new rhythmical scheme upon the older, smoother flow of the Gregorian chant.

Analysis of the intervals in the Chartres manuscript brings out some striking points: (i) there are, out of 241 intervals, only 15 fifths; (ii) there are as many as 67 thirds, 25 of these being set in seven chains of three each and one of four; (iii) the discord of the second occurs 23 times, but that of the seventh not at all. Unisons and octaves total 78; there are 48 fourths and 10 sixths. It may be remarked that the difference in the figures shown for the second and the seventh is characteristic of the music of this period and of that immediately following (see p. 297). There are 28 cadences, if we include in this figure all the half-closes marked in Bannister's transcript, adding two more at 'revolvit' and 'de morte' for the sake of consistency. Of these, 23 are closing cadences which approach the unison, and in 14 cases they approach through the third. Six cadences are 2–1, and out of the remainder 4–1, 5–1, and 6–1 occur once each. Of the five expanding cadences, four are 6–8 and one is 5–8. We have therefore 19 out of 28 employing the imperfect concord of third or sixth as an approach, only two using the fifth. The result of this analysis shows that the actual music of the eleventh century at Chartres at any rate was considerably different from what we have been taught to expect from the descriptions of the theorists, and that it is, from a later point of view, much in advance of it.

COTTON AND THE AMBROSIANA TREATISE

Before we pass on to the music of the twelfth century some mention should be made of two theoretical writers about 1100, one of whom is anonymous and the other, John Cotton, an Englishman.[1] An interesting point in Cotton's work is his recognition of the practical advantages of contrary motion. He says of *diaphonia* (which now means the same as organum):

> Ea diversi diverse utuntur. Caeterum hic facillimus ejus usus est, si motuum varietas diligenter consideretur: ut ubi in recta modulatione est elevatio, ibi in organica fiat depositio, et e converso.[2]

> (Different people treat it in different ways; but the easiest method is to pay careful attention to variety of movement, so that when the plainsong goes up the counterpoint goes down, and vice versa.)

What has been observed sporadically in the Winchester Troper and systematically in the Chartres organa has now been promoted to the position of a normal rule of composition. Cotton explains that organum is so called 'eo quod vox humana apte dissonans similitudinem exprimat instrumenti quod organum vocatur'[3] (because the human voice, by singing an independent part, produces an effect similar to that made by the instrument called the organ), which though a late testimony may be held to lend support to the theory of the instrumental origin of organum (see p. 276).

The other treatise—*Ad organum faciendum* (How to construct organum)—is in the Ambrosiana Library at Milan.[4] It contains similar

[1] Both his surname and his nationality have been disputed: see *Johannis Affligemensis De Musica cum Tonario*, ed. J. Smits van Waesberghe (Rome, 1950), pp. 22 ff.
[2] Gerbert, op. cit. ii, p. 264.
[3] Ibid. ii, p. 263.
[4] MS. 17.

instructions about contrary motion, and the parts are allowed to cross one another. This crossing of parts is a very necessary and desirable practice in a state of things where all the voices are what we should call 'baritones'. The internal evidence both of the Gregorian chant and of medieval harmony makes it quite certain that the bass voice, as we know it, was not used, and that the normal voice was of the nature of a baritone or tenor-baritone. To take a thirteenth-century example we find that the music shown in Ex. 202 in Chapter XI (about 1275) is written for three tenors and a baritone. The first tenor runs from middle c up to a', the second and third from G to a', and the baritone from F to f. This sort of compass is found throughout all the compositions of the twelfth, thirteenth, and fourteenth centuries. The theory propounded by Machabey,[1] that owing to the 'division of men's voices into two parallel lines, [harmony] must have followed as a matter of course', is not in accord with the facts.

[1] *Histoire et évolution des formules musicales*, p. 52.

IX

MUSIC IN THE TWELFTH CENTURY

By Dom Anselm Hughes

NEW CONDITIONS

As we approach the end of the eleventh century the conditions under which we can study polyphonic developments are very different from those obtaining in the days of the *Musica Enchiriadis* and the Winchester Troper. It is a change which may be compared to that which takes place from a night of darkness, varied only by passing phases of moonlight, to a dawn, at first indeed obscure but promising steady progress towards the full blaze of noontide. In this half-light the form and the position of objects can be distinguished, but the sharpness of their outline cannot be immediately seen, and their colour is not yet discernible with any degree of accuracy. Translated into the language of music, this is to say (1) that the manuscripts of both plainsong and polyphony have now begun to denote the actual pitch of the notes, and (2) that some sort of conventional agreement on a time-system must have come into existence, for there are now two or more notes in one voice against only one in the other. These two very significant changes must be considered in some detail later on, for they introduce us to (3) the vitally important subject of the relationship between the individual voices. From this point we shall be able to notice (4) the beginnings of the idea of harmonic cadence, (5) some results of the wider range of voices now in use, and (6) the first recorded instances of three-part writing. Before giving attention to these matters the sources of our information must be enumerated.

SOURCES OF THE PERIOD

In the last chapter the theoretical writers were mentioned before such few practical sources as were then available. Now that we are passing on from the period of mnemonic to that of definitive notation, it will be wiser to build our conclusions upon the actual music which survives, and to judge the reliability of the theorists by the degree of accuracy with which they describe and explain it. Two collections of music survive from this period, known respectively as the Codex

Calixtinus and the Martial-Tropers. There is also a group of nine pieces in the Cambridge University Library MS. Ff. i. 17; and there are eleven other more or less isolated specimens:

Madrid, Bibl. Nac. 19421 (from Catania).
Douai, 90 and 274.
Lille (see *Oxford History of Music*, i, p. 110; 2nd ed. i, p. 83).
London, British Museum, Burney 357 (from Thame).
Oxford, Bodleian, Bodley 572 (from Canterbury), Lat. Liturg. d 5 (from Alta Ripa in Switzerland).
        Corpus Christi College 59 (from New Lantony, near Gloucester).
Rome, Vatican, Ottob. 3025.
Burgos, Parish of St. Stephen (unnumbered).
Tortosa, Cathedral Library, C 135.

Transitional between this period and the next, but belonging more closely to the earlier stage than to the latter, and therefore treated at the end of this chapter, is the eleventh fascicle of the St. Andrews manuscript (Wolfenbüttel 677).

THE CALIXTINE AND ST. MARTIAL MANUSCRIPTS

The manuscript in the Cathedral Library of Compostella in north-western Spain which passes under the name of the Codex Calixtinus was written about 1137 according to Anglès,[1] or after 1139 according to Walter Muir Whitehill and Dom Germain Prado, who have published a complete edition in three volumes, with facsimiles, notes, and transcriptions of all the musical parts of the manuscript.[2] Thirteen years before this full edition appeared the music alone was edited and published by Peter Wagner.[3] The manuscript contains a plentiful collection of services with music for the vigil and feast of St. James the Great, the patron saint of Compostella, whose relics are there enshrined. To this place a vast number of pilgrims journeyed in the Middle Ages. The pilgrimages to Rome, to Compostella, and to Jerusalem were, and still officially remain, the three pilgrimages of greatest dignity in Western Christendom: in England they were out-rivalled only by the two best-loved national pilgrimages, to St. Thomas the Martyr at Canterbury and to Our Lady of Walsingham.

The Compostella manuscript thus contains a good deal of 'special music' in addition to the ordinary liturgical chants for the festival, and we may lawfully call some of its contents pilgrims' songs, and may suppose that they would have been sung on the road to and from

---

[1] *El Còdex musical de Las Huelgas* (Barcelona, 1931), i, p. 59.
[2] *Liber Sancti Jacobi—Codex Calixtinus* (Santiago de Compostela, 1944).
[3] *Die Gesänge der Jakobusliturgie zu Santiago de Compostela* (Freiburg, 1931).

Compostella as well as in the cathedral. The Offices, Masses, and Processions of the festival are liberally supplied with tropes, and twenty-one of the pieces are set in two parts, one of them having a third part added in a separate hand (see p. 303).

Nearly all the compositions of the Middle Ages have come down to us anonymously, but these Calixtine specimens enjoy the unusual distinction of having the names of their composers appended. Most of them are French archbishops and bishops, but according to Anglès[1] the ascriptions are apocryphal. A curious clef-sign ≣g≣ on fo. 190ᵛ for one line only of the four staves occupied by the piece 'Ad honorem summi regis' (To the honour of the King most high) has been interpreted by Dom Prado as indicating gymel, or song in parallel thirds (see p. 342). Wagner's comment on this peculiar passage wisely refrains from this suggestion: he is content to point out that

in the original [manuscript] two clefs, C and g, are set in a very curious way. The former seems to be of a darker colour and partly erased. If the G-clef is retained, the guide-mark at the end of the line for the f which follows *curia* at the end of that staff is correct.[2]

There is a collection of interesting eleventh- and twelfth-century manuscripts, most of them preserved at the Bibliothèque Nationale in Paris, which came originally from the monastery of St. Martial at Limoges and other places in the south of France. These are known among musicologists and liturgiologists as the 'Martial-Tropers'. The eighteen oldest tropers of the series contain no polyphonic music, but the nineteenth (Bibl. Nat. lat. 1139) has three specimens in two parts. This suggests that polyphony was unknown at Limoges before the date of this troper, which is usually given as the twelfth century; though Handschin[3] suggests that parts of the manuscript may date from the late eleventh century, without, however, giving the reasons for this opinion. A little later than this manuscript, about 1150, are three other 'Martial-Tropers' (Bibl. Nat. lat. 3549 and 3719, Brit. Mus. Add. 36881) which provide between them no fewer than 57 examples of two-part writing. This material has not yet been completely scored, but a sufficient number of the pieces have been reproduced or quoted for some idea of the style to be gained. Examples 148 and 150 are drawn from this source. The music of Brit. Mus. Add. 36881 has been dealt with in detail by Spanke and Anglès,[4] who

[1] Op. cit. i, p. 62.   [2] Op. cit., p. 125.
[3] *Revue du chant grégorien*, xli (1937), p. 15, n. 17.
[4] H. Spanke, 'Die Londoner St. Martial-Conductushandschrift'; H. Anglès, 'La

give transcriptions of eight pieces. The manuscript is attributed by the authorities of the British Museum, without finality, not to Limoges but to Narbonne.

NOTATION AND THE STAFF

The first traces of staff-notation have already been mentioned briefly in Chapter IV (p. 109). It is now time to deal with the matter in greater detail and to bring it into the general line of musical history.

First of all comes the line, in imagination or in dry-point or in ink, above the top of the text, and from this basis the heights of the notes are computed with more or less accuracy. This first occurrence of the notion of 'height' is possibly of no real value, but it is certainly not without interest. For the idea of 'high' and 'low' is so universal a principle of our notation that it is hard for us to realize that it is nothing more than a conventional manner of speaking, and has really nothing to do with height in the physical world. We might with almost equal justice reverse our terms, speaking of the 'high' notes as 'low', and vice versa, for the 'low' notes of an organ are produced by pipes which are very much taller than those of the 'high' notes. 'In music itself, our terms "high" and "low" are conventional attributes. The Greeks used the terms in reverse, as for them the high notes were those played on the long strings of the lyre, those which compelled the player to reach higher up on the instrument.'[1]

Before long the actual lines of the staff begin to appear—first the line for F, usually in red; then that for c, often in yellow; then lines intermediately for a and over the top of the c-line for e, usually in dry-point where red and yellow are used for the other two. Once the staff was established as a convention, men began to abandon the use of varied colours and to rule all four lines in red or in black. To decide where this practice originated seems to be impossible in the present state of our knowledge. In any case it is unlikely that its originators were aware of the full implications of the innovation. Guido of Arezzo (d. 1050) seems to have been the first to appreciate the practical advantages of definite notation. He says in his prologue to the Micrologus:

Quidam eorum [sc. puerorum] imitatione chordae et nostrarum notarum usu exercitati, ante unius mensis spatium invisos et inauditos cantus ita primo intuitu indubitanter cantabant.[2]

música del Ms. de Londres, Brit. Museum, Add. 36881', in Butlletí de la Biblioteca de Catalunya, viii (1928–32), pp. 280–303. Also published separately (Barcelona, 1935).

[1] W. D. Allen, Philosophies of Music History (New York, 1939), p. 255.
[2] Prologus Guidonis in Musicam (Micrologus), ed. A. M. Amelli (Rome, 1904), p. 17; Gerbert, Scriptores ecclesiastici de musica, ii, p. 3.

(Some of the boys, who had practised intervals from the monochord and from our notation, were able in less than a month to sing at first sight and without hesitation chants which they had previously never seen or heard.)

It is not easy to discern whether Guido regarded the staff or solmization as the more useful discovery. His name has come down to us in musical histories chiefly as inventor of the staff. As a matter of fact it would rather seem that his claim to renown should rest on his work as organizer and propagator of solmization, for which he is not so frequently given credit. The staff, on the other hand, was in existence before his day.

Guido's system of solmization has something of the simplicity of genius. A tune, presumably already well known, is found in which the opening syllables of six divisions (the seventh is ignored) give the notes of the scale in rising order:

Ex. 144[1]

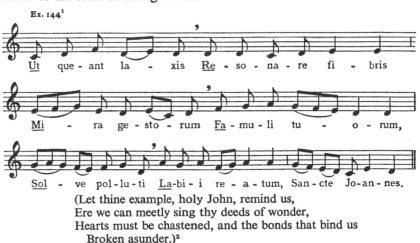

Ut que - ant la - xis Re - so - na - re fi - bris
Mi - ra ge - sto - rum Fa - mu - li tu - o - rum,
Sol - ve pol - lu - ti La - bi - i re - a - tum, San - cte Jo - an - nes.

(Let thine example, holy John, remind us,
Ere we can meetly sing thy deeds of wonder,
Hearts must be chastened, and the bonds that bind us
Broken asunder.)[2]

These syllables can be fixed in the memory, and reference can be made, if needed by the less musical learners, to the pattern tune. In these *incipit* notes of 'Ut queant laxis' we have a hexachord which, if extended for two notes to the octave, would give us the modern major scale. With the modality of the actual melody Guido is not concerned: his object is to show where the semitone occurs, using a method which can be applied to any mode, according to the position of the semitone, e.g.:

Dorian:	Re	mi	fa	sol	la . . .
Phrygian:		Mi	fa	sol	la . . .
Lydian:			Fa	sol	la . . .

[1] The version of this melody is printed as given by Guido. A purer and older form can be seen in *Antiphonale pro diurnis horis* (Rome, 1919), p. 619.
[2] Translation by R. E. Roberts in *The English Hymnal* (1906), No. 223.

Next comes the question of how to follow on after *la*, and for this the mutation of the hexachord is brought into play.

TYPES OF THE HEXACHORD

The Greek gamma (*Γ*) was used as a symbol for the note below the lowest A: hence the term gamut, or scale (= gamma-ut). Starting from this low G our first hexachord will be:

Γ	A	B	c	d	e
ut	*re*	*mi*	*fa*	*sol*	*la*

If we change over at *c* and begin again with *ut*, the semitone between *e* and *f* will fall in its right place (*mi–fa*): which must always happen, for this location of the semitone between *mi* and *fa* is the very kernel of the whole system. We now have:

c	d	e	f	g	a
ut	*re*	*mi*	*fa*	*sol*	*la*

and we reach the first fence, for the following hexachord would read:

f	g	a	b	c¹	d¹
ut	*re*	*mi*	?	*sol*	*la*

But the next semitone being *b–c*, not *a–b*, a convenience is made of the variability of *b*, and the third hexachord is:

f	g	a	b♭	c¹	d¹
ut	*re*	*mi*	*fa*	*sol*	*la*

This is called the *hexachordum molle* (soft hexachord). To get in step again the fourth hexachord begins one note above the last, instead of three notes, thus repeating the first an octave higher: and because it uses b♮, it is called the *hexachordum durum* (hard hexachord):

g	a	b	c¹	d¹	e¹
ut	*re*	*mi*	*fa*	*sol*	*la*

Repetition continues on this plan for another octave, going as high as is needed for the treble voice.

The explanations of this system in medieval treatises are very much more detailed and more involved than that given above: but as the singer of the Middle Ages had no mental picture of the keyboard with its black and white notes to work from, what seems child's play to us was to him a serious task. *Ut* was replaced by *do* in Italy during the early seventeenth century for reasons of euphony. But as Guido's original scheme gave the five open vowels for the first five notes (a duplication at *la* being unavoidable), the substitution of *tu* for *ut*, instead of *do*, would have been better. The significance of staff notation for the development of polyphony is obvious. Before it came into general use the transmission of music depended very largely on tradition and the example set by expert singers. This explains the emphasis laid by the chroniclers on the journeys made to St. Gall and Metz by the legendary Romanus and Petrus,[1] or by James, the papal precentor, to York. The acceptance of a new system of precise pitch-notation made it possible for singers to perform music at sight, and for authentic copies to be sent from one place to another. The *notator* was now as important as the *cantor*. Abortive attempts to denote actual pitch were also made in other directions, by alphabetical letters or by signs of one kind or another. They were experiments in answer to a demand, but as we have seen already (p. 278) they led nowhere.[2]

THE NOTATION OF TIME

So soon as two or more notes were to be sounded in one voice against one note in the other the singers had to agree upon some kind of a convention by which the voices could be held together in the intended relation. Passing over, as they were, from a period in which their notation was mnemonic, not descriptive, we should not expect to find the scribes using all at once an accurate temporal or mensural notation. For this reason there is, and always will be, a high degree of conjecture about our transcriptions of nearly all twelfth-century music. We must recognize the tentative and empirical nature of the notation employed, and the fact that apparently no two scribes used exactly the same system. Apel justly observes:

> Throughout the twelfth, thirteenth, and fourteenth centuries the mechanics of notation were in a state of continuous flux and rapid change, produced and paralleled by an evolution in musical style the progress of which lies mainly in the field of rhythm. . . . In place of methodical and systematic explanations, given frequently in the form of rules, we must treat the subject in a more flexible manner, and must approach it chiefly from the evolutionary point of view.[3]

[1] For a discussion of this journey see Dom Rombaut van Doren, *Étude sur l'influence musicale de l'abbaye de Saint-Gall* (Brussels, 1925), pp. 127–33.

[2] Those who are interested in examining them more closely will find a full account in Dom G. Suñol, *Introduction à la paléographie musicale grégorienne* (Paris, 1935).

[3] *The Notation of Polyphonic Music* (Cambridge, Mass., 1942), pp. 199–200.

It will be necessary to consider the matter of a time-scheme before taking up the equally important subject of the intervals between the voices. Until we arrive at some decision about what the scribes seem to have thought about time, we cannot provide ourselves with even tentative transcriptions of their music in order to study their intervals. That they had some sort of conventions about time-relations must be taken as axiomatic; otherwise the singers would have no means of keeping together or of sounding the concordances at key-points in the melody, a matter about which they were certainly careful. That these conventions were actually erected into a formal scheme as early as the twelfth century is by no means sure: and that the notation followed any such scheme consistently is out of the question.

To interpret the notation we have therefore to make our choice among different methods followed by various modern scholars; and we shall perhaps be most successful if we do not decide to follow one or other of these methods rigidly, remembering that we are watching the growth of a system, not examining a finished product. These various schools of thought consist of (i) those who wish to avoid the use of any modern notes with a temporal significance, and either print their scores in two-part plainsong notation or use crotchet-heads without tails throughout, with the modern staff and clef signs; (ii) those who follow the verbal rhythm of the text in iambic or trochaic fashion when dealing with a syllabic passage—two beats for an accented syllable, one for an unaccented; (iii) those who apply as much as possible of the systematic notation of the following century, usually known as 'modal notation'; and (iv) those who frankly attempt to apply the complete mensural notation which belongs to the fourteenth century and the later part of the thirteenth. In this chapter free use has been made of the third method in the analysis or presentation of material; but when there has been real doubt about the propriety of applying this, the first method has been preferred. It may be of interest to see a comparative specimen of (i) the free-rhythm transcription, both in plainsong and in tailless crotchets, and a very free interpretation of the same piece in a combination of methods (ii) and (iii). All that is claimed for the last version is that it is not inconsistent with the notation, seeing that the notation in question has as yet no method of denoting its time-values; and that we are justified in hunting for an interpretation which seems to give the most musical result. The following example is the *cantus firmus* of the two-part piece 'Nostra phalanx', which occurs in the Codex Calixtinus:

(i) In free rhythm, in plainsong notation:

Ex. 145

No-stra pha-lanx plau-dat læ-ta hac in di-e qua a-thle-ta Chri-sti gau-det

si-ne me-ta Ja-co-bus in glo-ri-a. ℟ An-ge-lo-rum in cu-ri- a.

(Our company applauds on this happy day in which James, the athlete of Christ, rejoices in glory without end in the court of the angels.)

(ii) In free rhythm, on the modern staff:

Ex. 146

(iii) Interpreted freely in accordance with rhythmic ideas not formulated until a slightly later period, but very likely existent at this time in the mind of the writer or the singers:

Ex. 147

* The apparent inconsistency between the interpretation of this group and that used at 'athleta' in bar 7 is dictated by the arrangement of the upper voice in the two-part setting; and is also artistically justified, as showing the difference between half close and full close.

THE RELATIONSHIP BETWEEN THE VOICES

In studying the part-writing of the twelfth century there are two main lines of inquiry, the contrapuntal and the harmonic. We have to ask first to what extent we can discern an individual melodic value in the upper (added) voice; and second, what are the intervals employed. It must be frankly admitted that as a general rule the upper parts seem to be without melodic interest. The voice-parts are, in the great majority of cases, homophonic and not polyphonic in character. As we shall see in the next two chapters, these pieces are the forerunners of the vertically conceived conductus, not of the horizontal part-writing of the motet. And it would appear that the 'organizers', as they are sometimes called, are often thinking more of their rules than of their music. There are, of course, exceptions— for example, in the upper part of 'Congaudet hodie':[1]

Ex. 148

Con - gau - det ho - di - e   cœ - les - tis cu - ri - a,   Quod

ho - mo per - di - tus   e - rit in glo - ri - a,   Na-

-to de vir - gi - ne   qui   re - git o - mni - a.

[1] Brit. Mus. Add. 36881, fo. 12. Transcription from Spanke and Anglès, op. cit., p. 309 (with slight alterations in the rhythm). The rhythm printed by Anglès is in even crotchets throughout. Another rhythm, which is in some ways more probable than either his version or the one given above, is:

Ex. 149

Con - gau -det ho - di - e   cœ - les - tis   cu - ri - a,   etc.

(The heavenly court rejoices today, for lost mankind shall come to glory, since he who ruleth all things is born of a virgin.)

And when the upper voice is frankly melismatic against a slowly moving tenor we find a melodic flow which has a 'Gregorian' beauty of its own, as in 'Prima mundi seducta sobole':[1]

(The first progeny of the world being led astray, heaven's inhabitants are troubled at the knowledge of the deceit.)

The principal facts emerging from a study of the intervals used in this early period are:
  (i) the frequent use of the unison or octave, especially at the beginning or end of a phrase;
  (ii) how frequently the second is used as an arbitrary discord, and how seldom the seventh by contrast;
  (iii) the free use of the third;
  (iv) the fourth and fifth used freely, but not so often as some writers would lead us to suppose;
  (v) the relatively infrequent use of the sixth by contrast with the free use of the third. This may be explained by saying that in

---

[1] Brit. Mus. Add. 36881, fo. 13ᵛ; Spanke and Anglès, op. cit., p. 311. The upper voice is transcribed above in plainsong 'quaver notation', and the lower voice accommodated accordingly.

the greater part of this music there is a tendency for the parts to keep close together, as though fearful of straying too far apart; and when the fifth has been reached it is seldom that the interval is extended to the sixth or the octave.

(vi) the apparent absence of any dislike for consecutive unisons, fifths, or fourths. The following is a rather extreme example, from 'Clangat coetus':[1]

Of these points (iii) above, foreshadowed by the Chartres music examined in Chapter VIII, p. 281, would hardly need mention but for the contrary statements of so many theoretical writers. But the conclusions given above have not been evolved from the information, sometimes obscure, supplied by the medieval theorists or the notebooks of their students: they are the result of a careful and extensive perusal of the actual material, and the evidence must be presented here, if only in summary. Study of the original sources gives rise to a suspicion, amounting at times to a certainty, that the empirical notation of the composer, scribe, or copyist does not always succeed in conveying to us what he has in mind. Laboratory methods in musical studies are in many cases unnecessary or even misleading, while in other cases they may be useful if not given too high a value; but in the case of eleventh-century music they seem to be the only possible way of arriving at the facts.

Forty-one pieces have been analysed, fourteen of which are Spanish and twenty-seven Anglo-French. The figures of these two regional divisions are given separately, as they display certain differences which are not without significance. They lend little support to the remark of Anglès[2] that the music of the Codex Calixtinus (from which twelve of the fourteen Spanish pieces have been taken) was written under strong French influence. His conclusion may well be right, but it must have been reached on other grounds. The total number of intervals analysed is 3,655 (Spanish 743, Anglo-French 2,912): and only by this full and mathematical analysis is it possible to decide

---

[1] Tortosa Cathedral C. 135, fo. 18ᵛ; facsimile in Anglès, *El Còdex musical de Las Huelgas*, i, p. 83.
[2] Ibid., p. 59.

upon the truly representative pieces of any of these early collections. Thus Besseler[1] gives 'Vox nostra' as an example of Calixtine harmony; whereas the intervals of that specimen are the most divergent of all from the normal average. 'Ad superni regis decus', from which a short quotation is given on p. 302, or 'Congaudeant catholici', in its original two-part version (see p. 303), can be shown by their actual figuring to approximate most closely of all to the norm.

Analysis shows:

	Spanish	Anglo-French
1. Unisons and octaves	283 (38·1 %)	1,078 (37·0 %)
2. Fifths	191 (25·7 %)	852 (29·3 %)
3. Thirds	103 (13·9 %)	510 (17·5 %)
4. Fourths	93 (12·5 %)	260 (8·9 %)
5. Sixths	29 (3·9 %)	95 (3·3 %)
6. Seconds	34 (4·6 %)	82 (2·8 %)
7. Sevenths	10 (1·3 %)	35 (1·2 %)

The 34 occurrences of the discord of the second in the Spanish sources analysed are all from the Codex Calixtinus, which has only 21 sixths and 7 sevenths. Probably some of the relatively frequent discords of the second revealed by the tables are due to copyists' errors, or to doubtful points in the transcriptions where editors have (rightly) refrained from reading a concord of unison or third lest they should be guilty of following a preconceived notion of euphony. In the case of the seventh, the greater distance on the page and the fact that the octave is used less frequently than the unison makes positive errors less likely than in the case of the second. Furthermore, if the twelfth-century Codex Calixtinus were transcribed with a more liberal interpretation of thirteenth-century practice, when the notation was adequate to express these ideas, many of these discords would tend to disappear, e.g.:

Rex im-men-se, pa-ter pi - e, e - lei-son.   Con-so-la-tor, dul-cis a-mor, e-lei-son.

[1] *Die Musik des Mittelalters und der Renaissance* (Potsdam, 1931), p. 96.
[2] Recorded in *The History of Music in Sound* (H.M.V.), ii, side 14.

Ex. 152 (ii)

Rex im - men - se, Pa-ter pi - e, e - lei - son.

Con - so - la - tor, dul-cis a - mor, e - lei - son.

(Mighty king, holy Father, have mercy: Consoler, dear love, have mercy.)

CADENCES

The normal melodic cadence, as inherited from Gregorian times, falls to the final by step. The fashion of rising to the final note came in with the *sequela* (see p. 129) where it is usually only an intermediate cadence. We find in these earliest specimens of part-music:

(i) The upper melody is frequently developed in melismatic form at the cadence. But this is nothing new: it is well known in Gregorian music, and is indeed a natural expression, part of a common musical instinct, e.g. the end of 'Per lethalis pomi partum':[1]

Ex. 153 (i)

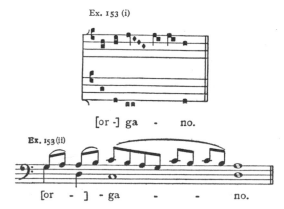

[or -] ga - no.

Ex. 153 (ii)

[or -] - ga - - no.

(ii) For the lower voice, in the Anglo-French group 73 per cent. rise to their final note instead of falling: in the Spanish group, 60 per cent. They rise by step, for it is quite a long time before the authentic or dominant cadence (V–I) is found. Nor should

[1] Brit. Mus. Add. 36881, fo. 1; Spanke and Anglès, op. cit., p. 305.

we expect this so long as the lower voice still retains a purely melodic contour and function, however much the upper line may bear the marks of 'filled-in' harmony. But the fact of their rising in so many cases betokens the passing of the older Gregorian custom of falling to the final. It is the lower voice that we have analysed, for that is the part in which the set melody (hardly ever borrowed from plainsong in this type of composition) is to be found. The upper voice, which is moving in contrary motion more often than not, will fall where there is a rising cadence in the lower voice, and vice versa.

THE RANGE OF THE VOICES

Examination of twenty-six Anglo-French pieces reveals that only three of them approximate to our conception of tenor and bass—or rather tenor and baritone, for the lower voice drops only very seldom below *c* to *A*. These three pieces are all found in Brit. Mus. Add. 36881: 'Gregis pastor Tityrus', *f* to *g'* and *d* to *d'*; 'Prima mundi seducta sobole', *g* to *g'* and *e* to *b*; and 'Res jocosa quod haec rosa', *c* to *e'* and *A* to *a*). Of the remainder, nineteen would be described today as for two baritones, the typical range being *c* to *c'* or *d* to *d'*. Four of them are abnormal: 'Cantu miro summa laude', *d* to *g'*, with the 'lower voice' ranging from *e* to *a'*, higher than the 'tenor'; 'Agnus qui pius es factus', *d* to *f'* and *f* to *f'*; 'Mira lege miro modo', *f* to *a'* and *c* to *g'*; and 'Viderunt Emanuel', *g* to *a'* and *f* to *g'*. From this it is evident that the discrimination between tenor and bass has not yet arrived, and that the slightly higher range of the upper voice is merely the result of the harmonic construction 'on paper', by which one voice is reckoned as 'above' the other (they cross frequently); and no special regard is paid as a rule to that marked difference between the characteristics of the tenor and bass voices which is axiomatic with us. Of twenty Spanish pieces, sixteen may be reckoned as for tenor and baritone, but three are for tenor and bass ('Cunctipotens', *g* to *b'* and *d* to *c'*; 'O adjutor', *c* to *g'* and *A* to *a*; and the first of three settings of 'Benedicamus Domino', *d* to *e'* and *A* to *a*). One—'Misit Herodes'—is abnormal: the upper voice sinks to *G* and rises to *d'*, while the lower voice has a compass narrower each way, running only from *Bb* to *c'*.

It is clear that the discrimination of voices was between solo and chorus rather than between tenor and bass. The older Gregorian tradition, by which the soloist was a tenor, is certainly present in the minds of some of these composers, notably the Spanish. The two-part sections in some pieces are obviously intended for two soloists; and it is in these sections that we find one, or occasionally both, of the singers rising to *g'* or *a'*. The pieces in question are the first six of the organa in the Calixtine manuscript (the other compositions belong to the class of conductus, to be described in the next chapter) by Ato and other composers: they consist of the *incipit*—the first word or two—for two voices, then (presumably, though it is not written) the rest of the text for unison singing by the chorus, in plainchant. The lower voice of the *incipit* has already begun the ordinary Gregorian melody, and this presumed unison passage will take it up and finish it. Then follows the verse, set for two voices.

There is one, and probably only one, example of imitation in the Calixtine manuscript. There is no reason for supposing that it was accidental, but as it does not seem to appear more than once, we cannot claim that it is yet a normal technical procedure. Example 154[1] shows that the imitation is of the type called interchange, which was a simple matter of exchanging strains between the two voices. Later on we shall see this interchange highly developed into the *rondellus* or roundelay (see p. 375); but until independent entry has come into use we can hardly claim as yet any direct connexion with canon, still less with fugue:

Ex. 154 (i)

Ad su-per-ni re-gis de-cus

Ex. 154 (ii)

Ad   su - per - ni   re - gis   de - cus

(To the glory of the heavenly king.)

THREE-PART WRITING

Three surviving examples of three-part writing have been assigned to this period: 'Congaudeant catholici', 'Custodi nos', and 'Verbum

[1] Codex Calixtinus, fo. 185.

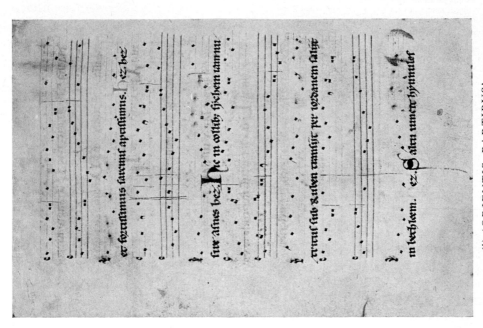

(a) 'VIRTUTE NUMINIS'

(British Museum MS. Cotton Titus A XXI, fo. 90.) Thirteenth century

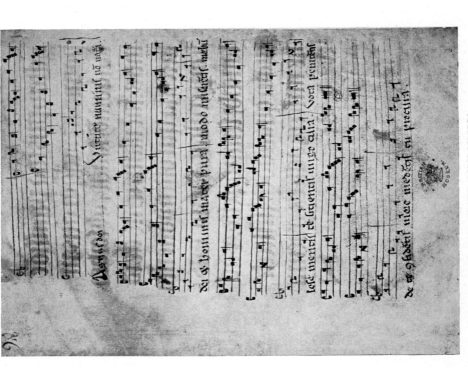

(b) 'ORIENTIS PARTIBUS'

Showing the second verse, with parts of the first and third verses. (British Museum MS. Egerton 2615, fo. 43ᵛ.) Thirteenth century

Patris humanatur'. The date *c.* 1137 for 'Congaudeant catholici', from the Calixtine manuscript, is fairly well established. But its middle voice has apparently been written in by another hand, and even if this is nearly contemporary, the fact makes it difficult to accept it as an original piece of three-part writing. The method of the insertion, however, is not without interest (see next page). 'Custodi nos'[1] was dated by Wooldridge[2] as early in the twelfth century—that is to say contemporary with 'Congaudeant'. He remarks:

It is not only a very primitive specimen of writing in three parts, but contains also the earliest attempts at present known to produce imitations by one voice of passages uttered by another. . . . It will be observed that again a large number of discords, including several tritone fourths, appear upon the weak beats of the rhythm, while with five exceptions, four of which are thirds and sixths, the strong beats are marked by concords.

The last point has already been underlined above (p. 297); and the two other questions raised by Wooldridge—imitation, and the treatment of the tritone which involves chromatic alteration or *musica ficta*—will have to be dealt with later; at present we are concerned only with the date. The manuscript from which 'Custodi nos' is taken has been described and catalogued by Ludwig,[3] and he categorically assigns it to the thirteenth century. There seems little doubt that the date suggested by Wooldridge, who was presumably following Coussemaker, must be laid aside.

The third piece, 'Verbum Patris humanatur', occurs among the music found in the fly-leaves of Cambridge University Library, Ff. i. 17. The part-music on these fly-leaves was reproduced in facsimile, with one short exception, by Wooldridge in *Early English Harmony* (1897). The date there given was 'thirteenth century', but there can be little doubt that Besseler[4] is right in assigning it to the twelfth. The internal evidence of the music and of the texts connects it with other collections of the twelfth century, and not at all with those of the thirteenth. Furthermore, the script is of a cursive character which is distinctive of a small number of manuscripts of this period, listed above (p. 288), and is not found later. This group conveys the impression that the staff has arrived, but not square notation, and its script is in appearance very much like some of the long series of Martial-Tropers of the twelfth century. Ludwig[5] remarks of it: 'The

---

[1] Paris, Bibl. Nat. lat. 15139 (formerly St. Victor 813); facsimile in C. E. H. de Coussemaker, *Histoire de l'harmonie au moyen âge* (Paris, 1852), pl. xxvii.
[2] *Oxford History of Music*, 1st ed., i, pp. 112–14; 2nd ed., pp. 84–85.
[3] *Repertorium organorum recentioris et motetorum vetustissimi stili* (Halle, 1910), i, p. 139.   [4] Op. cit., p. 95.   [5] Op. cit., p. 327.

notation displays a cursive script midway between neumatic and square notation':

Ex. 155[1]

Ver-bum Pa-tris hu-ma-na-tur, O, O, dum pu-el-la

sa-lu-ta-tur, O, O. Sa-lu-ta-ta foe-cun-da-tur

vi-ri ne-sci-a. He-i, he-i, no-va gau-di-a.

(The Word of the Father is made flesh, when the Virgin is hailed: hailed, she conceives, knowing not man. Hey, hey, for the news of joy.)

In three-part music one of the first questions we may ask is: 'What feeling is there, if any, for chords?' The answer, so far as it is supplied by 'Verbum Patris', is negative. The full triad occurs twice only, each time in the cadence (bars 10 and 12). The doubled third, on the other hand, is found four times (bars 2, 4, 5, 7) and the second chord includes a doubled fourth. The numerous discords are less striking than they may appear on paper: six out of nine are on unaccented notes. It may be observed that while the lowest voice carries the main melody, the middle voice is also melodic and contrapuntal: but the highest voice has comparatively little melodic interest and may be frankly described as a 'filling-in'.

When the middle voice was added to 'Congaudeant catholici' the scribe seems to have been working from a harmonic rather than from a contrapuntal point of view: the extra part, which has hardly any melodic interest of its own, is in strict accord with the 'bass' throughout, in octaves and fifths, except for three thirds on accented beats,

---

[1] Cambridge University Library, Ff. i. 17, fo. 4ᵛ; facsimile in Wooldridge, *Early English Harmony*, pl. 29. Recorded in *The History of Music in Sound*, ii, side 15.

with six thirds and a fourth on unaccented beats.[1] It will be instructive
to reprint here this pilgrim song, first in Ludwig's transcription and
then in a reconstruction freely based on the suggestive fact that several
groupings (marked x in the first version) reach a concord at the last
note:

Ex. 156

-Con - gau - de - ant ca - tho - li - ci, læ -

-ten - tur ci - ves coe - li - ci di - e

sta.

Ex. 157[2]

Con - gau - de - ant ca - tho - li - ci, læ - ten - tur

<hr />

[1] These figures are taken from Ludwig's version as printed in Adler's *Handbuch der Musikgeschichte* (1930), p. 182.
[2] Recorded in *The History of Music in Sound*, ii, side 14.

ci - ves   coe - li - ci   di - e   i

(Let catholics rejoice, let the citizens of heaven be glad this day.)

This approach to the problem of many passages in early medieval harmony is perhaps not wholly empirical. A similar practice was known in organum, where the *vox principalis* would enter on the second note to avoid a dissonance with the *vox organalis*, thus:

Ex. 158

vox organalis

vox principalis

The theorist who is known from his position in the first volume of Coussemaker's *Scriptores* as 'Anonymus IV' (*c.* 1275) says: 'Si fuerit discordans, ad primam sequentem concordantem erit inceptio'[1] (if it would make a discord the beginning [of the harmony] will be on the first following concord). The point is one to which no attention appears to have been paid, and it would seem to deserve further investigation. The principle has already been applied at bar 2 of Ex. 152 (p. 300), and it is followed in other quotations later, such as those from the eleventh fascicle of the St. Andrews manuscript.

[1] *Scriptores de musica medii aevi* (Paris, 1864), i, p. 363.

One short example from the main body of this manuscript is given here to show this principle clearly at work:

Ex. 159[1]

etc.

Ec - - - - - - -[ce sacerdos]

'UT TUO PROPITIATUS'

This curious short respond-verse in Oxford, Bodley 572,[2] has had to run the gauntlet of explanations and theories ever since its first publication in H. B. Briggs's *Musical Notation of the Middle Ages* (Plainsong and Mediaeval Music Society, 1890). Its interest lies not so much in the music as in the notation, which is alphabetical (see p. 277). According to Apel[3] it is 'the only specimen of part-music written in letter-notation preserved outside of treatises'. The date, originally given as tenth or eleventh century, is now generally agreed to be early twelfth century.

The lower voice is the plainsong of a respond-verse in the office of St. Stephen (26 December). The version of the plainsong quoted here is from the Erlyngham Breviary,[4] as being the nearest to the form of Bodley 572. The importance of the plainsong original is shown by the seventh and fifteenth notes in the lower voice, where a sign ♮ occurs, which Apel calls

vaguely reminiscent of a 5, the meaning of which has been variously interpreted. We suggest interpreting it as indicating prolonged duration of the preceding tone.[5]

The plainsong leaves no room for doubt. 'Ut tuo propitiatus' has usually been described as originating in Cornwall, as the main body of the manuscript is Cornish. But fo. 49[v], on which the piece occurs, has been ascribed in Bodleian catalogues since 1913 to St. Augustine's, Canterbury:

[1] Wolfenbüttel 677, fo. 40.
[2] Facsimile in Wooldridge, *Early English Harmony*, i, pl. 1.
[3] Op. cit., p. 207.
[4] Salisbury, Chapter Library 152.
[5] Op. cit., p. 208.

Ex. 160 (i)

Ut tu-o   pro-pi-ti-a - tus in-ter-ven-tu Do-mi-nus nos pur-

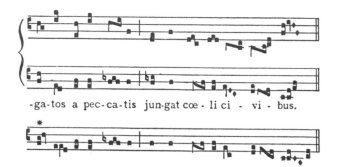

-ga-tos a pec-ca-tis jun-gat cœ-li ci - vi-bus.

* This B is marked ♮ in BM. Add 28598 fo.17v.

Ex. 160 (ii)

Ut tu-o   pro - pi-ti-a - tus

in - ter - ven - tu Do - mi - nus nos   pur-ga-

-tos a pec - ca - tis jun - gat coe - li ci -

-vi - bus. *or*

(... that the Lord, appeased by thy intercession, may join us, purified from sin, to the citizens of heaven.)

This verse clearly belongs to the twelfth- (or possibly eleventh-) century style of 'experimental plainsong in two parts', and this type of notation has therefore been chosen for the example.

THE ELEVENTH FASCICLE OF THE ST. ANDREWS MANUSCRIPT

The St. Andrews manuscript (Wolfenbüttel 677, formerly Helmstedt 628) belongs chiefly to the following chapter, where it will be quoted frequently for purposes of illustration. It has been chosen partly because it is the earliest of the main documents of the early or middle thirteenth century and partly for the sake of convenience, as it is the only one of those documents available in facsimile.[1] The eleventh and last fascicle (fo. 176–97) of this manuscript is admitted to be the earliest. It is in a different hand; and though perhaps written not much earlier than 1250, and so practically contemporaneous with the rest of the manuscript, its music belongs definitely to an earlier period, and falls within the scope of this chapter rather than of the next. Unlike the rest of the manuscript, its contents are not to be found in the other main sources of the list of Notre-Dame music

---

[1] *An Old St. Andrews Music Book.* Published in facsimile with an introduction by J. H. Baxter (London, 1931).

given below (p. 313), and it is therefore assumed to have been composed in Scotland or England, though there seems to be no particular
reason for this second alternative. It is a homogeneous collection,
consisting of music for the Masses of the Blessed Virgin Mary
throughout the year: seven Kyries, one Gloria, nine Alleluias, a
Tract, fifteen Sequences, seven Offertory antiphons, four settings of
Sanctus, and three of *Agnus Dei*. The items of the Ordinary (*Kyrie,
Gloria, Sanctus, Agnus*) are all troped, as are some of the Offertories.
Its music is in two parts, and shows a tendency towards regular
rhythm in places, especially in the Alleluias—presumably because of
their more melismatic character. One of its most interesting features
is the appearance of a third voice at a few of the cadences of these
Alleluias, a kind of ad libitum first tenor, e.g.:

Ex. 161[1]

Al - le - lu - - ia.

[1] Wolfenbüttel 677, fo. 182. For an explanation of the sign ∧ see p. 325, and for
a note on the instrumental suggestion conveyed by such passages see p. 327.

X

MUSIC IN FIXED RHYTHM

By Dom Anselm Hughes

PRELIMINARY REMARKS ON DATES AND DATING

THE period with which this chapter deals runs approximately from 1175 to 1275. It is different from what has gone before in one notable respect; whereas materials up to this point have been rather scanty, they suddenly become plentiful. This large body of early thirteenth-century music is described as being written in 'modal rhythm', so named because it is based on certain rhythmical patterns or 'modes' (see pp. 318–20). There is as yet no essential difference in the notation itself, but there are conventions by which the presence of various rhythmic systems can be ascertained and deciphered. This is a great step towards measured music. In fact it is measured music, though in the notation the mensuration is implied rather than expressed. But something must first be said on the question of dating.

It cannot be too often remarked that nearly all dates before the invention of printing must be regarded as little more than approximate or conjectural; and it is dangerous to build too much upon them when it is a question of a few years, or even of a few decades. We may say, for instance, that such-and-such a work dates from 1350 because we know that the composer was alive and active in that year. But he may have been fifty years old in 1350 and have written the music thirty years before; or alternatively he may not have written it until twenty years later. Over the fifty years' gap thus set up he may not have altered his method of notation or his script, though the style of his composition will presumably have developed. It is therefore rash to base any arguments upon statements of close dates, unless there is external evidence available, or internal evidence such as references to ascertained historical events.

The present position in the dating of music from the twelfth to the fourteenth centuries is not wholly satisfactory. It has been assumed hitherto that whereas on the one hand organa and conducti were composed and written at Notre-Dame in Paris from about 1170 under Léonin up to the death of his successor Pérotin in 1235, on the other hand manuscripts in which these productions are preserved must be dated about 1300 or later. No adequate explanation seems to be forthcoming to account for this unreasonable gap in time. Unreasonable it is, because styles and fashions changed and developed in the Middle Ages almost as rapidly as they do today, and this in notation as well as in composition. Nor was it usual in those centuries to preserve the remains of the past with the zealous care now shown by scientific historians. Fly-leaves of fourteenth-century music cut up and used as binding for fifteenth-century manuscripts provide one proof of this. Just as a modern choir-master destroys an accumulation of unwanted music of the past, so the medieval precentor was ruthless in making over disused parchments to workshops where the bindings were repaired. A very close parallel can be seen in Gothic architecture, where it is quite usual to find that not long after a church was built an aisle or a chapel was pulled down to make way for something better or larger in a later style.

Some explanation must be sought and offered for one very wide gap in time between the assumed date of composition and the ascribed date of the manuscript. This occurs between 1170 and 1300, in relation to the work of Léonin. Alternatively, the gap must be very substantially narrowed if not actually closed. Welcome indications are to be found, for example, in Apel's contention[1] that the famous manuscript Wolfenbüttel 677 ought to be dated about 1250, not in the fourteenth century, to which it is sometimes assigned. A more wholesale pushing back of the customary dates would agree with the estimates of non-musical palaeographers. Three leading experts who made cursory inspections of musical manuscripts in the Bodleian Library in 1945 and 1946 almost invariably suggested dates just about a hundred years earlier than those which ordinary musical canons would ascribe to them. It has been remarked on the other hand by Wellesz and others that the script of a choir-book or other formal musical composition is naturally executed in a careful style which may consciously or unconsciously preserve an archaic character; and this is especially true of ornamental initials, a detail to which palaeographers give attention when forming their opinions. A prudent revision of dates in the direction of earlier ascriptions would do something to narrow our gap.

References to such events as the exile of St. Thomas of Canterbury from 1164 to 1170,[2] and to Canterbury without any reference to St.

---

[1] *The Notation of Polyphonic Music 900–1600* (Cambridge, Mass., 1942), p. 200.
[2] 'In Rama sonat gemitus' (Wolfenbüttel 677, fo. 168ᵛ).

Thomas at all,[1] are highly significant. In the latter case it may be answered that the words may have been written a century or more before the music. But in most cases it is not at all probable. Composition of text and music usually (not always) went together, when the text was not liturgical: and frequently it is obvious that the composer made up his words as he went along. Many composers seem to have cared little or nothing about the literary value of their texts. That the highly orthodox Middle Ages permitted some of the extraordinary doctrinal statements or implications occasionally found in the texts is only explicable on the grounds that the words did not matter. If it is true that musicologists have been dating manuscripts rather too late, the explanation may be that they have been relying too much on theorists, forgetting that when musical subjects form part of an academic curriculum the lecturers are frequently a century or more behind the actual practice of contemporary composers. Until the serious revival of the study of sixteenth-century counterpoint in our own times it was usual for teachers in this subject to define contrapuntal doctrine in the terms of Fux (d. 1741) and Marpurg (d. 1795). This was not in any way supposed to describe the music of the nineteenth century, but only to explain its theoretical substructure.

SOURCES OF THE PERIOD

The following are the chief manuscripts displaying modal rhythm:

1. Wolfenbüttel, Ducal Library 677, fascicles 1 to 10 (*c.* 1250).
2. Florence, Bibl. Laur., plut. xxix, 1 (*c.* 1250).
3. Paris, Bibl. Nat. lat. 15139, formerly St. Victor 813 (*c.* 1250).
4. Madrid, Bibl. Nac. 20486 (*c.* 1300).
5. Wolfenbüttel, Ducal Library 1206 (*c.* 1300).

These are the largest and by far the most important in this period. The first has been reproduced in facsimile, edited by J. H. Baxter (London, 1931). It was written at the Augustinian monastery of St. Andrews in Scotland (see fo. 56). To these we should add a list of music which has since disappeared:

6. British Museum, Harley 978, fo. 160 (*c.* 1240).

This was probably written at Leominster in Herefordshire, a cell of Reading, by one William of Wycombe.[2] There are two other early collections, both of Norman-French origin:

7. British Museum, Egerton 2615 (1223–34).
8. British Museum, Egerton 274 (1275–1300).

[1] 'Solaris ardor Romulus' (Oxford, New College, MS. 362, fo. 89).
[2] Cf. B. Schofield in *The Music Review*, ix (1948), pp. 81–86.

A large collection of similar date, though its notation is mensural, is:

9. Burgos, El Còdex de Las Huelgas.

This has been published in facsimile, with transcription and notes, by Higini Anglès (Barcelona, 1931).

THE GENERAL PICTURE

In our mental picture of musical activities in western Europe from the end of the twelfth century it would be a mistake to think of a few advanced innovators working in isolated places. This might be nearer to the truth for the year 1000 or even 1100; but the scene has shifted a good deal since that time. The extensive and well-defined collections of music which are available for use here and in the next two chapters are no mere experiments by local groups of composers. On the contrary, they are the materials with which many of the cathedrals and larger monastic choirs of England, France, and Spain enriched their services. The list of churches where harmonized music is known to have been sung, whether we compile it from contemporary references or from actual remains, is a long one: so long, indeed, that we should be justified in saying that the practice was universal. The great minsters of those days were the scenes of extended activities by numerous bodies of clerics. Many of them have already been mentioned in these pages—Winchester, Chartres, Worcester, Notre-Dame in Paris, Compostella, St. Martial at Limoges, and St. Gall. Some were staffed by monks, others by a body of canons and minor beneficiaries. To the functions in the choir they devoted a good part of the day's work, especially on Sundays and festivals. Splendour of ceremonial and of ornament was matched by elaboration of music. The unadorned Gregorian chant, however protracted the melismata of Gradual and Alleluia, of Antiphon and Respond, was not enough for them: they sought new ways of enlarging the opportunities of the singers.

In England alone there is ample evidence of the practice of polyphony. We have seen already (p. 280) that Winchester had a complete collection of organa by the beginning of the eleventh century. In 1217 the General Chapter of the Cistercian Order noted that at Abbey Dore and Tintern they were singing in three and four parts, after the manner of the secular clergy.[1] Robertsbridge Abbey in Sussex, from which comes the earliest known piece of organ music, written in the following century, was also a Cistercian house; and so was Thame,

[1] 'Triparti vel quadriparti voce, more saecularium, canitur' (*Statuta Cap. Gen. Ord. Cist.*, ed. J. M. Canivez, i, p. 472, n. 31).

from which comes the manuscript quoted in Ex. 212 (p. 388). As
late as 1526 the Abbot of Waverley, the senior Cistercian house in
England, ordered Thame to lay aside pricksong.[1] And in 1320 the
General Chapter of the same Order had to censure 'syncopation of
notes, and even hockets'.[2]

If things were so in the abbeys of the Cistercians with their traditions of soberness and austerity, they were presumably even more
ornate in the choirs of the Black monks, as the Benedictines were
called, in order to distinguish them from their Cistercian offshoot. In
the thirteenth and fourteenth centuries we have music in parts known
or presumed to come from the Orkneys, Durham, Coldingham, York,
Addle, Selby, Tattershall, Rufford (Notts.), Dublin, Shrewsbury,
Coventry, Peterborough, Bury St. Edmunds, Hereford, Leominster,
New Lanthony by Gloucester, Worcester (including perhaps Led-
bury and Pershore), Reading, and Canterbury; and theoretical
writings from Bridlington, Doncaster, Tewkesbury, Evesham, Oxford,
Beaulieu, Canterbury, and Dover, some of which are extant and some
lost. Most of these place-names indicate a Benedictine house. It is
also significant that the manuscript Wolfenbüttel 677 was written in
the Augustinian Abbey of St. Andrews.

Of secular music-making in England at this period we know very
little. There is, however, some interesting information about popular
practice in the *Descriptio Cambriae* by Gerald de Barri, known as
Giraldus Cambrensis (*c.* 1147–1220). The passage has often been
quoted but is worth repeating in full:

In musico modulamine non uniformiter ut alibi, sed multipliciter
multisque modis et modulis cantilenas emittunt, adeo ut in turba canen-
tium, sicut huic genti mos est, quot videas capita tot audias carmina,
discriminaque vocum varia, in unam denique sub B mollis dulcedine
blanda consonantiam et organicam convenientia melodiam.

In borealibus quoque majoris Britanniae partibus, trans Humbriam
scilicet Eboracique finibus, Anglorum populi qui partes illas inhabitant
simili canendo symphonica utuntur harmonia: binis tamen solummodo
tonorum differentiis et vocum modulando varietatibus, una inferius sub-
murmurante, altera vero superne demulcente pariter et delectante. Nec
arte tamen sed usu longaevo et quasi in naturam mora diutina jam con-
verso, haec vel illa sibi gens hanc specialitatem comparavit. Qui adeo
apud utramque invaluit et altas jam radices posuit, ut nihil hic simpliciter,
nihil nisi multipliciter ut apud priores, vel saltem dupliciter ut apud

---

[1] A. Hamilton Thompson, *Song Schools in the Middle Ages* (London, 1942), p. 26.
[2] Rose Graham in *The Journal of Theological Studies*, xxxviii (1937), p. 295. For
hocket see p. 397.

sequentes melice proferri consueverit; pueris etiam, quod magis admiran-
dum, et fere infantibus, cum primum a fletibus in cantus erumpunt,
eandem modulationem observantibus.

Angli vero, quoniam non generaliter omnes sed boreales solum hujusmodi vocum utuntur modulationibus, credo quod a Dacis et Norwagien-
sibus qui partes illas insulae frequentius occupare ac diutius obtinere
solebant, sicut loquendi affinitatem, sic et canendi proprietatem con-
traxerunt.[1]

(In their singing of music they do not produce their songs in unison, as is done
elsewhere, but polyphonically, with a number of different melodies: so that in
a crowd of singers, as is customary in this nation [i.e. Wales] you will hear as
many melodies as there are people, and a distinct variety of parts, finally coming
together in a single consonance and harmony under the soft sweetness of B flat.
Also in the northern parts of Britain, that is, beyond the Humber and round
about York, the people who inhabit those parts use a similar sort of harmony
in their singing, but in only two different parts, one murmuring below, the other
soothing and charming the ear above. In the case of each nation this facility has
been acquired not by skill but by long-established custom, so that habit has now
become second nature. And this has become so strong in either case, and has
struck its roots so deep, that one never hears singing in unison, but either in
several parts, as in Wales, or at least in two, as in the north. And what is still
more marvellous, children too, and even infants, when first they turn from tears
to song, follow the same manner of singing.
But the English as a whole do not use this manner of singing, only the
northerners, so that I believe it was from the Danes and Norwegians, who very
often used to occupy those parts of the island and hold them for long spaces of
time, that the inhabitants derive their peculiar manner of singing, just as they
have affinities in their speech.)

The importance of this passage lies more in its geographical details
than in its musical information. It is interesting to note that Welsh-
men today still have a predilection for singing in harmony, and that
both Wales and Yorkshire have produced outstanding singers and
are noted for their choirs. As a primary source for musical practice
about 1200 the description is inadequate, because its terms are not
sufficiently precise. The language is that of an amateur. There is
nothing in it to justify the assumption that people in the north of
England were in the habit of singing in parallel thirds, though the
evidence of the thirteenth-century hymn 'Nobilis, humilis' (see p. 341),
which comes from the Orkneys, then part of the Norwegian kingdom,
suggests that they may have done so. Nor is it clear what is meant by
'sub B mollis dulcedine blanda'.[2] Davey may be right in suggesting
that the author meant 'that everything sounded well, and in its proper

---

[1] *Opera*, ed. J. S. Brewer and J. F. Dimock, vi (London, 1868), pp. 189–90.
[2] Cf. the description of instrumental playing in Ireland, from the *Topographica
Hibernica*: 'Seu diatessaron, seu diapente chordae concrepent, semper tamen a B molli
incipiunt, et in idem redeunt, ut cuncta sub jocundae sonoritatis dulcedine compleantur'
(op. cit. v, p. 154).

key'.[1] Elsewhere, in his *Topographica Hibernica*, Gerald de Barri compares Irish instrumental playing with English, to the disadvantage of the latter, which he describes as sluggish.[2]

CONDUCTUS AND ORGANUM

In the Calixtinus manuscript the two items vary in an important particular. In one there is a lower voice moving slowly in long notes, using an extract from a Gregorian chant, while the upper voice is melismatic and ornate. In the other piece the two parts keep step. We are here in the presence of a fundamental and far-reaching bifurcation. In the thirteenth century these two types of polyphony were known respectively as organum and conductus. The word organum is used now and henceforward in a sense quite different from that of the system described in Chapter VIII. The theorists speak of it as *organum proprie sumptum* (organum properly so-called). To call it 'formal organum' would be a satisfactory way of distinguishing it from the primitive organum. Formal organum is essentially a Gregorian tenor in long notes, with an upper part (sometimes two upper parts, or very occasionally three) broken up into short notes. The tenor of the conductus, on the other hand, is not as a rule a previously known melody. When the form is fixed and the theoretical writers begin to lay down rules for its composition, they prescribe that its lower voice shall be newly composed instead of being borrowed. The upper parts —one, two, or three—move in step with the tenor, which is not in long notes as in the organum. Sometimes these upper parts may be broken up to a moderate extent—two or three notes against one instead of twenty or thirty against one, as may occur in organum.

The tenor derives its name directly from the essential form of organum, where the notes of the lowest part are 'held' (Latin *tenere*) while the other part or parts moves forward. The second part is called *duplum*; if there is a third part above this it is called *triplum*, from which the English 'treble' is derived. On the rare occasions when there is a fourth voice, above the *triplum*, it is styled *quadruplum*. From 1198 onwards we meet with *triplum* and *quadruplum* used as titles for the whole piece, in three or four parts respectively.[3] We shall return to these terms when dealing with the motet in Chapter XI.

---

[1] *A History of English Music* (2nd ed., London, 1921), p. 18.

[2] 'Non enim in his, sicut in Britannicis quibus assueti sumus instrumentis, tarda et morosa est modulatio, verum velox et praeceps, suavis tamen et jocunda sonoritas' (op. cit. v, p. 153).

[3] B. E. C. Guérard, *Cartulaire de l'église Notre-Dame de Paris* (*Collection de documents inédits sur l'histoire de France*, Paris, 1850), i, p. 74.

Organum and conductus, and their immediate descendants, very seldom interlock in the same composition, and it will be convenient to treat them separately as soon as the notation has been dealt with. The immediate antecedents of the conductus, which were considered in the last chapter—the part-music of the Codex Calixtinus, the Martial-Tropers, and the Cambridge manuscript Ff. i. 17—shade off imperceptibly into the formal conductus (this name being actually applied to them by some authors of our own day), so that the form may be said to date back into the twelfth century. Organum, on the other hand, although it is also found in the twelfth century, is not so distinctive of that period, and belongs rather to the thirteenth century, at least in its documentary sources. During this period it gives birth to the motet, the dominating form in the subsequent period, discussed in Chapter XI. Organa, conducti,[1] and motets together form a very substantial literature, considerably larger than what is available in the twelfth and fourteenth centuries. This literature was elaborately catalogued by Friedrich Ludwig in his *Repertorium organorum recentioris et motetorum vetustissimi stili* (Halle, 1910), which is indispensable as a work of reference, in spite of the fact that it lacks an index. When Wooldridge wrote the first volume of the *Oxford History of Music* in 1901 he was under the limitation of having to work only from the Florence manuscript (see p. 313). In spite of this his discussion was notable in its day as a piece of pioneer work and has retained its value almost up to the present, chiefly on account of his very full explanations and examples of the rhythmic modes and their various combinations in the different voices. This information must be presented in some little detail. We are now in the presence of a definite school of composition with its own technique, and (we are bound to add) with its own mannerisms and its own clichés.

THE RHYTHMIC MODES

It will be necessary first to set out the rhythmic modes, with some information about the notational system in which they were written. Modal rhythm is nothing more than the embodying in formal music of natural regular rhythms common to all mankind, of which the dance-rhythms stand foremost, because they are so intimately connected with music, while the ballad and other types of rhythm founded on poetical metres will also find their place in this newly organized

---

[1] *Conductus* is sometimes found as a fourth-declension noun, but the second declension appears to be the more frequent form. Cf. L. Ellinwood in *Musical Quarterly*, xxvii (1941), pp. 169–70.

family. There is also the rhythm of toil. Many folk-songs are based
on this, notably those of the Hebrides. There is also a curious mention of music used by vine-dressers in Odington:[1] 'Celeusma est
cantus quem decantant vintores cum ad extremos antes pervenerint'
(the *celeusma* is the strain sung by the vine-dressers as they reach the
farthest rows of the vines). This may have been a work-rhythm; or
perhaps it was nothing more than a traditional incantation, though
in classical times the word *celeusma* was used in almost exactly this
sense of 'shanty'. Odington presents 'four shorts', ♪ ♪ ♪ ♪, as this
type of rhythm, with the technical name *proceleusmaticus*.

These rhythms were in existence long before the arrival of harmony
and of fixed pitch-notation, and their origin must be regarded as lost
in antiquity. But once composition had passed beyond the limitations
of that free-rhythm prose which forms the text of Gregorian chant,
and was no longer restricted to unison singing, the fixed rhythms
found their natural place in formal music. The musicians of the
period had therefore to find a notation for them and to classify them.
The material available consisted of the square notation of the ecclesiastical chant, on a staff of four or five lines, as the range of the voice
might require. The notes were written either singly—for syllabic
melodies—or in groups. These groups are called neums in plainchant literature: in harmonized music they are always referred to as
ligatures. Before setting out the actual interpretation of these ligatures, it will be necessary to explain the medieval modes of rhythm
and their numbering, together with the *ordines* in which they were
arranged.

The rhythmic modes are six in number. The first mode corresponds
to the classical trochaic verse, where the foot consists of a long syllable
followed by a short: – ◡. Translated into musical symbols, it appears
as ♩ ♪ or its equivalents in longer or shorter time-values.

The second mode is the iambic, the reverse of the first: ◡ – (♪ ♩).
This is not simply the first mode with anacrusis: ♪ | ♩ ♪ | ♩ ♪ | ♩;
the accent here falls on the short note: ♪♩ | ♪♩ | ♪♩ |.

The third mode, the dactylic (– ◡ ◡), would logically be written
♩ ♪♪. This is the rhythm of the galloping horse, represented by
Virgil's 'quadrupedante putrem sonitu quatit ungula campum',[2] and it
must have been perfectly familiar to people in the thirteenth century.
All the theorists of the time, however, prescribe the rhythm ♩. ♪♩.
The explanation which they give us is that triple time alone is used

[1] *De speculatione musice*, iv. 1; printed in Coussemaker, *Scriptores*, i, p. 211.
[2] *Æneid*, viii. 596.

out of veneration for the mystery of the Holy Trinity. This sounds like a pious *post hoc*, not a genuine *propter hoc*. It is far more probable that the difficulty of setting a series of ♩ ♪♪ over or under another voice which ran in a series of ♩ ♪ was solved by the simple expedient of dividing the unit as ♩. ♪♩ instead of ♩ ♪♪, and thus making the length of the dactylic foot exactly twice, instead of one-and-a-third times, the length of the iambus or the trochee.

The fourth mode, the anapaestic, is like the second, the reverse of its predecessor: ◡ ◡ – (♪ ♩ ♩.). It was very seldom used. An example may be found in Wolfenbüttel 677, fo. 44, at the second clausula on *Lux magna*.

The fifth mode consists entirely of longs, usually in groups of three, with a rest to complete the double unit of two bars: ♩. ♩. | ♩. r. ||. Note that the crotchet is dotted, because it has to be divisible by three, in order that ♩ ♪ or ♪ ♩ may be set in the upper part. The fifth mode is normally used in the tenor, or lowest voice, only.

The sixth mode, on the other hand, is ordinarily found in an upper part. It consists of groups of three shorts: ♪ ♪ ♪ | ♪ ♪ ♪, and is of infrequent occurrence, though not so rare as Mode IV.

The metrical units which constituted the rhythmic modes were grouped in *ordines*, corresponding to catalectic lines in verse, i.e. lines in which the last foot is truncated. It follows that every *ordo* must end with a rest. Thus, in the first mode the first *ordo* is ♩ ♪ | ♩ ↱, the second ♩ ♪ | ♩ ♪ | ♩ ↱, the third ♩ ♪ | ♩ ♪ | ♩ ♪ | ♩ ↱, and so on. The following table will make the application of the principle clear:

Ex. 162

Mode I, Ordo 1   Ordo 2   Ordo 3

Mode II, Ordo 1   Ordo 2   Ordo 3

Mode III, Ordo 1   Ordo 2   Ordo 3

Mode IV, Ordo 1   Ordo 2   Ordo 3

Mode V, Ordo 1   Ordo 2   Ordo 3

Mode VI, Ordo 1   Ordo 2   Ordo 3

The lower voice in the next example—a *cauda* from the two-part conductus 'Magnificat . . . qui judicat'—illustrates the use of the first and third *ordines* of the first mode, as well as the occasional substitution of two short notes (indicated in the original by the use of the *plica*) for the long note proper to the mode:

Ex. 163

The principle can also be illustrated by examples capable of transcription in duple time, e.g. the well-known *Prose de l'âne*, 'Orientis partibus':

Ex. 164[2]

O - ri - en-tis par - ti - bus   ad-ven-ta-vit   a - si - nus   pul-cher et for-

---

[1] Wolfenbüttel 677, fo. 121ᵛ. For the *plica* see p. 325.
[2] Cf. H. C. Greene, 'The Song of the Ass', in *Speculum*, vi (1931), p. 534. Recorded in *The History of Music in Sound* (H.M.V.), ii, side 15. See also plate facing p. 303.

-tis - si - mus,   sar - ci - nis ap - tis - si - mus: hez, va, hez, sire as - nez, hez.

(From the East has come the ass, beautiful and strong and fit to bear burdens. Hey, sir ass, hey!)

The system of the rhythmic modes, as presented by the theorists, is clear and logical. Its practical application, however, is not always so obvious. As Apel observes:

In turning to a study of the manner in which these modes were used in actual music and expressed in writing it must first be said that the theoretical system does not in every respect conform with the actual data. If considered from the standpoint of the musical sources of this period, it proves to be too complicated in certain respects and too much simplified in others.[1]

We must now return to the ligatures. It is only by the inspection of their forms and patterns that a composition written in modal or 'square' notation can be deciphered, as the notes in themselves have not so far acquired any temporal significance. Ligature is the binding together of square notes, two or more, into a bunch or group. Diamond or lozenge notes are included in a falling group of three or more, but are not actually joined together. In this period the binding follows in detail the Gregorian fashion current at that time. Thus, in a pair of notes ascending the second note will sometimes be placed above the first, instead of after it: while in a descending pair the first note has a tail, descending, on its left side. But if the descending group has three notes instead of two, the tail will be on the right side of the first note instead of on the left, and the two following notes will be rhomboid (diamond or lozenge is the term usually employed), not square. These refinements mean nothing at all: but they were the contemporary orthodox shapes which the plainsong copyists used, and they were practical, not arbitrary or fanciful. They saved time and space, and parchment was costly. It is necessary, however, to know these shapes in order to understand medieval notation, since later on the alterations in the position or direction of the tail were to transform modal notation into mensural notation, when the time-

[1] Op. cit., p. 231.

values were no longer merely hinted at but were precisely indicated. For the present it will be sufficient if we set down the series of ligatures in their orthodox, proper, form—*cum proprietate*, as the mensuralists later described them to distinguish them from their modified shapes without propriety or with opposite propriety (*sine proprietate, cum opposita proprietate*)—see p. 382:

Ligatures of—

two notes: Rising ▮ or ▮ †   Falling ▮

three notes: Rise & fall ▮   Rise & rise ▮ or ▮

Fall & fall ▮ ‡   Fall & rise ▮

four notes: Rise, fall, fall ▮ or ▮ †   Rise, rise, fall ▮

Four rising ▮ or ▮ †   Four falling ▮ § or ▮ †

Fall, rise, fall ▮   Rise, fall, rise ▮ or ▮ †

Fall, rise, rise ▮   Fall, fall, rise ▮ or ▮ †

† Forms so marked are not strict plainsong forms but are found in the modal manuscripts of this period.

‡ In polyphonic notation ▮ is more often used for this group in a modal passage.

▮ sometimes indicates ♪ ♪ ♪ as distinct from ♪ ♩ ♩. or ♩. ♪ ♩ , but this will normally occur in a syllabic text, not in a melismatic modal part.

§ This is the *conjunctura* (see next page).

Ligatures may in theory contain any number of notes: those with five or more are merely extensions or combinations of the above forms. In the florid or melismatic portions of thirteenth-century music we shall meet with certain formal 'patterns' of ligatures, repeated with more or less regularity. When this regularity reaches such a degree as is shown in Ex. 165 it is quite certain that we are in the presence of a notation which is systematic and intentional:

Ex. 165
Mode 1

Mode 2

Mode 3

Mode 4

Mode 5

Mode 6

The *conjunctura* is a falling group, usually of four notes when in the upper part (Ex. 166), sometimes of five (Ex. 167): but in the cadences there are often six, seven, eight, nine, or even more notes. This cadential occurrence, or *copula* as it is sometimes called, is so frequent in some manuscripts as to appear a cliché. The theorists—and the test of concordance in the manuscripts supports them—tell us that the last note of a *conjunctura* is equivalent to the sum of the time-values of the others. This is true of a *conjunctura* of four or five notes running in the text, but it needs modification in the case of some of the cadential forms employed. Ex. 168 is a cadence used dozens of times in Wolfenbüttel 677. Ex. 172 is a good instance of the actual use of the *conjunctura* in a composition of the period:

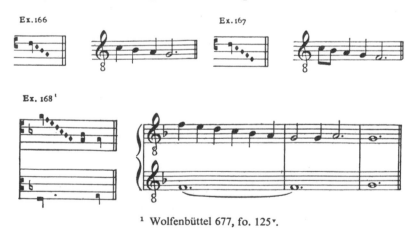

Ex. 166

Ex. 167

Ex. 168 [1]

[1] Wolfenbüttel 677, fo. 125ᵛ.

The falling three-note group must sometimes be interpreted as a
conjunctura ♪♦ = ♫ ♩ : practice is not uniform in this detail, and
the true interpretation can, as a rule, only be decided from the context.
During the thirteenth century, or at least in the fourteenth, the *conjunctura* began to lose its original significance, and to take on the
meaning—which seems more logical and more obvious to us today—
of a long followed by three shorts.

The *plica* (fold) is a sign which has caused an amount of trouble
wholly disproportionate to its small size. It is a short stroke which
modifies the single square note, leading either upwards or downwards, ♫, ♩, and these forms are substantially identical with the liquescent *semivocalis* of plainsong, which is printed as ♮ and ♩ today. If we
approach the interpretation of the *plica* with the knowledge of its
plainsong correlative in mind it will cause us less difficulty. The
instructions of the medieval theorists most often quoted are those
of the Anonymus of Paris, who in his *Quaedam de arte discantandi*
tells us that 'it should be formed in the throat with the epiglottis',[1]
and of Lambert, who wrote under the pen-name of Aristotle: 'The
plica is made in the voice by compressing the epiglottis, combining it
neatly with a repercussion of the voice.'[2] The practical but (in this
case) hardly more explicit Walter Odington merely remarks that it is
'inflexio vocis a voce sub una figura'[3] (sliding from note to note, but
using only one sign). Whether we prefer to execute polyphony (or
for that matter plainchant also) in the fashion recommended by the
first two of these quotations is a matter not only of skill in physio-
logical interpretation but also of musical taste. What must be seriously
noted is that the second, semi-vocal, note of the plica is not an ad
libitum ornament, ♩ ♪, but has a time-value of its own, one-third
or one-half of that which would belong to the parent note if it were
not plicated, according to whether that parent note is 'perfect', ♩·,
or 'imperfect', ♩ . It is usually represented today by the sign ∧,
thus ♩ ♪̂ or ♫̂ .

In the next century we shall see the *plica* becoming slightly more
complicated in its interpretation: for the present the only other point
to mention is that the interval between the first and second notes,

---

[1] 'Debet formari in gutture cum epiglotto' (Coussemaker, *Traités inédits sur la
musique du moyen âge*, p. 274).
[2] 'Fit autem plica in voce per compositionem epiglotti cum repercussione gutturis
subtiliter inclusa' (Coussemaker, *Scriptores*, i, p. 273).
[3] Ibid. i, p. 236.

which is very seldom even hinted at in the manuscripts, is most usually a tone or semitone, filling in the interval of a major or minor third,

Ex. 169

but that where the next full note is a tone or a semitone below the parent note of the *plica* a drop of a third is made,

Ex. 170

and similarly with a rising *plica*,

Ex. 171

The falling *plica* is much more frequent than the rising. Where the interval is greater than a third, the intervening step must be decided by the context. The following is an example of *plica* and *conjunctura* in actual use, with the first note of the second group in the lower voice interpreted as an anacrusis:

Ex. 172 [1]

THE CONDUCTUS

As we have seen (p. 317) the conductus was theoretically never, and in practice very rarely, written on a given melody: its tenor (the lowest voice) was freely composed. It had either one or two (very rarely three) upper parts, which are generally supposed to be wordless, though some authorities think that all the voices sang the text.

Two types have to be distinguished, the *conductus cum cauda* (with a tail) and the *conductus sine cauda* (without a tail). The *cauda* is more than the modern term 'coda' implies. It is an embellishment which

[1] Florence, Bibl. Laur. plut. xxix, 1, fo. 264ᵛ.

appears at the end of intermediate phrases and sections, or even in a short emphasis upon important words, and at the beginning as well as at the end of a composition. Some of the pieces which have been described as *conducti sine caudis* are, as a matter of fact, nothing more than the upper voices of motets, their tenors not having been written into the particular manuscripts in which they occur. A number of these have been already identified, and probably many others will be linked up to their tenors as time goes on. The reason for their appearance in the guise of conducti may be either that the upper voices of the motet were actually detached for separate performance: or alternatively, and this is perhaps more likely or more frequent, the manuscript in question was that used by the singers, or by the higher voices of the choir, alone, while the tenor volume would be needed elsewhere for an instrumental player or for a singer in a different part of the choir.[1]

As for the precise manner of performance, all that we can be sure of is that it was not precise. Outside the choir, theorists might make detailed rules as to what ought to be done, elaborate explanations of what had been done, or co-ordinate the new music into a system. But inside, the music-makers sang and played as convenient to the occasion or the performers available.[2] It is worse than useless to dogmatize and say this or that piece was performed in such-and-such a manner, by a choir composed of such-and-such elements, since it is fairly certain that many of the pieces we possess were executed in different ways at different times. In some cases we are quite sure that the music is all vocal, and that all the voices of the conductus sang the words: in others, it is possible that they merely vocalized (as, for instance, when the scribe has begun to write in the text to the upper part or parts and has crossed it out after a few words as being wrong), while in others the instrumental character of some parts, notably in the *caudae*, is unmistakable. The following is a good instance of this 'instrumental suggestion':

Ex. 173[3]

Hic   est   [ci - bus,]   hic   est *   po - - tus.

[1] For further details see *Musical Quarterly*, xxx (1944), pp. 462 and 471.
[2] Cf. G. S. Bedbrook in *Music and Letters*, xxvi (1945), p. 78, and Ernst H. Meyer, *English Chamber Music* (London, 1946), p. 16.
[3] Wolfenbüttel 677, fo. 196ᵛ. At (*) Wolfenbüttel gives E F; the correction is from Assisi 695 and Brit. Mus. Harl. 3965 (from Hereford).

Our next example (from the Offertory 'Recordare') is given in two forms: (1) in a purely vocal setting,[1] and (2) in a version with instrumental suggestion in the upper part.[2]

Compass or range of voice supplies an occasional indication: thus in the final *cauda* of 'Roma gaudens jubila'[3] both parts, which have remained within the octave *c–c'* during the texted portions, suddenly make use of *A*, an unusually deep note for voices at this period, and at the pitch then prevailing.

The 'instrumental suggestion' will appear even more strongly when we come to the motet in the next chapter. In so far as we can realize that all these interpretations are right, each on its own occasion, we shall have grasped the spirit of the Middle Ages. The point is presented in a very acute form by Rudolf von Ficker. He says that the works of the thirteenth century are

still dependent upon the old method of improvisation, which allowed the performers' subjective faculty for development wide latitude—a method now, together with the tradition, quite extinct. For the rigid note-forms of the manuscripts are only a sort of musical sketch, not a precise guide for actual performance, for number and kind of instruments and singers, for tempo, dynamics and agogics, for tonality and accidentals. The composer supplied merely the musical substance. To endow it with the breath of life was the function of the producer, whose task it was to add all details needed for a finished performance, in every case producing something new and different according to his artistic ability, while following traditional rules and usages.

The prehistorian, palaeobiologist or archaeologist nowadays no longer confines himself to chronicling the meagre finds of cultures of past millenniums in their nudely scientific aspect. He rather conceives it to be his chief mission to restore the scanty remnants of these sunken worlds to living

---

[1] Las Huelgas, fo. 8ᵛ; after Anglès.

[2] Wolfenbüttel 677, fo. 192ᵛ.

[3] Ibid., fo. 107ᵛ (transcription of the complete piece in Davison and Apel, *Historical Anthology of Music*, i, p. 41); Florence, Bibl. Laur. plut. xxix, 1, fo. 318ᵛ (facsimile in Reese, *Music in the Middle Ages*, facing p. 300).

reality. The same should be demanded of the musical scientist: he ought, with the aid of all critical resources, to reconstruct the long-lost music of old in a form approximating [to] that in which it was heard by the contemporaries of that age-old culture. Only then shall we be in a position to raise and answer the question respecting the aesthetic value of this art.[1]

Manfred Bukofzer has also pointed out that the idea of 'choir music' applied to thirteenth- and fourteenth-century polyphony may be misleading, as the parts in harmony were sung by soloists, the choral body responding in unison.[2] This restriction of the harmonized parts to solo groups is perhaps the one consistent factor in what we know for certain about medieval methods of performance.

A typical *conductus sine cauda*, or simple conductus, is 'Veri floris', selected chiefly because its brevity makes it possible to print it entire; also because it is known in no less than nine different manuscripts, a testimony to its diffusion and popularity. Eight of these manuscripts have music, and all, with the exception of a monophonic version in Stuttgart, Landesbibl. I Asc. 95, are in two-part or three-part harmony (see Ex. 175 on the next page).

Space does not allow full analysis, but inspection shows that the two-part version of Brit. Mus. Harl. 524 seems to have been written in 'quartal' harmony, i.e. harmony based on the fourth as the most important interval. This has already been noticed by Joseph Yasser.[3] The quartal harmony seems to have been changed to the 'tertian' system, based on the third and fifth, by the later composers or arrangers of the three-part versions. The quartal harmony has, moreover, been preserved in alternate sections, so that it is difficult to see here anything less than an intentional design, a contrast between the old and new styles.

The music of the conductus is written in square notes of indeterminate length. This has led some transcribers to read them all as equal longs: others, e.g. Anglès in *La Música a Catalunya*, have more wisely taken into account the fact that the notation is premensural, and have followed the verbal rhythm in a ternary form, on the analogy of the interpretation of troubadour songs (see pp. 225 ff.). A determination of this controversy between the 'isochronous' and 'ternary' systems of transcription seems to be now possible, since examination of the conductus-motet 'Serena virginum' (see p. 365) shows irrefragable evidence of a rhythmic treatment which is neither

---

[1] *Musical Quarterly*, xv (1929), p. 486.
[2] *Papers of the American Musicological Society* (New York, 1940), p. 23.
[3] *Medieval Quartal Harmony* (New York, 1938), pp. 87–89.

Ex. 175

Ex.175 contd.

Ex. 175 contd.

la - i - cum,   sen-sumtrahens tro - pi - cum   flo-ris a   na - tu - ra.

(Under the type of 'the true flower which the pure root brought forth', the pious care of our clergy has made a mystical flower beyond the experience of the laity, drawing a figurative meaning from the nature of the flower.)[1]

isochronous nor ternary. The same is true of the few others which supply definite first-hand evidence, such as 'Latex silice'[2] and 'Qui servare puberem'.[3] From internal evidence it can be clearly seen that 'Veri floris' (p. 330), 'Coelum non animam',[4] 'Trinae vocis tripudio',[5] and others fall neatly and convincingly into a rhythm of this kind; and it is to such rhythms that Bukofzer is presumably alluding when he speaks of 'certain lengthenings of "primary" accents in the verse which are not disclosed by the meter and which can be derived only from the music'.[6] Other specimens, as he has pointed out, can be classified under the various rhythmic modes by examination of the ligatures in the intervening melismatic sections, or *caudae*, when these melismatic sections repeat the melody of the syllabic sections.

When we turn from the *conductus sine cauda* to its more fully developed relation *cum cauda* we discover, to a degree not hitherto encountered, music which only needs to be known and interpreted to be widely appreciated. The *caudae*, those textless preludes, interludes, and finales to which we have briefly alluded above (pp. 326–7), have not hitherto been fully explored. As soon as these sections are scored on any considerable scale it becomes apparent that their chief interest lies not in the harmony but in the melody of the lowest voice. Some

[1] Recorded in *The History of Music in Sound*, ii, side 17. *BM* = Brit. Mus. Harl. 524 (see *Oxford History of Music*, 2nd ed., i, p. 164); *F* = Florence, Bibl. Laur. plut. xxix, 1; *Ma* = Madrid, Bibl. Nac. 20486; *StG* = St. Gall, Stiftsbibliothek 383; *Tort* = Tortosa Cathedral, 97; *W*[1] = Wolfenbüttel 677; *W*[2] = Wolfenbüttel 1206. The variants from *W*[1], *Tort* and *Ma* are from the transcript printed by Anglès in *La Música a Catalunya fins al Segle XIII* (Barcelona, 1935), p. 262. The words of the song are said to be by Herras of Hohenburg and are also found, without music, in Oxford, Bodleian, Rawl. C 510.

[2] Four-part motet in Florence, Bibl. Laur. plut. xxix, 1, fo. 230ᵛ; *clausulae* in Wolfenbüttel 677, fo. 49, and Florence, fo. 158; three upper parts in Wolfenbüttel, fo. 74; monophonic in Stuttgart, Landesbibl. I Asc. 95; text in Oxford, Bodleian, Rawl. C 510. See also G. M. Dreves, *Analecta Hymnica Medii Aevi*, xxi (Leipzig, 1895), p. 17, and *Musical Quarterly*, xxx (1944), p. 462.

[3] Three-part motet in Florence, fo. 381ᵛ; two upper parts in Wolfenbüttel, fo. 106, and Madrid, Bibl. Nac. 20486 (facsimile in P. Aubry, *Cent Motets du XIIIᵉ siècle* (Paris, 1908), pl. III); *clausulae* in Wolfenbüttel, fo. 49, and Florence, fo. 101ᵛ; text in Oxford, Bodleian, Add. A 44 and Rawl. C 510. See also *Analecta Hymnica*, xxi, p. 157, *Oxford History of Music*, 1st ed., i, p. 358, *Musical Quarterly*, xxx (1944), p. 462.

[4] Wolfenbüttel, fo. 11; Florence, fo. 223ᵛ; Munich, Staatsbibl. lat. 4660 (*Carmina Burana*), fo. 48. Text in Oxford, Bodleian, Rawl. C 510, fo. 18.

[5] Wolfenbüttel, fo. 68ᵛ; Florence, fo. 205. Text in Oxford, Bodleian, Rawl. C 510, fo. 16ᵛ.

[6] *Bulletin of the American Musicological Society* (1948), p. 65.

hundreds of these *caudae* have been examined and classified in the preparation of this chapter. Their origin is unknown. In some cases, doubtless, they have been written by the composer of the conductus in which they are embedded: in others, it is hard to avoid the conclusion that the composer was incorporating some older dance or song tune into his composition. Others again may be nothing less than the traditional music of instrumentalists who were already in the habit of playing in parts. Here is a typical example—the final *cauda* of 'Rosae nodum reserat':

Ex. 176[1]

Some of these melodies may well have a subsequent history, but so far, in spite of help from experienced students of folk-song, few of them have been positively identified. In the following example the lower part is probably an ancestor of the refrain of the Christmas carol 'In hoc anni circulo':

---

[1] Wolfenbüttel 677, fo. 54ᵛ. Recorded in *The History of Music in Sound*, ii, side 16. The first two notes in the upper part are written CB in the manuscript.

Ex. 177[1]

Another tune, where the first two bars suggest the opening strain of 'Country Gardens' (one of the best known folk-tunes, popularized in Percy Grainger's arrangement), provides the final *cauda* of the three-voiced *Sanctus* trope 'Perpetuo numine':

Ex. 178[2]

[lau]

---

[1] Ibid., fo. 121ᵛ. For the melody of 'In hoc anni circulo' see *Piae Cantiones* (1582), ed. G. R. Woodward (London, 1910), no. ii. The tune is found for one voice in Paris, Bibl. Nat. lat. 1139, fo. 48. This is a twelfth-century manuscript, but this piece, according to Spanke ('St. Martial-Studien', in *Zeitschrift für französische Sprache und Literatur*, liv (1930), p. 296), is in a later hand than the rest of the manuscript.

[2] Wolfenbüttel 677, fo. 83ᵛ. Extracts from this and the next example are recorded in *The History of Music in Sound*, ii, side 16.

One of the finest series of *caudae* is quoted at some length, in order to show the way in which ideas are built up. It will be noticed that the quality of the melodies seems to improve from beginning to end. The passages given are selections from the tenors of the many intermediate *caudae* and of the final section of the conductus 'Fraude caeca desolato', which is rather longer than the average. The reference numbers of the bars show the position of the extracts quoted in relation to the whole piece. Note the strong dance-rhythm at bar 200.

¹ Wolfenbüttel 677, fo. 120.

DANCE MUSIC

There are many other passages in the *caudae* of the conducti which deserve attention by students of old dances. If the metrical and rhythmical requirements of their forms can be settled they may prove to be a valuable source for thirteenth-century dance music. It is particularly interesting to compare with them three thirteenth-century dances preserved in the British Museum.[1] They are in two parts, marked *cantus superior* and *cantus inferior*. The form is clear-cut and symmetrical, and the rhythm falls naturally into 6/8 time. The melody is, generally speaking, in the lower part; but in the second piece the lower part of the first half becomes the upper part of the second, with a new part below it. The first half of this dance is given here:

Ex. 180

[1] Brit. Mus. Harl. 978, fo. 8ᵛ–9; facsimiles in Wooldridge, *Early English Harmony*, i, pls. 18–19. Recorded in *The History of Music in Sound*, ii, side 17. Transcriptions of Nos. 1 and 2 in Davison and Apel, op. cit., pp. 43–44; cf. J. Wolf, 'Die Tänze des Mittelalters', in *Archiv für Musikwissenschaft*, i (1918–19), pp. 10–42.

This is not a case of a *canto fermo* with an upper part; it is rather a genuine instance of two combined melodies. There appear to be no other independent examples of polyphonic dance music at this period. The three-part 'In seculum viellatoris',[1] which Wolf included in his collection of medieval dances,[2] is simply an instrumental motet; and the long dance-tune in the Bodleian Library[3] is almost entirely monophonic. The latter, however, is of interest on account of its vivacity and charm, and its strongly instrumental character. It falls into a series of sections or *puncti*, some of which have *overt* and *clos* endings, the repetitions being written out in full. The second of these, with its intervals based on the common chord, will give some idea of the liveliness of the piece:

Ex. 181

There is one short section in three parts, which provides a simple harmonization of the section immediately preceding it:

Ex. 182

---

[1] Bamberg, Staatsbibl. Ed. iv. 6, fo. 63ᵛ; facsimile in Aubry, *Cent Motets du XIIIe siècle.*

[2] Op. cit., p. 21.

[3] Oxford, Bodleian, Douce 139, fo. 5ᵛ; facsimiles in Wooldridge, *Early English Harmony*, i, pl. 24, and J. Stainer, *Early Bodleian Music* (London, 1901), pl. 7; transcription in Davison and Apel, op. cit., p. 43.

Its position in the manuscript leaves it uncertain whether it is to be regarded as a coda to the whole piece. The upper part, though noted on the stave with a B♭ in the signature, has all the appearance of a part for a percussion instrument. The notation indicates the third rhythmic mode; but as there can be little doubt that it was meant to be played *more lascivo* (in jolly style),[1] i.e. with the long equal to two (not three) breves, a transcription in 2/4 time is preferable to 6/8.

THE RELATIONSHIP OF THE INDIVIDUAL VOICES

The intervals of the third and, to a lesser degree, the sixth were now recognized by theorists. As early as the latter half of the twelfth century[2] Theinred of Dover explains why the major and minor thirds are admitted in organa, in spite of the fact that they are not strictly consonances:

Ditonus et semiditonus cum sibi condividentibus equisonas consonantias propter equisonantiam cum consonantiis admittuntur in organa.[3]

(The major and minor thirds, together with the intervals which combine with them to make octaves [i.e. the minor and major sixths] are allowed in organa as well as the consonant intervals, because of the octaves [which result from the combination of third and sixth].)

He adds that the major third and minor sixth are more common than the minor third and major sixth. The preference is interesting, though it is based on faulty mathematics. It is obvious that the reluctance of theorists to admit thirds and sixths as consonances was due to the fact that they did not fit into the acoustic theory which they had inherited from the Greeks. Thus, the *ditonus*, as its name implies, was reckoned as two (major) tones, i.e. $\frac{9}{8} \times \frac{9}{8} = \frac{81}{64}$; whereas the ratio of the major third in the harmonic series is $\frac{5}{4}$ or $\frac{80}{64}$. But as Theinred himself says, the difference is hardly noticeable to the ear;[4] and Odington in the late thirteenth century not only mentions that many people regard the *ditonus* and the *semiditonus* as consonant, on account of their close approximation to the major third and minor third of the harmonic series, but also observes that intervals like this which are not mathematically consonant can be made to sound so

---

[1] See Robertus de Handlo, *Regulae*, in Coussemaker, *Scriptores*, i, pp. 388 and 402 (the words 'in maxima quinte rubrice' in the latter place are an obvious error for 'in maxima quinta quarte rubrice'), and cf. *supra*, p. 227, n. 2.

[2] For the arguments in support of this date see C. C. J. Webb in the *English Historical Review*, xxx (1915), pp. 658–60.

[3] Oxford, Bodleian, Bodl. 842, fo. 20.

[4] 'Ditonus qui sesquiquartae sonorum proportioni quae prima sequitur sesquitertiam adeo propinquus est, ut octogesima prima tantum parte maioris termini hic superet hanc: quod auditu percipere difficile est' (loc. cit.).

if they are skilfully and beautifully sung.[1] This growing realization
that the ear, and not acoustics, must be the test of consonance is
important. A compromise was adopted, by which the thirds were
regarded as 'imperfect' concords. John of Garland (thirteenth century), a teacher of Oxford and Paris who seems to have held a position of great authority in his day and after his death, has a threefold
classification,[2] according to which the unison and the octave are
perfect (or complete) concords, the major and minor thirds imperfect,
while the fifth and fourth are 'intermediate' ('mediae concordantiae').
Corresponding to these are the perfect discords—semitone (or minor
second), tritone (or augmented fourth), and major seventh; the imperfect discords—the major sixth and the minor seventh; and the
intermediate discords—the tone (or major second) and the minor
sixth. The imperfect discords are described as those which are not
concordant but are tolerable to the ear.[3] A similar classification is
found in the works of Anonymus IV[4] (see p. 351) and the Anonymus
of St. Dié,[5] who differs from John of Garland in including the major
sixth among the imperfect concords, while he regards the minor sixth
as a discord.

Turning from theory to practice, we find that in a group of sixteen
two-part conducti selected at random for analytical purposes the third
is actually the most favoured interval, though it occurs mostly upon
the unaccented beats, in a proportion of about two to one. Out of
2,415 intervals, the third appears 704 times, unisons and octaves 645,
fifths 556, fourths 311, seconds 120 (the same remark as made above,
p. 299, holds good here also), sixths 67, sevenths 12. In the use of the
third the progressions unison–third–fifth and fifth–third–unison are
the forms most commonly used. The sixth is gradually coming to be
looked upon as more respectable, and we even find this passage in
'Austro terris influente':

Ex. 183[6]

The full triad of bass-note, third, and fifth has already been met at
two intermediate cadences of 'Verbum Patris humanatur' (Ex. 155,

---

[1] Coussemaker, *Scriptores*, i, p. 199.
[2] Ibid., pp. 104–5.
[3] 'Imperfectae dicuntur, quando duae voces junguntur ita quod secundum auditum
vel possunt aliquo modo compati, tamen non concordant' (ibid., p. 105).
[4] Ibid., p. 358.   [5] Ibid., pp. 311–12.
[6] Wolfenbüttel 677, fo. 112.

p. 304). It is not infrequent in the thirteenth-century conductus; the following instances of openings with the full triad may be cited:

Coe-lum non   Tri - - [nae] Ver - bum   Hic est

We may notice how in three out of these four the triad is formed not by building upon a bass but by fitting the *canto fermo* with a major third above and a minor third below. There are many examples which can be found with long passages in parallel triads in a manuscript which hails from Reading;[2] but they are not in the least typical of the music of the century, and their aesthetic effect is disappointing.

It does not follow from this recognition of the triad that there was an awareness of chord progressions in the modern sense. The individual voices in the conductus, however closely they might coincide with one another in rhythm and time-values, were still conceived mainly on a horizontal, not a vertical, basis. For this reason it is not surprising to find triads followed immediately by open fifths or by some other formation which by the standards of later centuries sounds like an incomplete chord. At the same time, it is significant that imperfect concords were felt to require resolution, e.g.:

La tierce de ton et demiton requiert unisson apres li, et celle de deux tons quint apres li. La sixte de demiton avuec quinte requiert apres li quinte, et celle d'un ton avuec quinte requiert double apres li.[3]

(A minor third must be followed by unison, and a major third by a fifth. A minor sixth must be followed by a fifth, and a major sixth by an octave.)

EARLY ENGLISH PART-SONGS

The practice of singing in consecutive thirds is well illustrated by the thirteenth-century hymn 'Nobilis, humilis',[4] which celebrates the

---

[1] (*a*) and (*c*) Wolfenbüttel 677, fo. 11 and 70; (*b*) Florence, Bibl. Laur. plut. xxix, 1, fo. 205; (*d*) Brit. Mus. Harl. 5393, fo. 80ᵛ.

[2] Oxford, Bodleian, Bodl. 257.

[3] Anonymus XIII, in Coussemaker, *Scriptores*, iii, p. 496. 'La sixte de demiton' is a necessary correction for Coussemaker's 'La sixte et demiton'.

[4] Upsala, C 233, fo. 19ᵛ–20; facsimile in *Music and Letters*, xx (1939), facing p. 353; transcription in Davison and Apel, op. cit., p. 22. The opening of the melody (in the

virtues of St. Magnus, patron saint of the Orkneys. This form of two-part singing was known as 'gymel', though the term was not applied to it in manuscripts before the fifteenth century.[1] It appears to have been particularly favoured in England: certainly its influence is very evident in English music of this period. The earliest two-part songs in the vernacular seem to be from English sources—'Edi beo þu' and 'Foweles in þe frith'. The lower voice of the first piece has only three notes, which may possibly indicate that it was intended for some instrument of a very limited compass:

Ex. 185[2]

E - di beo þu, he - ve - ne que - ne, fol - kes froure and en - gles blis:

Mo - ðer un - wemmed and mai - den cle - ne, swich in world non o - þer nis:

On þe hit is wel eþ sene of al - le wimmen þu ha - vest þet pris.

Mi swe - te le - ve - di, her mi bene and reu of me ʒif þi wille is.

(Blessed be thou, queen of heaven, comfort of men and joy of angels, spotless mother and pure maiden, there is none other such in the world. It is readily seen that of all women thou bearest the prize. My sweet lady, hear my prayer and have pity on me if it is thy will.)

upper part) is quoted by Robertus de Handlo with the words 'Rosula primula, salve Jesse virgula' (Coussemaker, *Scriptores*, i, p. 402).
[1] M. F. Bukofzer, 'The Gymel: the Earliest Form of English Polyphony', in *Music and Letters*, xvi (1935), p. 77.
[2] Oxford, Corpus Christi College 59, fo. 113; facsimile in R. Morris, *Old English Homilies* (Early English Text Society, O.S., liii), facing p. 261.

Fowe - les   in þe frith, þe   fis - ses in þe   flod: and I mon wa - xe wod, mulch sorw I wal - ke with for beste of bon and blod.

(Birds in the wood, and the fishes in the water, and I must grow mad, much sorrow am I troubled with for the best of bone and blood.)

Similar treatment occurs in 'Jesu Cristes milde moder'[2] (a translation of the sequence 'Stabat juxta Christi crucem'), which consists very largely of parallel thirds. The further influence of this type of writing is to be observed in the three-part pieces written in the style generally known as 'English descant' (see p. 350).

ORGANUM

In the earlier part of this chapter (p. 317) something was said about organum in the thirteenth century. This form must now be considered in greater detail, not so much for what it is as for what it produces later by way of the *clausula*. The original form of organum is simple enough. It consists of a tenor singing (or playing) a Gregorian melody in long notes of indeterminate duration while a voice above is descanting in florid melismatic passages. By conventional signs, to which allusion is made more than once in the treatises, the two voices co-ordinate with one another when the slow-moving tenor is about

---

[1] Oxford, Bodleian, Douce 139, fo. 5; facsimiles in Wooldridge, *Early English Harmony*, pl. 7, and Stainer, *Early Bodleian Music*, pl. 6. Recorded in *The History of Music in Sound*, ii, side 18. For other interpretations of the text see *Early Bodleian Music*, ii, p. 10, and *Oxford History of Music*, 2nd ed., i, p. 307; cf. Wooldridge in *Sammelbände der internationalen Musikgesellschaft*, iv (1902–3), p. 571.

[2] Brit. Mus., Arundel 248, fo. 154ᵛ; facsimile in Wooldridge, *Early English Harmony*, pl. 35.

to shift from one note to the next. This means that the idea of cadence has to receive theoretical attention, possibly not for the first time.

The upper melody in organum was at first entirely unmeasured,[1] and its melismata closely resemble those of a Gradual verse or a Responsory verse in the Gregorian chant. By degrees, however, this upper part is found to 'stiffen' into more set rhythmical patterns, feeling ahead towards that rhythmical modality which has already been described in relation to the *cauda* of the conductus. It seems impossible to determine finally the precise point at which organa must cease to be regarded as entirely free in rhythm and must be subjected (in modern transcriptions) to a mensural interpretation. The methods followed by the more cautious transcribers are shown in this short typical extract:

Ex. 187 (i)[2]

etc. (*about ¼ of the whole piece*).

Ex. 187 (ii)

---

[1] See W. Apel in *Journal of the American Musicological Society*, ii (1949), p. 145, where a case is made out for a considerable degree of rhythmic mensuration.

[2] Wolfenbüttel 677, fo. 39ᵛ.

The appoggiatura formation by which the fourth is sounded as a preparation for the fifth at the opening of the piece is representative of the technique of the period.

In addition to the gradual settling of the upper voice in the direction of a rhythmic regularity, we meet in the heyday of 'Notre-Dame' composition a convention by which certain passages of the organa stand out as having (a) more notes to the tenor, with at the same time (b) a discernible rhythmic pattern or patterns in the upper voice or *duplum*. Of this particular or modal sort of music Wooldridge wrote in 1901:

In some [organa] it occupies a very considerable portion of the composition, while in others it is much reduced; in some again it is concentrated in one portion of the work, in others it is distributed, and appears in small quantities from time to time. These passages are always in regular modes, in which the swing of the triple rhythm is extremely noticeable, while the true *Organum purum*, which constitutes the remainder of the composition, stands out, through the totally different character of its phrases, in striking contrast.[1]

Thus 'Laetabitur' in Ex. 187 is followed immediately by these seven bars on the first syllable of 'justus', after which the organum is taken up again. Another instance will be seen in Ex. 195 (p. 361):

Ex. 188

_____
[1] *Oxford History of Music*, 2nd ed., i, p. 117.

Passages of this sort, called *clausulae* or *puncta*, will occupy our attention in the next section: meanwhile it should be remarked that as soon as organum is found written for three voices, with a *triplum* above the *duplum*, there must of necessity be agreement between the two upper voices in the matter of time-duration. The system of modal notation is now, therefore, applicable throughout:

These earliest organa are very frequently associated in histories with the name of Léonin, a precentor of Notre-Dame at Paris, who flourished *c.* 1150–75. A certain number are known from before his time, notably those of St. Martial and those in the Codex Calixtinus (see p. 288). Our information about Léonin and his great successor

¹ Florence, Bibl. Laur. plut. xxix, 1, fo. 14.

Pérotin comes from Anonymus IV.[1] He mentions also the following composers and singers—Robert de Sabillon, Peter Trothun, John Primarius, another Peter, Thomas of St. Julien, a certain Anglicus who had an 'English method of notation and also to some extent of teaching', Theobald the Frenchman, Simon de Sacalia, a certain master of Burgundy, Probus of Picardy whose name was John the Falconer. 'And there were good singers in England', he goes on, 'and they sang most exquisitely, such as Master John *filius Dei*: and such as Makeblite at Winchester and Blakesmit at the court of the late King Henry' (Henry III). The chief points in the information conveyed by Anonymus IV can be checked from the Archives of Notre-Dame, though they are not found in any other medieval writer. Particularly useful are his notes on the variation, which approached confusion, in the various practices of notation in his day. The manuscript[2] is said to come from Bury St. Edmunds, which suggests that the writer was an English student at Paris, possibly a young monk of Bury, who brought his notebook home with him: if that is the case his interest in English music and musicians is natural. But no attempt at contrasting English music with Norman-French in this period can be pressed very far. By the time that William of Normandy had completed his plans for filling important posts in the English Church and State with Normans, the Channel had ceased to be the dividing line of two cultures which it had been in earlier centuries and was to be again later. The French language was widely used by the educated classes, and it was not until 1362 that English was ordered to be used in the courts of law.[3]

More recent discoveries of thirteenth-century music have tended to support the view that the so-called 'School of Notre-Dame' was in fact only one local, though perhaps a nuclear and important, production centre among many others from which a vast corpus of organum, conductus, roundelay, and motet music was spread throughout Britain, France, and Spain. The Low Countries do not seem to be strongly represented, which is rather surprising in view of the fact that Liége was a long-established centre of musical composition.[4] Of the eight or nine known manuscripts of the early two-part sequence 'Verbum bonum', the three earliest are Douai 90 and 274, and Jersey, Trinité 8; of these the first two are from Kloster

---

[1] Coussemaker, *Scriptores*, i, pp. 342 and 344.
[2] Brit. Mus. Royal 12 C vi.
[3] For further details see A. R. Myers, *England in the Late Middle Ages* (London, 1952), p. 80.
[4] See A. Auda, *La Musique et les musiciens de l'ancien pays de Liége* (Liége, 1930).

Anchin and the third either from Liége or from Antwerp, the latter according to Bannister. These, and an important manuscript now at Turin,[1] seem to represent the only contributions from a corner of Europe which was destined to play so important a part in music in the fifteenth century.

CLAUSULAE

Brief mention has already been made of the sections within organum where the lower voice moves more quickly and the upper voice takes on a regular rhythmic formation. In three of the leading manuscripts[2] these particular sections are written separately, or re-written, in another part of the same volume. To these excerpts is usually given the name *clausula*. There is an alternative title, *punctus* or *punctum*, which would be more attractive for the simple reason that the 'point', as a name for a short organ piece, survives so late as the Buxheimer (1451) and Mulliner (sixteenth century) manuscripts. But the word 'point' has so many other meanings, particularly in the notation of this and the subsequent centuries, that *clausula*, which denotes nothing else than this particular form, is the better choice and has come into general use. Research has shown that the *clausulae* of the 'Notre-Dame' group can be classified in two layers, the original excerpts and a later set of 'substitute *clausulae*'. The latter are assumed with no absolute certainty, but with a high degree of probability, to be from the hand of Pérotin as distinct from the earlier work of Léonin. Their main interest lies in the fact that they were the birthplace of the motet. Just as in the case of the sequence (see p. 148) so here it was apparently found that words would be useful to help the singer memorize and enunciate the upper part. The *clausulae* were music of a popular cast. Their actual form is closely similar to that of the conductus *caudae*, and they may likewise enshrine snatches of popular secular melodies in their upper parts; though, as they are built upon a given theme in the lower voice, this is not quite so probable as in the case of the conductus *caudae*, which are free throughout.

From very early times the added texts were of two kinds, for use in church or in hall: in Latin and in Anglo-Norman, Norman-French, or French respectively. This we may safely assume as a general rule, though as we know from sundry denunciations by bishops there were

---

[1] A. Auda, *La Musique et les musiciens de l'ancien pays de Liége* (Liége, 1930), p. 61; Besseler, 'Studien zur Musik des Mittelalters', II, in *Archiv für Musikwissenschaft*, viii (1926–7), p. 142.

[2] Wolfenbüttel 677; Florence, Bibl. Laur. plut. xxix, 1; Paris, Bibl. Nat. lat. 15139.

THE ST. VICTOR MANUSCRIPT

Showing cues of French motets in the margin of Latin *clausulae*.
(Paris, Bibl. Nat. lat. 15139, fo. 288.) Thirteenth century

also combinations of the two languages. Thus in Paris, Bibl. Nat. lat. 15139, one of the very oldest of the 'Notre-Dame series', the French *incipits* of the secular poems are to be seen written all down the margins of the pages which contain the *clausulae*. Neither Wolfen-büttel 677 nor Florence, Bibl. Laur. plut. xxix, 1, have any songs to French words. One of the oldest examples of this traditional state of things is a fragment in the Worcester Chapter Library,[1] where the organum, the original matrix of the *clausula*, has not yet been discarded: and the nascent motet is seen embedded in it at the section which would, in the normal state of things, have been taken out and written separately as a *clausula*. This piece will appropriately serve as the first example to be given in the next chapter, which deals with the motet (see p. 356), while we illustrate the subject here by a facsimile page from Paris, Bibl. Nat. lat. 15139, which shows a number of *clausulae* with their marginal cues in French. One such *clausula* is transcribed here in modern notation as Ex. 190, followed by another specimen (Ex. 191) from Wolfenbüttel 677, which is included for its high musical qualities. A third *clausula* is given as Ex. 214 (pp. 390–1), where will be found an explanation of the term *color* printed in Ex. 191:

Ex. 190[2]

<hr />

[1] Add. 68, xviii.
[2] Paris, Bibl. Nat. lat. 15139, fo. 290ʳ. Cf. Yvonne Rokseth, *Polyphonies du XIIIᵉ siècle* (Paris, 1936), ii, 197.

Ex. 191[1]

'ENGLISH DESCANT'

Before passing on to the wholly polyphonic style represented by
the motet there is one other member of the conductus family to be
mentioned—a form of composition related to the later fauxbourdon,
to which Bukofzer has given the name 'English descant'.[2] Its existence
was suspected by Riemann more than fifty years ago[3] but for thirty

[1] Wolfenbüttel 677, fo. 43.
[2] *Geschichte des englischen Diskants und des Fauxbourdons nach den theorischen
Quellen* (Strasbourg, 1936).
[3] *Geschichte der Musiktheorie im IX–XIX Jahrhundert* (Leipzig, 1898), p. 111.

years no confirmatory evidence was forthcoming, and as a result some scholars, led by Wooldridge, began to be suspicious of the fact. But from the publication of the Worcester manuscripts in 1928 onwards many dozens of specimens have been placed on record. The geographical position of Worcester links up with one of the most familiar passages in the medieval treatises, where Anonymus IV gives an early recognition of the third as a consonant interval:

Ditonus et semiditonus non sic reputantur. Tamen apud organistas optimos et prout in quibusdam terris, sicut in Anglia, in patria quae dicitur Westcuntre, optimae concordantiae dicuntur, quoniam apud tales magis sunt in usu.[1]

(The major and minor third do not rank thus [i.e. as perfect concords]: though with the best composers and moreover in certain countries such as England, in the region known as the West Country, they are held to be excellent consonances, for they are more frequently used by such composers.)

While Worcester still seems to be the most prolific source, other places have produced specimens, e.g. Bury St. Edmunds, Tattershall in Lincolnshire (the probable original home of Brit. Mus. Sloane 1210), and the unknown places in which Brit. Mus. Arundel 14 and many fly-leaves at Cambridge (University Library and Caius College) were written.

The form uses three voices and is essentially simple. A phrase is sung in a succession of six-three chords, two, three, four, five, or more in number, ending on an open fifth, the lowest voice falling a step while the others rise:

Ex. 192[2]

Be - a - ta vi - sce - ra   Ma - ri - æ vir - gi - nis   etc.

(Blessed is the womb of the Virgin Mary.)

It will be noticed that in this example the melody is in the highest voice. This feature is a novelty in the Worcester examples; and in most of them the melody remains in the lowest part. Sometimes it

[1] Coussemaker, *Scriptores*, i, p. 358.
[2] Worcester, Chapter Lib. Add. 68, xix a. Printed complete in Dom A. Hughes, *Worcester Mediæval Harmony* (Plainsong and Mediæval Music Society, 1928), p. 108. Recorded in *The History of Music in Sound*, ii, side 18.

migrates from one voice to another, as in 'Salve rosa',[1] where it is found interchanged in the two upper parts of the instrumental prelude and interlude, appearing in the lowest part for the vocal sections. But the fixation of the top line as the natural place for the principal tune had to wait until the fifteenth century: there intervened the great era of the motet, with its polyphonic and polytextual construction leading right away from the idea of harmonized melody.

[1] Hughes, op. cit., p. 125.

XI

THE MOTET AND ALLIED FORMS

By Dom Anselm Hughes

GENERAL CHARACTERISTICS

No form of medieval composition is more important than the motet. It is now generally agreed that the name is derived from the French *mot* (word), because the upper part is no longer a *vocalise* as in organum but possesses a text (*dictamen*, ditty) of its own. A very large proportion of the music which survives from the period 1250–1375 is motet music. It is a form which includes not only the motet proper but also a large quantity of music for the Ordinary of the Mass set in motet style. Indeed the motet form was used for almost every polyphonic item in church services of the time—hymns, the Proper of the Mass, the Magnificat—as well as for love-songs, banqueting songs, and compositions for great ceremonial occasions. Furthermore, the motet, alone among the various medieval forms, survived through an unbroken series of developments which led through the works of Dunstable and Dufay to the Netherland schools and the work of Fayrfax and Palestrina.

The medieval motet has certain differences which mark it off from the sixteenth-century type: the most noticeable is that whereas in the later motets all the voices are treated as equal partners in a harmonious combination (the only essential discrimination as a rule being that between 'high' and 'low' voices), in the medieval motet each voice has its own sharply marked characteristics. The most frequent number of voices is three. For example, in one collection— burnt during the siege of Strasbourg in 1870 but redescribed by the patient labour of Van den Borren[1]—the actual figures are 35 for two voices, 138 for three voices, and 9 for four voices. This proportion is typical, except perhaps for England, where the four-part motet was more popular (see p. 395). In the motet for three voices the melody of the highest voice will normally run in short notes, and that of the middle voice rather less so, while the lowest (the tenor) will move

---

[1] *Le Manuscrit musical M. 222 C. 22 de la Bibliothèque de Strasbourg* (Antwerp, 1924).

in very long notes arranged after formal patterns—the rhythmic modes and *ordines* which have been described in the preceding chapter. Thus, to take an example at random, in the Montpellier manuscript (see next page) the motet 'Salve virgo virginum / Est il donc ainsi / Aptatur' has 202 notes in the *triplum* (highest voice), 173 in the *motetus* (middle voice), and only 103 in the tenor. In the slightly different Turin version of this motet the disproportion is even more strongly marked.

The prevalent types of the earlier verbal texts, and the tenor melodies chosen as their foundations, give some indications of the actual surroundings in which the motet first appeared. The process by which many texts of the upper voices were formed is a fitting of words to a pre-existing melody, closely analogous to that which gave birth to the trope (see p. 129); while the tenor melodies are liturgical fragments in the oldest examples, usually from the Graduals of the Mass. In the case of the very earliest motets these fragments have done duty as tenors of the *clausulae* from which the motets are derived. Indeed the purest type of early motet consists of a liturgical tenor with two upper parts singing what is nothing more than a trope upon the words of the tenor. Sometimes these two upper texts are identical, at other times they vary slightly or altogether. Where the two upper texts vary, the name 'double motet' has often been applied. The need for this term seems rather doubtful, and it will not be used in this chapter. According to Ludwig's enumeration[1] of the contents of the Florence manuscript (see p. 313) sixty-four of its motet-tenors come from Graduals, only seven from chants of the Choir Office: one tenor (of 'Gaude rosa speciosa') has not yet been identified. In the Worcester collection are many tenors from Graduals, and from Alleluias with their verses, arranged in such a way as to indicate a connexion with the liturgy even more intimate than that of the Florence manuscript. These two, Florence and Worcester, are the two early collections of motets in which there is no occurrence of vernacular texts, and it is for that reason, as well as for palaeographical and other considerations, that they have been singled out for mention in this connexion.

The picture of the earliest motet performance that we can reconstruct will therefore be very similar to what occurred in the case of the *sequela*—an embroidery of the official chant during the interval between the Epistle and the Gospel: two or three skilled singers at the lectern facing the altar in the middle of the choir, and sometimes

---

[1] *Repertorium Organorum* (Halle, 1910), pp. 103–17 and *passim*.

an instrumentalist, either with them or on the organ bench, sustaining or reinforcing the lowest part. Perhaps in some places singers in the stalls on either hand will be maintaining the tenor: they will know the tune and will not need special books, and the metrical pattern of the tune needed for singing in the motet will be controlled by the hand or baton of one of the singers at the lectern. Manuscripts are known (the Madrid manuscript in particular) in which the upper parts are given without the tenor, and a practice such as that suggested (which is frankly hypothetical) would account for the existence of such incomplete part-books. But it was not long before the motet went out from this cradle into the wider range of choral singing on other occasions, not only in the church but also in the banqueting hall. French texts (which should often be more accurately described as Anglo-French, Anglo-Norman, or Norman-French) soon began to make their appearance for one or both of the upper voices, and still later on for the tenor. We shall return to these in the next chapter.

SOURCES OF THE PERIOD

To the list given at the head of Chapter X must now be added the following:[1]

Montpellier, Bibl. Universitaire, H 196
Bamberg, Ed. IV 6
Turin, Bibl. reale, vari 42
Paris, Bibl. Nat. fr. 146
　　”　　　”　　　”　　　844
　　”　　　”　　　”　　　12615
British Museum, Add. 27630
Worcester, Chapter Library, Add. 68, fragments ix–xxxv
British Museum, Add. 25031
Oxford, Bodleian Library, Lat. liturg. d 20
　　”　　　”　　　”　　Hatton 30
　　”　　New College 362

Of these manuscripts the first six are the most extensive: they are all French in origin. The seventh (Brit. Mus. Add. 27630) was probably written at Indersdorf in Bavaria. The others are all of English origin, but no large anthology of motets written in England has survived intact; there are traces of three collections of a hundred or so, of which the oldest is probably that listed in Brit. Mus. Harley 978. The music of this has all disappeared, though much of it can be reconstructed from other sources; but the titles remain. It contains the

---

[1] Other manuscripts, shorter or of minor importance, will be found listed in vol. iii.

names of eighty-one motets, besides many conducti and organa. They are stated there to be 'de W. de Wic', who is more likely to have been the compiler than the composer of the whole collection, and he has been reasonably identified by Schofield as a certain William of Wycombe, precentor of the Leominster cell of Reading Abbey.[1]

In addition to the many pieces (some of which are incomplete) in the Worcester Chapter Library, cognate sources in London and Oxford bring the total number up to well over 100, of which about 80 can be classified as motets.[2] The original foliation of one of the Worcester volumes now dismembered and scattered between Worcester, London, and Oxford runs up to 136; and judging from the rest of the contemporary literature in England and elsewhere there is not the least doubt that the whole of this volume contained polyphony. A third collection which shows signs of having once been of major rank is the New College manuscript: it now contains about twenty motets, some of them incomplete; but one of its foliations runs up to 90. Its origin is unknown, but it has affinities both in handwriting and in contents with the Worcester music. These numbers furnish some indication of what has disappeared from English sources.

THE ORIGINAL STRUCTURE OF THE MOTET

On p. 349 in the last chapter mention was made of a primitive motet, 'Ex semine Abrahae',[3] which has not yet shaken free from its parent organum. No less than thirteen manuscripts of this music have been cited with the different texts by Anglès;[4] he presents variant readings of all but the Worcester version, which is reproduced here:

Ex. 193

[1] B. Schofield in *The Music Review*, ix (1948), pp. 82–86.
[2] See A. Hughes, *Worcester Mediæval Harmony* (London, 1928).
[3] Recorded in *The History of Music in Sound* (H.M.V.), ii, side 18.
[4] *El Còdex musical de Las Huelgas*, i, p. 290, iii, p. 249. See also Yvonne Rokseth, *Polyphonies du XIIIᵉ siècle* (Paris, 1936), ii, pp. 20 and 142.

mo-de-ra-mi - ne   Ign-em pi - o   nu-mi-ne pro- du-cis, Do-mi-

-ne: Ho-mi-nis sa- lu- tem   pau-per-ta - te nu- da,   Vir-gi-nis na-

-ti- vi-ta-te de tri-bu Ju- da.   Jam pro-pi-nas o-vum   Per na-ta - le

no - vum: Pis-cem, pa-nem da- bis   par-tu si - ne se - mi - ne.

(From the seed of Abraham by divine overshadowing thou dost bring forth,
O Lord, in thy divinity a fire, and the salvation of man in his stark poverty, by
the birth of the Virgin of the tribe of Judah. Now on this new birthday thou
settest forth an egg and wilt give us fish and bread by this birth without seed.)

At the fifth bar the organum runs on into a section with syllabic text,
which turns the *clausula* into a motet. The parts within dotted brackets
are missing in the Worcester version and have been supplied from
other sources. The English mensural notation (see p. 368) and the

[1] Cf. Anglès, loc. cit.

lively form of the melody in the *motetus* are worth notice. Comparison with the other versions printed by Anglès suggests that Worcester, besides preserving the motet in its most archaic form, gives a better version: it seems to be less 'smooth' and to have more character, without losing that essential quality of euphony which we may expect in the early thirteenth century.

Whether this is so or not, the witness of this early English piece to the history of motet origins is of high value. Pierre Aubry wrote in 1908:

A curious text, which M. Wilhelm Meyer did not know of, goes to confirm his thesis and to show the close union existing between the organum and the motet. It is a fragment of manuscript from the thirteenth century in Worcester Cathedral Library. It consists of an adaptation in polyphonic style of the 'Alleluia, Nativitas', sung on the feast of the Nativity of the Blessed Virgin. The complete text of this runs 'Alleluia, Nativitas gloriosae Virginis Mariae ex semine Abrahae, ortu de tribu Juda, clara ex stirpe David'. Upon this melody the descanting musicians of Notre Dame, Pérotin and others, had composed melismatic variations in three parts: and the motet 'Ex semine Abrahae' was formed, we may say, by the arrangement of a new poetical text under the *vocalises* corresponding to the words 'ex semine' of the organum piece. Now the interest of the Worcester fragment is that it gives us the motet embedded in the organum: at these words 'ex semine' there is an interruption of the *organum triplum*, and the singers go on to execute, still in three parts, the motet in question. Unfortunately we know of no other examples of this arrangement.[1]

TENOR THEMES

When we come to look into the methods by which the earlier motets were built up, it will be obvious that their tenors ought to receive separate consideration before the upper parts are examined. The latter are new arrivals which look forward towards fresh and experimental treatment of their melodies and rhythms: they will bring us to points of imitation and interchange, already mentioned in speaking of the conductus; to a more liberal handling of the diatonic scale, involving augmented fourths and minor sevenths and opening the way to modulation; to close rhythmic or mensural interpretation of the text, sometimes referred to as 'declamation'; to suspension, syncopation, and variation.

To speak of the tenors as having been 'borrowed from Gregorian chant' is not strictly accurate in the case of the earliest motets, since these, as we have seen, are nothing but arrangements or harmoniza-

[1] Translated from *Cent Motets du XIIIᵉ siècle* (Paris, 1908), iii, p. 15, n. 2.

tions of the Gregorian chant, for use in its own liturgical setting. All that happened was that the section which had been taken out and given a separate existence as a *clausula* was now provided with words for its upper voice or voices. Later on, however, the favourite tags of the *clausulae* ('Flos filius ejus',[1] 'In saeculum', 'Manere', 'Latus', 'Aptatur', 'Et gaudebit' seem to be the six most popular) are actually borrowed for setting in one or other of the rhythmic formulas in order that new upper parts may be composed upon them: so that the whole repertory of the Gregorian chant-books comes to be used as a source from which to draw melodic subjects. The best way to illustrate this process will be to take one of these original *canti fermi* and trace it in detail. The two oldest collections in which motet-music is found are those of Wolfenbüttel 677 and Brit. Mus. Egerton 2615. Properly speaking, the first of these has no motets, but a number of the pieces ranked there as conducti have been identified as upper voices of motets, the tenor being absent. 'Serena virginum', 'Latex silice', 'Laudes referat', 'Deo confitemini', 'Gaudeat devotio', and 'Qui servare puberem' are six which have been identified so far, and there may be others. The first of these six occurs in the Egerton manuscript as well as in Wolfenbüttel 677 and later manuscripts; and as this 'Serena virginum' is built upon the tenor 'Manere', one of those mentioned above as being of most frequent occurrence, no more suitable *cantus* could be chosen for demonstration where space is not available for more than one full-scale example.[1]

'MANERE'

The point of departure is the Gregorian Gradual for the feast of St. John the Evangelist on 27 December. The Christmas season has very often been chosen by church composers from early times, perhaps more so than any other, Easter not excepted. This is not from any idea that Easter ought to take second place, but is explainable on the natural grounds that the northern European winter provides long hours of darkness indoors, whereas spring and summer and autumn festivals fall in days when all must be busy in the fields. The 'Notre-Dame repertory' of the Wolfenbüttel, Florence, and Madrid manuscripts suggests that the scheme proposed to set the Graduals for the entire round of church festivals to music in three and four parts, but that it got no farther than the winter feasts. It began ambitiously with the great four-voiced organa for Christmas Day ('Viderunt') and the

[1] For a selection of nine representative treatments of 'Flos filius ejus' see A. T. Davison and W. Apel, *Historical Anthology of Music*. i (Cambridge, Mass., 1946), No. 28.

following day, St. Stephen ('Sederunt'). The plan was carried no farther in the manuscripts which we possess, and the only other *quadrupla* remaining are four conducti with Christmas texts: 'Mors', a small piece which is probably an extract from a larger *quadruplum* which has not survived, coming from the Easter Gradual 'Christus resurgens ex mortuis jam non moritur, mors illi ultra non domina-bitur' (Christ being raised from the dead dieth no more, death shall have no more dominion over him), and the remains of a set of 'Spiri-tus et alme' tropes to 'Gloria in excelsis'.[1]

That the *quadrupla* were originally more numerous than the few remaining is indicated by these entries in the Notre-Dame *cartulaire*, showing that four-part organa once existed for the feasts of St. John (27 December), St. Thomas of Canterbury (29 December), and the Circumcision (1 January) at least:

(*a*) 'Responsorium et alleluia in triplo vel quadruplo vel organo . . . cantabuntur' (The responsory (i.e. the Gradual) and the alleluia shall be sung in three-part or in four-part or in [two-part] organum).[2]

(*b*) 'Qui vero in majori missa, eodem die, responsum vel alleluia in organo, vel triplo sive quadruplo, cantabunt, singuli sex denarios habeant' (But they who shall sing the respond (Gradual) or alleluia in organum, either for three or for four parts, at High Mass on that day [i.e. St. John's Day] are each to have sixpence).[3]

The former of these two quotations refers to ordinances for the Feast of Fools on 1 January 1198—a revision and tidying-up (probably overdue) of this popular carnival. The character of this celebration was of a style similar to that of the customs connected with the boy-bishop at Christmastide, when the seniors of the choir, out of rever-ence for the humility and simplicity of the Christ-child, performed the lower offices while the singing-boys wore the best vestments and sang the more dignified parts of the service (the celebration of Mass alone excepted).[4] The second quotation is dated about 1200. It is confirmed in similar terms in 1208,[5] and about the same time we have the same reward of sixpence conferred upon the 'four clerks who shall sing the alleluia in organum' on the feast of St. Thomas of Canterbury, 29 December.[6]

St. John's Day has no organum surviving in four parts, but we have

---

[1] Oxford, Bodleian, Mus. c. 60 (see Ex. 202, p. 375).
[2] B. E. C. Guérard, *Cartulaire de l'église Notre-Dame de Paris* (*Collection de documents inédits sur l'histoire de France*, Paris, 1850), i, p. 74.
[3] Ibid. iv, p. 121.
[4] Ex. 164 (p. 321) is taken from music for one of these carnivals, *c.* 1225.
[5] Guérard, op. cit. i, p. 358 and iv, p. 108.
[6] Ibid. iv, p. 105.

the Gradual for the feast, 'Exiit sermo', with its verse, set for two
voices[1] and also for three.[2] We may take this as our starting-point,
for the verse of this Gradual, 'Sed sic eum', contains the word
'manere', sung with a melisma which aroused the same interest and
admiration in medieval times as it does today. It is found, to another
text, in Ex. 41 (p. 120): and in this context it may be known to some
who are not familiar with the daily round of the Graduale, but have
listened to Tenebrae in Holy Week, where the strain is used for the
glorious paean of triumph when the third section is added to the
final 'Christus factus est' on the third night—'[Propter quod et Deus]
exaltavit illum' (Wherefore also God hath highly exalted him). It
may be remarked that there is not a note of difference between this
chant, as given from the modern Vatican text, and our polyphonic
example from the thirteenth century:

Ex. 194 (i)[3]

ma-ne-re

Ex. 194 (ii)

Ex. 195[4]

['Léonin' style]

vo-

---

[1] Wolfenbüttel 677, fo. 23ᵛ; Florence, Bibl. Laur. plut. xxix, 1, fol. 102ᵛ; Wolfenbüttel 1206, fo. 66ᵛ.
[2] Florence, fo. 18; Wolfenbüttel 1206, fo. 14.
[3] *Graduale Romanum* (Rome, 1908), p. 36.
[4] Wolfenbüttel 677, fo. 23ᵛ.

lo   ma - ne - re

do -

-nec.

From the verse of the Gradual the middle section of Ex. 195 has been extracted and rewritten as a 'substitute *clausula*', ascribed to the hand of Pérotin:[1]

Ex. 196

[color i]

Manere

[color ii]

Manere

[1] Wolfenbüttel 677, fo. 44. Also in Florence, fo. 151.

The tenor melody is repeated five times, with a different *duplum* composed above it each time. These five repetitions constitute a sort of *ostinato*.[1] Two other *clausulae* on 'manere' are found in the St. Victor manuscript,[2] for three and two voices respectively. Three-part *clausulae* are rare. Both of these St. Victor *clausulae* had their own motets written upon them later.

Returning to our own setting, the next stage is reached in the Egerton manuscript,[3] where a second upper part is written, to the text 'Serena virginum' shown in the lowest voice of Ex. 197; here there is a repeated rhythmic pattern (*talea*) instead of a melodic one (*color*). These two upper parts are also in the Madrid manuscript,[4] but without the tenor. Finally, a third upper part (*quadruplex*) is added in Wolfenbüttel 677, without the tenor, and in the Florence manuscript, with the tenor:

Ex. 197[5]

[TALEA 1]

Se - re - na   vir- gi-num, lux ho-mi-num ple - na,

---

[1] Cf. Rokseth, op. cit. iii, p. 238.
[2] Paris, Bibl. Nat. lat. 15139, fo. 288.
[3] Brit. Mus. Egerton 2615.
[4] Madrid, Bibl. Nac. 20486.
[5] Wolfenbüttel 677, fo. 9. The manuscript has 'patris' for 'paris' in line 6.

templum Tri-ni - ta - tis, pu-ri-ta-tis spe-ci-al-is tha-la - mus,

Ar- ca no-væ le - gis, thro-nus no-vi re - gis, vel-lus quod ri-ga-vit

qui nostrum por-ta - vit saccum,nostram car-nem ve-sti - ens.

[TALEA 2]

Ne - sci - ens vi-rum De-um pa- ris, o Ma-

-ri - a, ma - ter pi - a,   stel - la ma - ris sin - gu - la - ris

(Bright star of virgins, light and life of men, temple of the Trinity, chamber of rare purity, ark of the new law, throne of the new king, fleece that bedewed him who bore our sackcloth, clothing our flesh. Knowing no man you give birth to God, O Mary, holy mother, matchless star of the sea.)

These three upper parts do not concord with the tenor, but they do concord with one another. The musical solution of this problem would seem to be that the second and third parts (*motetus* and *triplum*, reading upwards) were sung with the tenor, that they got to be well known and appreciated, and that they had a third upper part added for performance as a conductus. This makes the form in which they appear in the Wolfenbüttel manuscript quite satisfactory: but to explain away the discordant appearance in the Florence manuscript is not so easy. The latter is a finely written manuscript, whereas the former, though accurate and careful, conveys the impression of being a working, singing copy. Possibly the copyist of the Florence manuscript did not quite realize what he was doing: or perhaps it was an understood thing that his four-part setting was not to be sung in four parts, but either parts one to three, or two to four, at choice.[1]

Many other motets upon the tenor 'Manere' could be cited, some with a greater degree of documentary fullness, some with less: this example of the 'Serena virginum' motet provides us with an inside view of the relationship of the tenor to the whole composition. It will be convenient to defer further consideration of the rhythmic *ordines* of the tenors until we come to see them as living parts of a practical working system in connexion with the isorhythmic motets described on pp. 390–5. It is now time to turn to the notation, and to some of the ways in which composition was developing at this period.

NOTATION

The system of notation is on the whole identical with that used for the conductus (see pp. 318–26), for the conductus is contemporary

---

[1] The whole of this intricate question is very adequately discussed by Hans Tischler in *The Musical Quarterly*, xxx (1944), pp. 470–1.

with the earlier motets. More complex points occur in the mensural interpretation of the tenors of some manuscripts.[1] In general, it is enough to say that the modal system is followed in the writing of the tenors, but that anomalous cases are often found in which the scribe or the composer has not followed the theorists' rules closely, or has so used them as to leave the door open for ambiguity. In the upper parts with their syllabic texts the modal notation, which rested upon ligatures, tends to disappear, and the single notes take on individual time-values, long or short. The short (breve) is still one-third of the perfect long; and in the third mode, where two shorts follow the long in dactylic form, the second of these two (*brevis altera*) is doubled in value, as explained on pp. 320 and 381. Otherwise the upper parts begin to look more straightforward and more in accord with our modern ideas of what notation ought to be—that is to say, a script which informs instead of mystifying the novice, which denotes the actual music instead of merely reminding the singer of what he had learnt before.

Long and breve are adequate equipment for the first motets. But as the independent upper parts begin to develop in their lyrical invention and subtlety the urge to subdivide the breve begins to make itself felt. The earliest indication of this is perhaps the group ⟨♪♦♦⟩, found in English manuscripts in place of ⟨♩♦♦⟩. Now ⟨♩♦♦⟩ is the subdivision of the long (♩ = ♩.) into ♩ ♩ ♩ or ♫ ♩. The new ⟨♪♦♦⟩, which seems to have no special name of its own, is the first subdivision of the breve, on the same lines, ♫ ♩ or ♫ ♪, according to whether the breve is perfect or imperfect. The semibreve has arrived, in fact, but not yet as an independent unit, for it occurs only in pairs for some considerable time. We shall meet it first as a separate entity in the seventh fascicle of the Montpellier manuscript (see p. 380).

Another group which seems to be rightly interpreted as showing a subdivision of the breve is that which opens a descending *conjunctura* (see p. 324) with a rising note, thus— [musical notation] . Concordances and other internal evidence suggest [musical staff notation] as the right translation of this group in a large number of cases.

Into the simplicity of an upper part noted in longs and breves (♩♦♦♩) there enters a slight complexity called by some authorities 'English mensural notation'. This consists of using the lozenge or

---

[1] See W. Apel, *The Notation of Polyphonic Music 900–1600* (Cambridge, Mass., 1942), pp. 253–60, 271–80, for a full discussion of these refinements.

diamond shape for the short note instead of the square form, thus: ◆◆◆◆ for ◆◆◆◆. It presents no special difficulties and appears to be confined to English manuscripts.[1] The English copyists very sensibly abandoned their own insular fashions in favour of the French methods about the end of the thirteenth century. Odington describes the lozenge-shaped notation of the breve (and also of the semibreve, with a short tail to the left, ♪).[2] This actual notation can be seen in *Worcester Mediaeval Harmony* (1928), pp. 128–9. Odington ends his short reference to the lozenge-breve and tailed-semibreve notation by saying: 'And this is very tiresome' (quod valde est inconveniens).

MUSICA FICTA

This period saw a considerable increase in the use of notes outside the diatonic scale. By about 1325 the following were all established: C♯, E♭, F♯, G♯, B♭. During the whole of the Middle Ages the accidentals were sometimes written in the script, sometimes not; it was assumed that the laws governing them were understood by the performers. It is this very assumption that sets up our present problem, because we have to recover and formulate the rules from a mass of practice which was not always consistent, and from theorists whose agreement with one another is not always apparent even when their meaning is clear. The great importance of these questions, leading as they do in the direction of modulation and towards the round of key-signatures used in transposition, calls for a reasonably full treatment here.

This system of 'implied accidentals' is known as *musica ficta*, or sometimes (less accurately) as *musica falsa*. It is a path that leads through a tangled thicket; and every attempt to clear it by laying down a guiding rule has to be qualified according to country, century, and predisposition or bias—that is, does the editor believe that the mentality of his composer or the copyist or the actual performers should be interpreted on the one hand as looking forward to the complete round of keys with the five semitones, or on the other hand as strictly controlled according to the current theory of the time and

---

[1] The French song in Oxford, Bodleian, Douce 139, fo. 179ᵛ, is an example presumably written in England: compare the comments made above, p. 347. See also J. Handschin in *Musica Disciplina*, iii (1949), p. 69, and K. J. Levy in *Journal of the American Musicological Society*, iv (1951), p. 227.

[2] Coussemaker, *Scriptores*, i, p. 244. Bukofzer has ascertained that the last example but one on p. 244, col. 1, is misprinted, and that it should read ◆◆◆ | ◆◆◆ for ▪▪▪ | ▪▪▪: and the last example is ♪, not ↑.

place, sometimes spoken of as 'the modal mentality'? Then, further, did practice vary according to whether the music was sung or played? And if played, should we take into account the possible limitations of the organ keyboard, not forgetting the varying limitations of other instruments? For the thirteenth century this last question may be legitimately posed, at least for the organ, but in the oldest piece of organ-tablature known—the so-called Robertsbridge fragment,[1] which dates from the early fourteenth century—all the twelve keys of the octave are already required. And are we to be governed by melodic proprieties and vocal scale-progressions more than by harmonic requirements? Finally, there is the relative importance of theory and practice, together with an elusive problem sometimes overlooked, viz. were the accidentals, when written in, inscribed in the manuscript in its original condition, or were they added by a later hand, either of the director of the music or of the individual performer?

All these strands are interwoven, and to reach anything like satisfactory conclusions it will be necessary to keep all of them in sight all the time. If this were not so, it might be possible to separate them, to work through them methodically, and to present the results in order. In this general picture, though there is lack of agreement on details among scholars a few general principles are agreed so universally that we may treat them as axiomatic: e.g. (i) that the accidentals were not always written, and (ii) that there must be some measure of predominance of melody over harmony—exactly how much is still a matter of discussion. The period we are concerned with is, roughly speaking, the thirteenth century, or more precisely 1175 to 1325. The latter date enables us to include the first documentary evidence of a twelve-semitone octave, the 'Robertsbridge fragment' just mentioned; though this is an organ part, not a vocal score, which makes it just a little less than perfect as a *terminus ad quem*.

The position which called for such a system as that of *musica ficta* is as simple as the processes of its working out are complex. It is the problem of the tritone. In pure melody the augmented fourth in a leap from F to B is avoided by flattening the B or sharpening the F, though the augmented fourth reached by step is in no way foreign to the Gregorian idiom in its most authentic form. Many examples of it can be found in the *Officium Majoris Hebdomadae* (Holy Week Office) published at Rome in 1922, the last of the series of Vatican chant-books to be revised, and therefore presumably the most

[1] Brit. Mus. Add. 28550.

scientific, and in the *Antiphonale Monasticum* of 1935 the tritonic passages are even more frequent.

A similar instance occurs in another common medieval convention, that of flattening the B when it is preceded and followed by an A. A familiar example of this is to be found in the version of the fourth line of 'Veni Creator Spiritus' as given in some hymnals:

This is the debased (Sarum) form. The authentic form as restored in the *Antiphonale Vaticanum* (1919), p. 427, is:

'The flat is an importation of later date, when harmonized music had introduced an aversion for the tritonic effect.'[1]

Medieval practice tended towards the softening of the tritone. The composition of music in two or more parts meant that the tritone might occur not as an occasional melodic feature but as a frequent harmonic problem. The problem was recognized, but apparently not resolved, so far back as the time of the *Musica Enchiriadis* in the tenth century (see p. 278): and it is first tackled seriously by John of Garland (*c.* 1195–1272). He does not speak of *musica ficta* but of 'error tertii soni'—the error of the third note. An elucidation of the passage in which this occurs in his *De Musica mensurabili*,[2] the classical starting-point for all theoretical treatment of *musica ficta*, was essayed by

[1] W. H. Frere, in *Historical Edition of Hymns Ancient and Modern* (London, 1909).
[2] Coussemaker, *Scriptores*, i, p. 115.

A. H. Fox Strangways in the second edition of the *Oxford History of Music*.[1] In the 'Introductio Musicæ secundum Magistrum de Garlandia, musicæ sapientissimum' there is a brief reference followed by a most disappointing gap in the manuscript. This belongs to the fourteenth century, and has sometimes been ascribed to a 'later Garland', but the title clearly suggests that it is lecture material 'after Garland'. The passage is clear, and may be translated thus:

We must now deal with 'false music', which is very necessary for musical instruments and especially so for the organ. It is 'false music', when we make a tone a semitone, and vice versa. Every tone can be divided into two semitones, so that signs to indicate semitones can be added to all tones.[2]

Magister Lambert, who wrote in the thirteenth century under the pseudonym of Aristotle, speaks of *musica falsa* (not *ficta*), but deals only with the semitones as noted, not as understood: and he rightly says that it is a question not of 'false music' but of mutation, 'for it is known by the signs ♭ and ♮'.[3] Walter de Odington (*c.* 1280) writes only of the current rules for flattening the B in plainchant. More precise rules are not reached until the period of *ars nova* (vol. iii, chap. i), when John de Muris and Philippe de Vitry give clearer information.

If we turn to the actual music of the period we shall find that the Wolfenbüttel and Florence manuscripts contain many instances of E♭ and F♯ (the F is marked with the ♮ sign, since the ♯ had not yet come into use). E♭ may be seen seven times in the conductus 'In rosa vernat lilium',[4] and six times in 'Jam vetus littera'.[5] These passages are not, strictly speaking, *musica ficta*, the essential idea of which is that the ♭ and ♯ are not written but understood: but they show how the inclusion of such semitones as E♭ and F♯ began at a date rather earlier than is implied in some histories. At the final *cauda* of 'In rosa vernat lilium' a direct light is thrown upon the question; the Wolfenbüttel manuscript marks E♭, while the scribe of the Florentine manuscript having scrupulously written in all the other occurrences of E♭ in this piece, does not think it worth while to mark the flats in the *cauda*, leaving them to be understood. It is a simple case where B♭ in the lower voice coincides several times with E, which must therefore be flat to avoid the tritone, in the upper voice. Both manuscripts occasionally use the two-flat 'signature' at the beginning of the line.

[1] Vol. i (1932), p. 331.
[2] Coussemaker, op. cit. i, p. 166.   [3] Ibid., p. 258.
[4] Wolfenbüttel 677, fo. 116ᵛ–117; Florence, fo. 271ᵛ.
[5] Wolfenbüttel 677, fo. 142ᵛ; Florence, fo. 272ᵛ.

Transcription and interpretation of such intervals as are uncertain in thirteenth-century music must remain, for the present, in a condition which is not entirely satisfactory. It would seem that we must be content to rely less upon definite rules than upon a general acquaintance with the music of the period. It is a welcome and healthy sign that editors of the last decade or two have diminished the number of the suggested accidentals which they have placed above the staff, with or without brackets. This means that students are no longer bidden to follow this or that school of interpretation, but are able to realize that the decisions are still open, liable to revision as knowledge increases; and furthermore that they may sometimes be lawfully made in different ways according to whether the music is to be sounded by voices or by instruments, in large or in small buildings.

VERNACULAR TEXTS

At the beginning of this chapter a reference was made to the appearance of French texts in the motets. Their first appearance seems to be in the St. Victor manuscript,[1] where 40 out of 42 Latin motets have cues or tags for sets of French words written down the margins of the manuscript. Contemporaneous with the manuscript, though usually listed after it rather than before, is Wolfenbüttel 1206, which has 98 motets with Latin words and 116 where French replaces the Latin text, instead of being an alternative, as in the case of the St. Victor manuscript. Later on (as, for example, very frequently in the Montpellier manuscript) the Latin is discarded in favour of the vernacular in one upper voice only, while the other, with no apparent sense of incongruity, retains the church text in the original Latin. Normally this Latin text is in the middle voice while the French is in the topmost: and this might suggest that in the banqueting hall a cleric from the choir sang the *motetus* part with a boy or a woman sustaining the *triplum*. This is, of course, a mere speculation: but some explanation ought to be offered for the preference given to Latin for the middle voice and French for the top. That the highest voice may have been added later in many cases is not denied, but this is a description of the process of growth, not a complete explanation of the form finally prevalent. When this practice is attempted in church, however, we are not surprised to find that the ecclesiastical authorities denounce it as improper, for the French texts are with a few exceptions frankly secular and deal for the most part with lovers and their lasses. The phase of the bilingual motet was a passing one, and it has received a

[1] Paris, Bibl. Nat. lat. 15139.

disproportionate share of attention in many accounts of medieval music.[1] One solitary example of a motet with an upper voice in English has been discovered—'Worldes blisce / Domino,[2] and what is probably an English tenor has recently been found in a fly-leaf at Princeton University.[3]

INTERCHANGE AND IMITATION

Composition of this period, with its more abundant opportunities for freedom of experimental treatment and development, is the cradle of various devices in counterpoint. Earliest in the order of time comes the very simple technique known as interchange, by which a phrase *A B* in one part is accompanied by *B A* in the other. This idea has been observed occasionally in work of the preceding century (see Ex. 154, p. 302), but it is now steadily developed, on the one hand

$$A B C$$

in the direction of a three-part form *B C A,* known as *rondellus* or

$$C A B$$

roundelay, and on the other hand in the direction of imitation, which leads through independent entry towards canon.

An example of interchange can be seen in the two-part sequence 'Ave virgo virga Jesse', which may well belong to a rather earlier period than that of the conductus and motet literature, and should perhaps be assigned to the twelfth century:

Ex. 201[4]

More distinctive of the thirteenth century are the second and third verses of this extract from a four-part 'Spiritus et alme' trope to 'Gloria in excelsis'. This is perhaps the oldest known piece of English four-part writing, and its origin is most likely Worcester:

---

[1] An example of an English motet with Latin *triplum* accompanied by Anglo-Norman tenor and contratenor is recorded in *The History of Music in Sound,* ii, side 19.

[2] Printed, with full comments, by Manfred Bukofzer in *Music and Letters,* xvii (1936), p. 225.

[3] See *Journal of the American Musicological Society,* iv (1951), p. 225, and vol. iii, ch. 3.

[4] Rouen 277 (Y 50).

(x) M S rises to C for this bar

The roundelay form is well displayed in full by 'De supernis sedibus'.[2]
A shorter specimen is given here from an interesting group of fly-
leaves recently discovered in a binding at Corpus Christi College,
Oxford. In this piece, 'Flos regalis', the first verse is in ordinary conductus style with a fine and extended introductory *cauda*. To the
corresponding *cauda* which precedes the second verse, 'Rex te Salem',
the text 'Rosa fragrans' has been added later (though not much later)
in three different coloured inks for the three voices: and a similar
treatment has been added to the final *cauda*. The original position
of this piece as a *cauda* introducing the second verse is definitely
established by the word 'Rex' still standing at its head, under the

[1] Oxford, Bodleian, Mus. c. 60, fo. 84. Recorded in *The History of Music in Sound*, ii,
side 18.
[2] Printed in Hughes, *Worcester Mediaeval Harmony*, pp. 134–8; facsimile on p. 127.

lowest line, a customary way of writing the initial syllable of a text
which was to be preceded by a long introduction:

(Fragrant rose, flower of spring, deliver thy servants from evil.)

Ex. 204 shows three short early instances of imitation, the third
exhibiting in its last three measures a further example of interchange:

¹ Oxford, Corpus Christi Coll. 489, No. 9. Recorded in *The History of Music in Sound*,
ii, side 20.
    ² (*a*) Wolfenbüttel 677, fo. 126ᵛ; (*b*) Florence, Bibl. Laur. plut. xxix, 1, fo. 204;
(*c*) Wolfenbüttel 677, fo. 120ᵛ.

These short passages are not long enough to be dignified by the name of canon. But a fragmentary fly-leaf in Oxford[1] has recently yielded up what certainly looks like a genuine example of canon:

Ex. 205

LATER *ARS ANTIQUA*

We have now reached the climax of the *ars antiqua*. This term is used here and elsewhere in this volume for the sake of convenience.

[1] Merton Coll. MS. 248.

It expresses very neatly the difference between the work of the thir-teenth and the fourteenth centuries. Needless to say it is not a con-temporary term: furthermore it was used in the following century in reference only to the immediate predecessors of the *ars nova*, from about 1280 to 1310. It is, however, convenient to apply the term *ars antiqua* to all harmonized work down to 1310 or thereabouts—perhaps even as far back as the Winchester organa and the Martial-tropers.

The later motets of the *ars antiqua* period, which are now to be considered, are not to be very sharply distinguished from the earlier. As to date, they may be described as belonging approximately to the second half of the thirteenth century, whereas those dealt with in the foregoing pages belong approximately to the first half. Some differ-ences they have in style, but these are the differences which must naturally accompany an advancing development, an ease in tech-nique, and that growing insistence upon euphony which may very well result from a prolonged experience of singing in parts. Where then is the dividing line to be drawn? In the notation is the answer to this question. And this stage in our inquiries may suitably be chosen for emphasizing the fact that throughout the Middle Ages notation was not just an extraneous affair, not a mere accidental matter of the machinery employed to express the sounds of music upon parchment or paper: on the contrary the forms of notation used had a vital connexion with the musical thought and system of each succeeding century.[1]

To take two points only. First of all it is a mistake to suppose that the notation of early centuries was in every respect cruder than our own. In many ways it was elementary, ambiguous, and incompletely equipped for denoting its subject-matter: but in the refinements of rhythm and (to follow for a moment the speculations of some scholars) in indications of quarter-tones it had that care for nuance which can be expected where all the melodies are in unison. These refinements tended to be lost in harmonized music, but the *plica* (p. 325) indicates that minute care in text-expression was retained. Secondly—and this is a point which arises in connexion with the later motets, when more adequate notation is available—there is the oppor-tunity for time-values to be broken up, and for melodies to be given some ornamentation. The melismatic flourishes in the tune, so charac-teristic of the Gregorian chant, had to be abandoned in the process of

[1] W. Apel, 'The Importance of Notation in solving Problems of Early Music' (American Musicological Society, *Papers*, 1938, p. 51).

evolving the conductus and the motet; for the conductus is essentially syllabic, while the very purpose of the original motet, according to one interpretation, was that a syllable should be given to each note of a florid melody. This process we saw at work earlier in the development of the sequence (Chapter V), and it will be found again later in attempts to devise a new genre in English church music in and after 1547. Only in the case of the sequences did the syllabic treatment endure: both in medieval composition and in Elizabethan church music it withered rapidly, for it had no real root in aesthetic principle.

The procedure in the later *ars antiqua*, with its advances in notation, seems to have been something like this: that so long as the written notes are of indeterminate length, as in those modal patterns which have been used hitherto, we cannot expect to find, and in practice we do not find, that it was feasible to think or to write in more than two degrees of time—long and short. It has been noted above (p. 368) that there is an occasional, sporadic appearance of very short notes in certain anomalous ligatures or *conjuncturae* of English modal notation. These are described as semibreves by later theorists, but not by the actual practitioners (*notatores*) themselves. It is true to say, broadly speaking, that the long and short notes were the sum total of the early thirteenth-century equipment in units of duration. And the time was ripe for a forward movement, possible now that musicians were free from the essentially ambiguous character of the modal notation in certain contexts: for in the modal period it would still have been necessary for the singers in many cases to know beforehand what the rhythm was, and sight-singing in parts could not yet have been an accomplished fact.

MENSURAL NOTATION

By stages, it would seem, and not by any flash of inventive genius on the part of any one man, the idea of attaching definite time-values to definite shapes of single or compound notes found its expression. As happens so often in ancient and medieval history, an eponymous teacher had to be provided, whose name could be a peg on which to hang the wreath of honour for the new doctrines. For this honour Franco of Cologne was selected, just as Guido of Arezzo had been chosen some two hundred years earlier as inventor of the staff, Notker for the sequence, and Boethius for alphabetical notation. The idea of mensural notation, however, was known and used some time before Franco, who wrote about 1260: the actual documents admitted to be 'Franconian' are now reduced to a very few, such as the *Roman de Fauvel*[1] and the seventh and eighth fascicles of the Montpellier manuscript.[2] Even so, we find some writers referring to 'Fauvel notation' as if to a sub-species of the Franconian: while Apel[3] detects in those last two fascicles of the Montpellier manuscript 'certain even later elements of notation, which are associated with Petrus de Cruce', who flourished at the end of the century. And these specimens of true Franconian notation are speedily made obsolete by the swift onset of the subsequent period, that of the *ars nova*. The mensural, 'pre-Franconian' collections, on the other hand, are now reckoned to include most of the more important sources of the period —the Las Huelgas, Bamberg, and Turin manuscripts, and fascicles 2 to 6 of the Montpellier manuscript.

The essential difference between the pre-Franconian mensural notation now under consideration and the modal notation which preceded it lies in the fact that there is a definite sign (⌐, the *virga* of plainsong) for a long note, and another distinct sign (■, the *punctum*) for a short or breve. The ligatures remain, with certain modifications which will shortly be treated in detail, but their use is mostly confined to the tenors, which do not require syllabic treatment because they are textless or melismatic: whereas the upper parts with their verbal texts run mostly in single notes. Manuscripts of this class can be quickly identified by the shape of their ligatures. But this does not mean that the changes in ligatures are the most significant developments of the period, which, as we have said, are the breaking up and the ornamentation of the upper parts, now made possible by the new mensural notation. The composer, having these single notes before him, material representing definite duration, begins to find it attractive, easy, and effective to subdivide his notes, to break up the breve into two and three parts, and to ornament his upper melodies with various time-patterns. While they conform to the 'greater measure' laid down by the tenor (which still is and will for a long time remain in a classical rhythmic *ordo*) these upper parts are in themselves free and do not necessarily follow a predetermined rhythmic formula. Here is an obviously great advance in the direction of lyric freedom for the composer, an opportunity which he took and used at times with great subtlety, until such time as the fashion of isorhythm spread to the upper parts also.

In the following pages the long is represented by ♩, the breve by ♪, the semibreve by ♪. The unit of measurement, known as the

[1] Paris, Bibl. Nat. fr. 146.   [2] Bibl. Univ., H 196.
[3] *The Notation of Polyphonic Music 900–1600* (Cambridge, Mass., 1942), p. 286.

tempus (later *tactus*), has moved from the *longa* to the *brevis*. In the subsequent period of the *ars nova* it will be seen shifting once more, from the *brevis* to the *semibrevis*. But for the present the semibreve occurs only in groups of either two or three, never singly; so that it is not yet a recognized unit in its own right, but exists only as a subdivision of the breve. When the group is a group of two, it represents an even division of the breve into two equal parts, as the name semibreve implies. Some writers have thought that the breve at this early period was already divided (when two semibreves occur as a group) in ternary fashion, ♪ᵌ♩ but Apel[1] has given good grounds for rejecting this interpretation. The new forms of the ligature are less significant than the new definite meanings of the single notes, long and breve: less significant, because they indicate no change in the music itself, only in the notation of the music. But they are very useful, for they enable us not only to read the rhythm of the tenor (or of any other part in which they may be used) with greater ease and certainty, but also to discern at a glance any isolated scrap of medieval music which is not only non-Gregorian but belongs to a polyphonic period later than that of modal rhythm.

These forms are worked out according to a definite logical system which (complicated though it may appear at first sight) is simplicity itself if we are careful to take the same starting-point as the medieval musician, that is the Gregorian notation. Reference to the table on p. 323 shows how some first or last notes have tails, pointing downwards. The new system of mensural ligatures takes all these forms as they stand, and says: 'These are proper forms' (*cum proprietate* is the technical term) 'and they shall indicate the normal course of the iambic rhythm and its compounds, thus: ♩, ♫ – ♩♩: but when it is desired to make the second note a breve they shall be written thus: ♪, ♩♩♩ .' Note that these last two forms are not *against* Gregorian propriety in the matter of the tails and their places: they are merely adaptations of the orthodox forms. The three-note ligatures *cum proprietate* are ♪, ♩♪ (most frequently now in the form ♩♩), ♩♩, ♩♩ = ♩♪ ♩. . The note marked *, shown as a minim here, is a *brevis altera*, i.e. a breve of doubled value, in accordance with the rules for the dactylic and anapaestic rhythms of modes III and IV (see pp. 319, 320). If all three notes are to be short the forms are ♩♪,

---

[1] Op. cit., pp. 295–6.

. All these three-note forms are quite consistent with the ligatures for two breves, and if the plainsong notation is familiar they can be easily committed to memory—a rising last note, if it is to be a breve, being turned away to the right instead of being written over the head of its predecessor, and a falling last note, if it is to be a breve, being written in oblique form as one piece with the foregoing note. If the logic of propriety could only be recognized as being quite simple and consistent, half the difficulty of knowing the ligatures at sight would vanish.

The principle of the ligatures without propriety is also simple. The removal or addition of a tail improperly (*sine proprietate*) means that the value of the note is changed from long to short or vice versa: thus the ligatures of two notes *sine proprietate* are , = . .: but where it is desired to make the second note a breve, then , = .

The three-note ligatures *sine proprietate* are given in the following table:

Long, breve, long	Long, breve, breve

The forms in the second column are of rare occurrence in this century, as they do not belong to strict rhythmic schemes in the ternary system which has been our only environment hitherto. When the duple or binary system, which is dealt with towards the end of this chapter, comes into general use they will be met with far more frequently.

We now come to the third class, ligatures of 'opposite propriety' (*cum opposita proprietate*). These need cause no difficulty whatsoever, as they are nothing but pairs of semibreves at the head of any ligature of three, four, or more than four notes, denoted by a tail pointing upwards instead of downwards:

Many, if not all, of the shapes given above are also found in the pre-Franconian period, which Apel[1] dates rather earlier than some authorities at about 1225 to 1260. They are practically universal in Franconian times, from about 1260 onwards, but in the transitional, formative period before 1260 many variants are found.[2] Ligatures of

[1] Op. cit., p. 282.   [2] Op. cit., pp. 296–7.

four or more notes follow the same rules: all extra interior notes are breves, unless they have tails pointing upwards to denote semibreves (in pairs), thus:

TECHNICAL DEVELOPMENTS

Before this short but necessary digression on notation it was said that composition is now distinguished by a more ornamental upper part. We are not obliged to ascribe this change solely to the more elastic notation now available for the first time. It may equally well have come about that in the upper parts of the motet, which are independent horizontal lines in a way that the voices of the conductus are not, the topmost voice stood out more prominently because of its clearer and more penetrating tones: so that it would begin to be regarded as the most important voice—an idea as radical in its own day as it is a commonplace with us—and would therefore receive fuller treatment. A fine musical result is often achieved, as in the following *triplum* from the motet 'In saeculum artifex / In saeculum supra mulierum / In saeculum',[1] where the final D makes us suspect that the C which we have been led to expect by the play on the triad C E G was in fact the original close of a secular song:

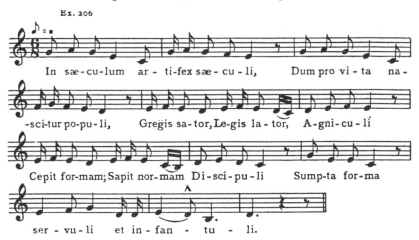

Ex. 206

In sae-cu-lum ar - ti-fex sae- cu - li, Dum pro vi - ta na - sci-tur po-pu-li, Gregis sa-tor, Le-gis la - tor, A-gni-cu - li Cepit for-mam; Sapit nor-mam Di-sci-pu-li Sump-ta for-ma ser - vu - li et in - fan - tu - li.

(The eternal creator of the universe, born to save the people, father of the flock and legislator, took the form of a little lamb; he knows the pattern of a disciple, having taken the form of a mere servant and a little child.)

[1] Las Huelgas, fo. 112ᵛ; facsimile and transcription of the complete motet in H. Anglès, *El Còdex musical de Las Huelgas* (Barcelona, 1931), no. 119.

The development of the technique displayed by the motet-com-
posers towards the end of the thirteenth century is by no means confined to the melodic ornamentation of the top line. There is an almost
equally important change in the contrapuntal direction, in that formal
relationship of one part to another which is known comprehensively
as imitation. The simplest and earliest instances of this have been
mentioned in Chapter IX (p. 302). The following example shows not
only a rather more subtle treatment, but is also an early specimen both
of *ostinato* and of duple rhythm (see p. 399):

(*Triplum*: Love may complain, seeing himself now suppressed, since faith [and
constancy] have begun to be reduced . . .
    Motetus: Faith and constancy follow love and keep him company . . .)

For an even more skilful and artistic use of *ostinato* compare the
following from 'Puellare gremium':[2]

[1] Montpellier, H 196, fo. 378ᵛ; after Rokseth, *Polyphonies du XIIIᵉ siècle*, iii, p. 238.
[2] *Worcester Mediæval Harmony*, p. 100. Recorded in *The History of Music in Sound*,
ii, side 19.

(x) Tenor repeats here: stated three times in all.

(*Triplum*: A maiden's womb spread joy throughout the world and happiness in heaven, when she bore the son of the great king and kept her chastity. O privilege . . .

Motetus: Mary becomes the spotless mother of the Lord, through the holy words of Gabriel, the faithful messenger sent from heaven. O spotless womb . . .)

The Montpellier and Worcester manuscripts also share the claim for the earliest instance of independent entry, though the Worcester manuscripts are probably about twenty years later than the Montpellier:

Ex. 209[1]

Deus! je n'i por-rai du-rer, Ce m'est a-

Se je voz pert, biau fins cuer douz, Co-ment por-

Manere

-vis S'il mi co-vient des-se-vrer De voz   etc.

-rai sanz vos du-rer?   On-ques n'a-mai fors   etc.

Ex. 210[2]

W 37

In tu-is lau-di-bus

W 35

Gau-de per quam cor-nu Da-vid Stel-la Ja-cob re-ve-la-vit.

W 37

lau-di-bus as-si-du-

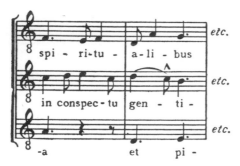

spi-ri-tu-a-li-bus   etc.

in conspec-tu gen-ti-   etc.

-a et pi-   etc.

[1] Montpellier, fo. 209ᵛ; Rokseth, op. cit. ii, p. 284.
[2] *Worcester Mediæval Harmony*, p. 77.

while the following striking quotation shows how firmly the contrapuntal idea has been grasped:

Ex. 211[1]

Las! n'on-ques ne de - ser - vi etc.

vos - tre cuer pi - tié n'en prent, Vo -

[Kyrieleyson]

HARMONY

The question of progression from chord to chord is one which does not seem to have aroused very great interest in the mind of the thirteenth-century composer. But we do find one very early enunciation of the classical doctrine about consecutive intervals, in the anonymous thirteenth-century French *Tractatus de Discantu* from St. Victor:

> Et ne doilt on point faire ne dire ij quintes ne deulx doubles, l'une après l'autre, ne monter ne descendre avec sa teneur, car ils sont parfais: mais par acors imparfais, tierces et sixtes, peut-on bien monter ou descendre ij ou iij notes ou plus ce besoing est.[2]

> (And one should on no account have two fifths or two octaves one after the other, rising or falling with the tenor, for they are perfect intervals: but one may quite well rise or fall two or three notes, or more if need be, by way of the imperfect concords, the thirds and sixths.)

These prohibitions, however, are either unknown to, or ignored by, the vast majority of writers in the period. Such avoidance of the consecutive progressions as they practise would seem to be due to artistic insight rather than to any reverence for regulations. As an example of this avoidance, in the early dawn of our present period, folios 179ᵛ to 182ᵛ of Wolfenbüttel 677 would repay study.

Contrast of unison and harmony would be a commonplace with choirs where the antiphony passed back and forth from the main body singing in plainchant to a semi-chorus of 'organizers' or 'discanters'. Emphasis by an occasional passage of unison is very rare:[3]

[1] Montpellier, fo. 123ᵛ; Rokseth, op. cit. ii, p. 176.
[2] Coussemaker, *Scriptores*, iii, p. 497.
[3] Brit. Mus. Burney 357, fo. 16.

Ex. 212

Et e - is ple - na - ri - æ fons ve - ræ sa - pi - en - ti - æ

per hunc ad - mi - ni - stra-[tur.]

(And to them is the fountain of true and absolute wisdom administered through him.)

This is the last of sixteen two-part phrases which make up the Pentecost sequence 'Amor patris et filii'.

In many primitive examples such as the conducti we have already seen the 'first species' of counterpoint, *punctum contra punctum*: and we have also met a type corresponding to the second and third species, that is to say a moving part over a stationary or slowly moving bass. The next development will be that which was formulated later on as the fourth and fifth species—syncopated and florid counterpoint. Early specimens are found both in conducti and in motets. Here are eight short examples from the former:

Ex. 213[1]

(a)

...e - ley - - - son.

(b) Three cadences from 'Hodiernæ lux diei'

[me]-mo-ri - a [patroci]-ni - a ne - sci - a

---

[1] (a) Wolfenbüttel 677, fo. 177ᵛ; (b) ibid., fo. 185ᵛ; (c) ibid., fo. 67ᵛ; (d) ibid., fo. 70ᵛ; (e) *Worcester Mediæval Harmony*, p. 108. The opening of this piece ('Beata viscera') is printed on p. 351, and the whole is recorded in *The History of Music in Sound*, ii, side 18; (f) ibid., p. 122.

A doubt has been cast[1] upon the suspension in the fifth of these
quotations, but the evidence of the manuscript is indisputably clear,
and the body of supporting evidence justifies the transcription. In
addition to the eight examples quoted above many others could be
adduced, especially from the eleventh fascicle of Wolfenbüttel 677.

Certain practices or methods of treatment, which were to develop
later on by a slow process into a system of key-relationship or modulation, can be discerned in this period: but their employment is so un-
methodical that it is hardly possible to look upon them as more than
instances occurring before their due time. It is a mistake to suppose
that we can find in the thirteenth century any real practice of modulation however rudimentary. As W. H. Frere has said:

The dominant and tonic relationship was very slow to develop. It is remarkable what a long period passed before the harmonic full close was
invented. Ideas of melody, not considerations of harmony, for a long time
dominated the closes.[2]

[1] G. Reese, *Music in the Middle Ages* (New York, 1940), p. 414, n. 123.
[2] 'Key-Relationship in Early Medieval Music', in *Proceedings of the Musical Association*, xxxvii (1910–11), p. 143.

There are many other examples which show that the idea of a full close by means of a 'dominant-tonic' progression was not completely unknown: but their witness is altogether discounted when we find that for each instance of this kind half a dozen can be produced in which although the lowest part moves C G C the second of the three chords is not the 'triad on the dominant' but the 'second inversion of the tonic'. Seeing that the leap of the fourth is comparatively rare in the Gregorian melodies used as tenors, Ex. 196 (p. 363) will be unusually fertile soil for examination, for the tenor twice has the progression C G C, and this occurs in each of the five *taleae*.[1] In these ten passages we find that only four make unmistakable use of the I V I progression, the G in the other six cases being taken as the inverted fifth of the root C or merely doubled at the octave.

ISORHYTHM

The example to which we have just referred shows a tenor melody, 'Manere', repeated five times. The repetition is exact, both in melody and in rhythm. At other times a melodic pattern is repeated in a different rhythm, and we get a result such as that shown in Ex. 215 (p. 392). In yet other cases the rhythmical figure is maintained, but the melody is broken up in a different manner: an early example of this is the following *clausula*:

Ex. 214[2]

[color i]

Do-ce-

---

[1] For an explanation of this term see opposite page.
[2] Wolfenbüttel 677, fo. 45ᵛ.

*P in MS.

Here is a new principle coming to birth—that of the variation of a
melody by setting it out in a new rhythm. This develops by the time
of the *Roman de Fauvel* (*c.* 1310) into what is now known as 'isorhythm'—the laying down of an artificial and often elaborate rhythmical pattern, with the cutting up of a melodic figure to fit it, after
a fashion which seems arbitrary but is not ineffective in the hearing.
The rhythmical pattern in this process is termed *talea*; the melodic,
color. Thus in four repetitions of the *talea* there might be two repetitions of the *color*, or there might be an uneven ratio, as three *taleae*
to two *colores*. In a fragment at Aberystwyth may be seen an example
of this, but with the second *color* overrunning the third *talea* by three
breves:

Ex. 215[1]

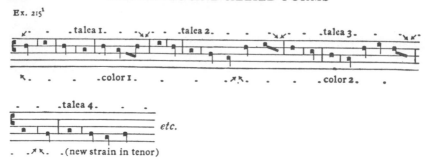

The relation of *talea* to *color* in the *Roman de Fauvel* has been worked out by Harold Gleason,[2] who tells us that the ratios are all simple except for the third motet, which has two *taleae* and a half to one *color*.

In the period covered by volume iii we shall see the isorhythmic principle carried to much greater lengths, with a degree of artificiality which may well be considered as swamping art: but for the present we need only notice the existence of isorhythm in the thirteenth century and list these few instances. Early traces of isorhythmic treatment in the upper parts also are discerned by Anglès in 'Amor vincit omnia / Mariae praeconio / Aptatur', a motet which occurs in several manuscripts of the period.[3]

In order to show the whole of a typical *ars antiqua* motet from the best period we give here 'O Maria virgo davidica / O Maria maris stella / Veritatem'. The grounds for its selection are first, its relative brevity: and second (more important), its apparent reputation in the thirteenth and fourteenth centuries. It is found in as many as ten manuscripts—mostly French, though one is English and one Spanish; and it is referred to in the anonymous contemporary treatise known as the *Discantus positio vulgaris*.[4] The version here given is that of the Montpellier manuscript and is taken from the transcription by Yvonne Rokseth in *Polyphonies du XIII**e siècle*,[5] where nine of the manuscripts are particularized and eight collated: the tenth is the Besançon MS. 716.[6]

---

[1] National Library of Wales, MS. Gwysaney 19.

[2] 'Isorhythmic Tenors in the Three-part Motets of the Roman de Fauvel' in *Bulletin of the American Musicological Society* (New York, 1943), no. 7, p. 8.

[3] Las Huelgas, fo. 116ᵛ (Anglès, *El Còdex musical de Las Huelgas*, i, p. 287; iii, p. 244); Montpellier, H 196, fo. 321ᵛ (Rokseth, *Polyphonies du XIIIᵉ siècle*, iii, p. 149); Bamberg, Ed. IV 6, fo. 36ᵛ (Aubry, *Cent motets du treizième siècle*, ii, p. 127).

[4] Coussemaker, *Scriptores*, i, p. 96.

[5] Vol. ii, p. 123. A conflate version is recorded in *The History of Music in Sound*, ii, side 19.   [6] Anglès, *El Còdex musical de Las Huelgas*, i, p. 263.

Ex. 216

O Ma-ri-a, vir-go Da-vi-di-ca,   Vir-gi-num flos,vi-tæ spes u-ni-ca,

O Ma-ri-a, ma-ris stel-la, Ple-na gra-ti-æ,

Veritatem

Via ve-ni-æ, Lux gra-ti-æ, mater clemen-ti-æ,   So-la jubes in ar-

Ma-ter si-mul et pu-el-la, Vas mun-di-ti-æ,

-ce cœ-li-ca, O-be-di-unt ti-bi mi-li-ti-æ,   So-la se-des in thro-

Tem-plum no-stri red-emp-to-ris, Sol jus-ti-ti-æ,

-no glori-æ, Gra-ti-a ple-na ful-gens de-i-ca.   Stellæ stupent de tu-

Por-ta cœ-li, spes re-o-rum, Thro-nus glo-ri-æ,

(*Triplum*: O Mary, virgin of David's line, flower of virgins, only hope of life, way of pardon, light of grace, mother of mercy, thou above givest thy commands in the heavenly citadel and the soldiery obey thee, thou alone sittest on the throne of glory, shining bright with divine grace. The stars are confounded by thy face, the sun and moon by thy power; all these bright luminaries thou dost surpass at noonday with thy face. With holy prayers appease thy son, thou who art in strange fashion his daughter, that judgement may not go against us but that he may give us the eternal rewards of life.

Motetus: O Mary, star of the sea; full of grace, mother and maiden in one, vessel of chastity, temple of our redeemer, sun of justice, gate of heaven, hope of sinners, throne of glory, consoler of the wretched, fountain of pardon, hear thy servants who beseech thee, mother of grace, that through thee their sins may this day be taken away—thy servants who praise thee in truth with a pure heart.)

ENGLISH MOTETS FOR FOUR VOICES

Reference has already been made (see pp. 353 and 359) to a predilection on the part of English composers for writing in four parts, with its resultant sonority. This is no mere passing phase of the thirteenth century, but is a feature which can be observed without difficulty in later work such as the Old Hall manuscript (vol. iii, chap. iv) and in the compositions of Browne and Ludford (vol. iii, chap. ix). From our present period there survive, in addition to the *quadruplum* quoted in Ex. 202 (p. 375), about twenty-seven of these English four-part motets, though many of these are incomplete portions from the Worcester collection. The opening of 'Ovet mundus'[1] is given as an example of this sonorous type. The characteristically English progressions of $\frac{6}{3}$ chords in bars 2 and 11 will be noticed:

---

[1] Oxford, Bodleian, Hatton 81, fo. 1ᵛ, 44. See also Vol. III, pp. 89–90.

(Let the glad world triumph, taboring in song, when the pure and fruitful child is born of a virgin.)

'Hostis Herodes impie', from the same manuscript, displays points of some interest: we have imitation between the upper parts, and the theme of the hymn-tune is preserved in a recognizable form and used as a basis for melodic treatment in the upper parts, instead of being cut into sections in the tenor according to the usual medieval technique. (A similar treatment is found in a manuscript from Bury St. Edmunds of about 1350[1] applied to the hymn-melody 'Deus tuorum militum'.) There is also a feeling towards a wider expansion and a better proportion of the vocal ranges:

Ex. 218[2]

[1] Oxford, Bodleian, E Mus, 7, pp. x, xi.
[2] Ibid., Hatton 81, fo. 44ᵛ–45. See also Vol. III, p. 90.

*D in the upper part is C in the MS.

(Herod, wicked foe, tyrant gnashing thy teeth.)

The melody of the hymn on which this is based is (in modern notation):

Ex. 219

etc.

HOCKET

Combinations of very short rhythmic figures such as ♩. ♩. ♩. ♪♪, when arranged on alternate beats in different voices, would seem to have originally suggested the technique known as *hoquetus* (spelt in every possible way) or hocket, in which rests and notes are set in alternation, usually ♩. ♪♪ ♩. ♪♪ in one voice against ♪♪ ♩. ♪♪ ♩. in the other. Four short examples are given below. The first is perhaps the earliest specimen on record: the second and third, also very early, have been selected to show how hocketing may be held to have grown naturally out of the rhythmic patterns in customary use, not out of the natural depravity of the singers, as most medieval and many modern writers would have us believe. The form could be more properly described as a form within a form (motet, conductus, *clausula*, &c.) and its complete development belongs rather to the next century. It was more at home in the hall than in the church, where its employment was soundly rebuked at times by bishops and other writers:

Ex. 220[1]

etc.

....et

[1] From 'Alleluia, hic Martinus pauper'. Vatican, Ottob. 3025; facsimile in H. M. Bannister, *Monumenti Vaticani di paleografia musicale latina* (1913), p. 521.

Ex. 221[1]

[1] Wolfenbüttel 677, fo. 48.

[2] Florence, Bibl. Laur. plut. xxix, 1, fo. 42ᵛ; after Anglès, op. cit. iii, pp. 125–6.

[3] *Motetus*, 'Triumphat hodie', Brit. Mus. Add. 24198, fo. 1, and Oxford, New Coll. 362, fo. 85; *contratenor*, Brit. Mus., loc. cit.; *tenor*, New Coll., loc. cit. Recorded in *The History of Music in Sound*, ii, side 19.

in va - cu - is al-mis pre - ci - bus.

The effect of the chanson 'Trop est qe fou', which has been heard repeated several times in the earlier, un-hocketed, part of this last motet, coming through with the emphasis of this staccato technique, is thrilling in performance.

DUPLE TIME

The rhythm of nature is binary, not ternary. It is hardly correct to speak of the later Middle Ages as having 'discovered' or 're-discovered' binary rhythm, for it was there all the time, not only in nature but also in the music. With the improvement in our modern methods of transcribing and printing old music, writing ♪ ♩ instead of ♩ ♩, we are now able to see more clearly how this 'greater rhythm' was in fact present, consciously or unconsciously, in the minds of the early musicians. Thus the following passage:[1]

Ex. 224

Ra - dix ve - ni - æ; ve - na gra - ti - æ;

Latus

Vi - æ dux et por - tus, por - ta pa - tri - æ.

(Root of pardon, fount of grace, guide and harbour, gate of our fatherland.)

[1] Florence, Bibl. Laur. plut. xxix, 1, fo. 285. Printed thus in *Oxford History of Music*, 1st ed., i (1901), p. 367.

has an appearance which is certainly ternary. But if the mode and *ordo* figures are taken into consideration, and if we leave in the background for the moment the ternary subdivision of the unit ◦—above all if we transcribe in crotchets and quavers instead of in semibreves and minims—the passage will then read as follows:

(Continuation of the Tenor line)

This is binary rhythm, if the tenor (always the dominating part in the structure, as the whole of the isorhythmic period shows) is taken as our guide. And this fifth mode is one of those which appears most frequently in the tenors of the motets. Allusion to this aspect of rhythm is infrequent in musicological works. Anglès[1] says it is clear that binary rhythm was known along with ternary in all times and in all countries. An opposite approach is made by such scholars as Apel, who does not seem to allow that duple rhythm existed earlier than the first known definite sample of it in notation. This he finds in the motet 'Je ne puis / Flor de lis / Douce dame' of the Montpellier manuscript.[2]

Wooldridge wrote in 1905 of the 'return to the duple measure' about 1280.[3] His position remains substantially sound after the inter-

---

[1] *La Música a Catalunya fins al segle xiii* (Barcelona, 1935), p. 349. Cf. J. B. Beck, *Le Chansonnier Cangé* (Paris and Philadelphia, 1927), ii, p. 45, and J. Handschin, 'Was brachte die Notre Dame-Schule Neues?', in *Zeitschrift für Musikwissenschaft*, vi (1923–4), p. 547.

[2] *The Notation of Polyphonic Music, 900–1600*, pp. 290–4. For another specimen of duple time from this manuscript see Ex. 207 (p. 384).

[3] *Oxford History of Music*, 2nd ed., i (1929), p. 229 (cf. pp. 59–60).

val of nearly fifty years, despite much subsequent advance in matters of detail. He is speaking, of course, of binary rhythm within the measure or bar, not of the *carrure* (or group of four bars)—the 'greater rhythm' with which we opened this subject. He rests his case upon one of the greatest of the medieval theorists, a man whose work is for the most part clear in its meaning, comprehensive in its scope, and adequately illustrated—Walter de Odington's *De speculatione musicae*.[1] It is to Odington, a monk of Evesham, fifteen miles east of Worcester, that we turn for the first sure evidence, and the earliest notational practice, of duple time. It is apparent that it was no new invention of the late thirteenth century: as he himself says:

Longa autem apud priores organistas duo tantum habuit tempora, sic in metris: sed postea ad perfectionem dicitur, ut sit trium temporum ad similitudinem beatissimae trinitatis quae est summa perfectio, diciturque longa hujusmodi perfecta. Illa vero quae tantum duo habet tempora, dicitur imperfecta.[2]

(Now with the older composers of organa the long had two beats, as in verse: but later on it is associated with the idea of perfection, so that it has three beats —after the likeness of the most blessed Trinity, who is the summit of perfection— and a long of this kind is called perfect. But the long which has only two beats is called imperfect.)

This is pure 'Franconian' doctrine, and the theological part of it is common stock with the theorists of the age: but the interesting part is the first clause about the older composers.

Odington later observes:

Alii autem, in his modis, utuntur longis et brevibus et semibrevibus et pausis secundum quod ego accipio, sed tantum dividunt longam in duas breves, ut duo tempora habentem, et brevem in duas semibreves, et raro in tres. Et pro longa dua spatia occupat pausa, pro brevi unum.[3]

(There are other musicians whose use of the longs, breves, semibreves, and rests in these modes is the same as my own, but they divide the long into two breves only, as if it contains two beats, and the breve into two semibreves, seldom three; also their long rest occupies only two beats, and the breve one.)

Wooldridge comments on this:

Odington makes no comment, but the passage itself is already most suggestive, for it is certainly a curious circumstance that this information should be given by the very author who also in another part of the same

---

[1] Cambridge, Corpus Christi College, 410; printed in Coussemaker, *Scriptores*, i, pp. 181–250. In the British Museum is a transcript of one short section only, taken from another manuscript (Cotton, Tiberius B. ix), which was burnt in the Ashburnham House fire. The transcript was made in 1729 for the use of Dr. Pepusch. Coussemaker also made use of this Pepusch transcript in the preparation of his text.

[2] Coussemaker, op. cit. i, p. 235.

[3] Ibid. i, p. 245.

work, and in treating of the same modes, refers as a matter of historical interest to the original alteration of the old duple long to triple value, as a necessity of the ternary system, which first revealed itself in those modes. May we not therefore, we are encouraged to ask, infer from Odington's statement, just given, that the constant distortion of the dactyl and anapaest in triple measure—always noticeable from the fact that apart from the *cantus mensurabilis* these metres must, of course, have maintained their propriety—had at length become so intolerably wearisome to musicians, that in the rendering of passages confined to the third and fourth modes the temptation to return to the true values proved sometimes irresistible?[1]

Wooldridge's question is perhaps unanswerable, but it is sufficiently provocative to be repeated here.

Acting on the hints of Odington, or on their own intuition, many specialists in early medieval music have been confident that they have discerned pieces where, although the notation admits of a ternary interpretation, the probabilities (both from the aesthetic and the general historical point of view) are heavily in favour of a binary reading. But the absence of definite time-values in the notation earlier than the 'pre-Franconian˙ types (*c.* 1260) makes the search for genuine specimens of duple time quite experimental. Where music can be transcribed either in ternary form by strict modal doctrine, or in binary form, the latter can be defended on the grounds that if the music really was (as its sound suggests) in duple time, this was the only way the *notator* could have written it with the materials at his disposal.[2]

'SUMER IS ICUMEN IN'

The best known of all medieval compositions is 'Sumer is icumen in',[3] from Reading Abbey. It was first described in 1709 by Wanley, and in 1770 was introduced to the musical world by Hawkins, followed by Burney in 1782. Its form, which is described in the manuscript itself as a *rota*, is that of an infinite canon at the unison for four voices which is accompanied by two lower voices who sing a short phrase in interchange. This interchange, and the fact that the part for these two lower voices is termed *pes*—the word used for tenor in the Worcester motets—brings the Reading *rota* into immediate relation with the main body of English medieval music. It has been alleged more than once that it is an instance of revolt against the domination of church musicians and the Gregorian chant; but this is to ignore the fact that

---

[1] *Oxford History of Music*, 2nd ed., i, p. 229.
[2] See further J. Handschin in *Musica Disciplina*, iii (1949), p. 72.
[3] Brit. Mus. Harl. 978, fo. 11ᵛ; facsimile in Wooldridge, *Early English Harmony*, i, pl. 10. Recorded in *The History of Music in Sound*, ii, side 15.

it is also provided with Latin words, 'Perspice Christicola' (thought by some experts to be older than the English), not to mention that the composer was presumably a monk of Reading, or possibly of its cell at Leominster in Herefordshire.[1]

As to its date, Madden gave the first expert palaeographical opinion in 1862. In assigning it to 1240 and not later he was in agreement with an estimate of the mid-thirteenth century made previously by Ritson and Chappell, and subsequently by Maunde Thompson and many other experts. Some interest has been aroused in recent years by an ingenious attempt[2] to assign a later date (about 1310), and to dispute the necessary connexion with Reading. But the arguments used in support of this thesis, and an accompanying suggestion that the original composition was in duple time instead of triple, have not found favour: and they have been completely refuted by Schofield.

'Sumer is icumen in' was (by modern standards) so far in advance of any other medieval music known up to twenty-five years ago that its existence was long regarded as an insoluble mystery. It is still in many ways unique, but as the rediscovery of thirteenth-century music proceeds, other pieces come to light which are worthy to take their place beside the Reading *rota*. Among these are 'Beata viscera'[3] and 'Puellare gremium'[4] from Worcester, with 'Triumphat hodie'[5] and the four-part 'Marionette douce',[6] the original provenance of which is not known. Perhaps the most effective of these later discoveries is 'Alleluia psallat',[7] which has been reconstructed from two Worcester manuscript leaves at Oxford, in the Bodleian Library and Magdalen College respectively—the latter now returned to its original home at Worcester.

The division between sacred and secular is a commonplace with us. But in the Middle Ages this dichotomy was unknown, as is shown by the story of the motets and by such things as the 'sacred' words written for 'Sumer is icumen in'. Such intelligent comments as were uttered in medieval times upon this topic are mostly confined to the texts and seldom deal with the music, hocket alone being a general

[1] B. Schofield, 'The Provenance and Date of "Sumer is icumen in",' in *The Music Review*, ix (1948), p. 81. See also Nino Pirrotta in *Musica Disciplina*, ii (1948), p. 205, and Handschin, loc. cit., p. 69.

[2] Manfred F. Bukofzer, '"Sumer is icumen in"—a Revision'. *University of California Publications in Music* (1944), ii, no. 2, p. 79.

[3] See p. 351.

[4] See p. 384.

[5] See p. 398, n. 3.

[6] Oxford, New College, MS. 362. Recorded in *The History of Music in Sound*, ii, side 20.   [7] Recorded ibid.

exception (see p. 397). 'Alleluia psallat' is a striking example of church music which sounds secular to us, although the lowest voice in the end portion is nothing but a Gregorian Alleluia melody written in long notes. As in the case of many other English motets of the period *c.* 1275–1325, its three vocal lines make continual use of that interchange which is so characteristic of English writing. This fact, coupled with the practical identity of the texts sung by each voice, produces a result which is a very welcome change from the rather confused complexity of text found in the more orthodox French motets of the thirteenth century.

BIBLIOGRAPHY

GENERAL

ADLER, GUIDO: *Handbuch der Musikgeschichte.* 2nd ed. 2 vols. (Berlin, 1930).

APEL, WILLI: *The Notation of Polyphonic Music, 900–1600* (Cambridge, Mass., 1942).

BESSELER, HEINRICH: *Die Musik des Mittelalters und der Renaissance* (Potsdam, 1931).

CHAILLEY, JACQUES: *Histoire musicale du moyen âge* (Paris, 1950).

COUSSEMAKER, C. E. H. DE: *Histoire de l'harmonie au moyen âge* (Paris, 1852).

—— *Scriptorum de musica medii aevi nova series.* 4 vols. (Paris, 1864–76).

DAVISON, ARCHIBALD T., and APEL, WILLI: *Historical Anthology of Music.* Vol. I (Cambridge, Mass., 1946).

GERBERT, MARTIN: *Scriptores ecclesiastici de musica sacra potissimum.* 3 vols. (St. Blaise, 1784).

GÉROLD, THÉODORE: *Histoire de la musique des origines à la fin du XIVᵉ siècle* (Paris, 1936).

—— *La Musique au moyen âge* (Paris, 1932).

KINSKY, GEORG: *Geschichte der Musik in Bildern* (Leipzig, 1929).

REESE, GUSTAVE: *Music in the Middle Ages* (New York, 1940).

RIEMANN, HUGO: *Geschichte der Musiktheorie im IX–XIX Jahrhundert* (Leipzig, 1921).

SCHERING, ARNOLD: *Geschichte der Musik in Beispielen* (Leipzig, 1931).

SCHNEIDER, MARIUS: *Geschichte der Mehrstimmigkeit.* 2 vols. (Berlin, 1934–5).

VIVELL, DOM CÉLESTIN: *Initia Tractatuum Musices* (Graz, 1912).

WOLF, JOHANNES: *Handbuch der Notationskunde.* 2 vols. (Leipzig, 1913–19).

—— *Musikalische Schrifttafeln* (Bückeburg and Leipzig, 1923).

CHAPTER I

EARLY CHRISTIAN MUSIC

(i) *History and Liturgy*

BAUMSTARK, A.: *Liturgie comparée* (Amay à Chèvretogne, 1939).

BAYNES, N. H.: *The Cambridge Ancient History.* Vol. XII (Cambridge, 1939).

BRIGHTMAN, F. E.: *Liturgies Eastern and Western.* Vol. I (Oxford, 1896).

CAYRÉ, F., and HOWITT, H.: *Manuel de Patrologie.* Vol. I (Paris, 1936).

COOK, S. A., ADCOCK, F. A., and CHARLESWORTH, M. P.: *The Cambridge Ancient History.* Vols. X and XI (Cambridge, 1934 and 1936).

DUCHESNE, L. M. O.: *Christian Worship: its Origin and Evolution.* Translated by M. L. McClure. 5th ed. (London, 1931).

FLICHE, A., and MARTIN, V.: *Histoire de l'Église.* Vols. I–IV (Paris, 1946–8).

GLOTZ, G. (ed. by): *Histoire du moyen âge.* Vols. I and III. 2nd ed. (Paris, 1944). Vol. IX (Paris, 1945).

KIDD, B. J.: *A History of the Church to A.D. 461* (Oxford, 1922).

(ii) *Music and Hymnography*

BAUMSTARK, A.: *Festbrevier und Kirchenjahr der syrischen Jacobiten* (Paderborn, 1910).

—— *Geschichte der syrischen Literatur* (Bonn, 1922).

EMEREAU, C.: *Saint Éphrem le Syrien* (Paris, 1918).

GASTOUÉ, A.: *Les Origines du chant romain* (Paris, 1907).

GÉROLD, TH.: *Les Pères de l'Église et la musique* (Paris, 1931).

HÖEG, C.: *La Notation ekphonétique. Monumenta Musicae Byzantinae, Subsidia*, i. 2 (Copenhagen, 1935).

JEANNIN, J. C.: *Mélodies liturgiques syriennes et chaldéennes*. Vol. I (Paris, 1927). Vol. II, in collaboration with J. Puyade and A. Chibas-Lassalle (Paris, 1928).

QUASTEN, J.: *Musik und Gesang in den Kulten der heidnischen Antike und christlichen Frühzeit* (Münster, 1930).

WELLESZ, E.: *Eastern Elements in Western Chant: Studies in the Early History of Ecclesiastical Music. Monumenta Musicae Byzantinae, Subsidia*, ii. 1 (American Series: Boston, 1947).

WRIGHT, W.: *A Short History of Syriac Literature* (London, 1894).

CHAPTER II
(a) MUSIC OF THE EASTERN CHURCHES

(i) *Sources*

Liturgical Books:

Μηναῖα τοῦ ὅλου ἐνιαυτοῦ. 6 vols. (Rome, 1888–1902).
Πεντηκοστάριον χαρμόσυνον (Rome, 1883).
Τριῴδιον κατανυκτικόν (Rome, 1879).

Facsimiles:

Hirmologium Athoum. Codex Monasterii Hiberorum 470. Monumenta Musicae Byzantinae, ii (Copenhagen, 1938).

Hirmologium e Codice Cryptensi E.γ.II. Musicae Byzantinae Monumenta Cryptensia, i (Rome, 1950).

Sticherarium. Codex Vindobonensis Theol. Graec. 181. Monumenta Musicae Byzantinae, i (Copenhagen, 1935).

(ii) *History and Liturgy*

BAYNES, N. H.: *The Byzantine Empire*. 3rd ed. (London, 1925).

BURY, J. B.: *A History of the Eastern Roman Empire* A.D. 802–867 (London, 1912).

DIEHL, C.: *Histoire de l'empire byzantin* (Paris, 1919).

FORTESCUE, A.: *The Orthodox Church* (London, 1911).

GOAR, J.: Εὐχολόγιον *sive Rituale Graecorum* (Paris, 1647; 2nd ed. Venice, 1730).

KRUMBACHER, K.: *Geschichte der byzantinischen Literatur*. 2nd ed. (Munich, 1897).

PARGOIRE, J.: *L'Église byzantine de 527 à 847* (Paris, 1905).

TREMPELA, P. N.: Αἱ τρεῖς Λιτουργίαι κατὰ τοὺς ἐν Ἀθήναις κώδικας (Athens, 1935).

(iii) *Music and Hymnography*

AYOUTANTI, A., STÖHR, M., and HÖEG, C.: *The Hymns of the Hirmologium*, Part I. *Monumenta Musicae Byzantinae, Transcripta*, vi (Copenhagen, 1952).

BOUVY, E.: *Poètes et mélodies* (Nîmes, 1886).

CANTARELLA, R.: *Poeti bizantini*. 2 vols. (Milan, 1948).

FLEISCHER, O.: *Die spätgriechische Notenschrift. Neumenstudien*, iii (Berlin, 1904).

GASTOUÉ, A.: *Introduction à la paléographie musicale byzantine. Catalogue des manuscrits de musique byzantine de la Bibliothèque Nationale de Paris et des bibliothèques publiques de France* (Paris, 1907).

HÖEG, C.: *La Notation ekphonétique. Monumenta Musicae Byzantinae, Subsidia*, i. 2 (Copenhagen, 1935).

KIRCHHOFF, K.: *Die Ostkirche betet*. 4 vols. (Hellerau, 1934–7).
—— *Osterjubel der Ostkirche*. 2 vols. (Münster, 1940).
PITRA, J.-B.: *Analecta sacra*. Vol. I (Paris, 1876).
—— *L'Hymnographie de l'Église grecque* (Rome, 1867).
TARDO, L.: *L'antica melurgia bizantina* (Grottaferrata, 1938).
THIBAUT, J.-B.: *Monuments de la notation ekphonétique et hagiopolite de l'Église grecque* (St. Petersburg, 1913).
—— *Origine byzantine de la notation neumatique de l'Église latine* (Paris, 1907).
TILLYARD, H. J. W.: 'Byzantine Music about A.D. 1100'. *Musical Quarterly*, xxxix (1953).
—— *Byzantine Music and Hymnography* (London, 1923).
—— *Handbook of the Middle Byzantine Musical Notation. Monumenta Musicae Byzantinae, Subsidia*, i. 1 (Copenhagen, 1935).
—— *The Hymns of the Octoechus*, Parts I and II. *Monumenta Musicae Byzantinae, Transcripta*, iii and v (Copenhagen, 1940 and 1949).
—— *The Hymns of the Sticherarium for November. Monumenta Musicae Byzantinae, Transcripta*, ii (Copenhagen, 1938).
WELLESZ, E.: *Aufgaben und Probleme auf dem Gebiet der byzantinischen und orientalischen Musikforschung* (Münster, 1923).
—— 'Early Byzantine Neumes'. *Musical Quarterly*, xxxviii (1952).
—— *Eastern Elements in Western Chant* (Boston, 1947).
—— *A History of Byzantine Music and Hymnography* (Oxford, 1949).
—— *Die Hymnen des Sticherarium für September. Monumenta Musicae Byzantinae, Transcripta*, i (Copenhagen, 1936).
—— *Trésor de musique byzantine* (Paris, 1934).

(*b*) RUSSIAN CHANT
(Works marked † are in Russian)

BUKETOV, I.: 'Russian Chant'. In G. Reese, *Music in the Middle Ages* (New York, 1940), pp. 95–104.
†FINDEISEN, N.: *Outlines of the History of Russian Music* (Moscow and Leningrad, 1929).
†GARDNER, I.: *A Forgotten Treasure* (On the Singing of the Prosomoia) (Warsaw, Synodal Typography, 1930).
KOSCHMIEDER, E.: *Die ältesten Novgoroder Hirmologien-Fragmente*, I Abhandlungen der bayerischen Akademie der Wissenschaften (Munich, 1952).
†METALLOV, V.: *Russian Semiography* (Moscow, 1912).
†NEVOSTRUYEV, K.: *Description of the Slavic Manuscripts of the Moscow Synodal Library* (Moscow, 1869).
PALIKAROVA VERDEIL, R.: *La musique byzantine chez les Bulgares et les Russes. Monumenta Musicae Byzantinae, Subsidia*, iii (Copenhagen, 1953).
PANOV, P.: *Die alt-slavische Volks- und Kirchenmusik* (Potsdam, 1932).
†PREOBRAZHENSKY, A.: 'On the Similarity of the Russian Musical Notations with the Greek in the Musical Manuscripts of the 11th–12th centuries'. *Russian Musical Gazette* (St. Petersburg, 1909), nos. 8–10.
RIESEMANN, O. VON: *Die Notationen des altrussischen Kirchengesanges*. Publ. d. Intern. Musikgesellschaft, Beihefte (Leipzig, 1909).
†SMOLENSKY, S.: *The Alphabet of Mesenetz* (Kazan, 1888).
—— 'Catalogue of the Collection of Russian Manuscripts in the Moscow Synodal School of Church Singing'. *Russian Musical Gazette* (St. Petersburg, 1899).
—— *On the Old Russian Musical Notations* (St. Petersburg, 1901).

SWAN, A. J.: 'The Znamenny Chant of the Russian Church'. *Musical Quarterly*, xxvi (New York, 1940).

—— 'Russian Church Singing'. In *The Orthodox Way* (Holy Trinity Monastery, Jordanville, N.Y., 1952).

CHAPTER III
LATIN CHANT BEFORE ST. GREGORY

(i) *Examples of Music*

Antifonario visigótico mozárabe de la catedral de León. Monumenta Hispaniae Sacra, v (Madrid, Barcelona, 1953).

Variae Preces, ed. Dom J. Pothier (Solesmes, 1901).

(ii) *Books and Articles*

BORELLA, P., and CATTANEO, E.: *Archivio Ambrosiano*. 3 vols. (Milan, 1949–50).

BROU, DOM LOUIS: Studies in Mozarabic Liturgy and Chant. *Revue Ephemerides Liturgicae*, lxi (1947), pp. 13, 309: *Hispania Sacra*, i (1948), p. 21; iv (1951), p. 21; v (1952), pp. 35, 341: *Anuario Musical*, v (1950), p. 3; vi (1951), p. 3: *Sacris Erudiri*, i (1948), p. 165; iv (1952), p. 226.

DUCHESNE, L. M. O.: *Christian Worship: its Origin and Evolution*. Translated by M. L. McClure. 5th ed. (London, 1931).

EISENHOFER, LUDWIG: *Handbuch der katholischen Liturgik*. Vols. I and II (Freiburg i. Br., 1932).

GARBAGNATI, EMILIO: *Gli inni del breviario ambrosiano* (Milan, 1897).

GASTOUÉ, AMÉDÉE: 'Le Chant gallican'. *Revue du chant grégorien*, xli–xliii (1937–9).

—— *Histoire du chant liturgique à Paris* (Paris, 1904).

—— *Ordinaire des saluts* (Paris, 1910).

HUGLO, DOM MICHEL: 'Source hagiopolite d'une antienne hispanique pour le dimanche des Rameaux'. *Hispania Sacra*, v (1952), p. 367.

LECLERQ, DOM H.: *Dictionnaire d'archéologie chrétienne et de liturgie*, vi (1924), cols. 475–593.

RIGHETTI, M.: *Manuale di storia liturgica*. Vol. I (Milan and Geneva, 1945).

THIBAUT, J.-B.: *L'Ancienne Liturgie gallicane, son origine et sa formation en Provence aux Vᵉ et VIᵉ siècles* (Paris, 1929).

CHAPTER IV
GREGORIAN CHANT

(i) *Sources*

ANGLÈS, H.: *La Música a Catalunya fins al segle XIII* (Barcelona, 1935).

Antiphonaire de Saint Grégoire. Facsimilé du manuscrit 358 de Saint-Gall, ed. L. Lambillotte (Brussels, 1851).

Antiphonale Missarum Sextuplex, ed. Dom R.-J. Hesbert (Brussels, 1935).

Antiphonale Sarisburiense, ed. W. H. Frere (London, 1901–26).

Le Graduel de l'église cathédrale de Rouen au XIIIᵉ siècle, ed. B. M. Loriquet (Rouen, 1907).

Das Graduale der St. Thomaskirche zu Leipzig als Zeuge deutscher Choralüber-lieferung, ed. P. Wagner. 2 vols. (Leipzig, 1930–2).

Graduale Sarisburiense, ed. W. H. Frere (London, 1894).

Manuscrits latins du Vᵉ au XIIIᵉ siècle conservés à la Bibliothèque impériale de Saint-Pétersbourg. 2 vols. (St. Petersburg, 1910).

Monumenti Vaticani di paleografia musicale latina, ed. H. M. Bannister. 2 vols. (Leipzig, 1913).

Paléographie musicale, cd. Dom A. Mocquereau. Series I: 15 vols. Series II: 2 vols. (Tournai, 1889 onwards—in progress).
The Winchester Troper, ed. W. H. Frere. Henry Bradshaw Society, viii (London, 1894).

(ii) *Books and Articles*

DAVID, DOM LUCIEN: *Analyses grégoriennes pratiques* (Grenoble, 1922).
DECHEVRENS, ANTOINE: *Études de science musicale.* 3 vols. (1898).
FERRETTI, DOM PAOLO: *Esthétique grégorienne* (Paris, 1938).
—— 'Étude sur la notation aquitaine'. In *Paléographie musicale*, xiii.
—— *Il cursus metrico* (Rome, 1912).
FLEISCHER, OTTO: *Neumenstudien.* 3 vols. (Leipzig, 1895–1904).
FRERE, W. H.: 'Historical Introduction'. *Hymns Ancient and Modern* (London, 1909).
GASTOUÉ, AMÉDÉE: *L'Antiphonaire grégorien* (Paris, 1907).
—— *Le Graduel et l'antiphonaire* (Paris, 1913).
—— *Les Origines du chant romain* (Paris, 1907).
GATARD, DOM AUGUSTIN: *Plainchant* (London, 1921).
GEVAERT, F. A.: *La Mélopée antique dans le chant de l'Église latine* (Ghent, 1895).
—— *Les Origines du chant liturgique de l'Église latine* (Ghent, 1890).
HOUDARD, G.: *La Science musicale traditionnelle* (St. Germain-en-Laye, 1912).
—— *Le Rhythme du chant dit grégorien* (Paris, 1898–9).
JACOBSTHAL, GUSTAV: *Die chromatische Alteration im liturgischen Gesang der abendländischen Kirche* (Berlin, 1897).
JAMMERS, EWALD: *Der gregorianische Rhythmus. Antiphonale Studien* (Strasbourg, 1937).
JEANNIN, DOM JULES: *Accent bref ou accent long en chant grégorien* (Paris, 1929).
—— *Études sur le rythme grégorien* (Lyons, 1925).
—— *Rapport de l'accent latin et du rythme musical au moyen âge* (Paris, 1931).
—— *Rythme grégorien: Réponse à Dom Mocquereau* (Lyons, 1927).
JOHNER, DOMINIC: *Wort und Ton im Choral* (Leipzig, 1940).
MOCQUEREAU, DOM ANDRÉ: *Le Nombre musical grégorien.* 2 vols. (Tournai, 1908, 1927).
—— *Monographies grégoriennes*, nos. i–vii (Tournai, 1910–26).
NICHOLSON, E. W. B.: *Introduction to the Study of the Oldest Latin Musical MSS. in the Bodleian* (London, 1913).
POTHIER, DOM JOSEPH: *Les Mélodies grégoriennes* (Tournai, 1880).
ROBERTSON, ALEC: *The Interpretation of Plainchant* (London, 1937).
SCHMIDT, J. G.: *Haupttexte der gregorianischen Autoren betreffs Rhythmus* (Düsseldorf, 1921).
STUIBER, A.: *Libelli Sacramentorum Romani* (Bonn, 1950).
SUÑOL, DOM GREGORY: *Introduction à la paléographie musicale grégorienne* (Paris, 1935).
URSPRUNG, OTTO: *Die katholische Kirchenmusik* (Potsdam, 1931).
VAN DIJK, S. J. P.: 'Medieval Terminology and Methods of Psalm Singing'. *Musica Disciplina*, vi (1952).
VAN DOREN, DOM R.: *Étude sur l'influence musicale de l'Abbaye de Saint-Gall, VIIIe au XIe siècle* (Brussels, 1925).
VAN WAESBERGHE, J. SMITS: 'The Musical Notation of Guido of Arezzo'. *Musica Disciplina*, v (1951).
—— *School en Muziek in de Middeleeuwen* (Amsterdam, 1949).
WAGNER, PETER: *Einführung in die gregorianischen Melodien.* 3 vols. Vol. I: 3rd ed., Vol. II: 2nd ed. (Leipzig, 1911–21).

CHAPTER V
TROPE, SEQUENCE, AND CONDUCTUS

(i) *Sources*

Analecta hymnica medii aevi, ed. G. M. Dreves, with the collaboration of C. Blume and H. M. Bannister. 55 vols. (Leipzig, 1886–1922). The following volumes consist of sequence texts: VII–X, XXXIV, XXXVII, XXXIX–XL, XLII, XLIV, LIII–LV. Vols. XLVII (1905) and XLIX (1906) contain *Tropi Graduales*, i.e. tropes for the Mass.

Anglo-French Sequelae, ed. from the papers of H. M. Bannister by Dom Anselm Hughes. Plainsong and Mediaeval Music Society (London, 1934).

DRINKWELDER, O.: *Ein deutsches Sequentiar aus dem Ende des 12. Jahrhunderts. Veröffentlichungen der Gregorianischen Akademie zu Freiburg in der Schweiz*, viii (1914).

PRÉVOST, H.: *Recueil des séquences d'Adam le Breton* (Ligugé, 1901).

Le Prosaire de la Sainte-Chapelle. Monumenta Musicae Sacrae, ed. Dom R.-J. Hesbert, i (Mâcon, 1952).

Les Proses d'Adam de Saint Victor, ed. E. Misset and P. Aubry (Paris, 1900).

Prosolarium Ecclesiae Aniciensis, ed. U. Chevalier. *Bibliothèque liturgique*, v (1894), pp. 1–63.

Tropaire-prosier de Montauriol, ed. C. Daux. *Bibliothèque liturgique*, ix (1901).

The Winchester Troper, ed. W. H. Frere. Henry Bradshaw Society, viii (London, 1894).

(ii) *Books and Articles*

ANDRIEU, MICHEL, *Les Ordines Romani du haut Moyen Âge*. 3 vols. (Louvain, 1931, 1948, 1951).

BANNISTER, H. M.: 'The Earliest French Troper and its Date'. *Journal of Theological Studies*, ii (1901).

—— 'Un Tropaire-prosier de Moissac'. *Revue d'histoire et de littérature religieuse*, viii (1903).

BARTSCH, K.: *Die lateinischen Sequenzen des Mittelalters* (Rostock, 1868).

BLUME, C.: 'Vom Alleluia zur Sequenz'. *Kirchenmusikalisches Jahrbuch*, xxiv (1911).

CLARK, J. M.: *The Abbey of St. Gall* (Cambridge, 1926).

ELLINWOOD, L.: 'The Conductus'. *Musical Quarterly*, xxvii (1941).

GAUTIER, L.: *Histoire de la poésie liturgique au moyen âge. Les Tropes*. Vol. I (Paris, 1886).

GERBERT, M.: *De Cantu et Musica Sacra*. 2 vols. (St. Blaise, 1774).

HANDSCHIN, J.: 'Conductus'. In *Die Musik in Geschichte und Gegenwart*, ii (Kassel, 1953).

—— 'Conductus-Spicilegien'. *Archiv für Musikwissenschaft*, ix (1952).

—— 'Gesungene Apologetik'. *Bibliotheca Ephemerides Liturgicae*, xxiii (1949).

—— 'Notizen über die Notre Dame-Conductus'. In *Bericht über den Internationalen Musikwissenschaftlichen Kongress der Deutschen Musikgesellschaft* (Leipzig, 1926).

—— 'St. Gallen in der mittelalterlichen Musikgeschichte'. *Schweizerische Musikzeitung*, lxxxv (1945).

—— 'The Two Winchester Tropers'. *Journal of Theological Studies*, xxxvii (1936).

—— 'Über einige Sequenz-Zitate'. *Acta Musicologica*, xv (1943).

—— 'Über Estampie und Sequenz'. *Zeitschrift für Musikwissenschaft*, xii (1929–30) and xiii (1930–1).

—— 'Zur Frage der melodischen Paraphrasierung im Mittelalter'. *Zeitschrift für Musikwissenschaft*, x (1927–8).

MOBERG, C. A.: *Über die schwedischen Sequenzen: I. Darstellung, II. 69 Sequenzen-weisen. Veröffentlichungen der Gregorianischen Akademie zu Freiburg in der Schweiz,* xiii (1927).

MULLER, H. F.: 'Prehistory of the Medieval Drama. The Antecedents of the Tropes and the Conditions of their Appearance'. *Zeitschrift für romanische Philologie,* xliv (1928).

REICHERT, G.: 'Strukturprobleme der älteren Sequenz'. *Deutsche Vierteljahrs-schrift für Literaturwiss. u. Geistesgeschichte,* xxiii (Stuttgart, 1949).

REINERS, A.: *Die Tropen-, Prosen- und Präfationsgesänge des feierlichen Hochamts* (Luxembourg, 1884–7).

SCHUBIGER, A.: *Die Sängerschule St. Gallens* (1858).

SESINI, UGO: *Poesia e Musica nella latinità Christiana* (Turin, 1949).

SPANKE, H.: 'Aus der Vorgeschichte und der Frühgeschichte der Sequenz'. *Zeitschrift für deutsches Altertum,* lxxi (1934).

—— *Deutsche und französische Dichtung des Mittelalters* (Stuttgart, 1943).

—— 'Rhythmen- und Sequenzenstudien'. *Studi medievali,* N.S. iv (1931).

—— 'Sequenz und Lai'. *Studi medievali,* N.S. xi (1938).

—— 'Die Sequenzen Adams von St. Victor'. *Studi medievali,* N.S. xiv (1941).

—— 'Über das Fortleben der Sequenzform in den romanischen Sprachen'. *Zeitschrift für romanische Philologie,* li (1931).

—— 'Zur lateinischen nichtliturgischen Sequenz'. *Speculum,* vii (1932).

STEINEN, W. VON DEN: 'Die Anfänge der Sequenzendichtung'. *Zeitschrift für Schweizerische Kirchengeschichte,* xl, xli (1946, 1947).

—— *Notker der Dichter und seine geistige Welt* (Berne, 1948).

VAN DOREN, DOM R.: *Étude sur l'influence musicale de l'Abbaye de Saint-Gall, VIIIᵉ au XIᵉ siècle* (Brussels, 1925).

WAGNER, P.: *Einführung in die gregorianischen Melodien.* Vol. I: 3rd ed. (Leipzig, 1911). Vol. III (Leipzig, 1921).

WELLESZ, E.: *Eastern Elements in Western Chant: Studies in the Early History of Ecclesiastical Music. Monumenta Musicae Byzantinae, Subsidia,* ii. 1 (American Series: Boston, 1947).

WERNER, J.: *Notkers Sequenzen* (Aarau, 1901).

WINTERFELD, P. VON: 'Rhythmen- und Sequenzstudien: I. Die lateinische Eulalien-sequenz. VI. Die ursprüngliche Form der Sequenz Pangamus creatori. VII. Welche Sequenzen hat Notker verfaßt?' *Zeitschrift für deutsches Altertum,* xlv (1901) and xlvii (1904).

WOLF, F.: *Über die Lais, Sequenzen und Leiche* (Heidelberg, 1841).

CHAPTER VI

LITURGICAL DRAMA

ADAMS, J. QUINCY: *Chief Pre-Shakespearean Dramas* (Boston, 1924).

BARTHOLOMAEIS, V. DE: *Le origini della poesia drammatica italiana* (Bologna, 1924).

CHAMBERS, E. K.: *The Medieval Stage.* 2 vols. (Oxford, 1903).

CLARK, J. M.: *The Abbey of St. Gall* (Cambridge, 1926).

COUSSEMAKER, C. E. H. DE: *Drames liturgiques du moyen âge* (Paris, 1861).

DU MÉRIL, E.: *Origines latines du théâtre moderne* (Paris, 1849).

GASTOUÉ, AMÉDÉE: *La Musique de l'Église* (Lyons, 1911).

GAUTIER, LÉON: *Histoire de la poésie liturgique au moyen âge. Les Tropes* (Paris, 1886).

LANGE, C.: *Die lateinischen Osterfeiern* (Munich, 1887).

LIPPHARDT, W.: *Die Weisen der lateinischen Osterspiele des 12. und 13. Jahrhunderts* (Kassel, 1948).

LUZARCHE, V.: *Office de Pâques ou de la Résurrection* (Tours, 1856).

PFEIFFER, H.: 'Klosterneuburger Osterfeier und Osterspiel'. *Jahrbuch des Stiftes Klosterneuburg*, i (1908).

SCHONEMANN, O.: *Der Sünderfall und Marienklage* (Hanover, 1855).

SCHULER, E. A.: *Die Musik der Osterfeiern Osterspiele und Passionen des Mittelalters* (Kassel, 1951).

SEPET, M.: *Le Drame chrétien au moyen âge* (Paris, 1878).

SMOLDON, W. L.: 'The Easter Sepulchre Music-Drama'. *Music and Letters*, xxvii (1946).

YOUNG, KARL: *The Drama of the Medieval Church*. 2 vols. (Oxford, 1933).

CHAPTER VII

MEDIEVAL SONG

(i) *Sources*

(Works marked * are facsimile editions, with or without transcription and commentary)

ANGLÈS, HIGINI: *La Música de las Cantigas de Santa Maria del Rey Alfonso el Sabio*. Vol. II (transcriptions). (Barcelona, 1942.)

*AUBRY, PIERRE: *Le Chansonnier de l'Arsenal* (Paris, 1909). Incomplete.

*—— *Le Roman de Fauvel* (Paris, 1907).

*BECK, JEAN: *Le Chansonnier Cangé*. 2 vols. (Paris and Philadelphia, 1927).

*BECK, JEAN and LOUISE: *Le Manuscrit du Roi*. 2 vols. (London and Philadelphia, 1938).

BÉDIER, JOSEPH, and AUBRY, PIERRE: *Les Chansons de croisade* (Paris, 1909).

BÉDIER, JOSEPH, and BECK, JEAN: *Les Chansons de Colin Muset* (Paris, 1912).

*BOURDILLON, F. W.: *Cest daucasī & de nicolete* (Oxford, 1896).

*BREUL, KARL: *The Cambridge Songs* (Cambridge, 1915).

GENNRICH, FRIEDRICH: *Rondeaux, Virelais und Balladen*. 2 vols. (Dresden, 1921, and Göttingen, 1927).

HOLZ, G., SARAN, FRANZ, and BERNOULLI, EDUARD: *Die Jenaer Liederhandschrift*. 2 vols. (Leipzig, 1901).

*JEANROY, ALFRED: *Le Chansonnier d'Arras* (Paris, 1925).

JEANROY, ALFRED, BRANDIN, LOUIS, and AUBRY, PIERRE: *Lais et descorts français du XIIIᵉ siècle* (Paris, 1901).

LANGLOIS, ERNEST: *Le Jeu de Robin et de Marion* (Paris, 1896).

*LIUZZI, FERNANDO: *La lauda e i primordi della melodia italiana*. 2 vols. (Rome, 1935).

*MEYER, PAUL, and RAYNAUD, GASTON: *Le Chansonnier français de Saint-Germain-des-Prés* (Paris, 1892).

*MÜLLER, K. K.: *Die Jenaer Liederhandschrift* (Jena, 1896).

*RIETSCH, HEINRICH: *Gesänge von Frauenlob, Reinmar von Zweter und Alexander*. *Denkmäler der Tonkunst in Österreich*, xx. 2 (Vienna, 1913).

RUNGE, PAUL: *Die Sangweisen der Colmarer Handschrift und die Liederhandschrift Donaueschingen* (Leipzig, 1896).

*SCHMIEDER, WOLFGANG, and WIESSNER, EDMUND: *Lieder von Neidhart (von Reuental)*. *Denkmäler der Tonkunst in Österreich*, xxxvii. 1 (Vienna, 1930).

*SESINI, UGO: *La melodie trobadoriche nel canzoniere provenzale della Biblioteca Ambrosiana R.71 Sup.* (Turin, 1942).

*VINDEL, PEDRO: *La siete canciones de amor* (Madrid, 1915).

(ii) *Books and Articles*

APPEL, CARL: *Bernart von Ventadorn* (Halle, 1915).

—— *Die Singweisen Bernarts von Ventadorn* (Halle, 1934).

AUBRY, PIERRE: *Iter Hispanicum* (Paris, 1908).

—— *Trouvères et troubadours* (Paris, 1909).

BECK, JEAN: *Die Melodien der Troubadours* (Strasbourg, 1908).

—— *La Musique des troubadours* (Paris, 1910).

CHAYTOR, HENRY JOHN: *The Troubadours* (Cambridge, 1912).

—— *The Troubadours and England* (Cambridge, 1923).

COLLET, HENRI, and VILLALBA, P.: 'Contribution à l'étude des "Cantigas" d'Alphonse le Savant'. *Bulletin Hispanique*, xiii (1911).

GENNRICH, FRIEDRICH: *Die altfranzösische Rotrouenge* (Halle, 1925).

—— *Grundriß einer Formenlehre des mittelalterlichen Liedes* (Halle, 1932).

—— 'Internationale mittelalterliche Melodien'. *Zeitschrift für Musikwissenschaft*, xi (1928–9).

—— 'Mittelalterliche Lieder mit textloser Melodie'. *Archiv für Musikwissenschaft*, ix (1952).

—— *Der musikalische Vortrag der altfranzösischen Chansons de Geste* (Halle, 1923).

—— 'Sieben Melodien zu mittelhochdeutschen Minneliedern'. *Zeitschrift für Musikwissenschaft*, vii (1924–5).

—— 'Trouvèrelieder und Motettenrepertoire'. *Zeitschrift für Musikwissenschaft*, ix (1926–7).

HANDSCHIN, JACQUES: 'Über Estampie und Sequenz'. *Zeitschrift für Musikwissenschaft*, xii (1929–30).

HILKA, ALFONS, and SCHUMANN, OTTO: *Carmina Burana*. 3 vols. (Heidelberg, 1930–41). Incomplete.

HUSMANN, HEINRICH: 'Das Prinzip der Silbenzählung im Lied des zentralen Mittelalters'. *Die Musikforschung*, vi (1953).

—— 'Die musikalische Behandlung der Versarten im Troubadourgesang der Notre-Dame-Zeit'. *Acta Musicologica*, xxv (1953).

—— 'Zur Grundlegung der musikalischen Rhythmik des mittellateinischen Liedes'. *Archiv für Musikwissenschaft*, ix (1952).

LIPPHARDT, WALTER: 'Unbekannte Weisen zu den Carmina Burana'. *Archiv für Musikwissenschaft*, xii (1855).

MOLITOR, RAPHAEL: 'Die Lieder des Münsterischen Fragmentes'. *Sammelbände der internationalen Musikgesellschaft*, xii (1911–12).

MÜLLER, HERMANN: 'Zum Texte der Musiklehre des Joannes de Grocheo'. *Sammelbände der internationalen Musikgesellschaft*, iv (1902–3).

POPE, ISABEL: 'The Medieval Latin Background of the Thirteenth-Century Galician Lyric'. *Speculum*, ix (1934).

ROHLOFF, ERNST: *Media Latinitas Musica II. Der Musiktraktat des Johannes de Grocheo* (Leipzig, 1943).

SCHNEIDER, MARIUS: 'A propósito del influjo árabe'. *Anuario Musical*, i (Barcelona, 1946).

SPANKE, HANS: *Eine altfranzösische Liedersammlung* (Halle, 1925).

—— 'Beziehungen zwischen romanischer und mittellateinischer Lyrik'. *Abhandlungen der Gesellschaft der Wissenschaft zu Göttingen: Philologisch-historische Klasse*, iii. 18 (Berlin, 1936).

—— 'Der Codex Buranus als Liederbuch'. *Zeitschrift für Musikwissenschaft*, xiii (1930–1).

—— 'Marcabrustudien'. *Abhandlungen der Gesellschaft der Wissenschaft zu Göttingen: Philologisch-historische Klasse*, iii. 24 (Göttingen, 1940).

TRAUBE, LUDWIG: 'O Roma nobilis'. *Abhandlungen der philosophisch-philologischen Classe der königlich-Bayerischen Akademie der Wissenschaften*, xix. 2 (Munich, 1891).

TREND, J. B.: 'The First English Songs'. *Music and Letters*, ix (1928).

—— *The Music of Spanish History to 1600* (London, 1926).

URSPRUNG, OTTO: 'Um die Frage nach dem arabischen bzw. maurischen Einfluß und die abendländische Musik des Mittelalters'. *Zeitschrift für Musikwissenschaft*, xvi (1933–4).

WAGNER, PETER: 'O Roma nobilis'. *Kirchenmusikalisches Jahrbuch*, xxii (1909).

WOLF, JOHANNES: 'Die Musiklehre des Johannes de Grocheo'. *Sammelbände der internationalen Musikgesellschaft*, i (1899–1900).

WUSTMANN, RUDOLF: 'Die Hofweise Walters von der Vogelweide'. In *Liliencron-Festschrift* (Leipzig, 1910).

CHAPTER VIII

THE BIRTH OF POLYPHONY

(i) *Sources*

Monumenti vaticani di paleografia musicale latina, ed. H. M. Bannister. 2 vols. (Leipzig, 1913).

Paléographie musicale, ed. Dom Mocquereau. Vols. I and IV (Tournai, 1889, 1893–6).

The Winchester Troper, ed. W. H. Frere. Henry Bradshaw Society, viii (London, 1894).

WOOLDRIDGE, H. E.: *Early English Harmony*. Vol. I (London, 1897).

(ii) *Books and Articles*

AMELLI, A. M.: *Micrologus ad praestantiores codices mss. exactus* (Rome, 1904).

APEL, WILLI: 'The Early History of the Organ'. *Speculum*, xxiii (1948).

—— 'The Importance of Notation in Solving Problems of Early Music'. *Papers of the American Musicological Society* (New York, 1938).

BANNISTER, H. M.: 'Un Fragment inédit de "Discantus"'. *Revue grégorienne*, i (1911).

BARALLI, R.: 'Un frammento inedito di "discantus"'. *Rassegna gregoriana*, xi (1912).

COUSSEMAKER, C. E. H. DE: *Histoire de l'harmonie au moyen âge* (Paris, 1852).

—— *Scriptorum de musica medii aevi nova series*. 4 vols. (Paris, 1864–76).

ELLINWOOD, LEONARD: 'John Cotton or John of Affligem?' *Notes*, viii (1951).

—— *Musica Hermanni Contracti* (Rochester, N.Y., 1936).

FARMER, H. G.: *Historical Facts for the Arabian Musical Influence* (London, 1930).

FICKER, RUDOLF VON: 'Der Organumtraktat der Vatikanischen Bibliothek (Ottob. 3025)'. *Kirchenmusikalisches Jahrbuch*, xxvii (1932).

GASTOUÉ, AMÉDÉE: 'Paraphonie et paraphonistes'. *Revue de musicologie*, ix (1928).

GERBERT, MARTIN: *Scriptores ecclesiastici de musica sacra potissimum*. 3 vols. (St. Blaise, 1784).

HANDSCHIN, J.: 'Aus der alten Musiktheorie'. *Acta Musicologica*, xv–xvi (1943–4).

—— 'L'Organum à l'église'. *Revue du chant grégorien*, xl–xli (1936–7).

—— 'The Two Winchester Tropers'. *Journal of Theological Studies*, xxxvii (1936).

—— 'Zur Geschichte der Lehre vom Organum'. *Zeitschrift für Musikwissenschaft*, viii (1925–6).

HUGHES, DOM ANSELM: 'The Origins of Harmony'. *Musical Quarterly*, xxiv (1938).

MÜLLER, H.: *Hucbalds echte und unechte Schriften über Musik* (Leipzig, 1884).

SCHNEIDER, MARIUS: *Geschichte der Mehrstimmigkeit*. 2 vols. (Berlin, 1934–5).

Sowa, Heinrich: 'Textvariationen zur Musica Enchiriadis'. *Zeitschrift für Musikwissenschaft*, xvii (1934–5).
Spiess, Lincoln B.: 'An Introduction to the Pre-St. Martial Sources of Early Polyphony'. *Speculum*, xxii (1947).
Spitta, Philipp: 'Die Musica Enchiriadis und ihr Zeitalter'. *Vierteljahrsschrift für Musikwissenschaft*, v–vi (1889–90).
Steinhard, Erich: 'Zur Frühgeschichte der Mehrstimmigkeit'. *Archiv für Musikwissenschaft*, iii (1921).
Van Waesberghe, J. Smits: *Joannes Affligemensis de musica cum tonario* (Rome, 1950).
—— 'John of Affligem or John Cotton?' *Musica Disciplina*, vi (1952).
—— 'Some Music Treatises and their Interrelation'. *Musica Disciplina*, iii (1949).
Wagner, Peter: 'La Paraphonie'. *Revue de musicologie*, ix (1928).
—— 'Über die Anfänge des mehrstimmigen Gesanges'. *Zeitschrift für Musikwissenschaft*, ix (1926–7).
Yasser, Joseph: *Mediaeval Quartal Harmony* (New York, 1938).

CHAPTER IX
MUSIC IN THE TWELFTH CENTURY
(i) *Sources*

Anglès, H.: *La Música a Catalunya fins al segle XIII* (Barcelona, 1935).
Baxter, J. H.: *An Old St. Andrews Music Book* (London, 1931).
Prado, Dom Germain, and Whitehill, W. M.: *Liber Sancti Jacobi: Codex Calixtinus* (Santiago de Compostela, 1944).
Wagner, Peter: *Die Gesänge der Jakobusliturgie zu Santiago de Compostela* (Fribourg, 1931).
Wooldridge, H. E.: *Early English Harmony*. Vol. I (London, 1897).

(ii) *Books and Articles*

Amelli, A. M.: *Micrologus ad praestantiores mss. exactus* (Rome, 1904).
Ellinwood, Leonard: 'The Conductus'. *Musical Quarterly*, xxvii (1941).
—— 'The French Renaissance of the Twelfth Century in Music'. In *Papers read at the International Congress of Musicology* (New York, 1939), p. 200.
Ficker, Rudolf von: 'Probleme der modalen Notation'. *Acta Musicologica*, xviii–xix (1946–7).
Hooreman, Paul: 'Saint-Martial de Limoges au temps de l'Abbé Odolric'. *Revue belge de musicologie*, iii (1949).
Laistner, M. L. W.: 'The Medieval Organ and a Cassiodorus Glossary among the Spurious Works of Bede'. *Speculum*, v (1930).
Ludwig, Friedrich: 'Die mehrstimmige Musik des 11. und 12. Jahrhunderts'. In *Bericht über den III. Kongreß der internationalen Musikgesellschaft* (Vienna, 1909).
Spanke, H., and Anglès, H.: 'Die Londoner St. Martial-Conductushandschrift' and 'La música del Ms. de Londres, Brit. Museum, Add. 36881'. In *Butlletí de la Biblioteca de Catalunya*, viii (1928–32), p. 280.
Waite, William G.: 'Discantus, Copula, Organum'. *Journal of the American Musicological Society*, v (1952).
—— *The Rhythm of Twelfth-Century Polyphony* (New Haven, 1954).

CHAPTER X
MUSIC IN FIXED RHYTHM
(i) *Sources*

Anglès, H.: *El Còdex musical de Las Huelgas*. 3 vols. (Barcelona, 1931).
Baxter, J. H.: *An Old St. Andrews Music Book* (London, 1931).

HUGHES, DOM ANSELM: *Worcester Mediaeval Harmony* (London, 1928).
HUSMANN, HEINRICH: *Die drei- und vierstimmigen Notre-Dame-Organa* (Leipzig, 1940).
WOOLDRIDGE, H. E.: *Early English Harmony.* Vol. I (London, 1897).

(ii) *Books and Articles*

APEL, WILLI: 'From St. Martial to Notre Dame'. *Journal of the American Musicological Society*, ii (1949).
AUBRY, PIERRE: *Iter Hispanicum* (Paris, 1908).
AUDA, ANTOINE: *La Musique et les musiciens de l'ancien Pays de Liége* (Liége, 1930).
BUKOFZER, M. F.: 'Interrelations between Conductus and Clausula' (Abstract). *Journal of the American Musicological Society*, vi (1953).
—— *Studies in Medieval and Renaissance Music* (New York, 1950).
ELLINWOOD, L.: 'The Conductus'. *Musical Quarterly*, xxvii (1941).
FICKER, RUDOLF VON: 'Polyphonic Music of the Gothic Period'. *Musical Quarterly*, xv (1929).
FRERE, W. H.: 'Key-relationship in Early Medieval Music'. *Proceedings of the Musical Association*, xxxvii (1910–11).
GASTOUÉ, AMÉDÉE: *Les Primitifs de la musique française* (Paris, 1922).
GENNRICH, FRIEDRICH: 'Perotins Beata viscera Mariae Virginis und die "Modaltheorie"'. *Die Musikforschung*, i (1948).
—— 'Three Centuries of French Mediaeval Music'. *Musical Quarterly*, iii (1917).
GREENE, H. C.: 'The Song of the Ass'. *Speculum*, vi (1931).
GRÖNINGER, E.: *Repertoire-Untersuchungen zum mehrstimmigen Notre-Dame-Conductus* (Cologne, 1939).
GUÉRARD, B. E. C.: *Cartulaire de l'Église Notre-Dame de Paris. Collection de documents inédits sur l'histoire de France* (Paris, 1860).
HANDSCHIN, J.: 'A Monument of English Mediaeval Polyphony: The Manuscript Wolfenbüttel 677'. *Musical Times*, lxxiii–lxxiv (1932–3).
—— 'Conductus'. In *Die Musik in Geschichte und Gegenwart*, ii (Kassel, 1953).
—— 'Conductus-Spicilegien'. *Archiv für Musikwissenschaft*, ix (1952).
—— 'Notizen über die Notre-Dame-Conductus'. In *Bericht über den Internationalen Musikwissenschaftlichen Kongreß der Deutschen Musikgesellschaft* (Leipzig, 1926).
HIBBERD, LLOYD: '"Musica ficta" and Instrumental Music'. *Musical Quarterly*, xxviii (1942).
HUGHES, DOM ANSELM: 'The Origins of Harmony'. *Musical Quarterly*, xxiv (1938).
—— 'Worcester Harmony of the 14th Century'. *Proceedings of the Musical Association*, li (1924–5).
LUDWIG, FRIEDRICH: 'Perotinus Magnus'. *Archiv für Musikwissenschaft*, iii (1921).
—— *Repertorium Organorum Recentioris et Motetorum Vetustissimi Stili* i, (Halle, 1910).
MÜLLER, HERMANN: 'Zum Texte der Musiklehre des Joannes de Grocheo'. *Sammelbände der internationalen Musikgesellschaft*, iv (1902–3).
ROHLOFF, ERNST: *Media Latinitas Musica II. Der Musiktraktat des Johannes de Grocheo* (Leipzig, 1943).
SCHMIDT, HELMUT: 'Zur Melodiebildung Leonins und Perotins'. *Zeitschrift für Musikwissenschaft*, xiv (1931).
SCHNEIDER, MARIUS: 'Zur Satztechnik der Notre-Dame-Schule'. *Zeitschrift für Musikwissenschaft*, xiv (1931–2).
TISCHLER, HANS: 'New Historical Aspects of the Parisian Organa'. *Speculum*, xxv (1950).

WOLF, JOHANNES: 'Die Musiklehre des Johannes de Grocheo'. *Sammelbände der internationalen Musikgesellschaft*, i (1899–1900).

CHAPTER XI
THE MOTET AND ALLIED FORMS
(i) *Sources*

ANGLÈS, HIGINI: *El Còdex musical de Las Huelgas*. 3 vols. (Barcelona, 1931).

AUBRY, PIERRE: *Cent motets du XIIIe siècle*. 3 vols. (Paris, 1908).

HUGHES, DOM ANSELM: *Worcester Mediaeval Harmony* (London, 1928).

ROKSETH, YVONNE: *Polyphonies du XIIIe siècle*. 4 vols. (Paris, 1935–9).

STAINER, JOHN: *Early Bodleian Music*. Vol. I: facsimiles. Vol. II: transcriptions by J. F. R. and C. Stainer (London, 1901).

(ii) *Books and Articles*

APEL, WILLI: 'On the Importance of Notation in Solving Problems of Early Music'. *Papers of the American Musicological Society* (New York, 1938).

AUBRY, PIERRE: *Iter Hispanicum* (Paris, 1908).

BESSELER, HEINRICH: 'Studien zur Musik des Mittelalters'. *Archiv für Musikwissenschaft*, vii and viii (1925, 1927).

BUKOFZER, M. F.: 'The First English Motet with English Words'. *Music and Letters*, xvii (1936).

—— *Geschichte der englischen Diskants und des Fauxbourdons nach den theoretischen Quellen* (Strasbourg, 1936).

—— 'The Gymel: the Earliest Form of English Polyphony'. *Music and Letters*, xvi (1935).

—— '*Sumer is icumen in*': *a Revision* (Berkeley, 1944).

FRERE, W. H.: 'Key-Relationship in Early Medieval Music'. *Proceedings of the Musical Association*, xxxvii (1910–11).

GLEASON, HAROLD: 'Isorhythmic Tenors in the Three-Part Motets of the Roman de Fauvel'. *Bulletin of the American Musicological Society* (New York, 1943).

HANDSCHIN, J.: 'The Summer Canon and its Background'. *Musica Disciplina*, iii (1949).

HUSMANN, HEINRICH: 'Zur Grundlegung der musikalischen Rhythmik des mittellateinischen Liedes'. *Archiv für Musikwissenschaft*, ix (1952).

LEVY, KENNETH JAY: 'New Material on the Early Motet in England'. *Journal of the American Musicological Society*, iv (1951).

LUDWIG, FRIEDRICH: 'Die Quellen der Motetten ältesten Stils'. *Archiv für Musikwissenschaft*, v (1923).

—— *Repertorium Organorum Recentioris et Motetorum Vetustissimi Stili*, i (Halle, 1910).

NATHAN, HANS: 'The Function of Text in French 13th-century Motets'. *Musical Quarterly*, xxviii (1942).

PIRROTTA, NINO: 'On the Problem of "Sumer is icumen in"'. *Musica Disciplina*, ii (1948).

SCHOFIELD, B.: 'The Provenance and Date of "Sumer is icumen in"'. *Music Review*, ix (1948).

STAINER, J. F. R.: 'The Notation of Mensurable Music'. *Proceedings of the Musical Association*, xxvi (1899–1900).

TISCHLER, HANS: 'English Traits in the Early Thirteenth-Century Motet'. *Musical Quarterly*, xxx (1944).

VAN DEN BORREN, CHARLES: *Le Manuscrit musical M. 222 C. 22 de la Bibliothèque de Strasbourg* (Antwerp, 1924).

WOLF, JOHANNES: *Geschichte der Mensuralnotation von 1250–1460 nach den theoretischen und praktischen Quellen*. 3 vols. (Leipzig, 1904).

INDEX